D1305711

cengage.com/wadsworth

cengage.com/wadsworth is the World Wide Web site
for Wadsworth Cengage Learning and is your direct
source to dozens of online resources.

At *cengage.com/wadsworth* you can find out about
supplements, demonstration software, and
student resources. You can also send email to
many of our authors and preview new
publications and exciting new technologies.

cengage.com/wadsworth
Changing the way the world learns®

5th EDITION

Job Search

Career Planning Guide, Book 2

Robert D. Lock

Jackson Community College

BROOKS/COLE
CENGAGE Learning

Australia • Brazil • Japan • Korea • Mexico • Singapore • Spain • United Kingdom • United States

BROOKS/COLE
CENGAGE Learning™

**Job Search: Career Planning Guide: Book 2,
Fifth Edition**
Robert D. Lock

Executive Editor: Lisa Gebo

Acquisitions Editor: Marquita Flemming

Assistant Editor: Shelley Gesicki

Editorial Assistant: Amy Lam

Technology Project Manager: Barry Connolly

Marketing Manager: Caroline Concilla

Marketing Assistant: Mary Ho

Advertising Project Manager: Tami Strang

Project Manager, Editorial Production:
  Catherine Morris

Art Director: Vernon Boes

Print/Media Buyer: Emma Claydon

Permissions Editor: Stephanie Lee

Production Service: Scratchgravel Publishing
  Services

Copy Editor: Toni Zuccarini Ackley

Illustrator: Christopher H. Lock

Cover Designer: Brenda Duke

Cover Image: Digital Vision/Getty Images

Compositor: Scratchgravel Publishing Services

© 2005 Brooks/Cole Cengage Learning

ALL RIGHTS RESERVED. No part of this work covered by the copyright herein
may be reproduced, transmitted, stored or used in any form or by any means
graphic, electronic, or mechanical, including but not limited to photocopying,
recording, scanning, digitizing, taping, Web distribution, information networks,
or information storage and retrieval systems, except as permitted under
Section 107 or 108 of the 1976 United States Copyright Act, without the prior
written permission of the publisher.

For product information and technology assistance, contact us at
Cengage Learning Customer & Sales Support, 1-800-354-9706

For permission to use material from this text or product,
submit all requests online at **cengage.com/permissions**
Further permissions questions can be emailed to
permissionrequest@cengage.com

Library of Congress Control Number: 2004108522

ISBN-13: 978-0-534-57421-5

ISBN-10: 0-534-57421-1

Brooks/Cole
10 Davis Drive
Belmont, CA 94002
USA

Cengage Learning is a leading provider of customized learning solutions with
office locations around the globe, including Singapore, the United Kingdom,
Australia, Mexico, Brazil, and Japan. Locate your local office at:
international.cengage.com/region

Cengage Learning products are represented in Canada by Nelson Education, Ltd.

For your course and learning solutions, visit **academic.cengage.com**

Purchase any of our products at your local college store or at our preferred
online store **www.ichapters.com**

Printed in the United States of America
2 3 4 5 6   23 22 21 20 19

To my family, students, and colleagues

Contents

Chapter 3   Using Your Writing Skills to Get a Job: Résumés and Cover Letters   67

Chapter 7   Using Your Speaking Skills to Get a Job: Interviewing for Information

196

Chapter 8   Using Your Speaking Skills to Get a Job: Interviewing for Jobs

218

Chapter 10   The Bigger Picture of Work   294

Preface

This book, *Job Search*, the second volume of the Career Planning Guide series, makes an assumption about you, the reader. It assumes that you have made at least a tentative career choice and feel fairly comfortable about it. The best job seekers are those who know exactly what occupation they want to enter. They have already completed a thorough investigation of their own personalities and of the world of work. If this does not describe you, obtain a copy of the first book in this series, *Taking Charge of Your Career Direction*, and move through it with the help of either a career-planning class, instructor, or counselor, or on your own. After you have established a career goal, come back to this book. *Job Search* concerns implementing your career decision. An occupational choice remains no more than a decision until you actively put it into practice.

This fifth edition of *Job Search* has incorporated a considerable amount of new material in its pages—enough to create five new appendices for the sake of shortening several chapters and adding flexibility to assignments by teachers and counselors. In Chapter 1, the segment on the characteristics of job applicants that employers want has been revised, and you will find some additions to the "20 thoughts." Because people lose jobs with increasing regularity these days, a new section on coping with job loss is included. For Chapter 2, new material has been added to the topics of job fairs, telephoning employers, and networking. Many more references to electronic sources of job leads through the Internet and the World Wide Web make up Chapter 2; these are constantly expanding, and it's a real effort to keep up with the changes. (Keep in mind, however, that less than 5 percent of all jobs are gained by going online; job seekers must still get out and meet people. Those "old" methods are a long way from being dead.) A new section on the curriculum vitae (CV) will be found in Chapter 3.

The information on electronic résumés has been lengthened. Not only are there scannable and plain text résumés, but also new software that allows you to create more colorful "formatted" résumés. (When will those software people ever stop?) Chapter 4 on application forms has expanded somewhat, with more current information about illegal questions and how to respond to them. U.S. metropolitan area data and state population figures and projections have been updated for Chapter 5, and a new cost-of-living index for selected U.S. cities has been added.

The structure of Chapter 6 is the same, but we've added new Web sites for obtaining information about companies; remember, though, the topic of researching organizations is always changing. Table 6-1 has been retained in Chapter 6, and although it is rather old (1992 data, published in 1995), nothing better has come along to illustrate the diversity of occupations in work organizations (in this case, hospitals). The bureaucratic-innovative-supportive classification of organizational cultures is the simplest yet most effective way of introducing this subject to young people who are not likely to be familiar with the structure of organizations. Chapter 7 on interviewing for information has a new exercise to expand a person's list of contacts if he or she is in a class or group. Chapter 8 on the job interview has more material on answering interviewer questions, but it is essentially the same because reviewers have rated this part very highly.

The last two chapters go into working on the job and encouraging a broader view of the world in which jobs exist. Chapter 9 contains new information on types of agreements a prospective new hire might be asked to sign and the transitional first year in a full-time job for a recent graduate. In the "concerns of workers" section of Chapter 9, new material appears about Hispanic/Latino workers, and we also look at the topic of office romances. Chapter 10 has been retitled "The Bigger Picture of Work," and it takes up the topics of the role of work in human affairs and the work ethic throughout human history, ending with the ever-increasing impact of the "free agent" on the workplace. The greater important of performance reviews, the effects of the 9/11 tragedy, and the force of "wild cards" (unexpected surprises) in human history are topics that have been added to the "Where Are We Headed?" section of Chapter 10. Appendixes A through E at the back of this book cover characteristics wanted in job applicants, electronic job banks, electronic résumés, Web sites for company information, and annual reports.

Scattered throughout the book are many updates and insertions of new material that are too numerous to mention here. The subject of the job search has expanded and become more complex with options that did not exist a few years ago. Methods of acquiring a position have undergone tremendous changes in the Information Age. All of this has caused the book to grow in order to be more comprehensive. There may be more in this book than a single person can use; if so, pick and choose. We call this book and its companion volume a "Career Planning Guide," so you can make choices in the methods you use.

I would like to thank the following reviewers for their constructive criticisms on this edition: Jodi Caldwell-John, Georgia Southern University; Robert Chope, San Francisco State University; Chris Clark, West Valley College; Lucy Crowell, Kansas State University; Margo A. Jackson, Fordham University; Christopher McCarthy, University of Texas at Austin; Jan Wencel, University of Southern Florida; and Keith Wilson, Pennsylvania State University.

Robert D. Lock

Chapter 1

Overview of the Job Search

The Job Search Mystery

Approaches to the Job Search

Coping with Job Loss

Twenty Thoughts about Undertaking a Job Search

Getting Organized for the Job Search

Summary

References

"So, what are you doing after graduation?" ask friends and family. It's the question that haunts most college grads. Jeremy Carroll tried to be witty about it. "I'll probably be the only sales associate in the store with a bachelor's degree—if I'm lucky enough to land that job." His field is journalism. He did an internship during the summer at a local newspaper.

> I thought I was as qualified as anyone else graduating this year, although there are 20 newspapers that would beg to differ. I have the rejection letters to prove it. But, I kept plugging away. And, in the end, it was networking that got me my first job. Relief does not begin to define what I felt. I did not "ask for a day to think about it." I wanted that job. I needed it. In fact, before "The Call," as I refer to it now, I was in panic mode. I was calling it quits on finding a full-time job in journalism. It's a tough job market out there, but it is possible to get a job. (Carroll, 2003)

Duane Davis (not his real name) has plenty of time on his hands. He has been looking for a job for months in his native city of Benton Harbor, Michigan, since coming back from a southern state where he had worked in a grocery store. Jobs are scarce, and even free time is difficult to fill in a place where half the population is under 25. "There's nothing to do," is the common complaint. A short time ago, protests about the actions of police officers had led to a riot where one person died. The death was the spark that ignited the anger, but poverty and unemployment were the real issues. Across the river, another town, St. Joseph, is relatively prosperous. Its median income is more than twice that of Benton Harbor. The two towns are often compared because they are so close to each other and the racial makeup is so different: St. Joseph is 90 percent white and Benton Harbor is 92 percent black. Alex Kotlowitz (1998) described the economic and racial division between the two towns in his book, *The Other Side of the River*, a probe into the death of a black teenager last seen in St. Joseph. Most young people in Benton Harbor do not approve of the violence. Yet, Duane concluded, "I guess that's what it takes to get people to notice us, to do something that's not right" (Associated Press, 2003).

Ruth Simmons grew up in a sharecropper's shack on a cotton farm in rural Texas. The black family lived in poverty. Christmas presents were an apple, an orange, and some nuts. Her mother worked as a maid and cleaned houses on weekends. "She went about her work with great dignity and treated everyone, even a racist, with extraordinary kindness," Ruth recalled. From both parents, she learned a strong work ethic. School became something special. "Here was a bright and orderly place. I could have a pencil and paper. I could have books to read." And there were her teachers, who took Ruth under their wing when her mother died of diabetes. "We knew poverty existed in Ruth's neighborhood," one of them said. "It was not an issue. You had a brain, you used it." Ruth excelled in school and went on to college. "There was still this myth that blacks were inferior to whites," Ruth noted. "I discovered the truth: I could do everything these very wealthy, very well prepared white women could do." She continued on to earn a Ph.D., taught at Princeton, and became a highly effective administrator. In 1995, Ruth was named president of Smith College, the first African American woman to head one of the "Seven Sisters" women's schools. In 2001, Ruth Simmons became the first African American president of an Ivy League university. "Nobody said it's great we have a woman, or a person of color," said Brown University Chancellor Stephen Robert. "People are happy about her coming here because of who she is" (Terry, 2002).

Three true stories—one of the frustrations of getting started in a chosen field of work, one of despair and hope of being noticed, and one of hardship leading to success. All of these stories have something to do with the job world, and like so much else in the world, they abound with hope, fear, fulfillment, failure, aspiration, desperation, tears, and joy. We are *in* the world (you and I didn't have much to do about that!), and most of us want to get into a part of that world called the *job world*, so we can earn a living. That is essential, a necessity we must do something about. But, how do we do it? Well, we must search for a job to be in that world. And *that* is the subject of this book.

Nearly everyone experiences the job search, but many people enter this enterprise with procrastination or a sense of foreboding. Job hunting is an activity a lot of us would just as soon avoid. We know we must work and find a job "when we grow up." We are also aware that in today's world, job hunting could become a necessity at any time in the future. Even the best workers, through no fault of their own, can be laid off or forced to resign. Or, we change our minds; we may have made a wrong occupational choice or the job that held such promise has turned to dust. The world of work changes quickly and seems not to offer the assurances it once did. The greatest job security is in knowing you have the skill to conduct a competent job search. Job-hunting skills are seldom taught, though, so job seekers often feel left out, with no one to help them. Most people recognize that they are responsible for their own job search, but they needn't feel isolated. Help is available, and some of it will come through this book.

One approach to the job search is to use traditional methods, such as answering want ads, writing and sending résumés, completing applications, and so on. Another approach emphasizes choosing your employers and getting through to the hidden job market, where (it is claimed) the great majority of jobs are found. Job search theories have many ideas in common, so you might try combining (in your opinion) the best features of them.

A discussion of the basic truths of the job search reveals many common elements in the different approaches. A brief survey of theories and ideas will start you thinking about the puzzles and problems of job hunting. Despite differences in method, no one really questions the fundamentals: give sufficient time to job search activities, know what you want, take personal responsibility, seek information, evaluate workplaces, persist, and show enthusiasm—to name just a few. No one argues about the need to be organized, either. An exercise at the end of this chapter will start you toward finding a job efficiently and systematically. Do it right; your job and your work are at the very heart of your life in this world.

THE JOB SEARCH MYSTERY

Few subjects are more vital to a person than the job search, but few topics are more shrouded with mystery. Nearly everyone has been frustrated by the job search, but everyone still has lots of advice to give.

No book or system can offer you a foolproof guarantee of landing a job. One fact can be stated with certainty, however: A job search involves work. No matter how easy you would like it to be, "it's a full-time job to get a job." You will need all your detective skills to win a job in your chosen occupation. As in any process of investigation and discovery, there will be times of discouragement and disappointment. Fear and anxiety are part of the picture, too, because a job seeker feels vulnerable and open to rejection. This book can help you acquire the skills you need to overcome many problems in the job search. A major purpose of the book is to reduce the fears and frustrations of job hunting and help you face the task of gaining employment in the occupation of your choice with hope, confidence, inventiveness, and mastery.

The phrase "occupation of your choice" implies that you are relatively certain of your career goal. If this is not so, you should first go through a career decision-making process such as the one described in the first volume of this Career Planning Guide series, and then come back to this book. To get the most benefit from this book, you will need to use a specific occupational choice as a target for the job search process this book describes. Your current major occupational choice will be used as an example. (Of course, you have the right to change your career goal. After all, the first book in this series, *Taking Charge of Your Career Direction*, leaves you with a ranked list of occupational alternatives, a set of backup occupations to which you can turn in case your number one career goal doesn't work out.)

APPROACHES TO THE JOB SEARCH

There are essentially three ways of going about finding a job: (1) basic, traditional methods; (2) newer, nontraditional methods; or (3) a combination of the two. A *traditional* approach to job hunting emphasizes communicating with as many employers as you can. For that reason, it is sometimes referred to as "the numbers game." The *nontraditional* approach involves identifying and targeting employers through personal research of the "hidden job market"—employment needs that are not officially advertised through regular communication channels. The two strategies share many features, such as self-assessment, researching work organizations, and adequate preparation for interviews. You may wish to take the common elements, add parts of each approach that appeal to you, and devise your own *combination* approach. All these techniques call for time, effort, planning, and preparation on the part of the job seeker. Still another job search method, which is favored by all too many people, is a no-approach approach. They would rather conduct a job search with no commitment of time, effort, planning, or preparation. We could call it a "punt" approach, because it's like a football team that doesn't know whether it wants to run or pass the ball on first down, so it punts.

Traditional Approaches: The Numbers Game

Traditional methods of job hunting involve contacting as many employers as possible in the hope that some of them will respond and suggest an interview.

The idea is that the more people you contact, the more you respond to help-wanted ads, the more résumés you send, the more electronic database services you use, the more employers you telephone, and so on, the more interviews and job offers you will receive. Talking with large numbers of employers over the telephone and posting your résumé or application with online job banks or sending them in large numbers of stamped envelopes requires time, expense, verbal skill, and persistence. This is the "numbers game," which its critics consider ineffective and unproductive, given the time and money spent on it. The job hunt has been streamlined by the Internet because of the ability of software to take the keywords embedded in the skills and experiences provided on your electronic résumé and match them with the needs of the employer. When a sufficient number of matches occur, a human being (the employer or an agent) notices you. Traditional approaches also involve getting help from career search professionals in placement offices and employment services, acquiring personal contacts and informal sources of job leads, and using advertised sources of job openings in newspapers and trade journals.

Because no single method of job hunting works very well, several job search techniques should be used. A while back, the Census Bureau conducted a study of 10 million job hunters and found that even the best job search method then—applying directly to employers—produced results less than half the time (Egan, 1976). Nothing has happened in the meantime to change that finding significantly. Because no one method is very effective, use more than one job search technique and contact as many employers as possible. For the most part, traditional methods operate by connecting job seekers with employers in the following ways:

- Using college career counseling and career center referrals
- Checking public and private employment agency listings of job vacancies
- Answering help-wanted advertisements in newspapers and magazines
- Placing position-wanted advertisements in trade journals

- Sending résumés and application letters in direct-mail campaigns
- Scanning the Internet for job openings listed by organizations
- Posting résumés with computerized database services
- Filling out application forms at personnel and employment offices
- Registering with professional and trade association job clearinghouses
- Attending career days and job fairs sponsored by various organizations
- Dropping in (or making cold calls) on people with hiring authority
- Telephoning businesses listed in the Yellow Pages or other directories
- Applying and taking tests for civil service positions in government
- Sending telegrams or mailing special-delivery letters of application
- Printing brochures that outline talents and credentials
- Going to places where employers come to meet or hire workers
- Registering at a union hiring hall
- Contacting friends, parents, relatives, acquaintances, neighbors, former employers, teachers, or anyone who may know about job leads

Obviously, using even a few of these job search techniques would entail a lot of hard work. You may agree with the critics of the numbers game and deride this approach as not worth the time, money, and energy required. However, if some solid leads develop and they bring in, say, three job interviews resulting in an attractive job offer, you might consider this work well worth the effort.

Nontraditional Approaches: Targeting Employers

Nontraditional job search approaches aim to make the job seeker more proactive than reactive. Job hunters select employer targets based on their own research, move into the hidden job market, and gain employment by demonstrating their ability to fill the unmet needs of employers.

The job seeker has a choice, says Richard Nelson Bolles, author of *What Color Is Your Parachute?* (2003). He calls his approach to the job search a "life-changing job hunt." (In past editions of *Parachute*, Bolles used the title "Finding Your Dream Job" and called the users of his methods a "creative minority.") A life-changing job hunt begins with your defining exactly what you are looking for. You may want to change your occupation, your field, the kinds of people you work with, your work environment, your profession to be more consistent with your goals and values, and/or the salary you are paid. Changing your occupation, field of work, or both are the pathways for making a life-changing job hunt. You must define exactly the occupation and field you want and then go find it. This approach involves homework that has three basic steps:

1. You must decide exactly *what* you have to offer to the world. This means identifying your favorite skills, the building blocks of your occupation, in order of importance to you.
2. You must decide exactly *where* you want to use your skills. This means identifying your favorite fields of interest and geographical preferences (where you want to live, researched through informational interviewing, books, or the Internet). Putting occupation and field together, a new career emerges.
3. You must "go after" the organizations that interest you the most, whether or not they are known to have a vacancy. How? Find out as much as you can about these organizations through sources on the Internet and from printed materials; these can be business directories, company literature, newsletters, trade magazines, government reports, business magazines, annual reports, and newspapers. When you have exhausted these resources, fill in your knowledge gaps by turning to your personal contacts: people who know or can refer you to those who know what's happening on the inside of companies that interest you. Keep learning about these organizations and employers until

you are satisfied you know everything you possibly can about them *before* you approach them about work. Be absolutely certain your skills can help the organization satisfy their needs or solve their problems. Then, through your research and/or your contacts, get an appointment with the person (or committee) in the organization who actually has the power to hire you for the job you want to do. Demonstrate to this person or committee how you can help with the needs and problems you know they have (because you have done your "homework"; that is, your research). Convince the employer, on the strength of your ideas and skills, to offer you a job or create a position that has not existed before.

If you are not hired, don't take it personally; the reason may have nothing to do with you. Persevere. You are not begging for a job; you are a "problem solver" or a "resource person." If a job is created, you may be the sole applicant for the position—after all, no one else may know about it. Your research, your demonstrated mastery of the subject, and the way you have presented your job hunt to the employer has carried the day. Control the process by developing alternative jobs and companies from which to choose. Even when a job is not forthcoming, you have gained vital information, created options, and devised a way to get a foot in the employer's door without getting your toes broken.

Nontraditional approaches emphasize an understanding of the hidden job market. Information about job vacancies is circulated mainly by word of mouth among people who have hiring authority, executives, department heads, friends, acquaintances, and a whole informal network of contacts a job hunter should cultivate. Most job openings are never publicized in employment agencies and help-wanted sections of the newspaper. The idea for a job opening may develop from the company's plans for expansion into a new product line, a problem that has arisen, changes in the marketplace, a promotion or retirement that leaves a job temporarily vacant, or a change in management policy. Meanwhile, months can go by before the human resources department publicizes the opening. This is the time when your personal contacts can help you penetrate the hidden job market by informing you of a job that is unknown to other job seekers.

When you interview people for information about companies and employers, you do not make a formal request for a job. For this reason, the informational interview strategy can go by other names such as "the non-job interview survey" (Billingsley, 1978) or the "remembering and referral (R & R) interview" (Haldane, Haldane, and Martin, 1976). At this point, you are not conducting a job interview. In the research phase of the job search, you interview people only to obtain information and to be remembered so that your name can be referred to other people. You can be remembered by stimulating interest in your proven skills—the abilities you have used to produce achievements. Creating a favorable impression will help people remember you. Solving problems, increasing the volume of business, or cutting the costs of producing things or services are achievements any employer will keep in mind. *Being remembered is the key to referral*; you don't get referred unless you are remembered.

Learning what to say in informational interviews takes time. It is based on information you have acquired about yourself, occupational targets, work organizations that interest you, and the people you want to interview. Asking for a job, if it happens at all, occurs only after you have been told for certain that a job is open or when you have been referred to a person who has a job to offer.

The life-changing job hunt, non-job interview survey, R & R, and informational interview techniques have advantages. You do a lot of thinking about who you are and what you want to accomplish with your life. Rejection is taken out of job hunting when you are not asking for a job. The pressures and tensions of a job interview are reduced or eliminated when a job is not on the line. Employers can be more relaxed, because there is no obligation to make a decision to hire you or turn you down.

William Bridges (1997) bases his approach on his belief that we are in a postindustrial work world where jobs as we have known them are gradually disappearing. Increasingly, we are working for ourselves, which may account for the rapid rise of entrepreneurial self-employment in our times. Instead of doing only what is within the confines of a job description, we should focus on doing work that needs to be done, either as a one-person business, in a growing company, or for a current employer. In the workplace of the future, people will merge their own resources (motives, abilities, temperament, and assets) with finding the best workplaces for the use of those resources, turning them into products employees market to employers. We will constantly launch ourselves into new career directions by looking for unmet needs wherever they appear, a process described in Bridge's *Creating You & Co.* (1997).

A Combination Approach

You can consider both traditional and nontraditional approaches to the job search and combine parts of each into your own unique method. Relying solely on creative nontraditional methods may strike you as impractical or difficult, but you may be able to connect some of those methods to more traditional approaches and develop a job search plan that is more to your liking and within your capabilities.

For those of you who have completed the first book in the Career Planning Guide series, the combination approach resembles the career decision-making process, with work organizations taking the place of occupational prospects. Create and expand a list of workplace prospects through research and informational interviewing. Reduce the number of alternatives as you investigate your workplace prospects, study your personal characteristics, and eliminate any alternatives that do not come close to your specifications.

A final step in the selection process would be to match your personal characteristics (work values and favorite skills) to the work organizations that remain on your list and arrange the organizations in an order of preference. You then have a prioritized list of workplaces, and can begin an active pursuit of the one at the top of your list. Unless you intend to be your own boss, the one factor you cannot completely control is the job offer, which must come from the employer. (This factor is much like the availability of jobs in the occupation of your choice in the career decision-making exercise completed in the first book in this series.) This is the reason you work with a list of alternatives rather than put all your hopes on one workplace (or one occupational prospect).

Honest questions about either approach can arise. Do traditional methods of job hunting adequately tap the hidden job market, make job seekers too dependent on career counselors or employment agencies, or cause job seekers to be rejected before they have a chance to see anyone with hiring authority? Can all job seekers identify prospective work organizations and research them thoroughly enough to discover their needs and problems? Can they appraise their own skills sufficiently to determine whether they have the ability to solve an organization's problems or satisfy its needs, and convince people who can hire to create a job position? Are nontraditional techniques more appropriate to professional and managerial types and of limited value to people who plan to enter specialized technical work, skilled trades, and semiskilled occupations?

Don't reject any job search method without giving it serious consideration. Some techniques are more complex than others. You may believe that you cannot follow an elaborate plan completely, but perhaps you can use certain parts of it. Questions and thoughts about both traditional and nontraditional approaches can lead to the formation of a combination approach tailored to your personal needs, interests, and abilities.

Traditional and nontraditional procedures may have more similarities than differences. For example, all job search approaches emphasize the importance of self-knowledge and occupational exploration. Making career decisions—knowing exactly what it is that you want to do—is an essential beginning to any job-hunting strategy. Another area of agreement is the importance of obtaining information about companies from personal research. No career counselor would want to see a client go into an employment interview without knowing the kind of product the company makes or the service it performs. Other broad areas of agreement include the following:

- Giving adequate time to the job search
- Developing a personal contact network
- Being honest and straightforward when interviewing employers
- Using the interview as a learning process
- Practicing answering and asking questions before a job interview
- Creating good first impressions with employers
- Writing thank-you letters after any kind of interview
- Showing enthusiasm about the prospect of working in your chosen occupation

These areas, and other ideas that reflect points of agreement among various approaches to the job search, are developed after the following section.

COPING WITH JOB LOSS

Losing a job you value is right up there with death of a loved one, divorce or separation, serious illness or disability, and being victimized by crime as one of the most devastating stressors of life. You feel destroyed, violated, wrongly treated, and robbed of your identity. Years ago, Elisabeth Kubler-Ross wrote about the five stages of dying (*On Death and Dying*, 1969) and people have noticed that these stages seem to have some application to the severing of relationships and other significant losses, such losing a job (Corey and Corey, 2002).

The first stage is one of *denial*. "Why didn't I see it coming?" you (or others) might ask. Perhaps denial at least partially explains why people are completely surprised when they are laid off or fired. There were probably dozens of clues. The boss never looked your way, your supervisor barely spoke to you, invitations to meetings were a thing of the past, no one exchanged gossip with you anymore, you were shoved into a dead-end corner, the role you once filled disappeared, and so on. The company had lost sales, reported budget deficits, downsized, been charged with "cooking the books" and investigated for fraud, contemplated bankruptcy, lost its reputation, closed plant sites, been threatened by hostile takeovers, and so on. Stockholders started bailing out, worker morale plunged, the board of directors publicly fought among themselves, the union hinted at a strike, middle management was decimated, customers complained, work loads doubled, and so on. You may have denied all this, and so you did nothing: no updating of the résumé, no networking, no job-vacancy searching on the Internet, no looking for job leads, no research of other companies, no scaling back on luxuries, no Plan B or C just in case disaster struck. And, when disaster struck, you "couldn't believe it; the loss of my job simply couldn't happen to me."

The second stage of the five is *anger*. "I gave my company so much; how could they be doing this to me now?" "It's corporate greed. The bosses give themselves hundreds of thousands of dollars and turn us out with nothing." "They used me, worked me to death, and now they throw me away!" The selfishness, the insensitivity, the injustice, the cruelty, the suffering—the unfairness of it all! Reality can no longer be denied. The pain crashes through, and your feelings turn to furious rage. Better to express it (and pity the poor person who listens to you) than to keep it bottled up inside where it is likely to become a form of self-punishment. Research on job loss suggests that individuals most attached to previous employers and professions respond most negatively to being laid off. For them, losing a job means more than losing money; it means losing a source of internal satisfaction and long-held social networks and structures to their lives (Leana and Feldman, 1992).

Bargaining is the third stage detected by Kubler-Ross. "If I go back to the company and promise to work overtime for no extra pay, maybe they'll take me back." Any glimmer of hope is seized and held tightly, however briefly. Usually, it vanishes like a mirage.

The shock, numbness, fiery wrath, and bartering of earlier stages gives way to *depression*, the fourth stage. You feel useless. Your spouse or a parent may become the breadwinner. "I've always provided for my family; now I can't. How can I look at my kids in the eye? I have failed them. What will others think of me? What could I have done differently?" Loss of self-esteem and expressions of self-blame, guilt, fear, and self-doubt (silent or verbalized) are common. The anger that was once directed toward your employer can be turned inward. Supportive counseling given by a psychotherapist, counselor, friend, spouse, or parent may be helpful at this point. It is important for the person who has experienced job loss to acknowledge and put into words the grief and bitterness they feel about it. When these emotions lie buried deeply within and are not worked through, it may be very difficult for a person to get on with his or her working life, which sooner or later involves a job search.

If people allow themselves to mourn their losses, the grieving process usually leads to a stage of *acceptance*. This is not resignation, a hopeless "giving up," or a sense of "what's the use" (Kubler-Ross, 1969). It is recognition that "what's done is done" and clinging to old resentments will not advance our interests, goals, and purposes in living. "It is time to move on. We all start out unemployed, so what else is new?" One cannot say that this is a time of great happiness or unalloyed bliss, but there are new possibilities and prospects out there. "I can make a new life for myself and provide for my loved ones again. I can learn from this experience and benefit from the knowledge I've gained in the school of hard knocks."

Each person going through a job loss experiences these stages in different ways. Some people express very little anger. Other people may not go through a bargaining phase. The value of a model such as this one is that it provides some understanding of how we can cope with a loss, like being laid off or fired from a job (Corey and Corey, 2002). It is important that we deal with a job loss in a constructive way. Perhaps you thinking you'll never be out of work. You should know that most people do not think about it until it actually happens, even though none of us are exempt from losing our jobs. Following are some ideas about getting through the trauma of being out of work. (Some of these suggestions apply to those who have a job as well as those who have lost their job.)

Apply for unemployment benefits as soon as possible—even if you are unsure about being eligible. You have already contributed to the benefits fund from your previous employment. Contact the nearest office of your state employment security commission or department of labor. You can collect benefits for up to 26 weeks (sometimes longer), depending on how long you have worked.

Determine your income and expenses. Monthly or weekly income: What will your benefits bring in? Are you entitled to severance pay, and if so, how much? What is your spouse's income (if any)? How much money do you have in your savings account? Do you have interest and dividends coming in, and if so, how much? Monthly or weekly expenses: Food and restaurants? Mortgage or rent? Clothing? Utilities (gas/oil, water, electric, sewer)? Taxes? Insurance? Telephone? Car (payments, fuel)? Medical/dental? School? Entertainment? Unexpected expense ("rainy day" fund)? Other expenses? Take a blank sheet of paper, and set up your income and expenses on a balance sheet. (Everyone could use this suggestion.)

Lower your expenses while out of work. Eliminate unnecessary items; keep telling yourself these can be restored once you're back to work. Avoid major purchases. Look for sales and discounts. Find the inexpensive places to eat and shop for food. Comparison shop for clothing and home/auto/life insurance. Now is not the time to buy a new car or stereo. Watch your credit card purchases, and pay that bill promptly to avoid the high interest charge. Look for lowered admissions for entertainment (some sports events, rock concerts, plays, and the like charge an arm and a leg—and a kidney to boot). You can deduct job-hunting expenses from your taxes. (Check with an accountant on this. Keep all receipts for producing résumés, transportation, employment agency fees, and the like.) Contact your creditors and ask them to help by stretching out payments to reduce the burden right now. Make life simpler; think of things you can do without, at least temporarily. Enlist everyone in the family on this project. (More about this to follow later in this chapter.)

Think of ways to bring in extra income. What items could you sell at a garage sale? Do you need the boat or extra car, and if not, how much money could you sell them for? (Plus think of the money you would save on insurance.) Consider painting houses and garages, selling or taking tickets, delivering newspapers, or cultivating gardens. (Take a look at the lists of interim jobs in Thought 18 in this chapter for more ideas.) Will any of your hobbies bring in extra cash? Would an employment agency have a temporary or part-time job for you? Can other members of the family help out by getting a job?

Stay healthy during a job search (and save money on medical expenses). Eat correctly; strive for a balanced diet. Cut down on or eliminate snacks and junk food. Take a daily multivitamin. Drink six or more glasses of water each day. Exercise in moderation. Walk, mow the lawn, make repairs, and/or clean the house. Relax and have fun. Try relaxation techniques such as deep breathing exercises, meditation, listening to quiet music, watching a sunset or sunrise, and so on. Recall past successes and imagine future ones. Maintain good posture. Get lots of regular sleep—seven to eight hours is the normal amount. Let go of that day's tensions (yes, easier said than done). If a sleep problem develops, consult with a doctor. Good health habits will help ward off becoming overstressed, one of your enemies in life as well as the job search. (Again, good advice for every job hunter.) And remember, using alcohol or drugs to fight stress just compounds the problem.

Interact with your family, and don't try to hide the fact you are unemployed. As hard as this is for some people to do, the alternative is to become cut off from those people who could help maintain your emotional balance the most. There is no reason to carry the weight of unemployment all by yourself. Tell them your unemployment will affect them for a while. Talk about your job search and how important it is to make plans and share anxieties together. This is the only way you can find out about their concerns. Reassure your children that they are not to blame for any of the problems you are going through now. Let them know how you will be spending your time. Who knows? Maybe they will have some worthwhile suggestions of their own.

Reach for spiritual connections. Spirituality is a hard subject to discuss or write about. To many people who have faith in a higher being, their spiritual life is a private matter. Spirituality can come through the beliefs and practices of a church, synagogue, or mosque—the elements of organized religion—although it is not absolutely necessary that it do so. Spirituality can take different forms: the transcendence of a quest for higher principles, the spirituality of a place, or the traditions, gatherings, and storytelling within a family (Hansen, 1997). Spirituality evokes a feeling of harmony with nature, humanity, and God. It was spirituality that allowed Viktor Frankl (1963) to survive the terror of Nazi concentration camps and create from that experience the psychological practice of *logotherapy*, helping people find meaning in their lives. Many other psychologists have integrated spirituality into their counseling: Gordon Allport, Abraham Maslow, Carl Rogers, and Eric Erikson just to name a few. Job loss is a time to ask and pray for support from sources outside oneself.

Get help from a support group, if needed. There doesn't seem to be any social or personal problem that doesn't have a support group organized to deal with it. Self-help group members support each other in a time of crisis. They know about the strain and stress you are going through; they are going through the same circumstance or have been there. As much as your family and friends want to help, they may not understand or comprehend all that is happening to you. Members of job clubs or cooperatives counsel one another about job searching, offer emotional support, and share information on the job hunt. These groups are covered more thoroughly in Chapter 2, the chapter on job leads. Support groups meet at libraries, restaurants, churches, government agencies, community centers, YMCAs, and YWCAs.

Understand that the only way you are going to eliminate your stress and frustration (that is, your joblessness) is to take action. Taking action means searching for a new job (the subject of this book), seeking education and/or retraining, investigating geographical relocation, getting into community activism, applying for financial assistance beyond unemployment insurance, and looking for social support. These six strategies and the frequency of their use were the focus of a study by Leana and Feldman (1992). During the mid-1980s, a total of 361 unemployed people in the Monongahela Valley outside of Pittsburgh, Pennsylvania, and Brevard County, Florida, responded to the research survey. The researchers found that 86.3 percent of those surveyed *engaged in job search activity* by following up on "help wanted" notices, trying to get a job through a government agency, and using community job bank services. They also found that 26.7 percent *sought education and retraining* at colleges, universities, and technical programs or took steps to learn a new trade or profession, and 45.2 percent *looked into relocating* by seeking a job in a different city, making plans to move to a new community, or searching for job opportunities outside their community. *Community activism* attracted 18.5 percent, who became active in efforts to help the unemployed or stop unemployment and went to a support group for the unemployed. Another 16 percent *sought financial assistance* beyond unemployment benefits by asking friends or relatives for financial help, applying for aid in making utility payments, and applying for food stamps. Finally, 79.1 percent *sought social support* by talking to their spouse about their feelings, keeping in touch with people on the old job, and talking to friends about the problems of unemployment (Leana and Feldman, 1992). This research is cited here to inform you about what people actually did after losing their jobs.

One way to start any job search, whether laid off or beginning, is to get organized—the subject of the last section in this chapter. This means setting aside space at home and structuring your time for (plus keeping accurate records of) job search activities—all of which will be explained later in further detail.

TWENTY THOUGHTS ABOUT UNDERTAKING A JOB SEARCH

1. Learn More

Job seekers can always learn more about job hunting. Most people know very little about how to search for a job. They think all you need to do is send out a few résumés, make some telephone calls, complete application forms, have an interview—and that's all there is to it! They are likely to overestimate their knowledge of the subject. Job search strategies are not usually taught in schools and colleges, and job seekers often take a "seat-of-the-pants" approach. There is more to the job search process than many people suspect. How many graduates have felt panicky or desperate in their job search and settled for something less than they were worth? That situation is called *underemployment.* Some underemployment may be structural (caused by the nature of the economy at the time), but some of it can be avoided with better job search information and techniques. Evaluate yourself on your job-hunting knowledge. Can you honestly claim you know the following?

- Precisely the work you want to do; you can accurately describe your job objective to an employer or on a résumé
- Information to include in your résumé and cover letter and how to design these kinds of business communications

- What most employers and human resources personnel ask on their applications
- Information you should obtain when you first interview employers
- Five to ten sources of job leads in your chosen occupation
- What you should know about a work organization before you apply to it
- The qualifications, achievements, skills, and motivations that would convince an employer to hire you
- Where you want to work and live, and where the jobs in your occupational choice are located
- Typical problems encountered by people like yourself who work in your chosen occupational field
- Social and economic trends influencing jobs in your occupational field

If you can answer yes to 5 of these 10 items, congratulations! You are in better shape than the average job seeker. (But what about the other 5 items—plus the others that could have been included?)

2. Sincerity and Energy

Give time and energy to a sincere and honest effort in your job search. The manner in which you conduct your job search will speak volumes to most employers. Job hunting that is frivolous and halfhearted will not impress any employer worth working for. No one is opposed to being humorous and lighthearted, but you become serious about getting a job in the occupation of your choice when the following statements apply to you:

- You are spending 30 to 35 hours a week in job-hunting activities (15 if currently employed).
- You have developed a daily action plan for your job search.
- You know exactly what you want to do in your work.
- You have options in case Plan A doesn't work out.
- You work on fine-tuning your job search message to employers.
- You are identifying organizations that interest you.
- You are researching at least three to five companies that appear to have what you want in your work.

- You are developing a network of contacts that could provide information for your job search.
- You are keeping a record or portfolio of proven accomplishments.
- You are collecting personal information you could use in résumés and cover letters and on job application forms.

Coming up with 35 hours each week for job search activities may be too much if you are working full time and have family responsibilities. Full-time workers may have to cut back to 15 hours, but this still means at least 2 or 3 hours of job-hunting activities per day. Use lunch hours, late afternoons, early mornings, Saturdays, evenings, vacation periods, and personal business days for writing and sending résumés, researching companies, developing contacts, and interviewing. It's surprising how many hours can be squeezed out of a busy week when you are dedicated to the task of getting a new job. The great majority of job seekers spend less than 5 hours per week on job-hunting activities (Bolles, 2003), perhaps thinking the computer can do it all for them (Challenger, 2003). No wonder job searches seem to go on and on! I won't sugarcoat job hunting as being all fun and frolic—there is hard work ahead as well as adventure, excitement, letdowns, elation, disappointment, stimulation, and frustration. Yet, there will be few times in life when you will be more absorbed and immersed in what you are doing than during the search for a challenging job.

3. Start Now

The time to start your job search campaign is now. Job hunting is hard work, and often frustrating. We'd rather procrastinate than face it. For example, college students are often tempted to say that they will start job hunting after graduation. After all, there *is* the Internet. Well, yes, cyberspace may give you some job leads quickly, but it won't get you a job offer because you must get out and interview people for that. As this edition of this book is being written, the U.S. Bureau of Labor Statistics reports that the average duration of unemployment is nearly 20 weeks (Geller, 2003)—close to 5 months. About 20 percent of the unemployed, nearly 1.6 million, have been without a job for 27 weeks or longer—more than 6 months (Challenger, 2003). Nearly a decade ago, the average time to find a job was 6.3 months (Mangum, 1996). Nothing much has changed. And that's only the unemployed the government knows about. The U.S. Department of Labor doesn't keep track of those who have become discouraged and quit looking for work.

You can do certain things to shorten the time span between graduation and full-time work. Do some serious thinking about what you want to do with the working part of your life. Establish your career goals: examine the occupational interests you have, the skills you enjoy using, and the values that mean the most to you, and learn about occupations that are most likely to express those values and use those skills—the subject of the first book in this series. Become knowledgeable about several sources of job leads (the subject of Chapter 2 of this book). Learn about job search methods now so you can move into action immediately when the time comes to search for a job (Chapter 2 again). Prepare your credentials for the career services office. Become acquainted with and keep a record of people who could serve as personal contacts (people who know about jobs, employers, and organizations) when you enter the job market (Chapters 2, 6, and 7). All career counselors will tell you to start building your network of contacts before you need it. Develop the right information to include in your résumé and cover letter (Chapter 3). Identify and research companies you believe would be desirable places to work (Chapter 6). Even get in some practice interviewing and asking people for career information before you start interviewing for a job (Chapter 8). Taking the time now to prepare an adequate information base for your job search campaign could spare you the grim cycle of initial enthusiasm followed by discouragement, desperation, and depression. Doing your homework on yourself and the job world enables some students to land jobs even before they graduate.

4. Continuity and Readiness

The job search is a continuous activity, and many job-hunting skills can be used much or all of the time. A job search is not an isolated event; it happens over and over again. It requires persistence and constant effort. The typical person today changes their jobs on an average of every three or four years; younger workers generally change their jobs more often than that. People no longer settle into one job for the rest of their lives. You may be perfectly happy in your present job, but life can be capricious at times. Industries suffer economic downturns, companies merge with new organizations, competition becomes intense, or the boss you like gets fired. No one ever plans to have an accident, to be laid off, or to become burned out or disillusioned, but these things do happen. You never know when the seemingly solid ground will shift underneath you. You never know when you will need to have your career-planning bag packed and ready to go. *The only true job security lies in being ready to search for a new job at any time.* (This statement touches on another aspect of security: options. Security parallels options. The more job options or alternatives you have, the more security you have.) Constant readiness is the only realistic approach for the job world of today.

5. Tell Everyone

Tell everyone you know that you are looking for a job. One exception may be your current employer if you are working full time (or a person who knows your boss). However, the more people who know about your job search, the more likely you are to learn about job positions that are or will be vacant. Keep talking to one person after another until you find one who knows of a vacancy. Don't be content with the discovery of one job—go on to find more than one possibility. A job lead does not necessarily lead to a job offer. You need a list of several jobs in several organizations from which you can select. Interestingly, job leads are more likely to come from acquaintances than from close friends or relatives, a phenomenon that researcher Mark Granovetter (1995) calls "the strength of weak ties." This insight seems to contradict logic, but the people you do not associate with as often are more likely to provide you with job leads. Further research has confirmed this finding.

Some people go it alone in the job search, too proud or afraid to involve anyone else. Most of us, however, need emotional support from others, particularly those who are close to us, when we face a tough situation. Pooling resources with others can be very helpful, especially if you get bogged down. This is particularly important for those who are job hunting because they have been fired. Some people conceal unemployment from their families. They carry the entire burden of guilt and embarrassment in their minds—an understandable reaction, but not a helpful or productive one. They simulate their former working days, getting up as usual and pretending to go to work. Don't let your pride get in the way. The truth becomes known sooner or later; therefore, it's better to be straightforward with your family from the start and ask for their support. Whether you are looking for a job for the first time or the twentieth time, your family can be a source of great strength. Your nuclear family and your extended family can provide you with moral and even financial support, and can be a rich source of job leads. But you must let them know what you are doing and how they can help.

6. Hidden Jobs

More job openings exist in the hidden job market than are visible and advertised to the general public. Ask people where they would start looking for a job, and most of them will mention the help-wanted ads in the newspaper. Others may mention listings in public and private employment agencies or college career centers, announcements in trade journals, or notices of examinations for civil service jobs posted on bulletin boards in government buildings. Many job seekers think most job vacancies are advertised to the general public. Actually, only 15 to 20 percent of all job openings on any given day are published and circulated. Many job search experts have long claimed about 80 percent of all employment comes through the "hidden job market" (Haldane, Haldane, and Martin, 1976; Jackson, 1991; Lathrop, 1998). Some labor economists consider these estimates too high, but understanding this concept can give you an advantage many others do not possess.

The hidden portion of the job market exists from the time an idea to create a job enters the mind of a person with hiring authority to the time the job is revealed to the public through newspapers, magazines, online bulletin boards, employment agencies, and college career services offices. The intervening time gives you the opportunity to penetrate the hidden job market through your own network of personal contacts. Many employers prefer to hire through an inside system of personal contacts rather than by any other method, feeling that it doesn't cost them as much and that the information they obtain is more reliable.

For example, let's say a person leaves a job in your occupation. The company needs a replacement. How could you find out about it? Who knows what has happened? The person leaving the job knows; so does management. Next to know would be coworkers; then, some of their friends hear that a job opening just might be created. In the meantime, a person (or people) with hiring authority must make a decision on how and when to fill the vacancy, and this process may take weeks or months. The job is still hidden from the general public. If any of your personal contacts learn about the potential job opening, that information is passed along to you because you have primed your contact to do this. You might help management make up its mind to offer you the job before it is advertised and made visible to the public.

The hidden job market may operate more extensively in small businesses than in large companies, which are more likely to have formalized hiring procedures. Job seekers often believe that big work organizations offer more employment opportunities. Actually, the reverse is true. Large firms have been and still are *downsizing* (shrinking their work force) and *outsourcing* (buying parts from independent suppliers, rather than making them themselves). Employment growth in recent years has been the greatest in small companies. Large companies are no longer the major source of employment opportunities in the United States (Wegmann, Chapman, and Johnson, 1989). Establishments in the United States are predominantly small. In 1999, 54.2 percent of all companies employed fewer than five workers; however, they hired just 5.9 percent of all workers. Organizations with more than 500 employees accounted for only 0.2 percent of all establishments; however, they employed 20.4 percent of all workers in the United States in 1999 (U.S. Department of Labor, 2002). Establishments with less than 100 workers employ about 54 percent of all workers (see Table 1-1).

The Bolles job-creation strategy illustrates another aspect of the hidden job market. After job seekers have researched workplaces and interviewed people for information, they can demonstrate their job search and problem-solving skills in the hope of creating in employers' minds job possibilities not perceived until now (Bolles, 2003). Employers are motivated to create jobs that may have been hidden even from themselves.

7. Use Several Methods

Use more than one source of job leads in your job search. The survey of 10 million job seekers cited earlier in this chapter reported that the most effective job search method, applying directly to employers, succeeded 47.7 percent of the time (Egan, 1976). Even this best method failed more than half the time. Fifteen other job search methods were even less productive. Because no single method of job hunting works very well, logic indicates that you should use several job search resources, certainly more than one—

Table 1-1 Percent Distribution of Establishments and Employment in All Industries by Establishment Size, 1999

Establishment Size (number of workers)	Percentage of Establishments	Percentage of Workers
Total	100.0	100.0
1–4	54.2	5.9
5–9	19.4	8.1
10–19	12.5	10.7
20–49	8.5	16.3
50–99	2.9	12.8
100–249	1.7	16.4
250–499	0.4	9.6
500–999	0.2	7.2
1,000 or more	0.1	13.2

Source: U.S. Department of Labor (2002). *Career guide to industries.* Washington, DC: Bureau of Labor Statistics.

but apparently most job hunters do not follow this advice. A 1992 study of the job search methods of 8 million job seekers revealed that the average number of methods used was 1.77, or less than two (Ports, 1993).

Another study reported that the likelihood of finding a job increased only slightly with each additional job search method, and actually declined somewhat when five or more methods were used (Bortnick and Ports, 1992). Of the 32,058 unemployed job seekers surveyed, 48 percent used one method, with 21.8 percent finding employment within one month. Another 34 percent used two job search methods; 23 percent of those job hunters successfully found a job after a month's time. Perhaps there is a reason for a decline in finding employment by job seekers using five or more job search methods. As Bolles (2003) suggests after pondering this peculiar finding, there may be a tendency not to give any method the time it needs to be effective. Bortnick and Ports (1992) also discovered that over two-thirds of the job seekers using five or more methods in the first month continued to look for work in the second month, whereas less than half of those using only one method continued their job search.

8. Job-Seeker Power

The job seeker has as much power in and control over the search process as the job-giving employer. Most job seekers believe they are powerless in their job search. Employers can give or withhold something that job hunters want—a job. However, job seekers also have the power to give or withhold something employers want—a worker's time and talent. Employers do have the power to hire, but it is a power they don't usually enjoy using. Hiring employees is often costly, time consuming, and full of tension and pressure. Often employers can't wait to give up interviewing job applicants and get back to their work. As one employer put it, "You ask, 'Are you living with your mother?' and you get sued for $20 million" (Brown, 1998). When their organizations can afford it or become larger, employers hire personnel specialists to do this work for them because they dislike it so much.

Pressure affects employers as much as (if not more than) job seekers. If they do not select good employees, their organization suffers. As for firing, employers would like to avoid that ordeal as much as anyone else. Employers and human resources departments work just as hard at finding good people as job seekers work at finding good jobs. Job seekers and employers pass each other on the street every day, both of them not knowing how much they need each other. You, as a competent job seeker, can help them out by the quality of your job search. Qualified, conscientious job hunters have far more power than they realize.

9. Screen Employers

Job seekers should screen employers and workplaces as much as companies evaluate prospective employees. It is clear that employers and their personnel departments screen applicants before they consider hiring them. A formal test, or some kind of informal, subjective test, may be administered. Employers want to feel that the chemistry is right before they hire. Job seekers, in contrast, are so anxious to pass the employer's screening devices that they forget to think about screening tests of their own until after they are hired. If employers screen you, there is no reason why you can't evaluate them.

Your screening, like that of the employer, should be performed before the question of a job comes up. You are not trying to discover if you are good enough for the job—you did that when you selected an occupation. Instead, you are trying to find out whether the employer's organization is good enough for you. Your attitude must not be like dropping to your knees and pleading with the employer to "please give me a job." When you first ask an employer for information so you can evaluate whether the workplace interests you, you avoid approaching the employer as a supplicant begging for help. While you screen the employer, he or she is also evaluating you as a possible job candidate, even though you haven't asked for a job. You and the employer are interviewing each other, and that is the way a job search ought to be.

10. Know Employer Needs

Learn the characteristics that employers want—before you ask them for a job. The best way to find out the attributes employers want is to ask them directly when you interview them for information about their companies.

Every employer has his or her own ideas, but employer organizations come up with skills and abilities on which most everyone would agree. Among these competencies are skills such as the ability to communicate clearly, manage information, use numbers, solve problems, hold positive attitudes, be responsible and dependable, learn continuously, be adaptable, work cooperatively with other people, participate in projects, and know a subject area of expertise.

Turn to Appendix A: *Characteristics Employers Want in Job Applicants* at the back of this book for more ideas about qualities employers are looking for in job applicants. You will notice that, although knowledge and technical ability are mentioned as characteristics employers want in workers, many of the listed skills involve attitude, teamwork, and cooperation—human traits that have more to do with who you are than what you can do.

11. Job Titles Conceal

In the job search, occupational titles often conceal more information than they reveal. Occupational titles are useful general indicators of the activities workers perform on the job in an occupation. We use job titles as a type of verbal shorthand so that we don't have to use lengthy descriptions to explain what we are talking about. Ask people about the work they do and they respond with a job title: secretary, manager, teacher, nurse, auto mechanic, detective. The title gives you some information and brings to mind some stereotyped images, both accurate and inaccurate, of what a person is like or does on the job. Take detective, for example. To really learn about what someone does in this line of work, you must go beyond watching Andy Sipowicz on TV's *NYPD Blue*. Andy may have been the perfect cop for the last century, but now that computers hold the key to uncovering evidence about crimes ranging from terrorist plots to accounting scandals, does he know how to glean secrets from a suspect's hard drive? How about auto mechanic? Popular knowledge about that occupation may still be the badly outdated "grease monkey" image. The average person does not have any idea of how technically complicated cars have become—some of them have 70 computers on them—which is probably why there are 60,000 unfilled auto-service jobs, slated to be 150,000 by 2010 (McGinn, 2002).

When you researched occupations to make a career decision, you discovered that the information from a job title was not enough. You had to ask questions and obtain information about the nature of the work activities, preparation, training, pay, working conditions, location, typical work associates, advancement opportunities, competition, personal satisfaction, problems to solve, and many other data that went well beyond the title of the occupation.

Sometimes job titles are used in a way that can be misleading or even deliberately dishonest. For example, a help-wanted ad for a computer programmer could be from an employer who actually needs a data entry clerk. You can cope with the problem of deceptive job titles by researching the company and interviewing for information to learn how your occupation is actually employed.

In some situations, you are forced to remove an occupational label. If your job becomes obsolete or is shipped out of town or overseas where you can't follow it, you must remove the old job label and repackage yourself as a pattern of skills to which you can affix a new job title after you are employed (Bolles, 2003). Those skills are then transferred to the new job title.

12. Know Your Objective(s)

The best job seekers are those who have their career goals clearly in mind. They think not only of a well-defined job objective, but also of a preferred geographical location and the names of several workplaces. By now you should have a ranked list of occupational alternatives based on knowledge of your important work values and your favorite, documented abilities. If this is not the case, you have some personal homework to do. Employers do not have the time to be your career counselor. Knowing what you want to do is the biggest hurdle in career planning. Once you have decided on a career goal, it is easier to take action in the search for a job in the occupation of your choice. Taking action means accomplishing a series of short-term goals, beginning with an entry-level position if you are just starting on your career path. The first job is not likely to be your ultimate dream job, which may be a while in the making. For those of you who worked through the first book in this series, return to the Basic Career Plan and the reality-testing exercises in Chapter 10 of *Taking Charge of Your Career Direction*. What were the short-term goals to be achieved on the way to your long-term career goal?

13. Desire and Enthusiasm

Demonstrating your desire for a job and your enthusiasm about the work impresses most employers more than anything else. Job seekers typically worry about how badly they need a job. Instead, they ought to think in terms of their desire for a job. Nothing captures an employer's imagination more than the job applicant's communication of enthusiasm about a job. No one has to say, "I want this job very much." Employers and interviewers can sense it without being told. Projecting apathy and indifference about your job search will kill your chances of getting a job faster than anything else. Many company recruiters openly wonder why so many students show no interest, drive, and ambition when they interview on campus. Projecting genuine enthusiasm will put you ahead of many competitors in the job search. A lot of people expect work to be a form of imprisonment, a monotonous grind, a life of quiet desperation, or an activity they will come to hate. Who could be creative or feel challenged by work with expectations such as these? Some jobs are too small, flat, dull, energy-draining, or unchallenging for you. Perhaps you can be spared from wrong jobs by the quality of your career planning. Develop desire and enthusiasm for your work by building reasonable expectations from a process of setting appropriate career and life goals.

14. Select Your Workplace

The selection of a place to work is just as important for job satisfaction as the choice of an occupation. Some people think that once they have chosen an occupation, they have completed their career planning. Actually, they have completed only one phase; more decisions remain for the job search. If you are serious about your future, your exploration of workplaces will involve as much effort as your research of occupations. Work organizations have their own distinctive products and services, group cultures, personality characteristics, and ways of employing people. The environmental context or social atmosphere of the place in which you work has as much to do with your career satisfaction as does the nature of the work in your occupation.

Some workers choose the right occupation, then find themselves in the wrong places of work. All too often, they think they have made the wrong occupational choice and never stop to consider that the problem could be the workplace. A change of work location could bring them the job satisfaction they had originally anticipated.

Competent job seekers research workplaces and organizations before they accept a job offer. They may even reject an organization's offer based on the information they have uncovered about it. Richard Irish (1978) once underscored the importance of selecting a work organization and an employer: "Hire yourself an employer. You'll be spending as much time with this person as with your wife or husband, and you'll want a good marriage" (p. xxii).

15. Research Your Chosen Industry

Researching your chosen industry is just as important as learning about occupations and work organizations. Why? One thing you may want to know is whether the industry that houses your occupation and job is expected to grow or decline. Some industries are booming because of an accelerated demand for their goods and services. Other industries may be declining as they become heavily automated and soon may need only skeleton crews. In the latter case, if you already are employed, you may decide your only defense against unemployment is to prepare for a new job search with a new job objective. If you are embarking on job hunting, you may want to reconsider the industry in which you are seeking a job. A good place to start is the *Career Guide to Industries* published by the Bureau of Labor Statistics (2002) of the U.S. Department of Labor. The *Guide* covers job opportunities in 42 industries, and when those industries are combined, they account for nearly three-fourths of the wage and salary jobs in the United States. For each industry, information is given on the nature of the industry, working conditions, employment data, occupations in the industry, training and advancement, earnings, and industry outlook. You can get a good idea of the kinds of industries that are covered in the *Guide* by looking at the lists of industries under each category of Table 1-2. This table provides employment numbers in major industry divisions and in certain industries as of 2000, and the projected change in percentages from 2000 to 2010.

16. Personal Responsibility

The best job hunters assume personal responsibility for finding a job. Make up your mind from the beginning to take responsibility for your job search. Professional career counselors, employment agency personnel, and college career services officials can help, but in the final analysis, the job seeker must put the words in the résumé, complete the application form, do the company research, and face the employer in the interview. If career counselors offer to relieve you of these burdens, flee from them as quickly as possible, for they are either charlatans or misguided. Before you pay a career counselor to help you, read the appendix on choosing a career counselor in *What Color Is Your Parachute?* (Bolles, annual editions). Get help when you need it, but get competent, ethical help.

Table 1-2 Wage and Salary Employment in Selected Industries, 2000, and Projected Change, 2000 to 2010 (employment in thousands)

Industry	2000 Employment	2000 Percent Distribution	2010 Employment	2010 Percent Distribution	2000–2010 Percent Change	2000–2010 Employment Change
All industries	133,896	100.0	155,872	100.0	16.4	21,977
Goods-producing industries	27,984	20.9	29,728	19.1	6.2	1,745
Agriculture, mining, and construction	9,514	7.1	10,682	0.0	12.3	1,167
Agricultural production	1,120	0.8	1,092	0.7	−2.5	−28
Agricultural services	1,099	0.8	1,524	1.0	38.6	425
Construction	6,698	5.0	7,522	4.8	12.3	825
Mining and quarrying	231	0.2	199	0.1	−14.0	−32
Oil and gas extraction	311	0.2	289	0.2	−7.3	−23
Manufacturing	18,469	13.8	19,047	12.2	3.1	577
Aerospace manufacturing	551	0.4	655	0.4	18.9	104
Apparel and other textile products	633	0.5	530	0.3	−16.3	−103
Chemical manufacturing, except drugs	723	0.5	691	0.4	−4.5	−32
Drug manufacturing	315	0.2	390	0.3	23.8	75
Electronic equipment manufacturing	1,554	1.2	1,657	1.1	6.6	103
Food processing	1,684	1.3	1,634	1.0	−3.0	−50
Motor vehicle and equipment manufacturing	1,013	0.8	1,100	0.7	8.6	87
Printing and publishing	1,547	1.2	1,545	1.0	−0.2	−3
Steel manufacturing	225	0.2	176	0.1	−21.6	−49
Textile mill products	529	0.4	500	0.3	−5.4	−29
Service-producing industries	105,912	79.1	126,144	80.9	19.1	20,232
Transportation, communications, and public utilities	7,019	5.2	8,274	5.3	17.9	1,255
Air transportation	1,281	1.0	1,600	1.0	24.9	319
Cable and other pay television services	216	0.2	325	0.2	50.6	109
Public utilities	851	0.6	893	0.6	4.9	42
Radio and television broadcasting	255	0.2	280	0.2	9.7	25
Telecommunications	1,168	0.9	1,311	0.8	12.2	143
Trucking and warehousing	1,856	1.4	2,262	1.5	21.9	407
Wholesale and retail trade	30,331	22.7	34,200	21.9	12.8	3,869
Department, clothing, and accessory stores	4,030	3.0	4,198	2.7	4.2	168
Eating and drinking places	8,114	6.1	9,600	6.2	18.3	1,486
Grocery stores	3,107	2.3	3,281	2.1	5.6	174
Motor vehicle dealers	1,221	0.9	1,366	0.9	11.9	145
Wholesale trade	7,024	5.2	7,800	5.0	11.1	776
Finance, insurance, and real estate	7,560	5.6	8,247	5.3	9.1	687
Banking	2,029	1.5	1,999	1.3	−1.5	−31
Insurance	2,346	1.8	2,497	1.6	6.4	151
Securities and commodities	748	0.6	900	0.6	20.3	152

Industry	2000		2010		2000–2010	
	Employment	Percent Distribution	Employment	Percent Distribution	Percent Change	Employment Change
Services	50,764	37.9	64,483	41.4	27.0	13,719
Advertising	302	0.2	400	0.3	32.5	98
Amusement and recreation services	1,728	1.3	2,325	1.5	34.5	597
Childcare services	712	0.5	1,010	0.6	41.9	298
Computer and data processing services	2,095	1.6	3,900	2.5	86.2	1,805
Educational services	11,797	8.8	13,400	8.6	13.6	1,603
Health services	11,065	8.3	13,882	8.9	25.5	2,817
Hotels and other lodging places	1,912	1.4	2,167	1.4	13.3	255
Management and public relations services	1,090	0.8	1,550	1.0	42.2	460
Motion picture production and distribution	287	0.2	369	0.2	28.7	82
Personnel supply services	3,887	2.9	5,800	3.7	49.2	1,913
Social services, except childcare	2,191	1.6	3,118	2.0	42.3	927
Government	10,238	7.6	10,940	7.0	6.9	702
Federal government	1,917	1.4	1,772	1.1	–7.6	–145
State and local government	7,461	5.6	8,318	5.3	11.5	856

Source: U.S. Department of Labor (2002). *Career guide to industries.* Washington, DC: Bureau of Labor Statistics, p. 4.
Note: Table 1-2 does not include nearly 11 million self-employed workers and about 180,000 unpaid family workers.

Another side of career responsibility can arise after you have accepted employment. If the job becomes monotonous, unchallenging, dreary drudgery, don't waste time blaming the system, those in power, the economy, or your horoscope. You have three options. (1) Do nothing. (2) Improve the quality of your job if possible. (3) Change jobs as soon as you reasonably can. The problem with the first option is that it leads to chronic complaining; the daily gripe session becomes your only job satisfaction. You can try to improve the nature of your work by thinking of ways to make it more challenging and rewarding, having your ideas evaluated by your coworkers and clearing them with your supervisors. Changing jobs, of course, requires a new job search, the subject of this book. Try to do it while you have a source of income from your current job. However bad the job may seem to you now, keep in mind that you can always learn something from it that might be useful later.

17. Support for—and from—the Community

The job seeker's relationship with the community cannot be ignored in the job search. As much as we pay attention to individual responsibility in job hunting, an equal emphasis should be given to a concept of community. "Community" is a hard subject to write about in today's world; people often regard it as a vague, nebulous idea that doesn't have much meaning for life in the 21st century. Many people think of choosing an occupation and getting a job in it strictly as a way of acquiring a prosperous private lifestyle, without thinking of the common good or anything else beyond their own personal interests. In addition to private values, your occupation is a means to express social values such as justice, health, and knowledge. In the interest of us all, we need lawyers to serve the value of justice, nurses and doctors to serve the value of health, and teachers to serve the value of knowledge (Bellah, Madsen, Sullivan, Swidler, & Tipton, 1988). An exclusive focus on personal advancement leaves people isolated from one another and confused about the requirements for a good society. Concern for the larger needs of the community may sound like starry-eyed philosophy, but there are down-to-earth, practical reasons for it. When you search for a job, you do not do it apart from the community. Your family, neighbors, work associates, social acquaintances, and job-finding groups, for instance, are part of a support network you can tap into as you hunt for a new job. The assistance you can receive from community organizations, such as a job club or cooperative, can be very helpful in finding work. As a worker or a business owner, you need customers, clients, students, patients, suppliers, coworkers, and so on—all from the larger community around you. If you forget these other people, you will soon be out of business. As much as we prize individual hard work and motivation in a job seeker or worker, we must acknowledge our dependence on other people in the community and our obligations to them. Self-reliance does not mean living in isolation from others.

18. Work as Education

Working on the job is an education in itself. People often assume that when their formal education in the classroom is completed, they are ready and equipped to do the work in the occupation of their choice. After you have worked on the job awhile, you discover that you have obtained most of your knowledge about the work on the job, not in school. This is not an indictment of the educational system, which has provided "generalist" skills that can be transferred to the job. Generalist skills, such as reading, communicating, researching, and analyzing, are learned in academic courses. These skills may in the future prove to be more adaptable to work than a specialty, which could become outdated because of advances in science and technology. Almost every job is learned through on-the-job training. Because skills learned on the job generally fall into the category of "specialist" skills, many companies provide an in-service education program to train workers in their specialties.

The best way to find out what jobs are like while you are in school is to gain work experience from a temporary, part-time, or summer job. If the work can be related to your career objective, so much the better. This is the idea behind cooperative work-study programs and internships; by all means, use them if you can. Work experience during school has advantages other than that of earning some spending money. It places you in situations where you can casually interview people for information you may need for your future job search and where you can develop personal contacts. Employers are more impressed with job seekers who have previous experience of paid work, internships, work-study arrangements, and volunteer work than with job seekers who have no work experience. Check with your college financial aid or career services office or public employment agency for part-time and temporary work opportunities.

Howard Figler, author of *PATH: A Career Workbook for Liberal Arts Students* (1979), suggests an **interim job** approach to career exploration and preparation for the job search. Interim jobs are temporary, part-time, and summer work experiences that meet the following requirements: the qualifications are minimal; the job is available; and it places you in contact with many people in different kinds of work situations. These jobs allow you to talk with people about their work, ask them questions to obtain information, and develop contacts that might prove useful in your future job search. Some interim jobs suggested by Figler include opinion poll interviewer, news reporter, retail store clerk, car driver, marketing research interviewer, bartender, museum guard, hospital orderly, security guard, golf caddie, short-order cook, comparison shopper, receptionist, photographer's helper, mail carrier, and temporary office worker.

Mariani (1998) lists occupations with the capability of being summer jobs, particularly in the service, sales, and retail trade categories. Specific occupations include waiter or waitress, tour guide, recreation attendant, janitor, ticket taker, golf course attendant, lifeguard, carpenter's helper, small-engine repairer, landscaping helper, greenhouse worker, animal feeder, lawn service worker, cashier, office clerk, and librarian assistant. Examples of companies or industries where summer work may be found are cleaning service, hotel/motel, day camp, fitness club, playground, amusement or theme park, bowling alley, movie rental store, computer or data processing firm, child care facility, grocery store, ice cream shop, bakery, pizza parlor, concession stand, department store, gas station, book store, souvenir shop, and hardware store. Self-employment opportunities may be found in washing cars, mowing lawns, garden care, tutoring, computer training, babysitting, house or pet sitting, house painting or cleaning, planning children's parties, and providing shopping services.

A summer camp counselor's job might be ideal for someone who likes the outdoors. A wide range of positions, from park ranger to recreation worker, can be found at the 350 sites of the National Park Service. Peterson's annual *Summer Jobs USA* lists more than 20,000 positions throughout the nation. Applications usually must be submitted between September and January for the following summer.

19. Persistence Pays Off

Persistence in the job search is the greatest strength of the job hunter. Without persistence and effort, no job search approach will work very well. The job seeker's greatest enemy is discouragement; people do give up on finding a job and quit altogether. The government's monthly unemployment figures include a special category for discouraged workers—those who have stopped looking for jobs. Rejection seems built into the job-hunting system. Even though you know it has nothing to do with you personally, your ego gets battered every time you are turned down. Your résumé draws no response, your letters don't get answered, phone calls are not returned, employers are not in, or someone else is chosen after the interview. That's the way the typical job search goes. Sooner or later, you are tempted to quit—but then you would certainly find no job.

Jackson (1991) suggests an innovative way of looking at the job search. He describes it as a NO NO NO NO NO NO NO NO NO NO NO NO NO NO NO YES! process. Every NO gets you that much closer to the YES. Be realistic about job hunting. Few job seekers connect with a firm job offer after only two or three hours of work. You can't just post a few résumés on a job board and sit back waiting for job offers to materialize. If you take seriously the hard work and persistence needed for job hunting, you'll be ahead of most job seekers on that factor alone.

Remember, most job hunters spend less than five hours a week on their job search. If you make job hunting a full-time, 35-hour-a-week job, you speed up the job search process by a factor of 7 and increase your chances accordingly. That may seem like a lot of time. But if you are not willing to give it your best shot, then you should ask yourself: How important is getting a job, anyway—to me and my family and loved ones?

20. The Universal Hiring Rule

The key to getting hired is convincing an employer that you will bring more value to the company than you will cost it. Tom Jackson (1991) calls this "the universal hiring rule." Can you show how you could cut the cost of producing something or providing a service? Can you show how you could increase a company's volume of business? The most effective sales technique in a job interview is to let employers know what you can do for them, quietly and confidently. This means you must be very knowledgeable about what the organization does—a practical argument for spending time researching the company. A majority of job seekers define the job search in terms of their own needs: "I need a job." Instead, take the straight and narrow path to your job search goal. Rehearse your answers to the employer's greatest concern and favorite question: Why should I hire you? Give the employer the reasons for doing so.

In Conclusion . . . Some More Thoughts . . .

Winning a new job is one of the best ways to develop self-esteem, whether you are seeking a first job or moving on to a better one. The feeling you get as you learn new techniques of job hunting and build confidence that you can always land a job is a liberating one. You can get help and support and pool your resources with others, of course, but you rely essentially on yourself. Perhaps the greatest feeling you can have about yourself is the inner knowledge that you can get a job, earn your own money, and take care of yourself.

If you currently work at a job you have come to hate, it's time to change jobs. Of course, there will be problems. It will cost money. You may think your family won't support you, that it's risky to change, or that it's suicide to change jobs in mid-career. But it may be more costly, risky, or suicidal to stay put. Yes, you will face new challenges and problems of adjustment, but you will also experience a rebirth of motivation, enthusiasm for life, and a sense of achievement. Today more people than ever opt for a mid-career job change, from the homemaker seeking a new life outside the home to the employee who suddenly needs to escape the comfortable work routine of the past 15 years. A new job can bring a new lease on life. One cautionary note: Job changing is not hopping helter-skelter from one job to another. Changing jobs should be a well-planned strategy, not change for the sake of change.

In addition to the 20 thoughts covered in this chapter, many more will be explored in this book, including the following:

- All interviews, informational or for a job, should be followed up with a thank-you letter.
- The job search campaign requires organization in order to be effective.

For now, 20 thoughts will suffice, and the ones you have just studied meet with widespread agreement. Others, such as the following, are more controversial:

- *Avoid personnel departments, because the only authority they have is the power to screen out job applicants, not to hire them, unless the job is in personnel.* This is true enough in a number of cases, but personnel (or human resources) departments are appropriate targets for entry-level positions, and they are still the main gate to jobs for the new college graduate (Shingleton and Bao, 1977).
- *It is easier to get a job if you are working than if you are not working.* This idea has its truth, but it is not as true today because too many worthy people have been unemployed recently, and being out of work doesn't carry the stigma it once did.
- *If other job-hunting techniques fail, offer to work for free and prove your worth to an employer.* The work-for-free method should be used only when you are unemployed and have found a job opening that is very close to being your ideal job. This method is a short-term strategy that has paid off for actors, singers, dancers, and comedians, and it is now being suggested to people searching for jobs in hundreds of kinds of occupations (Weinstein, 1994). Apprenticeships and unpaid internships have operated on a work-for-free principle. You make an offer to work for no pay for a limited time in exchange for an opportunity to demonstrate your talents, skills, and qualifications in the occupation you have prepared for. If the employer accepts your no-risk offer, you (naturally) perform your very best work. In effect, you are saying, "If I can do this excellent work for you for nothing, think what I can do for you when I am getting paid." Is this method a sure-fire way to get a job? There are no ab-

solute guarantees you will be offered paid employment. Working for free is a gamble, but it is unusual and creative enough that it just might work in the highly competitive labor market of today. Turn everything around and imagine you are the employer. You receive a work-for-free offer from a job seeker. "I want to work at your company, and I am willing to prove my value to you free of cost. You have nothing to lose and everything to gain—a hardworking, intelligent, productive employee. All I want is an opportunity to show you the good work I can do for you. This is a win–win situation for both of us." Would you turn down this person, or would you grant an interview to find out what this offer is all about? The working-for-free idea is no different from getting a free sample of a product from a manufacturer who is hoping to convince you of its benefits so you will buy it next time. You, the job seeker, are the seller in this case; you are proposing to give the employer a free sample of your work in the hope he or she will become a buyer of your services in the near future. Even if nothing happens as a result of your efforts, you will have spent only a small amount of your time and energy. (As for money, you could try to negotiate some of your traveling expenses. And keep in mind that the company cannot legally hire you without paying the minimum wage.) You will have gained on-the-job experience, valuable information about your chosen occupation, new friends and personal contacts, more confidence and skills, and (possibly) an employer reference—all significant contributions toward landing a job another time.

Well, that's 25 "thoughts" (we've just added five more). We could add hundreds of ideas, but that would make for a very long chapter. So, let's move on to the subject of organizing for the job search.

GETTING ORGANIZED FOR THE JOB SEARCH

Set up a job search office, or a place in your home for job search materials. Choose an area much like a place you would choose to study. It should include a desk or a table where you can keep supplies, notes, incoming mail, stationery, newspapers, books, and files.

Set a time for your job search efforts. Preferably, this should be 8:00 A.M. to 5:00 P.M. Job hunting is a full-time activity. If you are working or going to school full-time, reserve a couple of hours in the evening for such activities as visiting libraries, reading job search materials, and writing or completing letters, résumés, and applications. Use lunch hours, late afternoons, Saturdays, vacation periods, and personal-business days for contacting potential employers, conducting informational interviews, and researching work organizations.

Set aside space in a desk or on a corner of a desk or table for your supplies: paper for notes, stationery, stamps, envelopes, paper clips, stapler, and file folders. Use a file cabinet, desk drawer, or even a box to hold file folders into which you can put copies of correspondence sent and received, application forms, letters and résumés, newspaper and magazine articles, employer and organization information, and anything else that is pertinent to the job search. A portfolio could contain records of achievements. Whenever you accomplish something, give the experience a title and write a short account of the achievement. Put this note into the portfolio so you can use it to refresh your memory when writing a résumé or preparing for an interview. Consult Chapter 5 of *Taking Charge of Your Career Direction* for ideas on developing a portfolio.

You will need access to a computer or typewriter, Sunday editions of newspapers, a photocopier or printing service, a telephone and phone book, and transportation. If you are not home during the day, a telephone-answering machine would be helpful.

Keep accurate records. Use file cards on which you can write the names, addresses, and telephone numbers of contacts, employers, and organizations, or use your computer to maintain this kind of file. Make a copy of any personal or follow-up correspondence you send to employers; these records could help you remember items that may be discussed at later interviews. At the end of this chapter and throughout the book, you will find forms on which to keep records. You can photocopy these record forms for your personal use if you need more copies of them.

Travel expenses or fees paid to a career counselor or employment agency can be deducted on your tax return, whether or not you succeed in landing a new job. These expenses must be recorded and verified in case you are audited. Keep receipts to substantiate your transportation, telephone, stationery, lodging, and food costs. Even this book could be deductible. You cannot deduct the costs of education you need to qualify for a new job, nor are expenses deductible if you are job hunting for the first time or changing occupations. For expenses to be deductible, there must be substantial continuity between a new job and the last job. You cannot deduct expenses if you are changing from one career field to another.

EXERCISE 1-1 GETTING STARTED: A DAILY JOB SEARCH PLAN

Keep a record of your daily job search activities. First, make several photocopies of the Daily Job Search Action Plan form provided in this exercise to have copies available as you need them. Next, set your weekly goals, either week by week or over an entire month. How many hours do you propose to spend on your job search? How many sources of job leads will be explored, letters and résumés sent, telephone calls made, applications completed, areas and organizations researched, informational and job interviews held? After each day on your job search, fill out the Daily Job Search Action Plan. To do this, record the amount of time you spent on the job search that day and tally the number of job leads you explored, the number of letters or résumés you sent to job targets, and so on. Keep a count of employers who contact you; later chapters will supply forms for the names and addresses of contacts, employers, and organizations. A "miscellaneous" category, for job search activities not elsewhere classified, is also provided on the forms.

After a predetermined period of one or four weeks, check to see whether you have accomplished your goals. Were you too optimistic about how much you would do? Do you need to do more? Should you reset your goals in each category, considering the information you have received from your performance to date? Are your goals achievable, believable, controllable, and measurable?

EXERCISE 1-2 ESTABLISHING CLEAR CAREER GOALS

This exercise is intended for those who have not completed the career decision-making exercise in *Taking Charge of Your Career Direction*, the first volume of the Career Planning Guide series. Refer particularly to the chapters with lists of occupational interests, achievements, abilities (skills and aptitudes), and work values for help in supplying the information for this exercise. The first step in job hunting is in knowing what you want and what you can do. Fill in the following blanks.

A. (From Chapter 3) My strongest clusters of interests appear to be:

    1. _____   3. _____

    2. _____   4. _____

Daily Job Search Action Plan

Month: Day/Date	Time Spent on Job Search	Sources of Job Leads Explored	Number of Letters/ Résumés Sent to Job Targets	Number of Phone Calls Made	Number of Job Applications Completed	Pieces of Data Collected on Areas and Companies	Number of Interviews for Information	Number of Employer Contacts to you	Other or Miscel-laneous*
Weekly Goals									
Mon. __									
Tue. __									
Wed. __									
Thurs.__									
Fri. __									
Sat. __									
Weekly Total									
Mon __									
Tue. __									
Wed. __									
Thurs.__									
Fri. __									
Sat. __									
Weekly Total									
Mon __									
Tue. __									
Wed. __									
Thurs.__									
Fri. __									
Sat. __									
Weekly Total									
Mon __									
Tue. __									
Wed. __									
Thurs.__									
Fri. __									
Sat. __									
Weekly Total									
Reset Goals?									

*Network contacts, job search training or counseling sessions, and the like.

Photocopy this page if more Daily Job Search Action Plans are needed.

B. (From Chapter 5) Five achievements I have attained in the past are:

1. _____
2. _____
3. _____
4. _____
5. _____

On a separate sheet of paper, title these five achievements and provide details of how you made each one happen. Circle the skills, aptitudes, and abilities you used in producing the achievements.

C. (From Chapter 6) Ten of my strongest and most enjoyable abilities, documented or proven, are as follows:

	Name of Ability	Proof or Evidence
1.	_____	_____
2.	_____	_____
3.	_____	_____
4.	_____	_____
5.	_____	_____
6.	_____	_____
7.	_____	_____
8.	_____	_____
9.	_____	_____
10.	_____	_____

D. (From Chapter 7) Ten of my most important work values, defined or explained so that I know each one is distinct from the others, are as follows:

	Name of Work Value	Definition
1.	_____	_____
2.	_____	_____
3.	_____	_____
4.	_____	_____
5.	_____	_____
6.	_____	_____
7.	_____	_____
8.	_____	_____
9.	_____	_____
10.	_____	_____

E. (From Chapter 9) My number one occupational goal is _____
_____.

Typical jobs in this occupation are _____,
_____, and _____.

F. (From Chapter 9) My number two occupational goal is _____
_____.

Typical jobs in this occupation are _____,
_____, and _____.

G. (From Chapter 9) My number three occupational goal is _____

_____.

Typical jobs in this occupation are _____,

_____, and _____.

EXERCISE 1-3 THE PARADOXICAL JOB SEARCH

On the left side of the page, list all the ways you can think of to make certain your job search will *fail*. Really get into it—how could I make a complete mess of job hunting? After listing one blunder after another, come back to the right side of the page. On the same line as each failure method, write its exact opposite. For example, one way to ruin a job search might be "Arrive 45 minutes late for each interview." On the right side of the page, its opposite would be "Arrive on time (or 10 minutes early) for each interview." Another failure technique might be "Know nothing about the company to which I am applying for a job." Its opposite would be "Learn everything I can about the company before I go there for a job interview." When you finish, you should have quite a list of effective strategies for a successful job search.

	Ways to Make Sure My Job Search Will Fail	Their Exact Opposite— for a Successful Job Search
1.		
2.		
3.		
4.		
5.		
6.		
7.		
8.		
9.		
10.		
11.		
12.		
13.		
14.		
15.		

SUMMARY

1. There are three basic approaches to the job search. The traditional approach consists of including as many methods and contacting as many probable sources of job openings as possible. The nontraditional approach focuses on self-selected job targets (often hidden from the public view) through research of potential workplaces and employers. A combination of these two approaches can also be applied, using the shared ideas of the other systems of job hunting.

2. The loss of a job is similar to other kinds of valued losses. Job loss can be compared to the loss of a life. The five stages of grieving have been used as a model first proposed by Elisabeth Kubler-Ross. They are denial, anger, bargaining, depression, and (finally) acceptance. A number of coping techniques for a job loss situation were suggested: apply for unemployment benefits as soon as possible, determine income and expenses, lower expenses while out of work, bring in extra income, stay healthy, interact with the family, reach for spiritual connections, and get help from

support groups. Eliminate stress by doing one or more of the following: search for a new job, seek education and/or retraining, investigate new geographical areas, get into community activities, apply for financial assistance beyond unemployment insurance, and look for a support group that can help.

3. At least 20 basic ideas about the job search are common to all approaches. (1) Everyone can learn more about job hunting. (2) Give sufficient time and energy to make a sincere and honest effort in your job search. (3) Start your job search now, while you are in college or in a secure job position. (4) The job-seeking process is continuous and repetitive. (5) Tell everyone you know that you are looking for a job. (6) The majority of job openings are located in the hidden job market. (7) Use more than one source of job leads. (8) Job seekers have as much power in the search process as employers. (9) Screen employers and workplaces before seeking a job there. (10) Learn what employers are looking for in their employees. (11) Job titles can conceal as much as they reveal. (12) Develop a clear objective in your job search. (13) Show enthusiasm for your intended work. (14) Selecting a work organization is just as important as choosing an occupation. (15) Research industries along with exploring occupations and organizations. (16) Take personal responsibility in job hunting. (17) Nurture the relationship with your family and community as well as attending to your own personal interests. (18) Work is an education in itself. (19) Persistence may well be the most important job search skill. (20) Convince the employer that you will bring the company more value than cost. One other idea: If you have gone a long time without a job, consider working for free to prove your worth to an employer.

4. Organization and efficiency are the keys to job seeking. Establishing a job search office, setting aside time and space for gathering information and storing materials, and keeping accurate records will permit you to structure and analyze your job hunt. As you start your campaign, recording a daily count of job search activities will put into action the principle of being efficient and organized.

REFERENCES

Associated Press. 2003, June 29. Benton Harbor youth search for hope. *Jackson Citizen Patriot*, A-7.

Bellah, R. N., Madsen, R., Sullivan, W. M., Swidler, A., and Tipton, S. M. 1988. *Habits of the heart: Individualism and commitment in American life*. New York: Harper & Row.

ployed. *Monthly Labor Review*, 115(12), 33.

Billingsley, E. 1978. *Career planning and job hunting for today's student: The nonjob interview approach*. Santa Monica, CA: Goodyear.

Bolles, R. N. 2003. *What color is your parachute?* Berkeley, CA: Ten Speed Press, published annually.

Bortnick, S. M., and Ports, M. H. 1992. Job search methods and results: Tracking the unem-

Bridges, W. 1997. *Creating you & co.: Learn to think like the CEO of your own career*. Reading, MA: Addison-Wesley.

Brown, E. 1998, February 23. The job interview. *Forbes*, 161(4), 18–20.

Bureau of Labor Statistics, U.S. Department of Labor. 2002. *Career guide to industries*, Bulletin 2541. Washington, DC: U.S. Government Printing Office.

Carroll, J. 2003, Spring. The job hunt. *Contact*. Adrian, MI: Adrian College Bulletin, p. 20.

Challenger, J. E. 2003, April. Job seekers lengthen joblessness . . . Shut off computers and see employers! *Employment Review*, 15(4), 12.

Corey, G., and Corey, M. S. 2002. *I never knew I had a choice: Explorations in personal growth*, 7th ed. Pacific Grove, CA: Brooks/Cole.

Egan, C. 1976. Job search: There's a method in the madness. *Occupational Outlook Quarterly*, 20, 18–19.

Figler, H. E. 1979. *PATH: A career workbook for liberal arts students*, 2nd ed. Cranston, RI: Carroll Press.

Frankl, V. 1963. *Man's search for meaning*. Boston: Beacon Press.

Geller, A. 2003, May 31. After months, millions of Americans are still seeking work. *Jackson Citizen Patriot*, D-1 (from the Associated Press).

Granovetter, M. S. 1995. *Getting a job: A study of contacts and careers*, 2nd ed. Chicago: University of Chicago Press.

Haldane, B., Haldane, J., and Martin, L. 1976. *Job power now! The young people's job finding guide.* Washington, DC: Acropolis Books.

Hansen, L. S. 1997. *Integrative life planning: Critical tasks for career development and changing life patterns.* San Francisco: Jossey-Bass.

Irish, R. K. 1978. *Go hire yourself an employer.* Garden City, NY: Doubleday/Anchor.

Jackson, T. 1991. *Guerrilla tactics in the new job market,* 2nd ed. New York: Bantam.

Kotlowitz, A. 1998. *The other side of the river: A story of two towns, a death, and America's dilemma.* New York: Doubleday Anchor.

Kubler-Ross, E. 1969. *On death and dying.* New York: Macmillan.

Lathrop, R. 1998. *Who's hiring who: How to find that job fast,* 12th ed. Berkeley, CA: Ten Speed Press.

Leana, C. R., and Feldman, D. C. 1992. *Coping with job loss.* New York: Lexington Books.

Mangum, W. T. 1996, Summer. How job seekers should approach the new jobmarket. *Journal of Career Planning and Employment,* 56(4), 33–35, 60–61.

Mariani, M. 1998. Successfully seeking summer jobs. *Occupational Outlook Quarterly,* 42(4), 2–7.

McGinn, D. 2002, September 23. Brave new job hunt. *Newsweek,* 54–57.

Ports, M. H. 1993, October. Trends in job search methods, 1970–92. *Monthly Labor Review,* 116(10), 63–67.

Shingleton, J. D., and Bao, R. 1977. *College to career: Finding yourself in the job market.* New York: McGraw-Hill.

Summer Jobs USA. (annual) Princeton, NJ: Peterson's Guides.

Terry, W. 2002, December 22. The helping hand. *Parade Magazine,* 4–5.

U.S. Department of Labor. 2002. *Career guide to industries.* Washington, DC: Bureau of Labor Statistics.

Wegmann, R., Chapman, R., and Johnson, M. 1989. *Work in the new economy: Careers and job seeking into the 21st century,* rev. ed. Indianapolis: JIST Works, and Alexandria, VA: American Association for Counseling and Development.

Weinstein, B. 1994. *"I'll work for free": A short-term strategy for a long-term payoff.* New York: Henry Holt.

Chapter 2

Sources of Job Leads

Many people in many places are ready to assist you in your job search. Some are very helpful, some not so helpful. Some will offer assistance free of charge; others will charge you a fee. You should feel free to obtain help in finding a job, but it is important to remember that you are the only person who can convince an employer to give you a job.

Everyone needs help at some point in the job search. This chapter will describe where you can go and what you can do to obtain help in locating job leads. By way of introduction, we'll list some possible job-lead sources.

If you are in college or have attended college, contact your school's career services office, which arranges for students and graduates to meet with company recruiters and employers. State employment agencies and their local branches offer a free job-finding service. Private employment agencies provide job-finding services for a fee, usually paid by the employer, but sometimes by the job seeker, and sometimes by both. Temporary-help agencies can provide a route to a permanent, full-time position and extra money during the job search.

The help-wanted ads in newspapers, journals, and newsletters are often disparaged because of their visibility to everyone, but if employers as well as job hunters did not find them useful, they would have disappeared long ago. Some people place ads for themselves in these publications to indicate their availability. Other parts of the newspaper contain articles that can imply a job opening without actually announcing it, perhaps by reporting a retirement, a resignation, or the opening of a new business. Other publications, such as the National Association of Colleges and Employers *Job Choices* series, carry helpful information about companies and corporations. Computer technology has given job seekers the Internet with its electronic job banks and online information services that offer places to post résumés and look for positions listed by employers.

Some job seekers organize a direct-mail campaign of letters and résumés to hundreds of work organizations. Applying directly to human resources departments or personnel and employment offices has been named as the most extensively used job search method. Human resources departments represent a good source of job leads because personnel workers help managers and executives fill vacancies. Many professional and trade associations sponsor job clearinghouses and registers to connect job-seeking members and employers. A few executive search firms help people find jobs, but generally these firms work for employers to recruit for management positions people who are already employed. Good sources of contacts are career days or job fairs sponsored by schools, chambers of commerce, and the like. Drop-in visits or cold calls on heads of businesses or departments are quick and sometimes effective ways of reaching the person with hiring authority, if you are assertive enough. Instead of dropping in unannounced, you can telephone employers directly to get in touch with the person who has the power to hire. Job clubs use this approach; the telephone procedure you can use is outlined in this chapter.

Internships and work-study programs provide ways of gaining work experience and future employment. The government, the largest single employer in the country, should not be overlooked. Federal, state, and local governments employ nearly one-seventh of the U.S. labor force. More than 86,000 governmental units exist in the United States: one national government, 50 state governments, and the counties, cities or towns, townships, special districts, and school districts that make up local governments (Bardes, Shelley, and Schmidt, 2002). A competitive examination is usually required in the application process for government jobs. The military is also a source of employment, with its own recruiters and training programs.

Job clubs or cooperatives are guided by counselors and offer job hunters emotional support along with job leads. People have attracted employers through all sorts of unusual methods, such as long-distance calls, telegrams, artistically crafted brochures, and attending trade shows. Some unusual methods are creative and enterprising; others are just plain goofy.

Not mentioned yet is the most productive source of job leads, according to job search experts. They tell us that a majority of all employment is gained through the job seeker's personal contact network. A personal contact is someone you know who can give you valuable inside information about potential job openings or refer you to a person who may have a job to offer. Personal contacts can be parents, relatives, neighbors, friends, friends of the family, friends of friends, work associates, school alumni, present and former employers, teachers, and members of professional associations, service clubs, social groups, labor unions, and religious institutions. Methods of contact are often informal and casual. Make personal contacts for the purposes of friendship and helping others as well as for the purpose of job search. People will want to hear about how you are doing, but if you use them only as sources of job leads, they could come to regard you as self-serving, interested in your own career and nothing else. A personal contact network is like a mutual aid society; you help your contacts and they help you. Your contacts can give you information and advice and can often open doors to the hidden job market. Your initial approach to a potential personal contact can be like an informational interview, which will be discussed more fully in Chapter 7.

GETTING HELP IN THE JOB SEARCH

Some people are afraid to ask for help. Sometimes, that can be a tragic mistake. During the recession of the early 1980s, a 30-year-old man wrote an unsigned note to a newspaper columnist:

> I had to tell someone before I take my life. I am married with a family of three, religious, and never been in trouble with the law. For the past five months, I have been frantically searching for some kind of employment. I am now at the point of no return. My family and I are about to be evicted because I can't pay the rent. The debts are piling up. I would like to live longer and enjoy my family, but I can't support them. I have tried seeking employment. No matter what it may be, no one has a job opening. I'm not asking for charity or a handout. All I'm asking for is a chance to work and support my family. How do you explain to your children when they say, "Daddy, why can't I have boots for the snow?" When you don't have a job, you have to cut back on everything just to survive. But small children don't understand. I always believed that one must help himself before he can get help from someone else. I'm desperate, totally desperate. Please tell anyone who has a job that they are the luckiest people in the world, no matter what the pay or conditions. At least they can tell their family when payday comes that they can buy food and clothes and pay the rent. (Royko, 1982)

The columnist responded by acknowledging the man's plight and urging him to hang on. His wife and children would rather have an unemployed living husband and father than the memory of a dead one. He wasn't alone in his unemployed condition; it was nothing to be ashamed of. A lot of jobless people do not have control over the trends that cost them their jobs. Our welfare system, although far from perfect, would still provide the bare basics, so the family wasn't going to starve or be out in the freezing cold.

No one should be embarrassed to receive help in the job search; everyone needs it at some point, and plenty of people make their living giving job-finding assistance. You have been introduced to the sources of job leads. The following sections describe each one in more detail.

COLLEGE CAREER SERVICES OFFICES

A college's career services office develops contacts with employers, sets up interviews for students and company recruiters, and offers career counseling and job search information. Students can register with the career services office when they seek employment. Career services bring job vacancies to the attention of qualified student registrants. Faculty in a college may refer to this role as a placement function. The word *placement* can be misleading in that the career services office does not place people in jobs; it informs people where job openings exist. You must win the job through your own job search skills.

Companies send recruiters to colleges all over the country, mainly to interview graduating students for potential employment. During labor shortages for college-level jobs, recruiters by the hundreds and thousands descend on career services offices of colleges and universities in a given year. You should use this service while you are in college; probably, you'll never again have the opportunity to interview so many employers from so many different organizations so easily in one place.

You can register for company interviews at your college's career services office. To do so, complete a registration form for a quick review by employers. Open a credentials file that contains your transcript of courses and grades and letters of recommendation from former teachers, previous employers, and other people who know you well. Students can select the companies and the interviewers with whom they would like to talk. Career counselors in college emphasize that you need to begin using campus interviews about nine months before graduation—in other words, at the start of your last year of study. Before you meet with a recruiter, read all the information you can about the organization he or she represents. Most career services offices have annual reports of and descriptive information about the companies that send recruiters to them. Don't expect the recruiter to offer you a job on the spot, no matter how well the interview goes. If you are invited to visit the company's home office, this indicates a second phase in their employment process, and it usually means you have passed some kind of initial screening test in the college career services office.

Beyond the function of bringing recruiters on campus to meet with students, college career offices provide many other services, including career and academic counseling, job fairs, an occupational and employer information library, placement of students into summer and part-time employment, and career workshops. Other services are vocational testing, assistance with résumé and interview preparation, résumé referral to online job banks, storing credentials, placement of alumni, company site visits, and career-planning courses for credit. Some colleges have a computerized database of alumni who have agreed to help job seekers.

PUBLIC "ONE-STOP" CENTERS AND PRIVATE EMPLOYMENT AGENCIES

State and Local "One-Stop" Centers

"One-stop" centers bring together a wide variety of job services at the state and local levels in one central location. Established by the Workforce Investment Act of 1998, these centers gather job information and resources together, making them available to everyone so that more people can be linked to the services they need. The staff at one-stop centers emphasize finding jobs and summer employment opportunities in the local community, locating appropriate training, and developing job-seeking skills. Often, many different types of community-based organizations and services are connected to these centers. These centers also maintain a listing of job openings in the local area, the state, and the entire nation through America's Job Bank (http://www.ajb.org).

Any person 18 years of age and older is eligible for one-stop centers' core services. Centers focus their efforts on people who have faced serious barriers to being employed, such as living in low-income circumstances or having a disability. Other services go to those who experience difficulties in getting or keeping a job; have been homeless, a runaway, an offender, in foster care, or have a child; and are in need of help completing an educational program. There are one-stop centers in major population areas in every state.

Two sources can help find the center closest to you: America's Service Locator, U.S. Department of Labor, telephone 877-872-5627 (toll free) or use its Web site (www.servicelocator.org) or call your State Department of Labor (http://www. dol.gov/dol/location.htm). Another source could be your guidance counselor at school (NCWD/Youth, 2002).

Private Agencies

Some job seekers use private employment agencies on the assumption that they will work harder at uncovering employment opportunities because their agents work on a commission basis, not for a salary. They must produce results to stay in business. Who pays the costs for the use of private employment agencies? Most of the time, the employer pays. In the minds of agency managers, employers represent repeat business, whereas job seekers may be only one-time clients. When the employer pays the fee, the agency advertises its job vacancies free to job seekers. In this case, remember that the agency is working for the employer, not the job seeker. Other payment arrangements also exist. Sometimes you and the employer share expenses. If the agency collects a fee from you as a job seeker, you will be asked to sign a contract that requires you to pay them should they locate a job you accept. You could be billed 60 percent of your first month's pay, or 5 to 15 percent of your first year's salary. Many companies will reimburse you after you have been with them for a certain period of time.

How do you select a private employment agency? You need to do some research to answer this question. You can ask others who have been clients of an agency, but even this will leave you in some uncertainty, because an agency that worked for them may not be right for you. A local newspaper office could help. Chances are good that private employment agencies in the area have advertised in the paper, and the advertising editor may be able to give you information on the subject. Ask the agency to give you specific job information; however, do not expect the employment agency to give the name of the employer. A respected agency should tell you over the telephone the skills required for the job, experience needed, salary, and size of the company. If agents refuse, thank them for their time and hang up. One way to choose a recruiter or an employment agency is by checking if they are certified by the National Association of Personnel Services (10905 Fort Washington Road, Suite 400, Fort Washington, Maryland 20744; telephone 301-203-6700, fax 301-203-4346, Web site address http://www.napsweb.org).

If the agency asks you to sign a contract for the services, request to have a copy of the contract to look over before you make any decision about it. Take the contract to a lawyer or a local consumer protection agency to get legal advice before you sign. Before you leave your résumé with the agency, make sure the job openings they list actually exist. Some agencies, particularly if they are new to an area, are merely trying to fatten their bank of résumés to impress employers. Avoid any contract that demands "exclusive listing" or "exclusive handling"—it keeps you from using other job-finding services, and even if you find a job from your own efforts, you could still be required to pay the agency a fee. Be certain you understand the payment structure and the nature of the services offered before you sign an agreement.

Private employment agencies may concentrate on certain industries in a local area, or they may cover a wide assortment of occupations over a large territory. Reliable agencies can save you hours of time by referring you to only those job vacancies that match your job qualifications. Inexperienced agents can waste a lot of your time by inappropriate referrals. Ask your agent to be selective in suggesting job targets for you. Sending résumés in the hit-or-miss shotgun style is something you could do without the expense of the agency fee. Do not sign with any private agency that wants to sell you lots of extra services such as testing, résumé-writing workshops, and interviewing practice. Such services are often free or low in cost at a college career office.

Do not allow yourself to be pressured into applying for a job vacancy in an occupation other than the career objective you have established. Some agencies have been known to play the "bait-and-switch" game, luring you with one job prospect but later trying to entice you to apply for an inferior position. An agency staff member trying to put the squeeze on you by saying "you had better take what you can get" indicates that this person is interested only in a commission and not in providing reasonable service for you. Another objectionable tactic is to send a job seeker on numerous interviews for jobs in which he or she is not qualified, hoping the job seeker will become worn down and accept any job, and once again, the agency representative takes a commission. If you believe you have been treated unfairly, report your experience to your local consumer-protection agency, the nearest Better Business Bureau, or your state's attorney general. Some job search experts advise college graduates and other first-time job seekers to use private employment agencies only as a last resort. They believe that such agencies provide a better service for job changers—people who have been working for a number of years.

Temporary-Help Agencies

You can locate temporary-help services by looking in the Yellow Pages of the telephone book under "Temporary Help" or "Employment Contractors" and in the classified help-wanted ads of local newspapers. Make an appointment for an interview. Dress appropriately and prepare as you would for any other job interview. Temporary-help agencies bill their company clients for services provided. If hired for an assignment, the job seeker becomes an employee of the temporary-help agency. These private business services provide companies with workers for a limited time. Companies often need temporary help to fill in for permanent employees on vacation or sick leave or because of seasonal work needs or peak production periods.

At one time, most temporary-help agencies confined themselves to supplying clerical workers, but now they have expanded to include professionals such as temporary doctors, lawyers, engineers, accountants, legal assistants, systems analysts, programmers, and so on. Increasingly, downsized companies are using temporaries for several months instead of taking on a permanent hire (Boroughs, 1994). The number of temporary and part-time workers (technically called contingent workers) is growing rapidly, and temporary-help agencies such as Manpower and Kelly Services are growing with them.

The attractions of temporary and part-time employment for individual workers are flexible work schedules, supplementing regular income, exploring a variety of jobs and workplaces, trying out new work experiences, and interesting an employer in offering permanent full-time work by demonstrating excellent skills and work habits. Employers see temporary help as a way to lower labor costs, screen potential candidates for permanent jobs, and gain flexibility in adjusting to changing demands for labor. Disadvantages for workers are lower pay rates, limited benefits, less job security, and unpredictable hours.

Critics of temporary and part-time work trends charge business with shattering a tradition where loyalty to the company was valued and employees felt they had a secure workplace; instead, a nation of disposable, stressed, anxiety-ridden workers is being created. Former Secretary of Labor Robert Reich envisions the development of a two-level work force. The first step has been to increase the number of contingent workers, who get a smaller pay package and few or no benefits. The second step has been to reduce the ranks of middle management. Next is the reduction of benefits for all employees. Last is doing much more business by contract, whether by using contingent workers or by contracting out to independent suppliers (Castro, 1993). Noted over a decade ago, this trend has continued and is sadly creating divisions in the work force.

NEWSPAPERS AND PERIODICALS

Help-Wanted Advertisements

Many job hunters start by scanning the help-wanted advertisements in the classified advertising section of a daily newspaper. However, not all job openings are publicized in the local paper. Generally, the higher the salary paid for a job, the less likely it is to be advertised in the newspaper. The greatest disadvantage of help-wanted ads is that the publicity of a job opening in the newspaper means you will compete with many more job applicants. Because of the volume of replies an advertisement produces, you may need to answer many ads in order to bring about any response. Answer an employment ad promptly; job openings often fill up quickly, even before the ad stops appearing in the paper. Following up with a telephone call or writing a letter about a week after responding to an ad is often suggested as a way to outdo your competition and demonstrate your interest in the job. Sunday editions of daily newspapers contain the largest number of help-wanted listings. Local newspapers concentrate on local job vacancies. Large city newspapers such as the *New York Times,* the *Chicago Tribune,* the *Los Angeles Times,* and the *Wall Street Journal* carry large sections of help-wanted ads for all regions of the country as well as for local job openings.

In general, four types of want ads can be identified: (1) open ads, (2) blind ads, (3) employment agency ads, and (4) catch ads.

Open ads (Figure 2-1) are the best kind from the job seeker's viewpoint because they give the name of the work organization that offers the job opening. These ads often include the company's address and telephone number, the nature of the work, products and services of the organization, salary and fringe benefits paid, and the qualifications required of the applicant. One disadvantage of open ads is that they attract the largest number of responses, so you are likely to have more competition for jobs advertised this way. One possible way around competition is to learn from a personal contact or a business directory the name of the person who would most likely be your supervisor or manager. Your cover letter and résumé should go to that person, who is far more likely to be a hiring authority than someone in the personnel, human resources, or employment office.

Blind ads (Figure 2-2) do not reveal the name of the work organization advertising the job. The ad instructs the job applicant to send a letter of inquiry or a résumé to a box number at a postal address. Some information is usually given about the work and the kind of business the employer operates. Employers use blind ads when they don't want to deal with huge numbers of job applicants, some of whom are probably unqualified. By using blind ads, the company doesn't have to respond to all applicants and won't be bothered by unwanted telephone calls or walk-in applicants. A blind ad also allows an organization to maintain secrecy with respect to its competitors and its own employees. Sometimes an employed person makes the mistake of responding to a blind ad placed by his or her own company. If the boss finds out you are looking for a new job, you may be accused of disloyalty and fired. It has happened before. One way around this situation is to enlist another person to respond on your behalf. This third-party response strategy may not be as effective as the traditional response, but under the circumstances, it's a lot safer (Half, 1994). An employer can also use blind advertisements to test the job market for certain positions; the company may have no actual opening but wishes to discover the quality and numbers of job seekers available. Blind ads do have an advantage, though. Because they cut down on the number of responses, there is usually less competition for the jobs advertised that way.

Employment agency ads (Figure 2-3) are placed by public or private employment agencies for their employer clients. These ads function like blind advertisements, because you don't know the name of the employer who is using the agency. Sometimes an agency will run ads for fictitious job positions in order to attract résumés in

BROADCAST JOURNALIST

Professional broadcast journalist for reporter/editor/newscaster position at WJOB. Must have college degree, 3-5 years' experience in broadcast news, and demonstrated capabilities as a field reporter, writer, and broadcaster. Send résumé, letter, writing samples, and tape to: O. K. Doke, News Director, WJOB, 1000 Anystreet, Anytown, Anystate 99999. No telephone calls, please.

Figure 2-1   An open ad

QUALITY CONTROL DIRECTOR

Manufacturing company in southwest part of the state is looking for a person with a strong quality control background and supervisory experience. Must meet requirements in all phases of manufacturing, including plastics, die cast, stampings, finishings, and assembly operations. Degree preferred but not required if otherwise qualified. Send complete résumé to Box Z-101, Times Tribune, Anytown, Anystate 99999. All replies held in strict confidence.

Figure 2-2   A blind ad

CLERK/TYPIST

Experienced clerk/typist needed with typing speed of 60 wpm or more. Prefer one- or two-year community college or business school grad. Must be familiar with office practices. Apply at Ace Personnel Agency, 2222 Anystreet, or call 999-0000 for an appointment.

Figure 2-3   An employment agency ad

A CAREER IN ADVERTISING AND PUBLIC RELATIONS

Well-known national company seeking dynamic, enterprising people who desire an opportunity to earn up to $2000 per week and more with experience. Will train the right individual. No experience needed. Must have dependable auto. Call Buffalo Bart at 001-0001.

Figure 2-4   A catch ad

an effort to impress potential employer clients with the large number of hopeful job hunters they have on file.

Catch ads (Figure 2-4) should be avoided. They promise big money, easy working conditions, a need for few or no qualifications, or short work hours with large financial returns—but there's always a catch. They may use fancy titles such as "executive position" or "public relations manager," which appeal to vanity and status values. A catch ad hides the fact that the job often involves door-to-door selling. This type of ad sounds almost too good to be true, so you are tempted to respond and find out if it really is true. You may be required to buy the product you will sell. Companies that use catch ads often make their money by selling products to would-be salespeople, who must in turn sell them to would-be customers. You could end up stuck with a hundred hard-to-sell sets of encyclopedias (or whatever). Never sign on with a company that asks you to pay money first in order to get the job.

A study of the use of help-wanted ads found that 15 to 25 percent of all employers surveyed hired workers through help-wanted ads (Walsh, Johnson, and Sugarman, 1975). Employers who used want ads hired almost half their workers through them. Most want ads did not offer the job seeker adequate information. More than 85 percent failed to provide wage figures, 60 percent did not identify the employer, and 33 percent did not designate the industry. The authors of the study concluded that employment agency ads were mainly advertising for the agencies themselves. Two-thirds of the job seekers surveyed used want ads in their job search. Of these job seekers, one-fourth said they had actually found jobs through them. This study was conducted some time ago, but there is no evidence that this situation is any different now.

RECEPTIONIST/CLERK If you would like a friendly, tactful, well-dressed person to receive customers and visitors in your office, call (telephone number) or write (name and address). I have office management skills, can type 65 wpm, am well organized, and enjoy meeting people.

Figure 2-5 A position-wanted ad

Placing Advertisements for Yourself

This job-seeking tactic involves placing "position-wanted" advertisements in newspapers and trade magazines. Every week, thousands of job seekers place such ads in newspapers and magazines, hoping to attract a few potential employers. Most of the time, however, this strategy doesn't work. There are exceptions, but most people who have tried placing ads for themselves feel they have wasted their money. Those job seekers who do get responses from position-wanted ads tend to get them from small companies that offer lower salaries or from small employment agencies that want to sell their career-planning and job-finding services. If you plan to use this method of locating job leads, specialized trade publications may provide the best value for your time and money. There are thousands of trade magazines; you can obtain many of their names and addresses from libraries. A typical position-wanted ad in a newspaper is shown in Figure 2-5.

Some local newspapers run free position-wanted ads for young people as a community service at the beginning of summer, usually for about a week. If you choose to place such an ad, avoid sounding desperate for work. Emphasize your skills, achievements, and personal qualities.

Other Parts of the Newspaper

In using the newspaper in your search for job leads, read beyond the want-ad section. Many excellent job leads never appear in the want ads, but you can still find them in the newspaper. Look for articles on retirements, promotions, and resignations. Such announcements may indicate that there is an unfilled position at some level, possibly at an entry level if the chain reaction caused by a vacancy at a top level goes all the way through the organizational chart. Some people have even studied the obituary columns for notices of deaths of employed people; a new employee may be needed to fill the vacant position. Watch for new businesses that are opening or old businesses that are expanding; they will need employees. New building permits can result in construction jobs. When a lease is signed, this tells you that someone is moving to a new location; chances are they need more space for an expanding business. A new contract for a manufacturer or the development of a new line of products may mean that more people will be hired. Whenever you read about people leaving the community, their jobs may remain unfilled. The business and financial pages of the newspaper contain many such articles. Employers are likely to credit you with creative thinking if you turn information gleaned from articles of the newspaper into sources of potential job leads.

Other Publications

Business magazines such as *Forbes*, *Fortune*, and *Business Week* are excellent sources of industry information; their "positions open" sections are usually located near the last page of each issue. The Sunday edition of the *New York Times* advertises job openings in many locations nationwide and overseas. The *Job Choices* series, published each year by the National Association of Colleges and Employers, lists hundreds of companies by name and indicates the types of college majors they are looking for. Industrial directories, published in each state, list the names and addresses of companies located in each city. Higher education positions are advertised in the weekly *Chronicle of Higher Education*. You can find directories in the reference section of the library. The amount of material published each year on job openings in work organizations is truly staggering. The information is there; you have to dig it out.

THE INTERNET: ELECTRONIC JOB BANKS AND ONLINE SERVICES

Using the Internet requires knowing the occupation you want as a career goal, perhaps more so than with most other sources of job leads. It's easy to get lost in cyberspace, comparable to getting lost in the library stacks. If you don't know your career goal, you won't find it on the Internet. Simply typing the word "jobs" got the author 71,800,000 "hits" or matches in 0.14 seconds using the Google search engine. That's a few too many to deal with! Before you go online, know the names of occupations you have decided on and the skills you can honestly claim. It's also very helpful to know the geographic areas you want to live in and the names of organizations that interest you (the subjects of Chapters 5 and 6 in this book). You can narrow your scope by entering specific names of occupations or by following the search engine's directions.

If you decide to use the Web site of a job bank, you should ask several questions of it before signing on with it, using it, or paying for its services. These questions appear in Appendix B, *Electronic Job Banks: Questions to Ask and Web Sites*, at the back of this book.

An excellent resource is the *Guide to Internet Job Searching* by Margaret Riley Dikel and Frances Roehm (2002). It begins with chapters on using the Internet in your job search and posting a résumé on the Internet. *The Riley Guide*, as this publication is also called, goes on to give Internet sites for jobs in business, social sciences, humanities, natural sciences, engineering, and government. The URL for *The Riley Guide* is http://www.rileyguide.com. Another resource is Peter Weddle's *Guide to Employment Web Sites* (2002). These books and others list job bank Web sites considered the best in a variety of categories and industries. The authors are experts in the field of Internet searching for job leads. They update their books periodically, and their research can save you a lot of time clicking and scrolling over the far-flung expanse of the Internet universe.

A search engine is a good way to find information stored in databases of organizations. Meta Crawler (http://www.metacrawler.com) and Web Crawler (http://www.webcrawler.com), like several other search engines, combine the results of four or five engines with the click of a single button. However, when you want to really get at the heart of your search, go directly to a "stand-alone" search engine and use its advanced features to obtain your desired data (Dikel and Roehm, 2002). Several popular search engines are Google (http://www.google.com), Yahoo! (http://www.yahoo.com), AltaVista (http://www.altavista.com), Excite (http://www.excite.com), HotBot (http://www.hotbot.com), and Lycos (http://www.lycos.com).

Here are some tips for using keywords:

- You can use any mix of upper- and lowercase letters; the keyword field is usually not case sensitive.
- Skip using common words like *a, an, as,* and so on, as well as punctuation marks such as a period, colon, or semicolon. The search engine ignores them.
- If you really need to use common words and punctuation in your search, enclose them in double quotes; for example "Word for Windows" (Careerbuilder.com, 2003).

While using the Web, don't neglect other sources of job leads. Some job hunters think their computers will do all of the job search work for them and never do the most essential kind of work in landing a job: getting out and seeing people every day. The

Internet won't get you a job. It can help you uncover a job lead; that's why the Web is included in this chapter. Interviews win jobs. When companies are not coming to you, as they seldom do, it is crucial that you go to them in person (Challenger, 2003).

A list of Web sites for online job banks can be found in Appendix B: *Electronic Job Banks: Questions to Ask and Web Sites.* Computerized job banks and online information services offer job hunters two major options in their job-hunting campaigns. One option is to search a site designed to include desired job openings listed by employers who use electronic means to find job applicants. The other job search option is to post your résumé on one of these sites. (Constructing an electronic résumé is a topic that will be covered in the next chapter.) Online information services can also be used for acquiring knowledge about companies and organizations, the topic of Chapter 6 in this book.

Putting your qualifications into circulation electronically has its advantages. Job banks and online services give you the possibility of attracting hundreds of employers who otherwise would not know you exist. The computer in a résumé database service doesn't get tired; it works for you 24 hours of every day, freeing you up to use other sources of job leads and job search strategies. Then there is the element of speed. Computers can present your skills and qualifications to employers in a matter of seconds, a process that once took minutes or hours. The cost of entering your résumé into a database is relatively small compared with the costs of some other sources of job leads. The résumé database service of a job bank or online company classifies, codes, stores, retrieves, and transmits information from a group of résumés that have been entered into its system (Kennedy and Morrow, 1994).

When you use online information services, employment is usually only one item in a whole menu of services. Your computer puts you into contact with information about job openings listed in employer databases, job ad companies, and employment bulletin boards. There may be a monthly membership fee or a charge for each minute you are online. Your library may have the *Gale Directory of Databases,* Volume I (annual editions), which has a complete list of online information services. Most job ad services charge a fee, but some of the smaller or regional ones may be free. An electronic employment bulletin board run by volunteer help means it is free to users, but the quality of the job-finding service can vary considerably. Many commercial services offering online news, games, and hobby groups have employment boards posting job vacancies and space for your résumé at no additional cost. The chances that certain employers will check these public places can vary from often to never; there is no way of knowing that an employer you want to read your résumé will ever do so.

How do employers use electronic database services? When you send your résumé to a database service, the information is stored as you have sent it or (more likely) the résumé is summarized and entered into a standardized database format. Employers list their requirements for a given job. These specifications are then entered into the system using software that enables the computer to search for **keywords** on the individual résumés it is scanning. Keywords may be job titles, educational majors, functions performed, college degrees earned, equipment used, measurable skills, and so on—but, of course, what those keywords actually are and how many are needed to select a résumé are known only to the employer and the database service. If your résumé doesn't contain the prescribed number of "correct" keywords, it is passed over by the scanner. This is one disadvantage of electronic job searching and recruiting. If employers use only this fixed-format procedure (which can be a set of prejudged concepts), they can easily overlook candidates they might hire after a personal, face-to-face meeting. Obviously, this situation doesn't help the job seeker either.

The résumés (or their summaries) selected by the scanner are considered "most qualified" and sent on to the employer. Surviving this electronic cut does not automatically guarantee you will be called for an interview, but your chances of being contacted are greatly increased. In the electronic job market, employers appear to have an edge in the job search game. For you, the job seeker, to rely solely on electronic methods of job hunting is to take a great risk indeed. Your credentials and qualifications could remain buried in a résumé database for a long, long time.

Hundreds—and, in some cases, thousands—of résumés may arrive at personnel or human resources offices each week. These offices may have been targets for layoffs and terminations when their organizations have downsized. Those few remaining personnel workers can no longer handle the increased load of résumés. Enter the computer, with its capacity to inspect huge numbers of résumés in a fraction of the time it would take a human being to examine the experience, education, and abilities being sought for a particular position.

You get the picture: There are simply too many pieces of paper and too few people to read them. To those who too often have become bleary-eyed from reading hundreds of résumés, the computer and its scanning software must seem sent from heaven.

APPROACHING EMPLOYERS

Direct-Mail Applications

A direct-mail campaign usually consists of sending large numbers of résumés and cover letters to employers. A blanket mailing to companies can be time consuming, expensive, and produce only a low rate of response. It is like a mass sales drive. What happens to most advertisements you receive in the mail? They go into the wastebasket; you may not even look at some of this mail. What will happen to your résumés and cover letters? The more you personalize your letter and the better you design your résumé, the greater chance you have of your letter being read and answered. A *selective* direct mailing is based on your investigation of work organizations and your identification of the ones that impress you most. Choosing your targets carefully may take as much time as mass mailing because of the research involved, but the rate of response should increase.

Whom do you contact in the work organization? For entry-level positions, you would probably write to a personnel manager or a director of the human relations department—unless you have identified a person higher up in the organization who has the authority to hire. In your research of the company, if you discover the name of the vice president or manager in charge of the department in which you would work, you can send your letter to that person. Addresses of companies and names of executives and departmental managers can be found in directories of corporations. For the names of directories, refer to Chapter 6. You can find these directories in most public libraries or college career services offices.

If you know of a person who has been recently promoted in an organization, that person may want to recruit his or her own new team of people from outside the organization. Your source of names here could be from the business pages of newspapers, trade magazines, or college alumni magazines.

One strategy in the direct-mail campaign is to begin with a personal letter and follow it with a résumé and cover letter if your initial letter draws no response. Letters that are personally typed and signed will receive more attention than mass-produced ones; personal communication indicates a time commitment on your part (Powell, 1995).

What should you include in a personal (or "broadcast") letter that inquires about employment in an organization or indicates your interest in a company? You should briefly summarize your previous work experience and education, emphasize your past accomplishments, state what you can do for the organization, and express your interest in an interview. Use your personal stationery. If at all possible, send your letter to a person by name rather than by title alone. The personal touch makes a more favorable impression; the employer knows you took the time to locate his or her name. Keep sentences and paragraphs short; they are more likely to be read that way. Five or six sentences are enough for a paragraph. Do not start the letter by asking for or "wondering if there is" a job. Write about your achievements in a way that will indicate the benefits you can bring an employer. In your request for an interview, you might say that you have some ideas that may be of interest to the employer and could benefit the work organization.

If you do not hear from the employer in two weeks, consider following up your personal letter with a copy of your résumé and a cover letter. (These communications will be discussed in the next chapter.) Don't expect to hear from every employer. The direct-mail campaign offers a quick method for generating interviews, but the rate of response from employers can be discouragingly low. If you receive a 5 to 10 percent return rate, you have been doing something right. Generally, the higher the salary you seek, the lower the response. The low response figures for the direct-mail method are mentioned here because some job seekers rely on this method when other sources of job leads should be used as well, and they lose confidence in their ability to find jobs when this technique fails. Well-written letters and résumés and contacting the right person in the right work organization can greatly increase the effectiveness of a direct-mail campaign.

Human Resources, Personnel, or Employment Offices

Medium-sized and large work organizations have personnel offices or human resources departments. Personnel officers help managers and administrators fill job vacancies. They recruit applicants, screen candidates to eliminate the least qualified, and send the rest on to supervisors, managers, and executives who have hiring authority. Personnel officers seldom have the power to hire unless the job seeker is applying for a position in the personnel department itself. However, personnel recommendations often carry considerable weight, so it is important for job applicants to create good impressions in their contacts with them.

In your job search, consult with company employment officers. You should check whether they hire people with your particular occupational interests and skills, and determine if they have job openings in your particular field of preparation. You can ask them for the names of supervisors and administrators who hire people with your qualifications; most personnel officers can give you this information. Later, you can consider contacting these people in a direct-mail campaign or by telephone. Personnel departments represent the best single source of information about a company. However, they are not likely to know about all possible job openings in their organization, because some hiring authorities in the company may only be thinking about creating a new job position, waiting for the right applicant to come along.

If the personnel officer says flatly there are no job openings for you in the organization, ask him or her to suggest other work organizations, employers, or managers who could possibly be looking for a person with your occupational goals and abilities.

Professional and Trade Associations

Thousands of professional and trade associations act as intermediaries between job seekers and employers. They provide employment clearinghouses for their members. Your library may have directories that list the names and addresses of such associations. You send an association a membership fee that makes you eligible for placement help and notices of vacancies in their trade journals. These associations hold local or regional meetings and annual conventions that offer opportunities for job seekers to form relationships with people established in their field of work. Associations also print material that can help you discover job information available only through hidden job-market sources and networking.

Executive Search Firms

People working for executive search firms are often called "headhunters." They work for employers, not for job seekers. They concentrate their activities on people who already have jobs. When an employer hires an executive search firm to recruit applicants, the search firm's assignment is to find qualified candidates for a specific position that the employer has available. This job search method has limited value to job seekers. A direct application to an executive search firm will not usually receive much attention unless you know of an executive recruiter who gives time to job seekers.

Career Days or Job Fairs

You can make several contacts in a couple of hours at a career day or a job fair sponsored by a college career services office, chamber of commerce, or professional association. Job fairs are growing in popularity as a way of bringing employers and job seekers together. Many small companies send representatives to career days because they are less expensive than recruiting trips. You can talk with employers about your qualifications and ways you might contribute to their organizations. Obtain and review the list of employers scheduled to be at the career fair. Research employers' organizations ahead of time; you can then ask questions of company representatives based on what you know about their organization. Your questions are likely to indicate you have done your homework on the company without having to actually say so—and that's impressive because at this point many people are just browsing and few of them will have done this kind of research.

Come early, and beat the crowd. Waiting until the last half-hour is not a good idea; some recruiters may have packed up and gone home. Dress neatly, in "business-casual." Wear a suit if you would like to, but a good shirt and pressed slacks or a skirt will be appropriate. Bring extra copies of your résumé, and be sure you have proof-read it for typos. Carry your résumés in a folder or small briefcase to keep them neat and clean. Have paper and a pen or pencil ready for taking notes. Some recruiters suggest it's helpful to hear a short, 30-second "sales pitch"—hand them a copy of your résumé and give some basic information about yourself and your career objective or interests. Offer a firm handshake and maintain good eye contact. Ask probing questions to find out what you want to know from employers, such as names of people to contact for a job in the organization, current and future openings, availability of on-the-job training and internships, and academic credentials the company would like to see in its job applicants. One inquiry to avoid is "So, tell me about your company." You have just revealed that you really may be lazy, because you know nothing about the organization. Recruiters don't mind giving you information about the company and

Tight job market, eh?

the job opportunities there, but they do mind having to do *all* the work, which that question demands (Joell, 2003).

Obtain employers' business cards for follow-up purposes. For talks with recruiters that have gone well, a thank-you letter will be well received. (The thank-you letter is a topic in the next chapter and in the chapters on interviews.) Pick up any available information, such as brochures and other company data sheets, to review and evaluate after the career day is over.

Be aware of the time demands on employers at a job fair. Don't monopolize an employer's time if there are others waiting to ask questions. As in the case of interviews in the college career services office, don't expect employers to make firm job offers at a career fair. The most you could realistically expect is to be invited to the company's home office for further interviews. If that happens, you have done some things right and you've gotten the best you can get from a job fair.

Drop-in Visits or Cold Calls

Cold calling generally means trying to reach people with hiring authority without arranging for an interview ahead of time. This technique is suggested only for assertive job seekers not discouraged by rejection. Some people extol the virtues of cold calling, because your aim is to talk with a hiring executive rather than starting with a personnel worker in the human resources department. Who knows, a job opening may have just developed and you are in the right place at the right time.

Cold calling takes boldness and self-confidence. You must know exactly what you are doing once you are talking with the person who has the power to hire; otherwise, this method can easily backfire. It resembles door-to-door sales: If someone turns you down, there is always another potential customer waiting at the next door. Unannounced drop-in visits are sometimes effective because an executive may have been hoping to find a job applicant with an aggressive style. Some people get jobs this way, but most do not. You run the risk of being simply asked to leave; however, to some job seekers, this means you are no worse off than you were before. Pushing your way past "gatekeepers"—secretaries or receptionists—is a big gamble for beginning job hunters. Also, drop-in visits are not a particularly effective use of your time; you can make only a few of these kinds of contacts each day.

Employers, like most people, do not appreciate interruptions in their work, so a better method, particularly for those starting a first job search and/or seeking entry-level positions, is cold calling by telephone. You can contact more employers in a day through the telephone than by dropping in unannounced to employers' offices. Telephoning employers is a "numbers game," so you may be calling a lot of people before you obtain an interview.

A handwritten letter followed by a phone call may increase your chances of being able to talk with an employer, particularly in small companies. Be brief; write no more than three paragraphs. First paragraph: introduce yourself. Second: explain your reason(s) for contacting this person. Third: inform him or her you will be calling over the phone to ask if you could talk. Close with "If you prefer not to receive my call, please leave a message at. . . . Your wishes will be respected. Thank you for giving this request your consideration" (Pekas, 1990). (Be aware, however, that some companies consider a handwritten letter to be unprofessional.) Telephone the contacts in about five days if they haven't called to decline. State your name, then explain you are calling your contact (give first and last name), and refer to your letter. Plan your calls by preparing a script. Don't give a canned speech; try to be relaxed in your approach. Explain who you are, who you believe the other person is, and what possibilities you can see for working together. Ask if this is a convenient time. If not, offer to call back at a more suitable time. Assess how the other person sounds (Guiducci, 1992). Read the next section for more ideas about using the telephone for cold calling.

Telephoning Employers

The telephone call is a fast and direct way to find out if the employer will set up an interview with you. The original Job Club approach (pioneered in the 1970s and 80s with unemployed workers and copied by job seekers since then) is to use the Yellow Pages section of the telephone directory as a source of job leads. Job Club trainees learn about the job search and practice their telephone routine during the first week. In the second week, they start making up to 100 telephone calls per day in an effort to set up interviews with employers. Job Club counselors give the trainees lots of encouragement and support in the meantime. During the third week, they continue making calls in the morning and go out to an employer who has agreed to an interview with them in the afternoon. They keep going—calling and interviewing—until they are hired for a job. The job is seldom a "dream job," but any job with a paycheck looks good if you've been unemployed for a long stretch of time. Job Club counselors have claimed an 80–85 percent placement rate for this method.

After rehearsing the procedure, job seekers get on the phone and have a pad of paper on which to write notes. The script they follow for requesting an interview over the telephone goes like this:

- Give your name.
- Ask for the name of the employer (of a small company) or department head of the division in which you would like to work; this is the person who knows who may be leaving and whether the company needs your skills. Do not ask the secretary answering the phone about openings; secretaries are probably not authorized to give you this information and will probably refer you to the personnel department. If a secretary balks at connecting you to the department head or employer, say your request is about a very important matter.
- Address this person by name and introduce yourself.
- Describe your qualifications and briefly mention an achievement, if appropriate.
- Ask for an interview. If the employer agrees to it, try to schedule it as soon as possible—the same day in the afternoon or soon thereafter.
- If the person says, "There are no openings right now," ask for an interview in case a vacancy occurs later, and explain that you understand you are not being interviewed for a job at this time.
- If the person still says no, ask for other job leads in places you can contact that might be hiring. Because this employer is in the same general line of work, they may have a lot of information about what other businesses in the same industry are doing. If a place is mentioned, ask for the telephone number, address, and the person to ask for when you call.
- Ask for permission to use the person's name for leads; this gives you an introduction to other employers you contact.
- Ask for a good time to call back in case a job opens up later on; write down that date immediately (Azrin and Besalel, 1982).

You can list each step on a piece of paper before phoning and check steps off as you proceed with the call. The sequence we have just been through assumes you are calling a person you don't know. Be sure to ask for one or more referrals. "Warm" contacts and referrals improve your chances of gaining an interview somewhere else.

Using these guidelines, your conversations on the telephone might sound like this, beginning with the person who answers.

Example 1:

"Lakeland Wholesalers."

"Hello, my name is Sara Goodman. I would like to speak to the head of the sales department. Can you tell me the name, please."

"It's Mrs. Sanders; I'll connect you with her." (Mrs. Sanders answers.)

"Hello, Mrs. Sanders, my name is Sara Goodman. I have several years' experience in sales, and I am interested in meeting with you to talk to you about possible openings now or later in your department."

"Who did you say you were?"

"I'm Sara Goodman, and I'd like to make an appointment to talk with you about possible openings that might come up. Could you give me a few minutes this afternoon—perhaps, right after lunch?"

"You say you've had selling experience?"

"Yes, about three years' experience. Would 1 or 2 o'clock be OK?"

"Two o'clock would be all right. I can't promise anything, but there might be a job opening next week. Come to my office and we'll see what you can do. Do you know how to get here?"

"Yes, I have the address. I'll see you at 2 o'clock. Thank you."

Example 2:

"Jimmy's Service Station."

"Hello, my name is Tim Ryan. I would like to talk to the manager. However, I don't have the name."

"His name is Jim Stevens, and I'm him. What can I do for you?"

"Mr. Stevens, I've had experience in repairing foreign cars and I'd like to come over and talk with you about any jobs you might have open in car repair, or one that might come up later."

"What kind of cars have you worked on?"

"American cars and foreign cars, especially VWs and Toyotas—actually, most all of them. Could I come over and talk to you today if it's convenient with you?"

"Well, I don't think I need any help right now."

"I'd still like to talk to you. Something could come up later, even if there's nothing right now."

"Well, all right, but get here before 4 o'clock because that's when we get real busy. You've worked on Toyotas, you say?"

"That's right. I'll be over at 3 o'clock and we can talk about it. Thank you, Mr. Stevens, I'll see you at 3."

Example 3:

"City Sporting Goods."

"Hello, my name is Bill Smith. I'd like to speak to the manager. What is the name?"

"Susan. Susan Taylor. Can I help you?"

"No, I'd like to talk to the manager herself, thank you." (A moment passes. Bill writes the name of the manager on a notepad.)

"Hello, this is the manager. What can I do for you?"

"Ms. Taylor, my name is Bill Smith. I'm interested in meeting with you about any job opening you might have, now or in the future. I've had experience in selling sporting goods. Would you have any time this afternoon that would be convenient?"

"No, I'm sorry, we're very busy. Feel free to come over and fill out an application, but there are no openings."

"I'd be happy to complete an application form and would like to meet with you when you're not so busy."

"This is a small business, and everyone here has been with me for several years. There's no chance of a job here in the foreseeable future."

"I see, Ms. Taylor. I appreciate your not wanting me to waste my time. Could you tell me of any sporting goods store that might be hiring—or, any company that makes sports equipment?"

"Let's see. No, I can't think of any—unless it's the new store that recently opened in the Northtown Mall. Ken Rogers is the manager; he's a good man. He and I were classmates in school."

"Thanks, Ms. Taylor. That's really helpful. I'd like to check back with you in a couple of weeks, just in case something not anticipated happens. Could I call then?"

"Sure, but make it next month. Now that I think of it, one of my people may be looking around. Maybe something will have developed by that time."

"Thanks for your help, Ms. Taylor. I'll call next month."

(All three examples are adapted from Azrin and Besalel, 1982.)

Be prepared to deal with secretaries or receptionists who protect the boss from "unnecessary" calls. You may call at the wrong time; if so, ask the secretary to suggest a good time for you to call back. The best time to reach employers may be just after 5:00 P.M., the usual quitting time. The telephone switchboard is usually still open, the boss often stays late, and the secretary may have left for the day, so the person you most want to speak with just might answer the phone. Other good times to call might be just before the normal lunch hour or just before the workday begins, at 8:00 or 9:00 A.M.

The telephone is being used more and more by employers in their interview process. Sending company recruiters to colleges or paying the travel costs of job candidates for a series of interviews at the home office is expensive. Interviewing over the telephone is less costly in terms of both time and money.

INTERNSHIPS AND COOPERATIVE WORK-STUDY PROGRAMS

"Do you have any experience?" That question is often the hardest job search question for young people and recent college graduates. Internships and work-study programs give you a way to answer "yes."

Internships and cooperative work-study programs are agreements between schools and employers to provide students with supervised work experiences while they pursue an education. The arrangement is something like an apprenticeship, where a person agrees to work for a journeyman or master craftsman for a specified amount of time in order to learn a trade. Interns may or may not be paid. Employers like internships because they get a chance to evaluate a prospective employee at no risk. Interns can release experienced workers to perform more complex tasks. Work-study programs usually operate in one of two ways. Either you split the school day between classes and work, or you alternate between a semester devoted entirely to school classes and a semester of full-time work experience. Some work-study programs operate like apprenticeships in that you are paid for your work.

Students like internships and cooperative work-study programs because they give the opportunity for an on-the-job tryout of a prospective occupation. You gain valuable work experience before graduating, learn skills and gain confidence in your abilities, and acquire new contacts that could help you in your job search in the future. These programs can benefit you in several other ways. You don't have to commit yourself in this situation, because it is considered a learning experience. You can develop contacts to help in your job search. Your performance could lead to a job with the company that sponsors the internship or work-study program. Your school will award you credit for the experience. The experience looks good on your credentials or résumé. Employers want to hire people with experience. Possible disadvantages are (1) the length of your education could be increased if the internship credits are less than those of a normal course load, and (2) your program might include only lower-level skills rather than the cross-section of experiences you need to prepare adequately for an occupation.

For more details, consult your counseling office or academic adviser. More than 1,000 colleges, universities, and community colleges offer the plan. The National

Society for Experiential Education (9001 Braddock Road, Suite 380, Springfield, VA 22151; Web site: http://www.nsee.org) publishes the *National Directory of Internships*. Directories give you brief descriptions of sponsoring organizations; the type and number of positions available; benefits such as housing, meals, college credit, and training opportunities; eligibility requirements; and whom to contact. Use Internet search engines with keywords such as "intern," "internship," or "cooperative education" to locate internship and cooperative education programs (Dikel and Roehm, 2002). Several Web sites provide lists of internships. A few of them are:

- *Action Without Borders (http://www.idealist.org)*—If you are looking for opportunities with nonprofit and public service organizations, try this site. Search for internships as well as jobs and volunteer work by country or specialty.
- *Corporation for National and Community Service (http://www.nationalservice.org)*—The corporation provides opportunities for Americans of all ages and backgrounds to serve their communities and country through three programs: AmeriCorps, Learn and Serve America, and the National Senior Service Corps. Volunteers work with national and community nonprofit organizations, faith-based groups, schools, and local agencies to help meet community needs in education, the environment, public safety, homeland security, and other important areas.
- *Go Abroad (http://www.goabroad.com)*—This site contains just about everything a student would want to know about going overseas. Go Abroad has information on internships, volunteer work, job possibilities, study programs, teaching opportunities, language schools, and travel know-how.
- *MonsterTRAK (http://www.monstertrak.com)*—MonsterTRAK requires your college to be a member for you to gain access to the substantial resources this site offers.
- *Peace Corps (http://www.peacecorps.gov)*—The Peace Corps database has current open positions and an application form with guidelines to use in completing it. Currently, about 7,000 Peace Corps volunteers serve in 70 countries, working to bring clean water to communities, teach children, help start new businesses, and combat the spread of AIDS. Volunteers receive language and cross-cultural training to become a part of the community where they live.
- *Project Vote Smart (http://www.vote-smart.org)*—Scholarships are available for Project Vote Smart (PVS), a nonpartisan, nonprofit organization operated by interns and staff at the organization's Great Divide Ranch near Phillipsburg, Montana. PVS researches national and state candidates for elected offices and provides independent, objective information to the public about positions on issues, key votes, and interest group ratings of elected officials and candidates. Most Vote Smart workers are college student volunteers selected for two-week internships.
- *Student Jobs (http://www.studentjobs.gov)*—Operated by the U.S. Office of Personnel Management and the U.S. Department of Education's Student Financial Assistance Office, this Web site is open to high school, college, and graduate students. Here, you can learn about internships, co-ops, summer employment, the Outstanding Scholars Program, volunteer opportunities, temporary and permanent jobs, and full-time and part-time jobs. Post your résumé to bring up automated matching with posted job openings.

GOVERNMENT JOB OPPORTUNITIES: CIVIL SERVICE AND THE MILITARY

Civil Service

The U.S. government is the nation's largest single employer, with nearly 2.7 million workers distributed among the various government departments, agencies, commissions, bureaus, and boards. (Wal-Mart is the biggest private U.S. employer [Associated Press, 2003].) The largest growth in government employment in recent years, however, has been at the state and local levels. As with the federal government, each state government is the largest single employer in its particular state. Local governments hire more than half of all government employees in the United States. Together, all levels of government in the United States employ about 14 percent of the nation's labor force. Because of the publicity about government job openings, there is usually much competition for such jobs, but great opportunity also exists. For example, the turnover in federal positions produces approximately 300,000 job openings annually, even though total federal government employment has declined in recent years (Berman, 2001; Green, 1993).

The government hires people in almost every occupational group found in private employment. About 71 percent of all U.S. government workers are employed in professional specialty, administrative support, or executive, administrative, and managerial occupations. Approximately 41 percent of all federal workers have a bachelor's or higher degree. Systems analysts and computer engineers and scientists are employed throughout the government. Over three of every four federal health care workers are employed by the Veterans Administration. About 97 percent of all federal employees work in the 15 departments of the executive branch, excluding postal workers. (The U.S. Postal Service is an independent agency of the federal government.) The Department of Defense is by far the largest cabinet department, employing approximately 1.5 million military personnel and 670,568 civilian employees in 2001. About 84 percent of all federal employees work outside of the Washington, DC area (Damp, 2002). You can research departmental budgets on any level in government; all of this is public information. Budget increases or reductions affect the number of job openings in a department, agency, or bureau.

Working for the government has its advantages. First of all, the government is always hiring. About 10 percent of all currently filled federal jobs will become vacant in any given year due to retirements and promotions. (Even during a "hiring freeze" after politicians have proclaimed they will cut the "bloated federal budget," government continues to hire. Government agencies are experts in protecting their payrolls. These agencies provide real services to the public, and when they are cut, taxpayers complain loudly. With the prospect of losing votes, the politicians retreat and give way.)

Government jobs tend to be more secure than those in the private sector. The security of a government position allows you to make long-term career plans. Reductions in force (RIFs) occasionally occur, but the effects of this kind of downsizing are lessened by early retirements and attrition (not filling the jobs that have been vacated). Although promotions may seem slow at times, good work performance in government employment almost always guarantees opportunities for advancement. A career in public service offers job satisfaction, as well as opportunities for advanced professional training.

Another important advantage is that the government hires people at all stages of their career development. You can be a high school graduate with virtually no work experience, a student still in college, a recent college graduate, or a veteran separating or retiring from the military, and the government will have positions for which you can successfully apply (McKay and Lipson, 2003).

Government pay schedules are published. About half of the government workforce is under the General Schedule (GS) pay scale, which has 15 pay grades. Within each grade are 10 step increases. Each grade is defined by law, and is based on difficulty, responsibility, and the qualifications required for performance. About 20 percent of federal workers are under Postal Service rates. Federal employees receive wages comparable to the same job in the private sector of 32 particular areas of the United States having different costs of living. A great advantage of federal employment is the benefits package available to *all* government workers, including health benefits, the federal employees retirement system, group life insurance, and long-term care insurance.

It is only fair to mention certain features that some people will consider as disadvantages in working for the government. Look at any organizational outline of the federal government and you realize that government is a bureaucracy. Bureaucracy means hierarchy, and the actions you take must be approved by a chain of command. You will be regulated by procedures and guidelines established by others ahead of you, and sometimes they no longer may make sense. (However, these regulations protect you from being fired and protect your job from being eliminated.) You may want to take the initiative on some project, but the bureaucracy could regard your action as too risky. If you are entrepreneurial, the bureaucratic pace will probably challenge your patience. Change in most government agencies is a slow process. Keep in mind that in "carrying out the people's will," government bureaucracies must answer to the executive branch and to Congress (or the legislature on the state level).

Some people believe that government work is easy; they think government doesn't have much to do and its workers are overpaid and have an overabundance of benefits. This perception is a myth, and the truth can be quite a shocking surprise. For the most part, government employees work very hard and earn every penny they make. Any large bureaucracy, public or private, may carry a certain amount of "dead weight"—employees who go through the motions or are incompetent but have considerable job security, making it difficult to get rid of them. Trying to transfer to another governmental department could be as difficult as getting hired in the first place. Personnel actions in government involve paperwork, and will probably take months to process (McKay and Lipson, 2003).

Also, intense political pressures weigh on many government agencies. Decisions are often less than straightforward. The political and economic ideologies of the current administration must be taken into account. Many of the agencies' constituencies must be consulted. The media must be considered. Government bureaucrats must fill in many details of legislation directed to them by the legislative branch, which writes the law in more general terms.

Each federal agency does its own hiring. (There is no centralized personnel department for the federal government, as there was years ago when the Office of Personnel Management did all the hiring.) Following is a list of options for locating job opportunities with federal agencies of the executive branch.

1. *Federal agency Web sites*—The Internet has simplified locating federal job vacancies (Damp, 2002). Check one or more of the Web sites listed here:
    -   *USAJOBS (http://www.usajobs.opm.gov)* —This is the Office of Personnel Management's Internet employment Web site. It provides access to the national federal jobs database, job vacancy announcements, electronic and hard copy application forms, and a résumé builder that constructs a government-style résumé that can be printed, saved, and edited.
    -   *Federal Jobs Net (http://www.federaljobs.net)*—This site has links to over 200 agency sites. Not all federal job vacancies are listed in USAJOBS, so you should check with individual agency personnel offices in your area. The links in Federal Jobs Net are updated monthly. This center will guide you through the federal government job-search process.
    -   *Federal Career Central (http://www.fedjobs.com)*—This site contains a database of thousands of federal job vacancies updated each weekday. It is operated by Federal Research Service, Inc., P.O. Box 1059, Vienna, VA 22180-1059 (800-822-JOBS). Call or visit the Web site for subscription rates.
    -   *Federal Web Locator (http://www.infoctr.edu/fwl)*—A one-stop site for federal government information provided by the Villanova Center for Information Law and Policy.
    -   *FedWorld (http://www.fedworld.gov)*—Search by using various keywords such as occupational title, series, grade, or state. If you find USAJOBS overloaded, go to FedWorld for job lists.

- *FirstGov (http://www.firstgov.gov)*—Information on all aspects of federal government; this site has a jobs page offering links to sites you can explore.
- *Federal Jobs Digest (http://www.jobsfed.com)*—Arranged by job group titles, this site is a private source of federal job listings.
- *Student Jobs (http://studentjobs.gov)*—This Web site is sponsored by the U.S. Office of Personnel Management and the Student Financial Assistance Office of the U.S. Department of Education. It gives information about full-time and part-time jobs, summer employment, permanent and temporary jobs, internships, the Outstanding Scholars Program, cooperative programs, and volunteer opportunities for students in high school, college, or graduate school. You can post your résumé at this site and connect to many government departments and agencies.

2. Buy or subscribe to federal job vacancy listing periodicals. Call or write for current subscription rates.

- *Federal Career Opportunities*—(Published by Federal Research Service, Inc., P.O. Box 1059, Vienna, VA 22183; telephone 800-822-5027). This is a bi-weekly publication that lists thousands of currently available federal jobs.
- *Federal Jobs Digest*—(Regular Edition, Breakthrough Publications, P.O. Box 594, Millwood, NY 10546; telephone 800-822-5027). Federal job vacancies are published bi-weekly in a newspaper format.
- *Federal Times*—(6883 Commercial Drive, Springfield, VA 22159; telephone 800-368-6718). Some vacancies starting at the GS-7 level are briefly described.
- *Internships in the Federal Government* and *Internships in Congress*—(both published by the Graduate Group, P.O. Box 370351, West Hartford, CT 06137; telephone 860-233-2330).

3. Federal job hotlines.

- USA JOBS Automated Telephone System (478-757-3000; TDD: 478-744-2299)
- Department of Veterans Affairs (800-368-6008)
- U.S. Postal Service (800-276-5627) Web site: http://www.usps.gov

4. Directly contact the personnel office of each department, agency, or commission that interests you. This strategy requires targeting specific agencies and looking up their addresses, but these offices will have the most up-to-date information on current openings in their organizations.

5. Books written about government employment include *The Book of U.S. Government Jobs*, 8th edition (Damp, 2002), *Government Job Applications and Federal Resumes* (McKinney, 2001), *Federal Civil Service Jobs*, 14th edition (McKay and Lipson, 2003), *The Federal Resume Guidebook,* 2nd edition (Troutman, 1999), *Guide to America's Federal Jobs* (JIST editors, 2001), and *Post Office Jobs,* 3rd edition (Damp, 2003).

6. Two Web sites are available for Congressional jobs:

- *Congressional Quarterly (http://www.cq.com)*—Click on "News," where everything listed is free, including jobs with the Congress.
- *Roll Call (http://www.rcjobs.com)*—RCJobs provides a free employment service, including the posting of your résumé.

7. For state and local government jobs, try these two Web sites:

- State and local government on the Net (http://www.statelocalgov.net)
- Internet Job Source (http://www.statejobs.com)

Successful job hunting at all levels of government involves research of the specific agency in each branch of government. Departments and agencies have their own recruitment and examination procedures. (Researching organizations will be covered in more detail in Chapter 6 of this book.)

Federal job announcements are very complete (in contrast with employment ads of private companies in the classified section of the newspaper, which often provide little information about the job vacancy). These job announcements follow a general format and have several important parts to which you will need to pay close attention when filling out your application. At the top of the announcement is the name of the agency and the bureau within it that is doing the hiring. Each job opening has a "Vacancy Announcement Number," which is the number you will need to use in your application and in any correspondence about the application. Opening and closing dates of the vacancy are specified. A job title is given under "Position" (remember what was written about job titles in Chapter 1 of this book). The numbers after the job title refer to the job classification series. The salary range is indicated with a General Schedule (GS) number(s). The GS is the classification for white-collar jobs in the government. The "Duty Location" tells where the job is located. The next piece of information concerns who may apply: whether the job is open to all qualified applicants or if only current or former federal employees may apply. Major duties are described; read this section carefully to find out the job functions you will be asked to perform if you get the job. Basic requirements are covered indicating the experience needed for the job. "Substitution of Education" is the part of the job vacancy announcement that tells you the education at each grade level that could replace experience requirements.

The government's job announcements ask applicants to list their knowledge, skills, and abilities (KSAs)—the attributes required to perform the functions of a job. KSAs are usually demonstrated through qualifying experience, education, or training. Generally, you are asked to support each KSA listed by a narrative on a separate sheet of paper. Here is where some familiarity with the O*Net (Occupational Information Network) could be very helpful. The O*Net's knowledge, skills, and abilities are listed and described in Appendix H: O*Net List of Skills, Abilities, and Knowledge of *Taking Charge of Your Career Direction*, the first book in this series. Describing your knowledge, skills, and abilities will require careful writing on your part. (Don't just copy the definition of the knowledge, skill, or ability from the O*Net description; tailor your writing to the job being sought.) Although this step is somewhat time consuming, the request for KSAs may relieve you of taking a civil service test.

The "Basis of Rating" section tells you how applications will be evaluated. The pay, benefits, and work schedule section describes whether the job is full time or part time, if it is permanent or temporary, and which benefits you are eligible for if you are hired. A final section informs you where to mail your application or how to apply online, and provides a list of items you will need to submit (McKay and Lipson, 2003).

In applying for government jobs, you can use a résumé, the Optional Application for Federal Employment (OF 612), or any other format you choose. If the hiring agency prefers a certain format over others, it will state this in the job vacancy announcement. Also, you may be able to apply online. Either way, the choice of application is determined for you. If you use a résumé, be sure to include all of the information requested. If you have Internet access, the OF 612 form is available for printing. Go to the USAJOBS Web site (http://www.usajobs.opm.gov) and click on "Forms." Application forms can be obtained from 14 regional U.S. Office of Personnel Management Service Centers, Federal Executive Boards (located in 28 metropolitan areas), personnel offices of most federal agencies, many post offices, and state Job Service offices. Mailing addresses, telephone numbers, and Internet addresses of many of these offices can be found in the government blue-edged pages of your telephone book or in Dennis V. Damp's *Book of U.S. Government Jobs,* 8th edition (2002). Make photocopies before marking the original form. Consult Chapter 3 of this book concerning résumé writing for government job applicants and Chapter 4 on filling out an application for a government job.

The important parts of federal employment application forms are the work experience, education, and other qualifications sections. For these sections, use the functional-content, adaptive-skill format covered in Chapter 6 of *Taking Charge of Your Career Direction* to describe the functions you have performed in previous jobs and volunteer experiences. In the education section, include all education and training you have received—seminars, workshops, training programs, and vocational and adult education classes as well as schools and colleges. For references on résumés, obtain the permission of people not related to you who can give proof or evidence of your work ability.

The Military

The armed forces currently number over 1.5 million military personnel in the United States, not counting the nearly 700,000 civilians working in the Department of Defense (as of 2001). The numbers in each branch of the armed services are roughly as follows: Army, 530,000; Navy, 400,000; Air Force, 385,000; Marine Corps, 174,000; and Coast Guard, 37,000. Eighty-one different occupations are available to enlisted personnel, which make up 85 percent of the armed forces. Fifty-nine occupations are open to officers. Enlisted personnel and officers can qualify for more than 4,100 jobs. If your occupational goal reflects any type of military work, consider enlistment in the Army, Navy, Air Force, Marines, or Coast Guard after completing school. The Reserve Officers' Training Corps (ROTC) can help with expenses while you are in college; write for information from a college that offers ROTC programs. College catalogs and directories also provide ROTC information. The following are some of the Web sites you can use to find more information:

- U.S. Department of Defense, Recruiting Information and Career Opportunities from DefenseLink (http://www.dod.mil/other_info/careers.html).
- Today's Military (http://www.todaysmilitary.com).
- U.S. Army (http://www.goarmy.com). Information on 212 MOS (Military Occupational Specialties).
- U.S. Navy (http://www.navyjobs.com). The Navy's official Web site is http://www.navy.mil.
- U.S. Air Force (http://www.airforce.com).
- U.S. Marine Corps (http://www.marines.com). The main site for the Marines is http://www.usmc.mil.
- U.S. Coast Guard (http://www.uscg.mil).

The armed forces will assess your skills and interests to determine the kind of training program most appropriate for you. Most military occupations are transferable to the civilian labor force. Almost every military assignment teaches some kind of skill that can be useful to civilian organizations, including leadership, responsibility, technical know-how, management, experience overseas, loyalty, and discipline—skills that would be attractive to any employer.

SUPPORT GROUPS: JOB CLUBS AND COOPERATIVES

Job seekers, particularly those who have lost a job recently, are increasingly banding together in support groups sponsored and organized by state and local government agencies, community groups, vocational rehabilitation agencies, and churches. Many support groups target their services to a particular group, such as youth, minorities, women, ex-offenders, or older people. The mental state of the unemployed is often precarious at best. For an unemployed person who is feeling vulnerable and rejected, and is reeling from the blow of a job loss, a job club or cooperative offers much-needed assistance.

Joining a job club support group can be very helpful in finding a job. Job clubs are small groups of job seekers guided by a counselor. Club members exchange information about job leads, make phone calls, write letters, rehearse interviews, give each other rides, and offer emotional comfort. When members get jobs, they notify the others in the group, describe how they did it, and turn over their lists of job leads; the process then continues for other job seekers (Azrin and Besalel, 1982).

Check with your local community action agencies to locate job clubs in your area. Job clubs are sponsored by government agencies, women's resource groups, college career services offices, professional associations, religious institutions, individual churches, and adult education programs. A job club or cooperative can be an excellent way of getting help in the lonely, frustrating business of job hunting. Support groups provide the encouragement and reinforcement that you might otherwise lack. Job search support groups have spread to the Internet. Resources designed to address every possible career development issue, including unemployment and starting a new career, seem to exist in one form or another in the vast territory of the Internet. The quality of these resources, however, varies considerably (Kahnweiler and Riordan, 1998).

UNUSUAL METHODS

Creative job seekers continue to devise new ways of finding sources of job openings. For example, one young man put his résumé on a billboard; he received two job offers by the end of the second day. Some job seekers send employers telegrams asking for an interview because they know that a telegram will be read. This is an expensive method of uncovering job leads, as is the use of special delivery or registered mail. If these methods work, however, they're worth every penny. Long-distance calls have also been tried. Job hunters have prepared brochures to advertise their talents. Another source you might consider is editors or publishers of newsletters; they sometimes act as intermediaries between job seekers and employers because many newsletters are read by employers at all levels. One student got a job by picketing the company he wanted to work for (which succeeded that time, but is not recommended).

A few job seekers attend trade shows in their intended occupation's industry rather than go to job fairs or career days. Your purpose is the same in either case: You want to talk with company representatives. Your competition is less likely to think of a trade show as a means of developing job leads. Keep in mind, however, that at a trade show the company representative wants to talk with customers rather than job seekers. Wait for an opening, and make an appointment for an informational interview after the show. (The subject of Chapter 7 in this book is about interviewing for information.)

Open letters to all area employers have been posted on hundreds of bulletin boards. One college student began her open letter to all area business offices by introducing herself by name and stating, "I am skilled as a legal secretary and would like to do overflow typing work for your firm. Call me if your secretary is swamped or if your typing needs do not require a full- or even part-time secretary. My work is very neat. I can take dictation over the telephone and draft letters." She went on to describe her computer and dictaphone, which had a microcassette adapter for transcribing tapes. The message was typed as a business letter, thus serving to demonstrate her skills to any employer who happened to see it posted on the bulletin boards.

Perhaps showing persistence and constant dedication to getting a job qualifies as an unusual method of job seeking. One personnel director tells a story about an unemployed man, down on his luck, living in a community shelter during the winter. He walked three miles daily for two and a half months, appearing at 8:00 A.M. in the employment office of a local company to apply for a position as building custodian. Each day he was told there was no opening. Most job seekers would be discouraged to hear this message once or twice, let alone day after day for two and a half months. The employer was sufficiently impressed to create a job for the man. He had demonstrated his persistence and punctuality, which were important qualities to the job giver. The man had said by his actions, "If I can show up for work on time each day even when there is no job, think of what I will do for you when there is work for me to do and I am being paid for it."

PERSONAL CONTACTS/NETWORKING

In this chapter, you have read about many sources of help in locating job leads. However, none of these methods are as productive as your **personal contacts**: people who are knowledgeable about occupations and jobs that interest you, people who know others who are also knowledgeable, people with connections to other people who can hire you, and people with the power to hire. They can operate as a third party to bring the job seeker and job provider together. Personal contacts may be your friends and their friends, your parents and relatives and their friends, past and present neighbors, current and former classmates, teachers, counselors, administrators, religious leaders, youth club leaders, coworkers, employers, supervisors, customers you have served, club and association members, and so on. In fact, any person you know could potentially be a part of your personal-contact network.

Ask people to explain the meaning of **networking** and you are likely to get as many different answers as the number of people you ask. Some will say you network when you are looking for a job. Others may say that it is a way of contacting lots of people to help you with a problem. Yet others will reply that networking has a kind of hushed, "undercover" feeling to it. Each of these notions has a certain but limited truth about the meaning of networking. Each view centers on an aspect of networking, exaggerating and distorting it to the point of missing the essential nature of it. Networking involves interacting and exchanging information with people. Chances are very good, like 100 percent, that you have been networking all your life and will continue to do so. What do you do when you want to find out about something? How do you decide which movie to see, book to read, or TV program to watch? You talk to people, get their opinions, and work those ideas into your own thinking and decisions. You probably haven't thought of this activity as networking, but that's what you've been doing. You have done it intuitively. However, in certain areas of life, networking can be very purposeful and intentional, and used to achieve important goals (Lawson, 2000). In the first book of this Career Planning Guide series (*Taking Charge of Your Career Direction*), you used some aspects of networking in gathering information for making a decision for a career choice or change. In the book you are now reading, we focus on using networking for making a job search.

More jobs are obtained through a network of personal contacts than through all other sources of job leads combined (Granovetter, 1995). A **personal-contact network** is a structure of interlocking connections among people you know who could help you in your job search. Figure 2-6 helps you to visualize what a personal-contact network looks like. See how many names of people you can place on the lines in Figure 2-6. If you haven't done this before, this is the start of your personal-contact list. Don't stop when you have filled in the lines of Figure 2-6 with names. Keep going. Use the **referral question** (Who else do you know that might have information about jobs in the occupation I am interested in?). The idea is to enlarge the number of contacts you already have.

Aim to build and maintain a relationship throughout your life, not just for the length of your job search. Networking is a long-term project. The reason? A big part of it is systematic—setting up interviews, going out to meet a potential contact, and following up the initial meeting to maintain a lasting relationship. You never know when you will be job hunting again or need some other kind of help, and the people in your network could lend you valuable assistance. The problem with networking for a lot of people is that *it takes time*, and many people these days are in a hurry.

Keep in mind that individuals aren't the only ones that network. Organizations use their network of contacts to find people to fill their vacant positions.

Networking is a planned, strategic activity of developing relationships with people for a specific purpose and a desired outcome. However, there is another kind of networking that is *unplanned*, a chance encounter that leads to a mutually beneficial relationship. Planned networking can be nerve-wracking for some people; we think of what can go right, but we also have in mind the things that could go wrong. Every

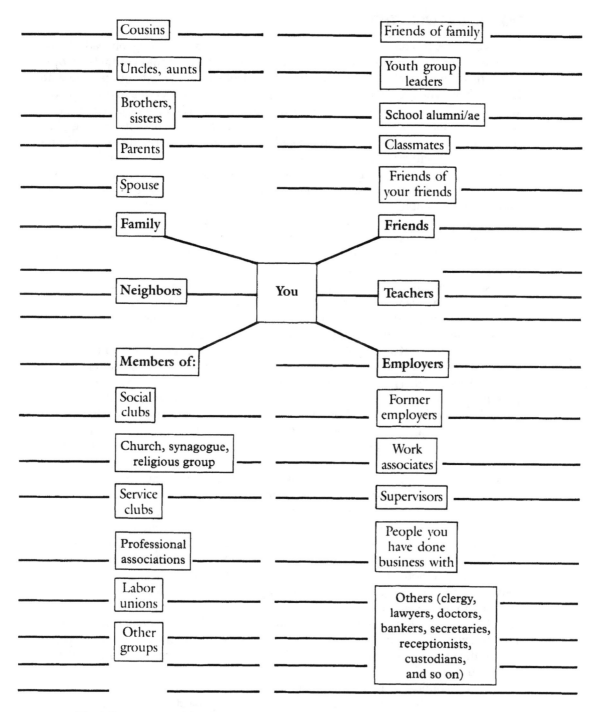

Blank lines are provided for you to insert the names of people as you think of them.
Remember, all these people have personal-contact networks of their own. Some may not realize this,
so you can share the idea of networking with them.

Figure 2-6   Personal-contact network

sentence and body movement is anticipated and, thus, we get nervous and anxious. Unplanned, chance meetings with people occur spontaneously. There are no expectations and no time to get nervous. Yet, there is a relationship between these two kinds of networking—the planned, strategic kind prepares us for spontaneous networking; when you are confident of your networking ability, you are ready to be natural and spontaneous (Darling, 2003).

Networking is *not* a crass cultivation or haphazard hounding of friends, acquaintances, and relatives for news of job vacancies. Cultivating people, in its best sense, means meeting people for the sake of getting to know them, possibly establishing a friendship, helping them when they are in need, and sharing information. In its worst sense, it means a one-sided manipulation of others in order to get something from them (in this case, a job or a lead on a job), without ever intending to do anything for them in return. Networking involves the art of conversation, an exchange of information and contacts. Networking is having something in common with another person and talking about it (Marler and Mattia, 1998).

Some people regard networking and acquiring contacts as degrading and vow not to "use" other people. This attitude can be just as unrealistic as the manipulative, selfish one. People like to do favors for others. Helping people is a worthy motive many admire and include in their own behavior. By going it alone in the job search, you could deprive some people of satisfying their need to assist others.

Other people are negative toward networking because they don't want to feel dependent on others or they think it requires being artificial. Networking has a bad reputation with some people; they have been burned by a job seeker who says they are looking for information and then asks if there are any job positions open (Lawson, 2000).

Unless you plan to live and work entirely alone without human contact somewhere on a lonely island, you cannot do without networking. (Read John Donne's *Devotions*, "No man is an island . . .".) The job search world floats on a sea of contacts. "Who you know" does help get you through the interviewer's door. "What you know" helps convince an employer to offer you a job. The research on job hunting has shown that people find more highly paid and prestigious jobs through personal contacts than through any other method. People who find jobs through personal contacts also report greater satisfaction in their work (Granovetter, 1995). The more you enlist people into your job search network, the better your success is likely to be. Richard Bolles (2003) gives using contacts the highest rating of all job search methods—an 86 percent effectiveness rate for getting a hiring interview and, after that, a job.

You can start right away to build a network of personal contacts. Don't wait until you graduate or are out of a job. In fact, networking is *not* getting a job, selling anything, receiving a donation, or securing funding. Start putting your network together *before you need it*. Build relationships before you need them. Otherwise, you run the risk of looking too manipulative.

If you haven't networked, Diane Darling (2003) suggests you stop reading about how to network and take a walk or go on an errand. Smile and make eye contact with at least two people you don't know. People with dogs are typically very friendly. Walk up to them, smile, and ask the name and the breed of the dog and how long the person has had the dog. (You do like dogs, don't you?) Ask if you can pet the dog and, if so, hold the back of your hand out for the dog to sniff. Then, say "thanks" and walk away. Next, go to the grocery or supermarket and shop for some food. While selecting a brand, ask someone next to you if he or she is familiar with the product or if there is another one that they prefer. Again, thank the person and walk away. The purpose of these exercises is to get you to talk with someone you have never spoken to before and ask a few questions. You are not asking anyone to do anything for you; you are asking about a dog and some groceries. When you are done, ask yourself a few questions: What did you think of the encounters? Did you like them? Did you find out anything about the people you contacted? How did you feel when the exercise was over? What didn't you like? How did it feel walking up to a total stranger? Could you talk to strangers all day—why or why not? What would you do differently? You have just accomplished an important step in networking: communicating with a stranger and making a connection. This is how and where networking begins (Darling, 2003). And remember, what you have begun is a lifelong process.

Work on Exercise 2-2, Record of Personal Contacts, at the end of this chapter. List the names, job titles, addresses, and telephone numbers of people who could be called your personal contacts. Indicate your relationship with each one (friend, relative, neighbor). Record the dates you have talked with each. Note the subjects discussed. List the names of those who suggested each personal contact and to whom they referred you. You start by brainstorming a list of potential contacts by yourself and then ask other people to suggest possible names for you. Of course, these "other people" could be contacts, too.

All it takes is one name to start developing a list of personal contacts. A natural way to begin a conversation with people is to ask them about their work. If their work is something in which you are also interested, so much the better. People love to "talk shop." Asking for details of their jobs is a time-honored way to obtain information. Keep in mind that the most important question in building your personal-contact network is the referral questions you should ask at the end of the conversation: "Can you give me the names of any other people who do the kind of work you do? How might I contact them? May I say that you suggested I get in touch with them?" Some people might even write a letter of introduction for you. These referral questions are the key to expanding the number of names in your personal-contact network. The success of a networking meeting is often measured by whether you have gained at least two more names of people to contact (Richardson, 1994). In theory, expansion of contacts is exponential. You talk with one person, who talks to another about your job search ($1 \times 2 = 2$). Those two each connect with two more people ($1 \times 2 \times 2 = 4$). And then ($1 \times 2 \times 2 \times 4 = 16$. Carry the networking equation one step further and you arrive at 256 people. Each link between two people generates an exponential expansion (Powell, 1995). Keep in mind, however, that not everyone you contact will have two or more names to suggest. Whether there is truth in the notion that any two people in the country are only six degrees of separation apart (Wildavsky, 2002), it says something about the power of networking and how connected we really are.

Courtesy is an essential factor in developing a personal-contact network. Good manners means keeping your discussions short, especially when you are talking to people at work. You are asking contacts for occupational information, job leads, and referrals to other people to expand your network, so acknowledging their efforts by saying and writing how much you appreciate what they have done for you is always appropriate. Expect to return favors by sharing relevant information gathered during your job searching with those in your network.

Always ask for permission to use your contact's name if he or she tells you about a job opening and/or suggests names of other people to contact. Ask also whether your contact would recommend using his or her name; it is possible that this person is not on good terms with the potential new contact. Express your thanks when you leave a contact that has expressed an interest in what you are doing and given information to help you. Write a thank-you letter or note of appreciation within a day or two. This is not only a mark of courtesy, but also practical. You can remind yourself that you may want to ask a favor of your personal contact again. If you have acted on a suggestion or a piece of advice from your contact, definitely tell him or her, either by letter or telephone (or in person if the opportunity should arise). Your follow-up activity and staying in touch with your contacts are important. The payoff for people who have given their time and advice is the knowledge and satisfaction of having helped someone (Richardson, 1994).

Giving a business card to a contact is highly recommended by many job-search experts. Always carry a few of them. Leaving your card with a contact is a reminder later on that he or she has a connection with you. The design of a business card must be attractive, allow for "white space," and identify you with your name and how you can be contacted (usually by telephone and/or e-mail). Home address is optional. It's not mandatory to put your home address on the card, particularly for women. If you have a business address, use it. Have your cards professionally made at a print shop so they are readable and strong enough to be used. Some people like to leave the back of the card blank for writing notes; others prefer to briefly explain what they do or their company does while leaving some space to write on. Make sure all information is up-to-date and correct.

You can hand out your card after a conversation, but don't just walk up to people at a gathering and distribute your cards. When you are at an event (workshop, convention, or any kind of meeting), carry your cards in a small case to keep them clean and looking good—just the image you want to convey. Ask for a card to keep in your referral file. Have a place to keep the cards you receive so you can easily retrieve them when necessary. Carry two pens; one may give out or not work. Have clean sheets of paper on which to write notes. Briefcases should look professional, be functional, open easily, and not be too bulky or weigh too much. Cell phones present a problem. If you are talking with someone and the cell phone rings, do you answer it or not? Your decision reflects your priorities. In this situation, it's best to leave the cell phone turned off for the duration of your networking conversations. If you are anticipating an important call, explain (early on) this expectation to the other person.

Be aware of what you are saying nonverbally while networking. The way we carry our bodies and the tone and inflection of our voices communicate more information than our words. This is a topic to which we will return in the chapter on interviewing for jobs (Chapter 8). Don't crowd people when you are talking to them; take your cues from them, but leave enough personal space for them to be comfortable with you. Maintain good eye contact, but don't stare holes through them. If you are standing, don't slouch. Use a breath mint before a meeting. Write down the questions you sincerely want to ask on a small sheet of paper, carry them with you, and refer to them, if you cannot remember them while you are in a conversation. Diane Darling (2003) gives a few pointers for starting conversations. Prepare neutral questions to ask. (Stay away from politics, religion, sex, inappropriate jokes, weight, height, age, and your relationships with others at work.) Talk about the business you or they are in, movies, sports, books, or the event you are attending. Read the newspaper or watch or listen to news broadcasts to know what's going on. Ask open-ended questions. Listen carefully; you were given two ears and one mouth, take the hint!

Interviewing will be covered in later chapters, but here is a quick rundown of the format that can be used. Express appreciation for the time your contact is taking to meet with you. If you were referred to this person by someone else, say so if you have permission. Explain why you are here (you are trying to get information for your job search), but don't ask this person for a job! Mention something about yourself: career interests, personal qualifications, an accomplishment or two, but don't go on and on—make this no more than two minutes. Ask appropriate questions; here, you can refer to your list if you need to. Jot down notes—a word or two to refresh your memory later. You may need to look at your notepad, but remember the importance of eye contact. Ask for referrals and get information about them if possible. If you get no contacts, be grateful for what you do receive. Assume the person is giving whatever he or she can (Wendleton, 2000). Thank the person for the time spent with you. Say you want to keep in touch and ask how this might best be done. After the interview, follow up with a thank-you note within a day or two and remember to stay in touch later on.

When you approach a personal contact to obtain information about jobs and job openings, the rule is: *Never ask for a job*. We have said this before, and we'll say it now because it's important. Asking a contact for a job is an absolute no-no. Your contacts are not likely to have hiring authority, much less have an unfilled job just waiting for you. All you will do by asking for a job is put your personal contact on the spot, make him or her uncomfortable, and possibly create negative feelings toward you. This is an information-seeking exercise, not a job interview. If, by some miracle, any of your contacts have a job waiting for you in the wings, let the initiative come from them. You can say to your contacts that if they hear of a job opening they believe you would be interested in, you would greatly appreciate knowing about it.

What could you ask or discuss with a personal contact in a conversation about work? After making clear the nature of your occupational goal, the following suggestions could be helpful:

- What attracted you to your occupation in the first place? What are the personal rewards of the work for you at this time? What do you enjoy about your job?
- How long have you worked in your job? How long have you been with your present employer?
- What are your major responsibilities? What skills are needed in your work?
- What qualifications would you look for in a new employee?
- What are the major frustrations and the most frequently recurring problems in your job?
- How is the industry changing now?
- If you learn of any job openings in (name of your career goal), would you please let me know?
- Who else could I talk with about your field of work? How can I get in touch with them? May I give them your name and say you suggested I talk with them?

The referral question is always your last question in a networking meeting. A major purpose in talking with people is to generate more personal contacts and keep expanding your network.

EXERCISE 2-1 RECORD OF JOB LEADS

Where have you found job vacancies in the occupation of your choice? Fill in the following information on the blank Record of Job Leads form that accompanies this exercise:

1. Write the name of the company or organization, and indicate the source of the job lead.
2. Enter the name of your contact person in the organization, with address and telephone number.
3. Keep a record of the actions you took concerning the job opening. Write the date you made each contact with an organization and make a note of what happened.

Photocopy the Job Leads form if you need more copies. Another option is to record your job lead information on 3-by-5 or 4-by-6 inch cards.

EXERCISE 2-2 RECORD OF PERSONAL CONTACTS

First, refer to Figure 2-6, where you are encouraged to list the names of contacts as you think of them. Then, on the blank Record of Personal Contacts form that accompanies this exercise, fill in the following information:

1. Write down the name of the person, address, and telephone number.
2. What is this contact's job title?
3. What is this person's relationship to you?
4. Record the date you talked with this person.
5. What subjects did you talk about?
6. Who suggested or referred you to this person?
7. To whom did this personal contact refer you?

Photocopy the Personal Contacts form if you need more copies. Another option is to keep a record of your personal contacts on 3-by-5 or 4-by-6 inch file cards.

Record of Job Leads

Name of Work Organization (source of job lead)	Person's Name	Address/Telephone	First Contact		Second Contact		Third Contact	
			Date	Result	Date	Result	Date	Result

Record of Personal Contacts

Name of Personal Contact Address/Telephone Number	Job Title	Relationship	Date of Interview	Subjects Discussed	Suggested by Whom?	Referred to Whom?

SUMMARY

1. Traditional sources of job leads are college career services offices, public and private employment agencies, newspaper and magazine help-wanted advertisements, electronic job banks and online services, direct-mail applications to employers, direct application to personnel or employment offices, telephone calls to employers, career days or job fairs, government civil service announcements, and job clubs. These methods have their critics because job vacancies from traditional sources are usually advertised and made visible to the public, which places the job seeker in competition with large numbers of applicants. Most of these sources are free or inexpensive (with the exception of some private employment agencies), so most counselors suggest using various sources in a multiple approach to finding job openings.

2. Some sources of job leads are more selective, in the sense that they are not as well known or used as much by the general public. Examples are drop-in visits, personal (or "broadcast") letters, work-study programs, telegrams, or a special brochure targeted to a number of employers. You can make some traditional sources of job leads more selective by researching organizations, eliminating those that do not interest you, and communicating only with those on which you wish to focus your job search.

3. More people discover job openings from personal contacts than from all other sources combined. Anyone you know can be a personal contact. You should always try to expand your contact network by asking for referrals from your current contacts. Many questions about work are appropriate, but one question you never ask a personal contact is "Do you have a job for me?" Your purpose is solely to obtain information. If an idea for a job develops, it comes from your contacts, not you. You can tell personal contacts, however, that if they encounter a job opening in your occupational field, you would appreciate hearing about it.

4. Keep a file of your job leads and names of your personal contacts on the forms provided in this chapter or on 3-by-5 or 4-by-6 inch file cards. Your job search will be more organized and effective if you maintain written records of your progress.

REFERENCES

Associated Press. 2003, July 2. Wal-Mart extends anti-discrimination policy to include gays. *Jackson Citizen Patriot*, A-6.

Azrin, N. H., and Besalel, V. B. 1982. *Finding a job*. Berkeley, CA: Ten Speed Press.

Bardes, B. A., Shelley, M. C., and Schmidt, S. W. 2002. *American government and politics today: 2003–2004*. Belmont, CA: Wadsworth.

Berman, J. M. 2001, November. Industry output and employment projections to 2010. *Monthly Labor Review*, 124(11), 39–56.

Bolles, R. N. 2003. *What color is your parachute?* Berkeley, CA: Ten Speed Press.

Boroughs, D. L. 1994, July 4. Business gives in to temptation. *U.S. News & World Report*, 56–58.

Careerbuilder.com. 2003. Tips for using keywords. Chicago: Career Builder Corp. (Retrieved July 2, 2003.)

Castro, J. 1993, March 29. Nobody is safe. *Time*, 141(3), 46–47.

Challenger, J. E. 2003, April. Job seekers lengthen joblessness . . . shut off computers and see employers. *Employment Review*, 15(4), 12.

Damp, D. V. 2002. *The book of U.S. government jobs: Where they are, what's available & how to get one*, 8th ed. McKees Rocks, PA: Bookhaven Press.

Damp, D. V. 2003. *Post office jobs*, 3rd ed. Moon Township, PA: Bookhaven Press.

Darling, D. C. 2003. *The networking survival guide: Get the success you want by tapping into the people you know*. New York: McGraw-Hill.

Dikel, M. R., and Roehm, F. 2002. *Guide to Internet job searching*. Chicago: VGM Career Books. ("The Riley Guide")

Granovetter, M. S. 1995. *Getting a job: A study of contacts and careers*, 2nd ed. Chicago: University of Chicago Press.

Green, K. 1993, Summer. Working for the U.S. in the 1990s. *Occupational Outlook Quarterly*, 37(2), 2–17.

Guiducci, J. 1992. *Joan Guiducci's power calling: A fresh approach to cold calls & prospecting*. Mill Valley, CA: Tonino/Power Calling.

Half, R. 1994. *How to get a better job in this crazy world*. New York: Signet Books.

Holmberg, E. E., and Kumar, L. 1998, annual editions. *Gale directory of databases,* 2 vols. Detroit, MI: Gale Research.

JIST editors. 2001. *Guide to America's federal jobs,* 2nd ed. Indianapolis, IN: JIST Publishing.

Joell, P. S. 2003. How to get the most out of career fairs. Bethlehem, PA: National Association of Colleges and Employers JobWeb.com. (Retrieved July 4, 2003.)

Kahnweiler, W. M., and Riordan, R. J. 1998. "Job and employee support groups: Past and prologue. *The Career Development Quarterly,* 47, 173–187.

Kennedy, J. L., and Morrow, T. J. 1994. *Electronic job search revolution.* New York: Wiley.

Lawson, K. 2000. *Guide to managing your career.* New York: Dorling Kindersley.

Marler, P., and Mattia, J. B. 1998. *Networking made easy.* Lincolnwood, IL: VGM Career Horizons.

McKay, D. R., and Lipson, M. 2003. *Federal civil service jobs,* 14th ed. Lawrenceville, NJ: Peterson's/Arco/Thomson.

McKinney, A. 2001. *Government job applications and federal resumes.* Fayetteville, NC: PREP Publishing.

NCWD/Youth. 2002, September. *Information brief: How young people benefit from one-stop centers.* Washington, DC: National Collaborative on Workforce and Disability.

Pekas, M. D. 1990. *Telephone mastery: A text on effective use of the phone in business.* St. Paul, MN: Paradigm.

Powell, C. R. 1995. *Career planning today,* 3rd ed. Dubuque, IA: Kendall/Hunt.

Richardson, D. B. 1994. *Networking.* New York: Wiley.

Royko, M. 1982, January 21. This is not the time to give up on life. *Jackson Citizen Patriot,* A-7.

Troutman, K. K. 1999. *The federal resume guidebook,* 2nd ed. Indianapolis, IN: JIST Publishing.

U.S. Department of Defense. 2001. *Military careers: A guide to military occupations and selected military career paths.* Washington, DC: U.S. Department of Defense.

Walsh, J., Johnson, M., and Sugarman, M. 1975. *Help wanted: Case studies of classified ads.* Salt Lake City, UT: Olympus.

Weddle, P. D. 2002. *Weddle's guide to employment Web sites: The job seeker's edition.* Stamford, CT: Weddle's.

Wendleton, K. 2000. *Targeting the job you want,* 3rd ed. Franklin Lakes, NJ: Career Press.

Wildavsky, B. 2002, April 1. Small world, isn't it? *U.S. News & World Report,* 134(33), 68.

Chapter 3

Using Your Writing Skills to Get a Job: Résumés and Cover Letters

"I thought I'd dash off my résumé and cover letter in less than an hour. After all, I'm writing about myself. I can list my schools and places where I've worked. I can tell what happened at each one of them. Imagine my surprise when my best friend told me she had been working on her résumé off and on for the past five days, and wasn't finished yet! How could anything so simple be so complicated?"

The personnel director of a well-known local company looked at a class of 25 students as he started a presentation. He had been sent a photocopy of each of their résumés and cover letters before coming to speak about the job search to a career-planning class. "I've read your résumés," he began. "Two of you would have been invited to an interview for a job opening. The rest of you would have been sent a polite rejection letter." There was a gasp from the students.

Improbable scenarios? No, your author has witnessed them on several occasions in recent years. Writing about yourself isn't easy. In a job search, you want to attract the attention of recruiters and employers, and that takes a certain amount of assertion and confidence, but you don't want to overdo it and set up expectations you cannot fulfill.

Writing a résumé and cover letter is a standard feature of most job search campaigns. A résumé is a summary of your personal, educational, and employment experiences and qualifications. Résumé preparation may seem a rather prosaic subject, but it is controversial. Some authorities state that résumés are more likely to get in the way of your job search than to help it (Fox, 2001). Certainly, a poorly written résumé will work against you, and a well-designed résumé by itself will not get you a job. Its intent is to obtain a job interview. If you can get an interview without a résumé, more power to you; however, some employers will not see you without a résumé. For many job seekers, résumés are the best way to get job interviews.

No less controversial is the question of what should be included or emphasized in the résumé. Some people advocate omitting a job objective on the theory that it limits the use of your résumé; others state that it must be included because it indicates to employers that you know what you want. Opinions differ over the preferred type of résumé—chronological or functional. The **chronological résumé** arranges the schools you attended and your job positions in reverse time order, starting with and emphasizing your most recent experience. This chronological approach is considered the most appropriate choice for job seekers with limited experience (Fry, 2001). The **functional résumé** accentuates the functions of job positions you have held, displaying the skills you have used and the qualifications you possess. Some writers discourage use of the chronological format and encourage something close to a functional style; one writer calls it a **qualification brief** (Lathrop, 1998). Still another type of formal summary of education and work background is the **curriculum vitae**, used mainly for academic positions in higher education.

As if the debate about which style of résumé to use and what to include in it weren't enough, now comes the electronic revolution to complicate the subject of résumé writing. Computers respond differently from people to the contents of a résumé, and job seekers need to be aware of those differences. For example, in a conventional résumé you can use italicized print and graphics, but these devices can cause a computer to transmit a distorted message to the employer. Use of the **electronic résumé** format will only increase in the future. Most companies no longer have sufficient personnel to sort manually through the massive numbers of résumés they receive. Your résumé is now more likely to be placed in an electronic database from which a list of qualified candidates can be quickly produced for the employer.

A **cover letter** accompanies the résumé. It introduces you to the employer and clearly states your application for a specific job, particularly if your job objective has been expressed in broad, general terms in your résumé. Other functions of the cover letter include presenting particular achievements and personal skills and requesting an interview with the employer. Some job seekers omit the personalized cover letter when they mail hundreds of résumés in a direct-mail campaign. The research on this subject indicates, however, that presenting a résumé with a cover letter is much more effective than presenting a résumé alone.

The skills discussed in this chapter and the next one are part of your general communication abilities. Words are used in special ways to get ideas across to other people, something you have spent a great deal of time on in school. You will relate to other people not only through résumés and cover letters but also when you write a letter of inquiry, a thank-you letter, or a letter accepting or declining a job offer. Of course, writing is not the only method of communication in the job search. You use your reading skills when you look for job leads and research organizations, and you use your speaking skills when you interview for information and for a job.

THE RÉSUMÉ

A résumé is a self-designed information sheet written about yourself—a brief statement of your qualifications for a job. The terms *personal data sheet* or *curriculum vitae* have been used in place of *résumé*. The word *résumé* has an accent mark over each letter *e*, but standard usage allows you to spell the word without the accent marks. Résumé is derived from a French word meaning "summary." A résumé generally summarizes your job objective, education, work experience, and any other pertinent information you want to emphasize to employers and personnel officers. The résumé should answer certain questions for the employer: "Who are you? How can you be contacted?" (answered in the heading). "What do you want?" (explained in the job objective). "What can you do?" (described in a qualifications section). "What have you learned?" (covered in the section on education). "What have you done?" (indicated in the section on work experience).

One great advantage of writing a résumé over filling out application forms is that it allows you to present yourself in your own way. Employers' application forms require you to disclose yourself on their terms, but a résumé can honestly emphasize your strong points while minimizing limitations. An employer will be impressed if you have prepared a résumé even if the employer has not asked for one. It shows that you are well prepared and serious about applying for a job. If an employer asks you to complete an application form before an interview, the résumé will help you supply accurate information you might overlook or remember incorrectly. The résumé can be thought of as a verbal picture of yourself that stays with the employer after you leave the interview.

The basic purpose of the résumé is to introduce yourself and secure an interview. It will not get you a job by itself; few, if any, employers are going to hire an applicant on the basis of a résumé alone. Résumés and cover letters are meant to get you through the employer's door.

A good résumé is written only by the individual searching for a job. Do not rely on an outside résumé preparation service; experienced personnel workers can easily recognize this sort of résumé because it follows a formula, lacks spontaneity, and may present a misleading picture of the job seeker. You can do a better job of writing the résumé yourself. It takes time, however; the résumé is part of your campaign to persuade an employer to hire you, and you must spend several hours—even days—working on it.

Neatness and correct spelling are essential. Neatness projects your qualifications on paper, but a messy résumé conveys the image of a careless worker in the minds of many employers. Mistakes in spelling, punctuation, and grammar reflect on your competence and can cost you a job opportunity. There is no argument about this point. Study after study over the years have shown the obvious: Employers prefer résumés that are neat, grammatically correct, and free of spelling errors (Meyers, 1984). If you are unsure about the spelling of a word, use a dictionary. If you are using a computer as a word processor, don't rely entirely on the word processor's spell checker. It helps, but it isn't 100 percent foolproof. Which of these words are spelled correctly: *peace* or *piece*? *poll* or *pole*? *right, write,* or *rite*? To the computer, all the words are spelled properly. Only a human mind can determine the correct spelling of a word by the way it is used in the context of a sentence. Nor will the spell checker help you if you leave out a letter in a word that becomes another correctly spelled word used inappropriately, as in these two cases of missing *r*'s: "I am a quick leaner," "My efforts gave me a fist in the class." Proofread, proofread! Then have someone else proofread your résumé before you send it to employers.

Punctuation marks may seem like little things, but they can easily change the meaning of an entire sentence. Consider Bill, caught in a sentence with no commas: "We are going to eat Bill before we do another thing." Quick! Get a couple of commas and place them before and after "Bill." Would a semicolon help in the following sentence? "Teachers eat chicken, students, fish." Yes, it would—right after "chicken." (Students will appreciate it.) As you can see, little things (like punctuation marks) mean a lot.

When you refer to activities in which you are currently engaged, use the present tense. Use the past tense when you mention anything previous to your current activities. Watch abbreviations; in most cases, it is best to write out the full spelling of a word.

The writing style should be factual and concise. Avoid the use of the personal pronoun "I." The reader of your résumé already knows you are the subject of each sentence or phrase. Start each sentence with an action verb. (Table 3-1 provides a list of over 200 action words to consult when you are writing your résumé.) Then complete the sentence by using a word or a phrase as an object to complement the action verb, and add an adjective or adverb to describe your action. (Table 3-2 offers a list of self-descriptive words.) Readers who have completed Exercises 6-1 through 6-4 in Chapter 6 of *Taking Charge of Your Career Direction* will recognize the functional, content, and adaptive skills that form the structure of résumé writing.

Always be honest and accurate about the information you give in your résumé. Personnel managers tell us that approximately one-third to one-half of the résumés they receive contain false information. Don't claim a skill you do not have or an accomplishment you cannot support with evidence. An academic record can be easily

Table 3-1 Action Verbs for Résumé Writing

achieved	authored	comprehended	decreased
acquired	awarded	computed	defined
acted	balanced	conceived	delivered
adapted	bargained	conceptualized	demonstrated
added	brought about	condensed	depicted
adjusted	budgeted	conducted	derived
administered	built	confined	designed
advanced	calculated	confronted	detailed
advised	cared for	conserved	detected
aided	carried out	consoled	determined
analyzed	caught	consolidated	developed
anticipated	chaired	constructed	devised
applied	changed	consulted	diagnosed
appraised	checked	contacted	diagrammed
approved	clarified	controlled	directed
arranged	classified	converted	discovered
articulated	cleaned	convinced	displayed
assembled	coached	cooperated	distributed
asserted	collaborated	coordinated	dissected
assessed	collected	corresponded	drafted
assisted	colored	counseled	drew
assured	communicated	created	drove
attained	compared	critiqued	earned
attended	compiled	cultivated	edited
attracted	completed	dealt	educated
audited	composed	decided	elected

enabled	initiated	participated	revamped
encouraged	innovated	perceived	safeguarded
enforced	inspected	performed	saved
enhanced	inspired	persisted	scheduled
enlarged	installed	persuaded	secured
enlisted	instituted	piloted	served
ensured	instructed	pioneered	set up
entertained	interpreted	planned	shaped
equipped	interviewed	played	shipped
established	introduced	positioned	shopped
estimated	invented	prepared	simplified
evaluated	inventoried	presented	sketched
examined	investigated	presided	sold
exceeded	judged	prevented	solved
exhibited	kept	printed	sorted
expanded	launched	processed	sparked
expedited	lectured	produced	spoke
explained	led	programmed	sponsored
explored	lifted	promoted	stabilized
expressed	listened	proposed	started
fabricated	located	protected	steered
facilitated	logged	proved	simulated
fashioned	maintained	provided	straightened
filed	managed	publicized	streamlined
finalized	manufactured	published	strengthened
financed	marketed	purchased	structured
fixed	mastered	questioned	studied
followed	maximized	raised	summarized
forecast	measured	read	supervised
forged	mediated	realized	supplied
formed	memorized	reasoned	supported
formulated	mentored	recognized	surpassed
fostered	minimized	recommended	surveyed
founded	moderated	reconciled	synchronized
fulfilled	modernized	recorded	systematized
furthered	modified	recruited	targeted
gained	molded	redesigned	taught
gathered	monitored	reduced	tended
generated	motivated	referred	tested
graduated	moved	rehabilitated	tracked
guarded	multiplied	reinforced	trained
guided	navigated	remedied	transformed
halved	negotiated	remodeled	translated
handled	nourished	renewed	traveled
harnessed	nurtured	reorganized	treated
harvested	observed	repaired	turned around
headed	obtained	reported	uncovered
helped	offered	represented	understood
identified	opened	researched	updated
illustrated	operated	resolved	utilized
imagined	orchestrated	restored	visualized
implemented	organized	restructured	volunteered
improved	originated	retrieved	won
improvised	outlined	reversed	worked
increased	overcame	reviewed	wrote
influenced	packaged	revised	
informed	painted	revitalized	

All of these action verbs are expressed in the past tense. For your current job or experience, use the present tense. Of course, you can consult a thesaurus to find replacements for these specific words.

Table 3-2   Self-Descriptive Words for Résumé Writing

accurately	disciplined	liberally	reasonably
actively	discreetly	logically	reflectively
adeptly	distinctively	loyally	reliably
aggressively	eagerly	maturely	resourcefully
alertly	effectively	meaningfully	responsibly
ambitiously	efficiently	methodically	responsively
analytically	eloquently	meticulously	rigorously
articulately	empathically	moderately	securely
artistically	energetically	modestly	self-reliant
attentively	enterprising	naturally	sensitively
attractively	enthusiastically	notably	seriously
businesslike	entirely	objectively	significantly
calmly	ethically	observantly	sincerely
candidly	exceptionally	optimistically	skillfully
capably	exhaustively	orderly	sociably
carefully	expressively	originally	spontaneously
cheerfully	extremely	painstakingly	stalwartly
clearly	fairly	patiently	steadily
cohesively	firmly	peacefully	strategically
competently	flexibly	perceptively	strongly
completely	forcefully	persistently	sturdily
comprehensively	formally	persuasively	successfully
confidently	generously	pleasantly	supportively
conscientiously	genially	politely	systematically
conservatively	gently	positively	tactfully
considerately	gregariously	practically	tenaciously
consistently	helpfully	precisely	thoroughly
constructively	highly	productively	thoughtfully
continuously	honestly	professionally	urgently
cooperatively	hopefully	proficiently	verbally
courageously	humorously	profitably	vigorously
creatively	imaginatively	progressively	virtuously
decisively	immediately	prudently	vitally
deliberately	incisively	punctually	vivaciously
delicately	independently	purposefully	voluntarily
dependably	industriously	quickly	warmly
determinedly	intelligently	quietly	watchfully
dexterously	intensively	radiantly	wisely
diligently	judiciously	rationally	zealously
diplomatically	kindly	realistically	

Most of these words are stated as adverbs, and for the most part, they can be changed to adjectives by dropping the suffix *-ly*. Again, you can consult a thesaurus to find replacements for these specific words.

checked by a request for school transcripts. Previous employers can be contacted for verification. A résumé will be rejected immediately if a false claim becomes evident. Be very careful about the accuracy of your information. The résumé reader does not know if inaccurate information is deliberately misleading or an unintended error. Typical errors on résumés (and applications) are wrong employment dates, reasons for leaving a company, and dates of school attendance.

Reasons for Writing a Résumé

There are many reasons for preparing a résumé. Ten are listed here:

1. A résumé can be a requirement for a personal interview. Some employers and interviewers will not talk to job applicants without first looking at their resumés.

2. A résumé lets you tell your story in your own way. You can be assured that your most attractive features will be presented to the employer. An employer's application form makes you tell your story in a way that might not allow you to present yourself as you would like.

3. The preparation of a résumé reminds you of things about yourself that you should remember as you search for a job. The process of constructing a résumé encourages you to make an inventory of your experiences and abilities. Job hunters learn about themselves as they prepare their résumés.

4. A résumé represents you when you are not on hand to speak for yourself. An attractive, well-written résumé can help you survive an employer's screening of candidates, especially when the competition is relatively equal in other respects. A résumé can help you be remembered after the interview has taken place.

5. If you apply for a job through the mail, the employer generally expects a résumé whether one is asked for or not. Sending a résumé that has not been requested obtains more job interviews than responding without a résumé (Washington, 1996).

6. A good résumé can be the most effective piece in a direct-mail campaign. With the advent of word-processed résumés and the computer's potential to send out hundreds of résumés and cover letters, the direct-mail campaign has been revived. Use original copies, not photocopies (Smith, 2000). Your appeal may include a personal letter or a work sample, but the résumé often gets the most serious attention from prospective employers (Biegeleisen, 1982).

7. A résumé can function as a business card or a detailed calling card as you research organizations (Rosen and Paul, 1998). Just as salespeople leave their cards, so can job seekers leave their résumés in order to be remembered. Give copies of your résumé to your personal contacts. They can distribute it to their contacts and thus widen the scope of your job search. A résumé makes it easier for those who know you to recommend you to potential employers.

8. You can transfer information from your résumé to an employer's application form and know that it is accurate because you have spent time making sure the material in your résumé is correct. If you arrive for an interview and are asked to complete an application form on the spot, you are already under pressure, and it's helpful to have a source of reliable information.

9. A résumé helps ease the transition of introducing yourself and getting acquainted with the employer or interviewer. It can provide an outline for discussion during an interview.

10. Even if you are not looking for a job, you should prepare a résumé. The majority of desirable job positions are offered to people who are satisfied in their work and are not seeking a new job (Rosenberg and Hizer, 2003). The job opportunity of a lifetime might suddenly appear—or you could lose a job in an economic downturn. Either way, it is advantageous to have an updated résumé to use in an unexpected situation.

Physical Appearance of the Résumé

The résumé must be typed; use a word processor or typewriter. Advice from employers and career professionals is virtually unanimous that job applicants should limit their résumés to one or two pages (Washington, 2003). Two-page résumés may be more appropriate for people with several years of work experience and many achievements and responsibilities to cover. (An exception to the one-or-two-page length is the curriculum or professional vitae, discussed later in this chapter.) Most employers will not take the time to read a long résumé. Use good quality 8½- by 11-inch paper. Larger sizes are difficult to handle, especially when inserted in a file folder; smaller sizes could get lost in the shuffle. Plain white bond or an off-white textured bond is usually recommended. Balance the material on the page so that the total effect is attractive and pleasing to the eye. Leave adequate margin space so the page will not appear crowded; margins should be at least one inch on all sides. Always have a space between information sections. Avoid careless erasures.

Extra copies of your résumé can be reproduced through high-quality printing and photocopying processes. Good paper, typesetting, and an excellent printing job are well worth the cost. The mechanics of a résumé must be perfect, and the material must be 100 percent accurate. Any mistake could be duplicated 200 or 2,000 times.

Should you enclose a photograph of yourself? There are positive and negative answers to this question. If you include a photo, it is easier for an employer to remember you after the interview, especially if the interviewer has talked with 10 other people that day. However, there is the problem of job discrimination. Usually it is illegal for an employer to request photographs from job applicants. A photograph identifies sex, age, and race, although this information can be discerned from other parts of the résumé or through an interview.

Sending your résumé in a large envelope can preserve its good appearance. That way, it will stay flat and not have to be folded. The larger envelope will be a little more costly, but it will give the employer a better looking résumé (and cover letter) to read. It is also more likely to be noticed, because many people use a smaller (#10) envelope and fold their résumés to fit it (Half, 1994).

INFORMATION SECTIONS WITHIN THE RÉSUMÉ

There is no single way to write a résumé; you must create one that is right for you. Some people advocate a chronological résumé; others believe a functional résumé is better. Some say a job objective must appear in the résumé; others prefer to leave it out. If you learn from your personal contacts that an employer in a target company prefers to see certain material included in or left out of a résumé, follow that format, regardless of what you read in this or any other book. Because the chronological résumé is the most widely used and accepted format (Rosen and Paul, 1998) and most people begin with a chronological résumé, that format will be described in this section with the sequence of parts in their typical order. (In following sections, salient points about the functional résumé, curriculum vitae, and electronic résumé are covered.)

The Heading

The heading includes your name, address, and telephone number (and e-mail address, if you have one). It is usually placed at the top center of the page. If you have two addresses (home address and school or business address), you can place your home address on the left side of the page and balance it with your other address on the right side. The title "Résumé" above the name is not needed. Give your full name, spelling out your first name and surname. Type your name in capital letters if you want to make it more noticeable. Place your address(es) on the second line. City, state, and ZIP code appear together on the next line. The telephone number of your home address goes on the last line of the heading, unless you have an e-mail address (which would then finish the heading). Include the area code. If you are currently working, do not list your work number unless you have your employer's permission to do so. Most people prefer to be contacted at home. Use your cover letter to suggest when and how this can be done.

The Job Objective or Career Goal

Different opinions exist as to whether a specific job objective or career goal should be a part of the résumé. Most people suggest including it. Stating a job objective on your résumé demonstrates that you are focused. Résumé adviser Tom Washington (2003) comments that he uses an objective statement for approximately 85 percent of the résumés he helps people write. Rogers (1979) found 87 percent of employers prefer to have job objectives included in résumés they received; only 5 percent said there is no need for it to appear. Communicate your goal clearly. Employers are impressed with people who know exactly what they want. You can give copies of the résumé to personal contacts without constructing a cover letter to introduce yourself and explain the job position you are trying to obtain.

Some people, however, prefer to omit the job objective, believing it restricts the scope of their employment possibilities. You could be considered for similar positions rather than just the one you had in mind. The problem with this approach is that employers are left to guess: "What does this person really want?" You can prepare a separate résumé for each job position sought, or the job objective statement can be expressed in more general terms so as to include an entire occupational field.

The job objective is the hardest part of the résumé to write if you have not defined your career goals and abilities. When résumé writers use uncertain, hazy, or overly general terms, they inadvertently reveal that they really don't know what they want. For example, "To obtain a challenging position in a dynamic company where my skills will be put to use" is a job objective statement that doesn't say anything. Your reader knows you don't want a dull, dead-end job in a company about to go belly-up (Roper, 1994). Never write "anything available" for an objective; employers will not take the time to figure out the meaning of those words.

Practice writing your career goal in brief, understandable language before putting it in your résumé. State the job position you are seeking. A job title may be enough, or you can put it together with your hopes for the future. You can indicate the kind of business or combine the job title with a particular type of occupation. Keep this section short. A well-constructed phrase or sentence is sufficient. Despite its brevity, the job objective statement is important. Your entire résumé revolves around it (Weinstein, 1982).

The following are some suggested frameworks for a career objective statement:

- A beginning job in _____, leading to a position in

  _____.

- Begin as a _____ in the

  _____ industry. A future goal is a move to

  _____, where I can be involved in

  _____.

- Interested in joining the _____ staff of

  _____ company (or firm, business, agency). Long-term

  ambition is to _____.

- A _____ position in _____ involving

  _____ responsibilities.

- Interested in becoming a _____, with advancement to _____.

- Desire a position that uses my experience (or education) in

  _____ with an eventual move up to _____.

- Seeking a _____ position in a (an) _____

  organization, with hopes of advancement to _____.

- Major interest is in _____, with advancement opportunity to specialize in _____ in the future.

You can express your job objective statement simply in terms of a job title. (Some employers prefer it that way.) Two or three titles could be mentioned as long as they are related. Don't try to cram too much into your job objective; you risk losing the attention of your reader or looking unfocused. If you have two or three job objectives, it is probably better to write two or three résumés, changing only the job objective and perhaps some qualifications. Other than these caveats, you are in charge of the design, and that's the nice thing about a résumé.

Qualifications (or Keyword) Summary

The "qualifications" section summarizes your preparation, experience, and strong points that are relevant to your job objective, usually in four to six lines. It contains positive statements that are more difficult to insert in any other section of your résumé. Highlights of your qualifications can do more than any other section to create a favorable impression about you and will set the tone for the remainder of your résumé. Your value to an organization will be strengthened, because employers are constantly asking for information about what you can do for them. This section can be written last. You may find it the most difficult part of your résumé to write. Once you have completed the education and work experience sections, you are in a better position to know the best accomplishments to include in your qualifications summary (Washington, 2003).

Complete sentences are not necessary; phrases of three to six words are sufficient. More people are using a "qualifications summary" with its short keyword phrases because of the increasing use of computers to read résumés. Your aim is to match as many of the employer's keywords as you can; the more "hits," the more likely your résumé will be brought up for a human being to read. If you know or believe your résumé will be scanned electronically by a computer, turn to "The Electronic Résumé" section later in this chapter, then come back to this section and continue reading. A few possible phrases for the qualifications summary section include:

- Bachelor's degree (or any other type of degree) in _____.
- Strong experience in _____.
- Excellent knowledge of (or skill in) _____.
- Effective handling (or managing) of _____.
- Special talent(s) for _____.
- Proven ability to _____.
- Developed outstanding program in (or for) _____.
- Saved money for a company by _____.

You can leave off the adjectives and verbs, and simply go with the qualification itself; typically, it's the nouns the computer is looking for. Watch repeating a word too much, such as "outstanding" or "excellent." Consult a thesaurus to find a substitute if you have already used a given word two or three times.

Education

Start with your current or most recent schoolwork and go back in time. If you have college, technical, or business school experience, it is usually not necessary to go further back than that. Military training, special seminars or workshops, correspondence courses, in-service industry training, or on-the-job training can be a part of your educational record. Insert a space between names of schools.

Items that can be covered in the education section include dates of attendance (use first and last month and year), names of schools and their addresses (with city, state, and ZIP code), degrees and diplomas earned (here, you can use abbreviations for the best known degrees), and educational majors. (Dates can be excluded if you do not want to reveal your age.) Mention specific subjects from which you received high grades, particularly if they are relevant to the position sought. If you are short on work experience, emphasize your education. Achievements in school should be mentioned. Some people add a section titled "Accomplishments in College (or High School)" or "Extracurricular Activities." And this should go without saying, but we'll say it anyway: Never claim attendance at a school you didn't attend or declare you have a degree you don't have.

If you graduated in the upper third, quarter, or tenth of your class, say so. Include a high grade point average (GPA). If it's not high, leave it out. The GPA can be omitted if you have been away from school for over five years (Washington, 2003). Your employment record says more about you by that time. The GPA can be computed in different ways to show you in your best light. You may have changed your career and educational direction and established a better record in your last one or two years of college. You could figure your GPA only from the courses you took in your educational major. Notice how the same data can be presented in significantly different ways.

GPA—four-year senior college:

Overall (all four years)—2.73

Upper division (last two years)—3.07

Upper-division courses in major—3.31

Senior-level courses in major—3.40

GPA—two-year college:

Overall (both years)—2.88

Last year of school—3.12

Courses in major—3.48

Give the figure that shows you to your best advantage (Figgins, 1976; Washington, 2003). Don't overdo these GPA tactics, however. Many personnel workers are aware of this strategy.

Did you work your way through school? Highlight that fact if you did. A perfect or near-perfect attendance record will have a favorable effect on any employer. List any scholastic honors received, scholarships won, or special recognition earned. Definitely include extracurricular activities, particularly those in which you excelled. Did you hold any class or club office, work as a library aide, or help publish the school paper or yearbook? Were you on an athletic team, in a musical group, or in a school play? Anything that will indicate leadership, teamwork, artistic talent, physical dexterity, or creative ability will strengthen your case. The great strength of a résumé is that it allows you to present your qualifications without saying a word about weaknesses or limitations.

The following are some sample statements of educational achievement:

- Graduated in highest _____ of my class.

- Earned special recognition in class for _____.

- The _____ team(s) of which I was a member won

  _____.

- Financed _____ percent of my educational (or college) expenses.

- Awarded a _____ scholarship, which partially covered school expenses.

- Wrote _____ for school newspaper.

- Performed _____ enthusiastically (or creatively).

- Managed _____ reliably.

- Participated in _____, _____, and

  _____.

Work Experience

If your employment history is your strongest appeal to an employer, place it ahead of your education section. Again, use reverse chronological order. Your most recent job is usually given the most space, because it probably represents your highest level of achievement and is of greatest interest to the prospective employer. Provide the following information: dates of employment (months and years), name and location of each work organization, your job title, results and accomplishments on the job, duties and responsibilities, skills used, and special abilities developed. Insert a space between each work experience. Be consistent; give the same information for all your places of employment. Construct descriptions of your work experiences to indicate you have the ability to manage the work in the job you are seeking. Present evidence for jobs well done or responsibilities carried out, especially if you helped your organization achieve its goals. Names of supervisors need not be given for job positions unless you have a special reason for doing so. Give their names *only* if you know they will give you a good recommendation and still work for the company.

If your employment record is long, you might consider subtitling a section "Representative Job Positions" after describing your last three or four places of employment. Indicate that your work experience section has been shortened for the sake of convenience (Figgins, 1976). A recent college or high school graduate is more likely to have the opposite problem and must describe each position more thoroughly. A waiter or waitress, for example, might say: "Had face-to-face contact with people. Suggested food items that would appeal. Took orders and remembered them correctly. Served people the meal they ordered. Made sure customers had a pleasant time. Totaled the check or bill without making errors. Brought the correct change to customers and thanked them for coming. Cleaned the table and neatly set it for the next patron. Dressed attractively to make a good appearance."

List your part-time, summer, and volunteer work, particularly if you have little full-time work experience. Homemakers, for example, may think they haven't had much work experience until they start to remember how they managed the family and held volunteer jobs. Treat the volunteer effort like any other job; think of the skills you used to complete the volunteer work. Try to show how your previous work experiences can be applied to your present job objective and your future occupational goals.

You can include military information in the work experience section, or you could construct a separate section for this. Be certain to mention military experience, because some private employers and many civil service positions give preferred status to former military personnel when hiring. List your branch of service, dates of entry and discharge, your rank, your Military Occupational Specialty (MOS), your duties, and other items such as promotions, honors, awards, proficiency ratings, and how your military skills could be applied to civilian jobs.

Whenever possible, show evidence or proof that others can depend on you to carry out your duties and responsibilities. Claiming that you were successful at your last job is only a generality. Supporting that statement with figures, such as a percentage increase in the volume of business or the organization's profits, will be more impressive. A representative sample of activities that brought about the results stated will make your claims more convincing to the employer.

Some writers advise that you list your work experience functionally rather than chronologically. A functional résumé features responsibilities, achievements, abilities, and experiences classified by category instead of by time sequence. Reviewing personal achievements and job successes to discover the skills that made them happen prepares you to write a functional résumé.

Some job seekers wonder whether they should give reasons for leaving jobs. It is not necessary to put this information in your résumé; definitely leave it out if it will work against you. It *is* worthwhile to write your reason for leaving a previous job on a separate piece of paper as preparation for a job interview or for filling out an employer's application form.

Always write something about each work experience after giving basic information (dates of employment, name and address of company, and job title). If you were an employer, which applicant would you choose to interview?

Applicant A: Store checker and bagger. "Took customer's money and bagged groceries."

Applicant B: Store checker and bagger. "Greeted customers courteously, managed hundreds of business transactions accurately, operated cash register reliably, bagged purchased goods carefully, trained new employees thoroughly, and reported to work punctually each business day for 22 months."

Applicants A and B may have done the same work, but B gets the interview, being the better communicator.

Another controversy in résumé writing is whether to use bullets or write paragraphs in describing your accomplishments and results in the work experience section. The main argument for using bullets is that this style makes your résumé easier and quicker for an employer to scan. The employer may look at a résumé for only 20 or 30 seconds before deciding whether to put it in the "reject pile" or the "will read" batch. Quick scanning by the employer seems to favor the bullet format. However, when the employer returns to the résumé, the bullet style may lack the information or enough detail that a more complete paragraph could provide. (Bullet items usually run one or two lines; paragraphs are often four or five lines.) Paragraph writing runs a risk in that it could become long-winded and laden with unnecessary words; you must edit your presentation. Which style should you choose? It's your decision. Choose the style that you believe works best for you (Washington, 2003).

A lot of people dread the work experience section because they say to themselves, "I don't have any accomplishments" or "I can't think of any achievements." You are writing about your work history and that means *any* work you have done, whether it's paid, volunteer, parenting, or hobby—anything that will show the employer you have the skills and knowledge to do the job. You must learn to recognize your achievements, most of which you may have overlooked. Did you get a bonus, or an award, or good feedback on a performance evaluation? Were you ever asked to take on more responsibility, or did you receive compliments from customers or coworkers? You might uncover some accomplishments through the "P.A.R." approach of Yana Parker (2002). Look at what you did on your jobs in terms of problems, actions, and results. What *problem* existed in your workplace? What *action* did you take to resolve the problem? What were the beneficial *results* of your action?

Refer to the list of action verbs in Table 3-1 for help in starting the sentences that describe your previous job positions. These words may trigger memories of problems you solved by taking actions that produced beneficial results. Use the action verb (or functional skill) first. Next, list the object that completes the action; these are work-content or special-knowledge skills. Finally, add a self-descriptive adverb or adjective if you can; see Table 3-2 for a list. Other sample sentences or phrases that could go into the work experience section are the following:

- Achieved (accomplished, attained, fulfilled, succeeded in) _____

  _____ (finish with a self-descriptive adverb or adjective).

- Operated _____ capably.

- Planned (produced) _____ effectively.

- Created _____ imaginatively.

- Started as _____, promoted to a

  position of _____ within _____ years.

- Developed a working knowledge of _____, operation and maintenance of the following equipment: _____.

- Directed _____ employees in a supervisory capacity as

  _____.

- Responsibilities as _____ included

  _____.

- Have the following clerical skills: can type _____ words per minute; can take and transcribe dictation; can operate the following office machines:

  _____, _____, and _____.

- Organized and developed a new class in _____,

  which enrolled _____ students.

If you are reading this book and have not actively begun your job search, write a short summary of each job or volunteer experience you have had while it is relatively fresh in you mind. File these descriptions in a folder labeled "for future résumés." When the time comes to put the words into a work experience section of your résumé, you will have already made a start on it under much less stress and time pressure. You'll probably have more material than you will need, but then you can use only those experiences that relate to your job objective.

Other Information (optional)

Most résumés have information sections for the heading, qualifications, job objective, education, work experience, and (possibly) references, but this is not a rigid format. You can include other sections in the résumé under titles such as "Special Skills and Activities," "Professional Associations, Awards and Honors," or "Miscellaneous Data," and place them just below the education and work experience sections.

All of this information is optional; therefore, select only those items that will strengthen your résumé. You can show your involvement in professional functions, civic projects, volunteer work, memberships and offices held in clubs or organizations, travel experiences, and recreational activities. You can also emphasize special skills: proficiency in a foreign language, ability to operate specialized equipment, typing or shorthand speed, knowledge of computer languages, skills in first aid or lifesaving, or possession of special certificates and licenses. The subject of pay is best left for the interview.

Information concerning your availability for work can be included. If you are currently unemployed or can start a week after you accept a job offer, you can indicate that you are available immediately. If you are employed, state the amount of time you need to notify your employer and close out your affairs. You can write "Availability: _____ days notification required," or indicate the date you would be available.

The old personal data section, once a standard feature of résumés, has become outdated and is no longer used. Asking for pre-employment information about a person's age, height, weight, marital status, and health was legislated out of existence. You still could include some personal items, such as willingness to relocate or travel or hobbies and interests, if you believe they would be attractive to employers.

If you have a medical problem or physical disability that you believe must be explained, direct the reader to "see attachment." The situation can then be explained in greater detail on a separate sheet of paper attached to your résumé, with doctors' statements if necessary. An alternative would be to include disability information in a paragraph of your cover letter. If an employer has expressed a concern about how you are going to get to work, you can state you have a car or have made arrangements for transportation.

Avoid filling a résumé with nonessential or irrelevant information. If you have any doubt about the relevance of an item, leave it out. Long lists of factual data are boring to read and detract from the important things you want to say.

References (optional)

You should be able to list the names of at least three people who will attest to your good character, professional competence, or potential in your chosen occupation, but you are not required to include this information in your résumé. You may simply state, "References furnished upon request," but most people now omit a reference to "References" entirely.

However, have names of references ready if you expect to complete an employer's application form. Always secure permission from your references to use their names before you list them. Whom can you ask? References can be neighbors, former teachers, clergy, previous employers or supervisors if not already listed in the work experience section, or almost anyone who knows you well or remembers you and will give a good recommendation. Do not use relatives as references. If you have recently changed your surname or reverted to a former or maiden name, you will need to inform prospective employers that your references will remember you by a different last name.

One reason to include references in your résumé is to guide a potential employer to people who will express good things about you. Suppose you ended a previous job under less than desirable circumstances. Your prospective employer might contact your former company or supervisor and get a negative report—unless the list of references suggests easier ways to communicate with people who know you. Your potential employer can still reach a disapproving supervisor, but your references may be able to offset harmful comments with something more positive.

Examples of Chronological Résumés

Figures 3-1, 3-2, and 3-3 are sample chronological résumés that can serve as models. Do not repeat them verbatim; use your imagination to create your own résumé. Figure 3-1 is an example of a chronological résumé for a student still in college, Figure 3-2 shows an example for a student graduating from college, and Figure 3-3 gives an example for an experienced worker.

Exercise 3-1 provides a worksheet for preparing a chronological résumé. Exercise 3-2 (later in this chapter) concerns preparing a functional résumé. You may wish to work on Exercise 3-2 first in order to make a better presentation of your previous (or current) job functions, achievements, and skills. If you believe your résumé will be scanned electronically by a computer, move ahead in this chapter and review Exercise 3-3 on developing keywords for an electronic résumé. Always prepare a rough draft of your résumé before you type your final copy. Your résumé must be perfect before you send it to an employer. How perfect? "Nobody's perfect," you could say, but think of what would happen if 99.9 percent was good enough. Twenty-two thousand checks would be drawn from the wrong bank accounts and 18,322 pieces of mail would be mishandled in the next hour; 1,314 phone calls would be misplaced in the next minute. Twelve babies born today would be given to the wrong parents. Two and a half million books would have the wrong cover, and 20,000 medicine prescriptions would be written incorrectly this year. *Think 100 percent perfect for your résumé.*

JASON M. JORDAN
2780 N. Hillside Road
Hometown, PA 16812
(814) 651-7325

OBJECTIVE	Interested in becoming a science and social studies teacher in a secondary school. Long-term goal is to become a college professor. Plan to complete college education at Pennsylvania State University.
EDUCATION August 2000 to present	**Hometown Community College,** 1915 S. Fairview Ave., Hometown, PA 16814. Currently enrolled for 15 credits and have registered for 16 credits in winter semester. Courses of study: College Algebra, Writing Experience, U.S. History, Geology, and Career Planning. Student Government representative. Future Teachers of America. Expect to earn Associate in Arts degree.
August 1996 to May 2000	**Hometown High School,** 1111 W. Main St., Hometown, PA 16812. Graduated in upper fifth of class of 312. Received "A" grades in Biology, Chemistry, Psychology, U.S. History, American Government, Algebra II, Spanish, and Drafting. Active in Science Club, Varsity Basketball, Track and Field, Drama Club, and the student newspaper. Vice president of senior class.
EXPERIENCE June 2000 to present	**Valley Lawn & Garden Center,** 2234 County Farm Road, Hometown, PA 16823. *Landscaper.* Taught landscaping techniques to new employees. Demonstrated ability to follow directions while building interlocking brick walls. Directed landscaping crews in planting trees and shrubs. Trained new employees in tractor and machinery safety.
May 1998 to present	**Hometown Boy Scout Troop #35,** Hometown, PA 16812. *Assistant Scout Master.* Achieved rank of Eagle Scout. Adapted campsite plan to accommodate extra people. Supervised other scouts in selecting and setting up a campsite. Encouraged scouts in judged activities such as first aid and orienteering. Guided scout troop in winning camporee.
August 1998 to May 2000	**Hometown High School,** Hometown, PA 16812, *Teacher's Assistant.* Guided students in constructive educational activities such as preparing for tests and reading maps. Educated students in American History enthusiastically. Assisted substitute teachers during the regular teacher's absence. Corrected student test papers efficiently and accurately.
December 1996 to March 1998	**Hometown Athletic Department,** Hometown, PA 26812. *Basketball Coach.* Gained valuable teaching knowledge as an upper elementary basketball coach. Taught shooting, dribbling, and rebounding to fifth and sixth grade students. Coached a team to a six and two record. Played every team member equally. Acquired significant experience in being a worthy teacher and mentor to these children.
REFERENCES	Available upon request.

Figure 3-1 Example of a chronological résumé for a student in college

TERESA M. MORGAN

Campus Address
1252 River St., Apt 808
East Lansing, MI 48823
(517) 555-0123

Permanent Address
1111 W. Franklin
Jackson, MI 49203
(517) 555-1234

OBJECTIVE

To pursue a career in interior design or a related field in which I can use my design training. Willing to relocate after June 2000.

KEYWORD SUMMARY

Artistic. Design. Decoration. Photography. Business oriented. Management aptitude. Computer literate. European study. Worked during college. Scholarship winner. Held office. Publications. Theater. Drama.

EDUCATION
Sept. 1997
June 2000

Michigan State University, East Lansing, MI 48825. Bachelor of Arts in interior design, with emphasis in design communication and human shelter. Courses include lighting, introduction to computers, public relations, and history of art. (F.I.D.E.R. accredited) 3.0 GPA (4.0 A).

July 1999
Aug. 1999

Michigan State University overseas study, England and France, decorative arts and architecture. 4.0 GPA (4.0 A).

Aug. 1995
May 1997

Jackson Community College, Jackson, MI 49201. Associate in Arts. 3.5 GPA (4.0 A).

EMPLOYMENT
June 1998
Present

Interior Decorator, H. R. Smith Decorators, 210 S. Brown, Jackson, MI 49203
- Contacted clients to determine decorating preferences for offices and homes
- Ordered fabrics and materials
- Supervised installation of design

Sept. 1998
May 2000

Food Service and Maintenance, Owen Graduate Center, Michigan State University
- Prepared and served food
- Managed upkeep of adjacent Van Hoosen Residence Hall

Dec. 1997
June 1998

Food Service and Maintenance, McDonel Residence Hall
- Served food and cleaned facility
- General building maintenance

HONORS AND ACTIVITIES

- Community College Transfer scholarship from MSU
- American Society of Interior Design Publicity Chair; Executive Board, MSU chapter
- Wharton Center of the Performing Arts (MSU), usher
- MSU Student Foundation member
- Sigma Chi Little Sisters
- Independent European travel, summer 1999
- Stage manager and performer in plays and musicals
- Jackson High School Senior Class Treasurer
- Jackson High School Yearbook Assistant Editor

References and portfolio available upon request.

Figure 3-2   Example of a chronological résumé for a student graduating from college

WILLIAM D. MASTERS
937 N. West Avenue
Riverside, California 92514
(909) 555-0000

JOB OBJECTIVE
Teaching political science and history, with opportunities for career and academic counseling at the community college level.

QUALIFICATIONS SUMMARY
Teacher. Counselor. Coach. Social Science. American Government. History. Career guidance. Therapy assistant. Administer/explain interest inventories and aptitude tests. Physical education. Track. Basketball. Recreation work. University of Southern California. California State University. San Jose State University. Military service.

WORK EXPERIENCE
July 1991 to present, Riverside Community College, Riverside, CA 92506. Experience includes teaching political science, Western civilization, and psychology courses, and counseling students in student services office. President of Faculty Association. Coordinator of nine Government Days for area high schools. Adviser for Student Senate.

September 1980 to June 1991, Modesto High School, 4000 Seventh Ave., Modesto, CA 95350. Head counselor; organized a complete guidance program; administered school-wide testing program; taught career guidance courses; coached basketball and track.

September 1976 to June 1980, Northern High School, 2489 Foothill Drive, Santa Barbara, CA 93109. Taught American government, U.S. and world history, and psychology. Coached varsity basketball, track, and cross-country. Served as faculty adviser to National Honor Society chapter.

March 1973 to February 1975, U.S. Army, Basic training, infantry and artillery; counterintelligence training.

Other part-time and summer work experience: *Recreation director*, Central Methodist Church, 1145 N. Pacific Ave., San Jose, CA 95192. *Playground supervisor* in San Jose summer recreation program. Mowed lawns, painted houses, delivered newspapers, and cleaned rooms to pay for college expenses.

EDUCATION
September 1985 to March 1990, University of Southern California, Los Angeles, CA 90089. Educational Specialist degree in counseling and educational psychology. Participated in counseling and guidance institutes at University of Maryland and San Francisco State College.

April 1975 to June 1976, California State University, Fullerton, CA 92634. Master's degree in counseling and guidance, with minor in psychology. Assisted in group and individual therapy sessions at Community Counseling Center. 3.7 GPA (4.0 A).

September 1969 to December 1973, San Jose State University, San Jose, CA 95192. Bachelor's degree in political science, with minors in history and physical education. 3.4 GPA (4.0 A). Member of Spartan YMCA.

REFERENCES

Dr. John H. MacPherson	Robert C. London	Dr. Wilma R. Curry
Professor	Principal	Associate Professor
Political Science Department	Modesto High School	Department of Counseling
San Jose State University	4000 Seventh Ave.	and Educational Psychology
San Jose, CA 95192	Modesto, CA 95350	University of Southern
		California
		Los Angeles, CA 90089

Figure 3-3   Example of a chronological résumé for an experienced worker

EXERCISE 3-1 DRAFT YOUR OWN RÉSUMÉ

Before you begin, make several copies of the following blank worksheet so you will have extras when you need them. Fill in the information where indicated on the worksheets. You will then use this information to develop a final copy of a résumé that you can send or give to potential employers.

Worksheet for Developing a Chronological Résumé

Name _____

Street Address _____

City, State, ZIP Code _____

Telephone (_____) _____

Job Objective

_____

_____

Qualifications Summary

_____

_____

_____

_____

_____

Education (List in reverse chronological order.)

Dates: _____ to _____ School Name _____

    City/State _____

    Degree/Courses _____

    _____

    Activities _____

    _____

Dates: _____ to _____ School Name _____

    City/State _____

    Degree/Courses _____

    _____

    Activities _____

    _____

Work Experience (List in reverse chronological order.)

Dates: _____ to _____ Company Name _____

Address _____

Title/Duties _____

_____

Accomplishments/Skills Used _____

_____

_____

_____

Dates: _____ to _____   Company Name _____

Address _____

Title/Duties _____

_____

Accomplishments/Skills Used _____

_____

_____

_____

Dates: _____ to _____   Company Name _____

Address _____

Title/Duties _____

_____

Accomplishments/Skills Used _____

_____

_____

_____

Dates: _____ to _____   Company Name _____

Address _____

Title/Duties _____

_____

Accomplishments/Skills Used _____

_____

_____

_____

Other Information (optional) Professional associations, awards and honors, special skills, etc.

_____

_____

_____

_____

_____

Military Information (if applicable)

Dates: _____ to _____ Branch of Service _____

Rank (when separated) _____ MOS/Duties _____

References (optional)

Name _____   Name _____   Name _____

Address _____   Address _____   Address _____

_____   _____   _____

Telephone _____   Telephone _____   Telephone _____

THE FUNCTIONAL RÉSUMÉ

The functional résumé highlights work functions rather than summarizing education and work experiences chronologically. It provides a way to display your abilities and relate your strengths to the job you are seeking. The reader concentrates on your achievements. Some résumé writers prefer the functional style, claiming it is more interesting to read and more likely to attract attention. They believe the chronological résumé tends to obscure a person's accomplishments and skills with too many names, dates, addresses, and positions held.

The functional résumé emphasizes different abilities, depending on the qualifications required by the job goal. Those who have had years of work experience often favor the functional résumé because they have accumulated many skills from work they have done. College graduates can emphasize the skills they developed in school, on part-time and summer jobs, and from life experiences. Functional résumés may work better for people who have changed jobs frequently. A chronological résumé would reveal many job changes; not listing jobs in order can disguise the frequency of changing from one job to another. If your career direction has changed several times or you have several gaps in your employment record, a chronological résumé could make some employers think you are unstable or unreliable.

A functional résumé could make your job changes appear more logical and sensible. You should not mislead your reader, however. Personnel workers are aware of the ability of the functional résumé to withhold information about your work history. If your employment background does not have frequent interruptions, you are probably better off using a chronological résumé.

Title each part of the work experience section with the name of a work function, and capitalize it to make it more prominent. (Don't underline, because so many résumés are now electronically scanned.) For example, you could write:

ADVERTISING EXPERIENCE   PUBLIC RELATIONS SKILLS
HOSPITAL NURSING   RESEARCH FUNCTIONS
MERCHANDISING MANAGEMENT   TECHNICAL ACCOMPLISHMENTS

If you have had just one kind of work experience, you could divide it into several titles highlighted by bullets. For example:

ADMINISTRATIVE SKILLS   ACCOUNTING EXPERIENCE
- District sales manager   - Develop annual budget
- Purchasing director   - Cost accounting
- Retail store manager   - Billing and collection

Then describe your achievements, responsibilities, and skills under each title. Exercise 3-2 organizes your work experience into a presentation of important qualifications for your job objective.

JAMES K. JEFFERSON
1077 Second Avenue
Miami, FL 33161
(305) 592-8170

CAREER OBJECTIVE
Sales management position that uses my experience in motivating people and creating effective programs contributing to increased sales and greater profits for the organization.

EXPERIENCE

Management	Directed and coached twenty representatives in sales and customer service, improved staff morale and reduced turnover rates, administered quality control program, implemented two-year plan to upgrade operation efficiency of a production unit, identified errors made by employees before they became a liability to the company.
Sales Representative	Sold advertising and promotional campaign services in a territory covering Central and Southern Florida, increased sales volume over 50 percent in a two-year period, trained and motivated a sales force of 12 people, successfully introduced new product lines.
Public Relations	Designed advertising artistically for a major retail company, developed media and promotional materials, established contacts with editors and producers, wrote press releases and program scripts imaginatively.
Training	Supervised training procedures for office personnel, prepared training manual, produced 30-hour training programs for field representatives, taught sales and retailing class at a local community college.
Sales Clerk	Assisted customers with orders and purchases of appliances and furnishings for their homes, placed orders on worldwide network, cleaned and displayed merchandise creatively, won salesman of the year and month awards.
Financial	Tallied daily sales receipts accurately, deposited monies carefully, prepared monthly and quarterly financial reports for management, assisted in budget preparation.
Cooperative Relationships	Negotiated settlements for customer complaints courteously, organized nonprofit child-care center for employees, served as consultant for small minority-owned businesses, counseled employees supportively.

EMPLOYMENT

1998 to present	Johnson Advertising Services, Inc., 1221 N. Adams St., Miami, FL 33167. Sales manager.
1994 to 1998	Emory Home Furnishings Company, 508 Beaufort Avenue, Atlanta, GA 30314. Personnel and public relations director.
1991 to 1992	J.C. Hill and Company, 163 Fourth Street, Tampa, FL 33606. Sales clerk.

EDUCATION

1994 to 1999	University of Florida, Gainesville, FL 32611. Master of Business Administration degree.
1992 to 1994	University of South Florida, Tampa, FL 33620. Bachelor of Arts degree. Majored in Business Administration.
1989 to 1991	Seminole Community College, Sanford, FL 32773. Associate degree in Arts and Science.

Figure 3-4   Example of a functional résumé

Figure 3-4 provides an example of a functional résumé. Notice that the focus of this type of résumé is on the work experience section. Each sentence begins with an action verb (the functional skill), which is followed by the object (a work-content or special-knowledge skill) and, often, a self-descriptive adverb (an adaptive skill).

JASON R. SMITH
4121 Howard Road
Carlson, Michigan 49210
(517) 787-0899

EMPLOYMENT OBJECTIVE

Major interest is in office management with an opportunity for advancement to a manager of a Sales, Purchasing, or Payroll Department.

BUSINESS EXPERIENCE

May 1999 to present. XYZ Corporation, 126 W. Storybook Lane, Carlson, Michigan 49212. Supplier of machine parts to Ford Motor Co. James Littlefield, manager.

Bookkeeping—Perform simple accounting, posting accounts, statements, payroll tax reports (state and federal), weekly payroll, invoicing, accounts payable, accounts receivable.

Purchasing—Purchased office machines and supplies for a 25-person office, purchased stamping machines and drill presses for manufacturing division.

Sales—Established sales organization of independent dealers in Michigan, Ohio, and Indiana; set sales policies and dealer discount schedules.

Collections—Set credit limits for dealers, terms of payment, collection procedures on late accounts.

Inventory—Instituted card system on 150–200 items for fast cost analysis and control.

Pricing—Determine list and net prices on manufactured goods such as machines, accessories, and replacement parts; prepare price lists for end users, stocking and nonstocking dealers.

Advertising—Handle layout and design of product literature, with photographs, descriptions, and specifications of product; direct mail advertising to dealer and end user; coordinated publicity campaign with an advertising agency.

June 1995 to May 1999. ABC Corporation, 3480 Donneybrook Road, Turkeyville, Michigan 49998. Manufacturer of farm equipment. Alan Praeger, supervisor.

Bookkeeping—Performed simple accounting, posting accounts, payroll, book closing (monthly and annually), control of cash receipts and disbursements.

Financial Statements—Prepared depreciation schedules, tax returns, annual partnership returns.

Invoicing—Prepared invoices for sales and miscellaneous labor sales.

Purchasing—Purchased machinery, tools, and operating supplies.

EDUCATION

September 1992 to June 1995. Carlson Community College, 1112 Emmons Road, Carlson, Michigan 49201. Associate in Applied Arts and Science degree with a major in Business Management. Grade point average: 3.25 (4.0 A). Distributive Education club member; Track and Field athlete; received scholarship from Business Department.

September 1988 to June 1992. Carlson High School, 445 Wildwood, Carlson, Michigan 49210. National Honor Society vice president; Track and Field team captain; Cross-country athlete; Junior Class Treasurer; Junior Achievement member.

REFERENCES

Furnished upon request.

Figure 3-5   Example of a combination functional and chronological résumé

Figure 3-5 is an example of a résumé that includes both functional and chronological features. The business experience section is in the functional style for each place of employment; everything else is arranged chronologically.

EXERCISE 3-2 FUNCTIONAL RÉSUMÉ WORKSHEETS I AND II

This exercise contains two worksheets. On the first worksheet you will find four columns. In Column 1, give the title of your job objective and identify its major functions. The current *Occupational Outlook Handbook* (U.S. Department of Labor, biennial editions), the electronic Occupational Information Network (O*Net), the published *O*Net Dictionary of Occupational Titles,* 2nd edition (Farr et al., 2002), or the older *Dictionary of Occupational Titles* (DOT) can help you specify the functions performed in the job you are seeking. (The DOT is published by the U.S. Department of Labor [1991] and can be found in many libraries and career resource centers.) Another approach is to obtain an organization's description of a position that interests you.

In Column 2, record your work experiences by job title and name of organization. Include any volunteer work. (Homemakers can consider their home responsibilities as work experience.) Add any educational experiences that are related to your job objective.

Describe your work experiences in Column 3 by listing the functions you performed in them. Functions are responsibilities, duties, and achievements in the work you have done.

Where any function listed under your job objective in the first column is the same as or similar to any function already performed in the third column, record it in Column 4. Refer to Figure 3-6 for an example of this first worksheet.

Column 1	Column 2	Column 3	Column 4
Your Job Objective: Title and Functions	Work/Educational Experiences: Titles and Locations	Description of Each Work and Educational Experience (List Functions Performed)	Work/Educational Experience Function Same as or Similar to Job Objective Function
Title: Social Services Aide *Functions:* Assisting caseworkers cooperatively Counseling individuals and families supportively and empathically Gathering information about personal and family problems Compiling records about clients' past histories and experiences Developing programs for small groups of clients on topics such as substance abuse, employment and family problems, interpersonal relationships, etc. Organizing, coordinating, and leading small groups Referring clients to other agencies Providing other services to caseworkers as needed, such as caring for children of clients while they are talking with the caseworker	1. Volunteer, Emergency Counseling Center 2. Teacher aide, Western Elementary School 3. Church school teacher, United Community Church 4. Homemaker, 1033 Adams Street, Homeville, Texas	1. Counseled, interviewed, listened to, and referred people; collected information on clients 2. Assisted regular teacher, instructed small groups of students, helped individual students with learning problems, developed programs for students with special needs, maintained records for student evaluation 3. Taught units on religious subjects and supervised care for babies and small children in nursery school 4. Gathered and prepared food for the family, mended and cleaned clothing, maintained a home, budgeted money, supervised and participated in various family activities, counseled and advised members of family	Counseling, inteviewing, and listening to individuals Referring people to other agencies Compiling and maintaining records on clients accurately; assisting supervisors (teachers and caseworkers) cooperatively Organizing and leading small groups in programs that meet their needs and interests Creating and developing programs of instruction that deal with personal and family problems Instructing students competently Caring for small children responsibly Teaching clients about buying and preparing food, mending and cleaning clothes, maintaining a home, handling money, supervising and participating in family activities, counseling family members empathically and supportively

Figure 3-6   Example of the first worksheet for the functional résumé

On the second worksheet, transfer the job objective title and functions from Column 1 of Worksheet I to Column 1 of Worksheet II. The functions can be expressed in a shorter form on Worksheet II.

Next, find the functions in Column 4 of Worksheet I that match the functions in Column 1 of Worksheet II and write them in greater detail in *Column 2* of Worksheet II. See Figure 3-7 for an example.

When you have completed the second worksheet, you have the basis for the work experience section of either a functional or a chronological résumé. Work experience should be 80–90 percent of the functional résumé. The job objective functions in Column 1 become your work experience titles on the résumé. The list of responsibilities, duties, and achievements in Column 2 can be fleshed out in greater detail under these functional titles. An employer knows from a glance at your titles and descriptions for each job function that you understand to a great extent what the job involves. As you complete these worksheets, you will begin to realize that you have already performed many functions of your future job in various ways during your previous work experiences (Angel, 1980).

Column 1	Column 2
Your Job Objective: Title and Functions	List the Same or Similar Functions in the Form of Responsibilities, Skills, and Achievements from Previous Work and Educational Experiences. (Use past tense unless currently using the function.)
Title: Social Services Aide Functions:	
1. Assisting caseworkers	1. Assisted and followed directions of supervising caseworkers and teachers competently and cooperatively. (Specific responsibilities can be listed here.)
2. Counseling individuals and families	2. Counseled, interviewed, and listened to people in an emergency counseling center and in my family. (More specific counseling skills could be indicated such as reflecting feelings, paraphrasing or summarizing statements, asking appropriate questions, giving advice or feedback, etc.)
3. Gathering information	3. Collected information about clients in performing responsibilities at an emergency counseling center. Assembled data about students in an elementary school for grading and evaluation purposes.
4. Compiling records	4. Maintained precise records about clients' and students' past family, school, work, and learning experiences.
5. Developing programs	5. Created programs for student, church, and family members on personal, religious, and special needs topics.
6. Organizing groups	6. Coordinated small-group activities in programs designed to meet the needs and interests of group members. (The names of specific groups and subjects of programs should be cited here.)
7. Referring clients	7. Learned the functions of 20 other social agencies in order to accurately refer clients from an emergency counseling center.
8. Providing other services	8. Experienced in (and could teach about) buying and preparing food for a family, mending and cleaning clothes economically, maintaining a home efficiently, caring for small children, handling money carefully, coordinating small-group and family activities, and counseling family members supportively. (With these "other" or catch-all functions, possibilities are limited only by your imagination!)

Figure 3-7 Example of the second worksheet for the functional résumé

Functional Résumé Worksheet I

Step 1. Complete columns 1, 2, and 3. If any column does not give you enough space, use separate sheets of paper.

Step 2. In Column 4, write the name of any job objective function from Column 1 beside any same or similar function (or responsibility) you have performed in an experience listed in Column 3.

Column 1	Column 2	Column 3	Column 4
Title of your job objective: _____	Record work and educational experience (title, location).	Describe each work and educational experience. List the functions you performed.	List work and educational experience functions that are the same as or similar to a job objective function.
Functions of your job objective: _____	1. _____ _____ 2. _____ _____ 3. _____ _____ 4. _____ _____ 5. _____ _____ 6. _____ _____ 7. _____ _____ 8. _____ _____ 9. _____ _____	1. _____ _____ 2. _____ _____ 3. _____ _____ 4. _____ _____ 5. _____ _____ 6. _____ _____ 7. _____ _____ 8. _____ _____ 9. _____ _____	_____ _____ _____ _____ _____ _____ _____ _____ _____ _____ _____ _____ _____ _____ _____ _____ _____ _____

Functional Résumé Worksheet II

Step 1. Complete Column 1. This column is the same as Column 1 on the first worksheet. You may shorten the descriptions of your job objective functions by using only the action verb and its object.

Step 2. In Column 2, list and briefly describe each function from Column 4 of the first worksheet next to the job objective function that is the same or similar to it. (Column 2 of this worksheet expands on and reorganizes the information in Column 4 on Worksheet I.)

Step 3. Transfer this information to the work experience section of your résumé. Titles of functions will come from Column 1, and descriptions of those functions already performed in work experiences will come from Column 2.

Column 1	Column 2
Title of your job objective:	List the same or similar functions—in the form of responsibilities, duties, skills, and achievements—from your previous work and educational experiences. (Use the past tense unless you are currently performing the function.)

Functions (brief titles):

1. _____ 1. _____

2. _____ 2. _____

3. _____ 3. _____

4. _____ 4. _____

5. _____ 5. _____

6. _____ 6. _____

7. _____ 7. _____

8. _____ 8. _____

9. _____ 9. _____

A RÉSUMÉ OR A CURRICULUM VITAE?

The term **curriculum vitae (CV)** refers to the course of a person's life, a detailed autobiographical summary of one's career. People in institutions of higher education, publishing, research and development divisions, government service, or professional associations often use a CV. The curriculum vitae is sometimes called a professional vitae or professional summary. It is a comprehensive account of significant events in one's life history, usually covering 3–5 pages, but it could take up to 10 pages, whereas the traditional résumé is usually 1–2 pages in length. The curriculum vitae has been compared to a videotape produced over a period of years, rather than a quick snapshot (McDaniels,1997).

The sections of a CV are somewhat similar to those of a résumé, but it contains additional material usually not found in a résumé. The heading typically includes your name, address, telephone number, fax number (if applicable), and e-mail address. The work and home addresses are usually placed on opposite sides at the top of the first page. It is appropriate to insert your title in your business address, such as "Assistant Professor, Art History Department." The date you wrote or updated your CV can be used instead of the page number on the first page (but the page number should be included on all subsequent pages).

The education section includes names, locations, and ZIP codes of institutions; degrees attained and dates awarded; and field(s) of study in reverse chronological order. Give the date you expect to receive the degree for any major program you are currently enrolled in. Also include the name(s) of your adviser(s) and the title of your dissertation or thesis. Name all relevant certificates and the year in which you received them. Next, a section or separate sections follow concerning scholastic honors, awards, grants, fellowships, publications, presentations, research, internships, courses taught, and related professional experience (such as committee work, student groups supervised, or tutoring). Try to relate all this material to your career goal(s). These subjects can greatly expand a CV, depending on the length and depth of your experiences.

Publications can include chapters in books, articles in journals, and research reports. For professionals with an extremely long list of publications, it is appropriate to write, "Selected listing—a full list is available on request." Put abstracts in a separate section to avoid the appearance of padding. Be careful not to pad your CV; this can occur in a "projects in progress" section when a CV writer has several activities started but no actual publications to back them up. Exaggeration invites a negative reader reaction, which is likely when the importance or substance of an item is not obvious (Hayes and Hayes, 2003). Keep copies of your transcripts and records of related workshops, seminars, and extended study periods as a part of gathering material for these sections of your CV.

Optional sections are items such as memberships in professional organizations, educational travel or study abroad, community involvement, and volunteer work. Qualifications and skills, now standard features in résumés, are an option for CVs. Significant volunteer activity can be mentioned. The greatest consideration here is *significance*. A volunteer job as district party chairperson would have career relevance for a political scientist, but not nearly as much for a chemist (McDaniels, 1997). Civic and religious activities can be important for people in business to show career-related community involvement. Leadership and service activities should be displayed in a CV.

Other optional possibilities are foreign language skills, computer skills, appointments to offices, special recognition occurrences, accomplishments in creative writing outside your professional field, and hobbies or leisure interests. Professional references are more likely to be inserted in a curriculum vitae than in a résumé. Before using a person's name as a reference, always ask for permission. Three references are expected with full names, titles, institutional addresses, and contact numbers. More names can be added, especially if they would contribute important information. Keep your CV up to date and timely. Addresses and contact numbers must be current. Check for accuracy. Knowing what to add and what should remain in your document is always a prime consideration, and calls for good judgment.

One guide to writing a curriculum vitae (Hayes and Hayes, 2003) suggests the following sections, in this order:

- Personal history (name, college address and telephone number, home address and phone number, and so on)
- Educational history with major, minor, degree (type and date), honors received, title of dissertation, and chair of advisory committee
- Professional positions including research assistantships, practicum appointments, and consultations
- Membership in professional associations
- Professional activities such as committee and departmental memberships and in-service training programs, important guest lectures, and workshops presented
- Editorial activities such as reviewing manuscripts
- Grants received
- Papers presented
- Publications
- Papers currently under submission
- Projects underway
- Statement of professional interest
- Professional references

THE ELECTRONIC RÉSUMÉ

An electronic résumé (or e-résumé) can be inserted into the body of an e-mail message, sent as an attachment to an e-mail message, posted on a commercial or a company's Web site, or put up on a Web page created by a job seeker. Since the advent of electronic résumés, three technological "waves" have marked the employee recruiting industry. First, job seekers were coached to write "scannable" résumés. Next came plain text (or "bare bones") résumés. Now, because of new software enhancements, formatted e-résumés and online screening are the latest developments, particularly in large and medium-sized companies (Kennedy, 2003). Thanks to the hundreds of Web sites where job seekers can post their electronic résumés in hopes of being contacted by employers, the recruiting system has been swamped with résumés. Thousands of companies have created their own Web sites where résumés can be sent. Employers do not have the staff to review the mountains of résumés that flood their personnel or human resources offices. Computer technology has provided an answer as well as added to this problem, and résumé writing has had to adjust.

An electronic résumé is similar to a conventional résumé in that it focuses on your work experience and educational background. The major difference in preparing a résumé intended for electronic scanning is that it is not read by a human being until it is "approved" by a computer. The computer reads your résumé, stores it in a database, retrieves it when there is an appropriate job opening, and prints and sends a copy of it to a prospective employer. When you write an electronic résumé, your goal is to include enough *keywords* that match the employer's requirements so that the computer will pull your résumé from a database, print it, and bring it to the employer's attention.

Applicant Tracking and Management Systems

Employers use an electronic **applicant tracking system** as one of their resources when looking for new people to hire. The computer can track your résumé in a fraction of the time it takes a human being to find the document. Many companies have recently reduced their workforces. Particularly hard hit have been the personnel, employment, or human resources offices where résumés are usually sent. At the same time, the number of résumés received has steadily increased. Although computer technology is very impersonal, at least electronic tracking will enable hiring executives to find your résumé. Before, your résumé could have been buried in a pile of hundreds or thousands, never to see the light of day. Another advantage is that the computer will generate as many copies of your résumé as needed, lessening the chance that one person will put your résumé in a drawer and forget it.

Newer **applicant management systems** feature **online screening**. This is an automated process of creating a pattern of requirements for a given job, thus obtaining data from each applicant to determine whether the candidate matches the job requirements. The system automatically evaluates the match between the contents of résumés and a job's requirements, ranking the most qualified résumés at the top. The screening system also may include tests that measure a candidate's knowledge and skills in a specific area of expertise. A controversial type of online screening is a battery of inventories that attempt to measure work-related personality traits to predict job success. Behavioral and managerial assessments where candidates are given problems for which they recommend solutions are also used to forecast an applicant's job performance. Applicants may be asked to prepare, deliver, and defend a presentation related to the job they are seeking. The system may administer an "integrity test" where candidates answer a series of questions designed to measure their honesty. Another aspect of online screening is the background check made with the applicant's permission. Results of a company's online screening system are sent to recruiters and hiring managers. In theory, online screening is completely based on the job in question and fair to all concerned; however, those people who are not "Web-savvy" may be screened out of a job that they could do well, tests can be faked, and the process is vulnerable to human mismanagement (Kennedy, 2003).

You need to know the technology (if any) that is being used by the company to which you want to send your résumé. In most cases, you will not know unless you contact the company's human resources department or receptionist by telephone or e-mail to find out. You can ask one or two questions. (1) "Do you accept résumés sent in electronically?" If the answer is no, you will send your paper résumé by regular mail. If the answer is yes, then ask the second question: (2) "Will you convert my résumé to plain text, or will managers see my résumé in its original format?" If the answer is plain text, you will need to send it as an ASCII form, explained later in this section. If the answer is original format, you can use your normal résumé.

One other question you could ask is: "Should I send my résumé as an e-mail attachment, or would you rather I paste it into a separate form?" Some companies ask you to attach your résumé, but many companies prefer that you cut and paste your résumé into a standard form or use the company's résumé builder form, fearing the possibility of a virus accompanying the attachment.

The Scannable Résumé

When you send your résumé to a company that uses scanning technology, it will be electronically scanned for keywords that correspond to specifications considered essential or desirable by the employer. Nearly all large (5,000+ employees) and medium-size (500–5,000 employees) companies use computerized résumé-scanning software. Many small companies (under 500 employees) are turning to independent database service companies to do their résumé screening for them. Don't assume your résumé won't be subjected to electronic screening just because you are applying to a small company (Kennedy and Morrow, 1995).

An electronic résumé needs to pass two screening tests: (1) the "cold" test of a computer, and (2) the "warm" test of a human. Without passing the first test, you won't get to the second. Both screening tests can be met with one résumé. After your heading (name, address, telephone number) and job objective statement, think of your qualifications section as a *keyword summary,* which needs to emphasize nouns (job titles; names of schools, companies, and departments; and skills and abilities). That's the information the computer is seeking. Then, in the main body of the résumé (education and work experience sections), emphasize action verbs (your functional/transferable skills) along with your keywords (usually content or knowledge skills) describing skills and accomplishments. That's the information a human reader is seeking.

The Keyword Summary

When electronic résumé writing first began, its distinctive feature was the keyword summary (or qualifications summary) placed after the heading and job objective. Now, a summary of key qualifications is standard for all types of résumés. Writing a résumé with a keyword summary is like writing a news article: You put your most important information first. Keywords sought by computers are generally nouns or short phrases. They describe the knowledge, skills, abilities, and experience an employer is hoping to find. Keywords are created from your experience and matched with a job description composed by a hiring executive. To get an idea of the keywords to write, start with the job announcement, examining it for the qualities in job candidates the employer is trying to find. Some keywords will be designated as requirements, without which a person will not be considered a qualified candidate. Other keywords will be abilities that employers would like to see in a candidate but that are not absolutely required (Weddle, 1995).

Not all job announcements will give you the information you need, so where else could you find an employer's keywords? Employers are not necessarily going to distribute a list of these words to the public. Often the only people who know the keywords for a job position are the employer and the database manager. Some creative thinking may pay dividends. Try to envision the kinds of abilities and educational and work experiences the employer could be looking for. Check job descriptions that are usually on file in the personnel or human resources office. Study help-wanted ads in the newspaper, especially those that go into detail; they may contain abilities, credentials, and experiences that employers want in their applicants. Those of you who have read through the content-skills section of Chapter 6 in *Taking Charge of Your Career Direction* encountered many keywords used by employers. The latest edition of the U.S. Department of Labor's biennial *Occupational Outlook Handbook,* the electronic Occupation Information Network (O*Net), the *O*Net Dictionary of Occupational Titles* (Farr et al., 2002), or the older *Dictionary of Occupational Titles* (U.S. Department of Labor, 1991) may help. Job titles and descriptions of occupations include keywords the computer may recognize. Employers may be searching for certain personality traits they want in their employees; the self-descriptive words listed in Table 3-2 earlier in this chapter could be useful. Your knowledge of the industry and the organization (the subject of Chapter 6 in this book) can be a source of keywords. Other knowledge-based keywords come from academic majors, names of licenses and certificates, school degrees, names of schools, names of companies and departments, and special awards or recognition. Whatever your occupational goal, try to anticipate the keywords the employer would use to describe a person in the job position. If those words describe you, then go after the vacancy. About 15 to 30 keywords (words or phrases) should appear in your summary of qualifications.

Some job seekers mistakenly load their résumé with an enormous barrage of keywords, whether or not the words accurately describe their qualifications. They think this tactic will create more "hits" with the tracking system and raise their résumé to the top layer of candidates. To complicate things further, they conceal the inappropriate words by changing the font color from black to white, making those words invisible against the white background of a computer screen. Recruiters discover this trick by highlighting and copying the entire résumé, pasting it into a Microsoft Word document, and then changing the font color to black—thus revealing the deception. The offending applicant is considered desperate, and desperation is not a good impression to make in the job market. Out of the company's database goes that person's résumé. Not only does the applicant lose a job opportunity, but also prospects for all other jobs in that company (Kennedy, 2003).

Personnel recruiter. Employment interviewer. Applicant screening. Public relations experience. Contract negotiation. Grievance settlement. Training representative. Job analyst. Staff morale work. Career development program. Communications facilitator. Customer service. University of Florida. Bachelor of Arts. Psychology major. Journalism minor. Teamwork seminar certificate. Newspaper reporter. Market research. Employee motivation.

Figure 3-8　Example of a keyword summary for an electronic résumé

Two sample keyword summaries, for a human resources specialist and a recent graduate in criminal justice, are shown in Figure 3-8. Remember, before you include any keyword, be sure you can back up your claim with solid proof in the main body of the résumé. Then go on to your work experience, education, and other subjects such as awards, recognition, and professional association membership in the main body of the résumé. Here, use synonyms (equivalent words) for keywords already used in the summary.

The Main Body of the Résumé

Keywords should continue to appear in the education and work experience sections of your résumé. Synonyms will reinforce keywords that have already appeared. The computer may not have recognized some of your keywords. By using synonyms, you increase the chances of producing "hits" or matches with the employer's required qualifications.

Electronic résumés can be a hybrid, or combination, of the chronological and functional styles used in conventional résumés. The chronological résumé arranges your employment and educational history in reverse time order. The functional style groups your qualifications according to function without regard to time sequence. A hybrid format tries to use the best features of both; it presents your work experience and education in reverse chronological order, combined with the knowledge and abilities you demonstrated in each case. First, list the names of employers and dates of employment, followed by the title of each position held. After that, give the major tasks or functions performed and the skills you used to accomplish those tasks. The words used to do this must include the keywords used in your summary or their synonyms; otherwise, the qualifications you claim to have may not be believed. Each account of a job position should be limited to one paragraph of three to five statements (Weddle, 1995). In the education section, list your degrees, certificates, training experiences, licenses, and successful completion of courses, seminars, or workshops, and then give the name of the school attended, with dates. Any special skills developed, outstanding grades, and classroom and extracurricular accomplishments should be included here. A final section can list names of associations to which you belong (including offices held) and any awards or special recognition you have received. These titles and labels may be keywords that match those of the employer. Always deliver proof for any skills or achievements claimed. Use measurable quantities and proven facts to write about your achievements and qualifications.

Design of the Electronic Résumé

An electronic résumé should be one or two pages long. Two pages may be an advantage in that you have the opportunity to use more keywords. Your name should be the first item the computer encounters. Do not place any other information on the same line as your name; everything else goes below your name. If you use a second page, your name should appear again at the top. Use a paper clip to hold your pages together, not a staple. Staples must be removed to scan a page; removal may produce holes and tears, which will cause problems for the computer that will, in turn, cause problems for future readers.

Paper size should be the standard 8½ by 11 inches printed on one side only. Do not use 11- by 17-inch paper folded to create a pamphlet-like résumé (Smith, 2000). Paper that has been folded is often not handled well by the computer. Use lots of white space; margins should be at least one inch. White paper and black ink give the greatest contrast between paper and print; this helps the scanner recognize letters and words. Send only clear, sharp résumés. Have your original reproduced at a print shop or on a laser printer. Many print shops and copy centers offer the use of computers and laser printers for reasonable hourly rates. Owners of small portable computers can find stores that allow them to attach a printer cable to their machines and print out a résumé on professional-quality equipment, eliminating the need to purchase printers of their own. Send original printed copies, not photocopies.

For older applicant-tracking systems (and there are still many in use), stick with standard typefaces in which the letters and words are clearly distinct from each other. The typeface should be without serifs, those small lines that finish off the main stroke of a letter at its top or bottom. Type size needs to be between 10 and 14 points. Forget extra frills on an electronic résumé, no matter how nice they look to the human eye. Italics, script, and underlined words or phrases may touch each other and confuse the computer. Do not use vertical or horizontal lines, parentheses, brackets, and compressed lines. Avoid bold-face text, shading, and the use of graphics (Smith, 2000). When the computer scans your résumé, it is set to read words, not pictures. Do not use bullets to begin a line, such as one describing an achievement or a skill; the computer may read a hollow bullet as the letter "o." Use an asterisk (*) instead. Avoid most abbreviations; standard abbreviations used by everyone are considered safe. Keep clear of vague, florid language and excessive use of generalities. The computer is searching for factual, unadorned statements about things you know and can do.

When you send a paper résumé to a company or a commercial online databank service, send it (and the cover letter if needed) *unfolded* in a large envelope. Creases on a line can destroy the clarity of your copy and baffle the computer. A bewildered computer will prepare a copy that will also bewilder the reader.

For résumés sent electronically by e-mail to company and commercial Web sites, keep in mind that when you post your résumé on the Web, you lose control over the information in it; anyone with a computer and Internet access can look at it. When e-mailing your résumé, include the word "Résumé" followed by your name on the subject line. This becomes your résumé title, which is often the first item a recruiter notices. E-mail, of course, has the advantage of being much faster than traditional mail ("snail mail"), taking seconds instead of days. Do not send your résumé as an attachment to an e-mail message, unless the employer instructs you to do so. Instead, paste the résumé directly into the e-mail. This means no virus will be transmitted along with your message; recruiters and employers will appreciate your thoughtfulness.

ASCII or Plain Text Résumés

If you have already created a paper résumé using a word processor and have saved it on your computer, you can strip it of all codes and save it as a plain text or ASCII (pronounced *as-kee*) text file. ASCII stands for American Standard Code for Information Interchange, a code that is understood by nearly all computers. The most popular ASCII file format used on the Internet to transfer résumés across computer networks is Plain Text or Text Only, which is identified by the *.txt* file extension (Smith, 2000).

Plain text or ASCII means producing a résumé that is designed for electronic transmission, a résumé (as described earlier) without italics, underlining, graphics, and so on—features we like to use to make our documents more attractive. If you don't use plain text, you risk having your résumé look like hieroglyphics or gobbledygook. There are some cautions to observe when you send your résumé to employers electronically. For example, be sure your lines are 65 characters or less; this includes spaces and punctuation as well as letters. If the lines in your electronic résumé are longer, your sentences may wrap to a new line, making your résumé look sloppy on the computer screen. Most word processing software has an option to convert a file to an ASCII or text-only file.

Appendix C: *Word-Processed Résumés into Electronic Résumés: Converting, Pasting, Improving, and Formatting* contains instructions for the following: (1) converting your word processed résumé into an electronic résumé, (2) converting your résumé into an e-mail message, (3) improving the readability of your ASCII text (within the limitations of a plain text résumé), (4) pasting your résumé into an e-mail message, and (5) formatting résumés.

Formats such as hypertext markup language (HTML), portable document format (PDF), and rich text format (RTF) and the construction of Web-based résumés and portfolios are best left to books whose entire subject matter deals with résumés. The following five books go into more detail and answer more questions about the writing and transmitting résumés and cover letters:

1. *Resumes for Dummies,* 4th edition, by Joyce Lain Kennedy (2003)
2. *Resume Power* by Tom Washington (2003)
3. *eResumes* by Susan Britton Whitcomb and Pat Kendall (2002)
4. *Resumes That Knock 'em Dead,* 5th edition, by Martin Yate (2002)
5. *Electronic Resumes and Online Networking* by Rebecca Smith (2000)

Paper Résumés in an Electronic World

With all the ballyhoo about electronic résumés, you would think paper résumés were a dying breed. However, paper résumés are alive and well, and will continue to be used in local and regional job markets over the next decade and perhaps even longer. Paper gives hiring managers something they can feel, see, and save. Paper résumés come in handy at a job fair because they are easy to distribute. Many job advertisements contain postal addresses, meaning they expect to receive paper résumés. And there are companies that have not converted employee referrals to Web processes. They often have a form that tells referring workers to clip a paper résumé to the form before giving a name to the human resources department. A majority of small businesses in the United States do not use electronic methods of receiving résumés, and only half of the population uses the Internet for any form of job search (Kennedy, 2003).

You can give your e-mailed résumé and cover letter double exposure by also sending a printed, hard-copy version transmitted by the post office. It will arrive at its destination a few days later, so you should attach a note that you have already sent a résumé and cover letter via e-mail. The subject of cover letters has not been "covered" yet (see the next section of this chapter), but you must include this letter with your electronic résumé just as you would for a conventional résumé. Your cover letter could help if your résumé is pulled from a database file. Continue using keywords in your electronic cover letter.

EXERCISE 3-3 DEVELOPING KEYWORDS FOR YOUR ELECTRONIC RÉSUMÉ

Use the keywords you develop in this exercise for any résumé you think may be scanned electronically and placed in a résumé database. The sequence of your material will likely be as follows: heading (name, address, and telephone), job objective, keyword or qualifications summary, education, work experience, and professional activities. This exercise focuses on using nouns and short phrases for keywords. The keyword or qualifications summary is placed near the beginning of your electronic résumé because it contains most of the words the computer is seeking and distinguishes the electronic résumé from more conventional ones.

Worksheet for Developing Keywords for Your Electronic Résumé

A. What are the qualifications employers would require or find desirable for the job position or cluster of positions in the occupation of your choice? Look for these qualifications in employers' job descriptions; help-wanted or recruitment advertising in newspapers and industry journals; O*Net descriptions and the *Dictionary of Occupational Titles*; required degrees, certificates, diplomas, and licenses; essential work experiences; academic majors; and so on. List these qualifications below.

_____	_____
_____	_____
_____	_____
_____	_____
_____	_____
_____	_____
_____	_____
_____	_____
_____	_____
_____	_____

B. Identify the keywords you can write about yourself that will describe the qualifications you have for the job position in the occupation of your choice. These are the nouns or short phrases that describe your work abilities and skills. Derive these keywords from the following sources:

- Achievements you have described previously (and placed in an achievement file)
- Lists of content skills and adaptive skills that identify you; be certain you can provide evidence that proves you have these skills
- Results of aptitude tests
- Awards and recognition
- Licenses and certificates
- Academic records (transcripts), degrees, diplomas, and honors
- Previous work experiences
- Performance evaluations from current and past supervisors
- Abilities you can develop from further education and training

List these keywords in the left-hand column. In the right-hand column, list synonyms (equivalent words) that can be used interchangeably with the keywords.

Keywords	**Synonyms**
_____	_____
_____	_____
_____	_____
_____	_____
_____	_____

(continued)

Worksheet for Developing Keywords for Your Electronic Résumé (continued)

Keywords	Synonyms
_____	_____
_____	_____
_____	_____
_____	_____
_____	_____
_____	_____
_____	_____
_____	_____
_____	_____
_____	_____
_____	_____
_____	_____
_____	_____

C.   Which keywords are common to both List A and List B? Use 15 to 30 of these words or phrases in the keyword summary of your electronic résumé. Save synonyms for the main body of the résumé (the work experience and education sections).

_____   _____
_____   _____
_____   _____
_____   _____
_____   _____
_____   _____
_____   _____
_____   _____
_____   _____
_____   _____
_____   _____
_____   _____
_____   _____
_____   _____

For the remainder of your résumé, follow the directions given earlier in this chapter for the chronological and functional styles (or the hybrid or combination résumé).

THE COVER LETTER

A cover letter (sometimes called a letter of application) should introduce you to a prospective employer, call attention to your résumé, and create a desire in the employer to schedule an interview with you. The cover letter is the first item employers notice when they open your envelope. Most organizations receive letters from many more job seekers than they could ever interview. Many employers or personnel officers will immediately start looking for reasons to reject your application and not grant you an interview. Therefore, only correct, concise, and carefully composed cover letters stand a chance of getting through the screening maze.

Cover letters are usually sent to discover job openings, initiate contacts, respond to an advertisement, or follow up a referral by a personal contact or an employment agency. In some cases, you must make a judgment call on whether to send your cover letter without a résumé. Some job seekers prefer to use the cover letter as a letter of application and present the résumé only after an interview has been held. Cover letters are not necessary for on-campus interviews in a college placement office or when arrangements for an interview have already been made.

Addressing a cover letter to a specific person by name is far more effective than using "Dear Madam," "Dear Sir," or an official title. If you do not know a specific name, telephone the organization and request the name and title of the appropriate person to receive your letter. Explain the reason for your call; a secretary or receptionist will give you this information. You can also find names in business and industrial directories from libraries, but verify this information because directories can become outdated very quickly. Not addressing a specific person by name makes your letter impersonal; some employers say they would rather have the wrong name on the address than "Dear Madam or Sir." A better impression is made when the job seeker has taken the time to learn the name of a person in the organization.

The cover letter should not exceed one page; three or four paragraphs are all that is needed. Almost all personnel managers in one survey agreed that one page is sufficient (Meyers, 1984). In your own words, it should say, "I am interested in your organization; let me give you some reasons why you should be interested in me. I would like to have an interview with you." Always type your cover letter. If you can't type or don't have a word processor or typewriter, find someone who can do the job correctly for you, and pay for it if necessary. Résumés can be mass-produced by a print shop; cover letters are more personal.

Heading, Inside Address, and Salutation

In the upper right corner, about 10 or 12 lines from the top of the page, depending on the length of your letter, type your return address and the date. If you prefer the block-style letter, it is equally correct to type the return address and date even with the left margin. See Figures 3-9 and 3-10 for examples of both styles. The block style aligns everything in the letter at the left margin.

The inside address is the same information you place on the outside of an envelope. It includes the name of the person to whom you are writing; his or her title, if available; the name and address of the organization; and the city, state, and ZIP code.

The salutation should read "Dear Ms. Smith" or "Dear Mr. Doe," followed by a colon (:). Use "Dear Madam or Sir" if you cannot find out the name of a specific person, as in the case of a blind ad. Some people have difficulty framing a salutation. A few years ago, the late newspaper columnist Ann Landers received suggestions from her readers for substitutions for the traditional approach. One was "Ladies and Gentlemen," but it sounded too much like the opening of a speech. "Good morning" is a homey touch, according to another suggestion. One reader wanted to replace the salutation with the company's name: "Dear Sears" or "Dear General Motors." The prize went to "Yoo-hoo. Yes, I'm talking to you." Save yourself the trouble; obtain the person's name.

4811 N. Pacific Avenue
Anyville, California 94201
Telephone (408) 011-0011
September 15, 2000

Ms. Jane Thompson
Personnel Director
Crown and Smith Publishing Company
1001 Woodland Avenue
Anytown, California 94901

Dear Ms. Thompson:

I am seeking a junior management position with a progressive company in the publishing business. My education and experience in writing and publishing could be valuable to your organization. I have earned a college degree, majoring in journalism at the University of California, Berkeley. Practical, on-the-job experience includes working as an assistant editor with a university press and as a teaching assistant in a college English department. I am capable of learning quickly and can grow with an organization such as yours.

As a trainee for a management position, I could contribute much while learning how a private publishing company operates. I have prepared several authors' manuscripts for publication by the university press. My experience includes delegating work assignments and arranging schedules of employees. I have taught four courses for the Communications Department at Oregon State University.

I am articulate, a good correspondent, and able to motivate people. I am eager to put my ideas and experience to work for you. I am willing to relocate and travel as required.

The enclosed résumé summarizes my education and work experience. Please contact me by phone or mail; I would be pleased to meet with you at your convenience.

Sincerely,

Daryl K. Jones

Daryl K. Jones

Figure 3-9   Example of a cover letter (regular style)

Body of the Letter

First paragraph. State why you are writing and why you want to work in that job position and for that particular organization; attract attention and create the desire to read further.

The first two or three sentences of the cover letter are very important. They must attract attention and motivate the reader to continue. The first paragraph is the hardest part of the cover letter to write. You must use words and phrases that will cap-

4312 Carlton Blvd.
Atlanta, Georgia 30341
Telephone (404) 933-5980
April 18, 2000

Mr. William A. Harrison
General Manager
Machinery Installation Systems
P.O. Box 560
Atlanta, Georgia 30342

Dear Mr. Harrison:

I am a resourceful, diligent, achievement-oriented person looking for a challenge. I can bring experience of a varied and thorough business background to your growing company. Please consider this letter and the attached résumé as my application for a management position within your organization.

While researching potential employers relevant to my aspirations and career goals, I was intrigued by the presentation of your unique product offerings and varied engineering services in the latest issue of the *Journal of the Fabricator*. My innovative and creative skills, talents, and interests, as well as my experience and education, would fit well at your company and operate to our mutual advantage.

It would be a pleasure to meet with you at your convenience to discuss your firm's employment opportunities, particularly coordination and/or supervision of your clerical, accounting, and financial processes. I can be reached at the above telephone number after 5:00 P.M. and on weekends or at my present office number (404) 934-8060 between 8:00 A.M. and 5:00 P.M. Monday through Friday.

I shall look forward to hearing from you. Thank you for your attention and consideration.

Sincerely,

Ruth A. Davisson

Ruth A. Davisson

Enclosure (Résumé)

Figure 3-10 Example of a cover letter (block style)

ture the imagination of the employer or personnel manager. Some writers estimate that you have an average opportunity of about 10 seconds with the reader. Within that time span, the reader will decide whether to continue reading or to go on to something else. Develop active language and powerful action verbs to persuade the employer to read further, to identify the purpose of your message, and to express what motivated you to write. However, you should do this in a way that is not so flamboyant it brands you as a show-off.

Here are some suggested openings:

- My education and experience in the field of _____
  could be valuable to your company (or organization).

- With _____ years experience in the _____ field, I am
  suitably qualified to apply for . . .

- I am an energetic, hardworking college graduate interested in a (an)

  _____ position.

- I know the _____ business! For the past _____

  years, I have been working in the _____
  industry. I began as a . . .

- _____, a former supervisor with your
  organization, suggested that I contact you for . . .

- My _____ skills and _____

  abilities in the field of _____ may be of interest
  to you.

- A recent advertisement for your company in the (name of publication)

  _____ indicated your desire to hire a

  _____ for _____.

Whatever the opening, it needs to generate enough interest to make the employer continue reading. Some writers prefer a very simple, straightforward approach. Some readers do, too! For example:

- Please accept my application for . . .
- I am qualified to be considered for . . .
- My background and experience prepare me for . . .
- I am applying for . . .

Second paragraph. State your qualifications for the job opening; emphasize an achievement (or two), particularly if it is relevant to the job being sought.

The second paragraph gives the employer reasons why he or she should hire you. Some writers might want to use two paragraphs for this. You should briefly summarize your qualifications, your skills and abilities, and one or two achievements, especially if they are appropriate to the position you are seeking. Review significant aspects of your education or previous work experience. Some writers like to identify their strongest abilities or reinforce a strength that is mentioned but not highlighted in the résumé. Consult any achievement experiences you have written and kept in a file folder for just this sort of occasion. Exercise 3-2, earlier in this chapter, contains worksheets for the functional résumé that could help you state your qualifications. Never misrepresent yourself by stretching the truth or exaggerating your talents and experience.

The following are examples of sentences you could use in this paragraph:

- At (name of company or school) _____ I was

  responsible for _____, using my

  _____ skills.

- I handled the following details for (name of organization or employer):

  _____.

- Sales increased by _____ percent when I _____ for

  (name of organization) _____.

- I was able to produce _____ more efficiently, saving (name of employer or organization) _____ time and money.
- My skills in _____ were demonstrated at (name of school or workplace) _____ when I
_____.

Third paragraph. Urge the reader to continue the correspondence, bring attention to the enclosed résumé, request an interview, and state how the employer can contact you (or how you will contact the employer).

The last paragraph summarizes the purpose of your cover letter. You want the employer to contact you and grant you an interview. A more assertive style is to inform employers that you will contact them for an interview; a less assertive style leaves the interview to the employer's discretion. The following are examples of statements that you could adapt:

- I hope to hear from you as soon as possible.
- Please send me information regarding employment with your organization.
- The attached résumé should prove to be of interest to you.
- Enclosed is a copy of my résumé, which summarizes my qualifications, education, and work experience.
- I am willing to discuss my qualifications with you in person at your earliest convenience.
- If you are interested in my qualifications (or application) for this position, I will be available _____ to meet with you in person.
- I will make an appointment for a personal interview with you next
_____.
- I will telephone your office next _____ in the hope of setting up an appointment with you.
- I can be contacted at the above address or by telephone (days)
_____ after (time) _____ or on weekends. My telephone number is _____.

There is no one right way to write a cover letter. Some people write four or five paragraphs; others are content with two.

Complimentary Close and Signature

The signature and closing are a brief, simple courtesy. Merely say "Yours truly," "Sincerely," or "Respectfully." Follow the close with a comma. About four lines below the complimentary close, type your name. An optional item is to type the word "Enclosure" in the lower left corner of the cover letter. This refers to the résumé, alerting the reader to the fact that more is included in the envelope. "Enclosure: résumé" or "Enclosure (résumé)" is also correct. Finally, remember to sign the letter, in ink (preferably blue or black), above your typed name.

Physical Appearance of the Letter

A cover letter is placed on top of a résumé and is received before a job interview occurs, so it conveys a first impression to the employer. The impression you want to create is that you are a competent person with a lot to offer. The way to do this is to send a clean, neat, and technically perfect cover letter. The same type or printing used on your résumé should also be used for your cover letter. Spelling mistakes, awkward sentence structure, grammatical errors, and typographical oversights detract from the quality of your letter; not paying attention to these details will cause your cover letter to work against you rather than for you.

Always use a current dictionary to check the spelling and definition of every word you are not sure of. Misspelled and mistyped words may be regarded as evidence of the job applicant's carelessness and inattention to detail, even though the applicant is normally intelligent and proficient.

Proofread your cover letter and résumé very carefully, word for word. A typographical error is as bad to the reader as a misspelled word. Ask a friend, spouse, or parent to proofread your work critically and catch all errors while there is still time to correct them. Never mail your letters and résumés without proofreading them.

Always type your cover letter on high-quality 8½- by 11-inch white or off-white paper. The importance of neatness cannot be overemphasized. When employers begin to look through cover letters and résumés, they often begin by eliminating those that look messy or contain misspelled words and errors in grammar.

EXERCISE 3-4 DRAFT YOUR OWN COVER LETTER

Your address _____

City, state, ZIP code _____

Date _____

_____ Employer's name

_____ Name of organization

_____ Address

_____ City, state, ZIP code

Dear _____ (name) _____ :

First paragraph (Attract attention and create the desire to read further; state why you are writing and want to work in that job and for that organization.)

_____

_____

_____

_____

_____

_____

Second paragraph (State your qualifications for the job; mention an achievement or two, particularly if they are relevant to the job being sought.)

_____

_____

_____

_____

_____

_____

Third paragraph (Urge the reader to respond; bring attention to the enclosed résumé; request an interview; state how you can be contacted.)

_____

_____

_____

_____

_____

_____

Sincerely yours,   Sincerely yours,

_____   _____
          (Your signature)   (Your signature)
(Type your name below your signature)   (Type your name below your signature)

Enclosure (résumé)

Note: Heading, complimentary close, and signature are placed on the left margin for the block style of business communication or in the right margin for the "regular" style.

OTHER TYPES OF WRITTEN COMMUNICATION

Résumés and cover letters are not the only communications you will write when you seek a job. Thank-you letters, follow-up letters, an acceptance letter, and letters declining offers are also part of the job search. Ideas for and models of these letters are presented in this section. After reading this section, you should have a general idea of how to write these kinds of business letters, but do not copy these models word for word.

Thank-You Letters

Within one day of each interview, you should write and mail a brief note to the person with whom you talked, expressing your thanks for the time he or she spent with you. You never lose when you say "Thank you." You can mention something specific from the interview to indicate that your letter is personally written to the reader, not just a form letter. Two or three short paragraphs are usually enough. (See Figure 3-11.) Use good quality notepaper and a matching envelope. Assuming your writing is legible, the thank-you letter can be handwritten, giving it a more personal touch. Make sure your signature is legible, so your reader will know who sent the letter.

> I am grateful for the opportunity to meet with you last ____(day)____. I value the information you gave me concerning _____.
>
> Should any opening occur in a job position for which you believe I would be qualified, I would greatly appreciate being informed about it. Let me know if I can provide you with any additional facts about my career goals and qualifications.
>
> Thank you once more for the interview. I hope we can meet again soon.

Figure 3-11   Example of the body of a thank-you letter

Writing a thank-you note takes only 5 or 10 minutes, yet it is one of the most important things you can do in your entire job search. The employer notices that you are a courteous person. You are probably the only one of a hundred job seekers who writes this kind of a letter. All career counselors advise it, and almost all job hunters forget it. Some people have obtained jobs on the strength of their thank-you letters. The thank-you letter was the one thing that set them apart from the other job candidates; it made the essential difference. Also, keep secretaries or receptionists in mind. Get their names and send them thank-you letters. You probably had to go through a secretary to see the employer. The secretary will appreciate your simple courtesy and remember you for it.

Follow-Up Letters

You write a follow-up letter when you do not receive any response from an employer after sending an application or résumé and cover letter. The purpose of the follow-up letter is to remind employers of your contact with them, show interest in their organization, and give additional information that could strengthen a previous impression. (See Figure 3-12.) There is no standard amount of time to wait before writing a follow-up letter. Some career counselors advise giving the employer two to three weeks to reply to your original letter. You can also write a follow-up letter when you receive no response after an interview. Follow-up activities are important; they indicate to employers a desire for the work in the job. One person got a job offer after writing three follow-up letters; the persistence and obvious interest in the company shown by the job seeker impressed the employer. One caution: Don't become an annoying nag. Hounding an employer immediately after sending a résumé or application will not improve your chances of landing a job.

Accepting or Declining a Job Offer

Accepting an offer. Start with a statement accepting the job offer and follow with any necessary details, such as additional papers needed and when you can report. End with a sense of optimism about the time when you will be working for the employer. See Figure 3-13 for an example.

Declining an offer. Decline the offer and express appreciation for the organization's interest in you, and thank them for the time they have given you. Indicate this was a difficult decision after giving it serious consideration. Leave an opening for future opportunities with the company. (See Figure 3-14.)

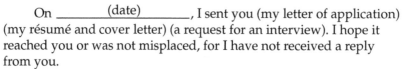

On _____(date)_____, I sent you (my letter of application) (my résumé and cover letter) (a request for an interview). I hope it reached you or was not misplaced, for I have not received a reply from you.

I have done some research on your organization and am very interested in learning more about it. I hope I have the opportunity to meet with you in the near future.

(You can finish by furnishing the details of how to contact you. Refer to the instructions for the third paragraph of the cover letter.)

Figure 3-12   Example of the body of a follow-up letter

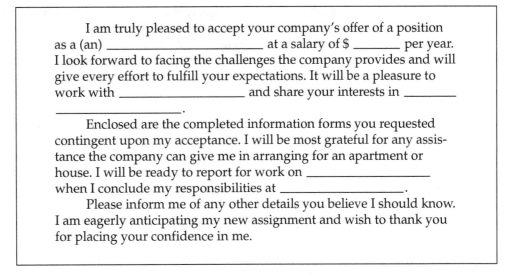

I am truly pleased to accept your company's offer of a position as a (an) _____ at a salary of $ _____ per year. I look forward to facing the challenges the company provides and will give every effort to fulfill your expectations. It will be a pleasure to work with _____ and share your interests in _____ _____.

Enclosed are the completed information forms you requested contingent upon my acceptance. I will be most grateful for any assistance the company can give me in arranging for an apartment or house. I will be ready to report for work on _____ when I conclude my responsibilities at _____.

Please inform me of any other details you believe I should know. I am eagerly anticipating my new assignment and wish to thank you for placing your confidence in me.

Figure 3-13   Example of the body of an acceptance letter

After considerable thought and deliberation, I have decided not to accept your offer of a position with _____. This decision was a very difficult one to make.

I am very impressed with your organization and hope the door will be open for future opportunities. I sincerely appreciate the time and consideration you have given me.

Figure 3-14   Example of the body of a letter declining an offer

SUMMARY

1. The résumé is a self-designed personal data sheet that contains information about your job objective, qualifications, education, and work experience. The two major styles of résumés are chronological and functional. Chronological résumés present your education and work experience in a time sequence, whereas functional résumés highlight work functions you performed on previous jobs. The strong features of both styles can be put together in a "combination résumé."

2. A curriculum vitae (CV) is an extensive autobiographical account that is usually longer than a traditional résumé. The CV is used to attract employers in higher education, publishing houses, research departments, professional associations, and government services. It is more detailed than a résumé and includes such subjects as degrees, dissertations, scholastic honors, academic awards, grants, scholarships, publications, courses and seminars taught, research conducted, workshop and conference presentations, and so on.

3. Résumés must be prepared for the likelihood they will be read by an electronic scanner before they are read by human eyes. The distinguishing feature of an electronic résumé is the keyword summary. Keywords are qualifications required or desired by the employer. Résumé writers must try to anticipate the keywords that will attract an employer (or, rather, the employer's computer). If the job seeker's résumé contains enough keywords to match those of the employer, the computer will bring up the résumé from a database for the employer to read.

4. A cover letter should accompany the résumé when you communicate with employers. The cover letter introduces you to the employer, explains why you are writing, states your qualifications for the job, and asks for an interview.

5. Other forms of communication with employers are a thank-you note after interviews, follow-up letters when you have received no response to your letter or résumé, and letters accepting or declining job offers.

REFERENCES

Angel, J. A. 1980. *The complete résumé book and job-getter's guide.* New York: Pocket Books.

Biegeleisen, J. I. 1982. *Job résumés: How to write them, how to present them, preparing for interviews.* New York: Putnam.

Farr, J. M., and Ludden, L. L., with Shatkin, L. 2002. *O*Net dictionary of occupational titles.* Indianapolis, IN: JIST Works.

Figgins, R. 1976. *Techniques of job search.* San Francisco: Canfield Press.

Fox, J. J. 2001. *Don't send a resume: And other contrarian rules to help land a great job.* New York: Hyperion.

Fry, R. 2001. *Your first resume: For students and anyone preparing to enter today's tough job market,* 5th ed. Franklin Lakes, NJ: Career Press.

Half, R. 1994. *How to get a better job in this crazy world.* New York: Signet Books.

Hayes, S. C., and Hayes, L .J. 2003. Writing your vita. In *A psychology student handbook.* Hanover, IN: Hanover College. Available online at http://psych.hanover.edu/handbook/vita2.html. Accessed July 25, 2003.

Kennedy, J. L. 2003. *Resumes for dummies,* 4th ed. New York: Wiley.

Kennedy, J. L., and Morrow, T. J. 1995. *Electronic résumé revolution: Create a winning résumé for the new world of job-seeking.* New York: Wiley.

Lathrop, R. 1998. *Who's hiring who: How to find that job fast,* 12th ed. Berkeley, CA: Ten Speed Press.

McDaniels, C. 1997. *Developing a professional vita or resume,* rev. ed. Chicago: Ferguson.

Meyers, H. H. 1984, Spring. Writing résumés right. *Journal of College Placement,* 44(2), 19–21.

Nutter, C. F. 1978. *The résumé workbook: A personal career file for job applications.* Cranston, RI: Carroll Press.

Parker, Y. 2002. *The damn good resume catalog: A crash course in resume writing with 200 damn good examples.* Berkeley, CA: Ten Speed Press.

Rogers, E. J. 1979, Fall. Elements of efficient job hunting. *Journal of College Placement,* 39(4), 55–58.

Roper, D. H. 1994. *Getting the job you want . . . now!* New York: Warner Books.

Rosen, S., and Paul, C. 1998. *Career renewal: Tools for scientists and technical professionals.* San Diego, CA: Academic Press.

Rosenberg, A. D., and Hizer, D. 2003. *The resume handbook: How to write outstanding resumes and cover letters for every situation,* 4th ed. Avon, MA: Adams Media.

Smith, R. 2000. *Electronic resumes and online networking: How to use the Internet to do a better job search, including a complete up-to-date resource guide.* Franklin Lakes, NJ: Career Press.

U.S. Department of Labor. 1991. *The dictionary of occupational titles,* 4th ed., rev. Washington, DC: U.S. Government Printing Office.

U.S. Department of Labor. biennial editions. *Occupational outlook handbook.* Washington, DC: U.S. Government Printing Office.

Washington, T. 1996. *Resume power: Selling yourself on paper.* Bellevue, WA: Mount Vernon Press.

Washington, T. 2003 *Resume power: Selling yourself on paper in the new millennium,* 7th ed. Bellevue, WA: Mount Vernon Press.

Weddle, P. D. 1995. *Electronic résumés for the new job market.* Manassas Park, VA: Impact Publications.

Weinstein, B. 1982. *Résumés for hard times.* New York: Fireside/Simon & Schuster.

Whitcomb, S. B., and Kendall, P. 2002. *eResumes: Everything you need to know about using electronic resumes to tap into today's job market.* New York: McGraw-Hill.

Yate, M. 2002. *Resumes that knock 'em dead.* Avon, MA: Adams Media.

Chapter 4

Job Applications

Giving information about yourself on an employer's application form is the most common element of the job search. Because filling out application forms is so much a fact of life, the importance of this document can be easily overlooked. The words you write on the form are permanent. They can be verified or refuted, and they will be used as part of your evaluation. The application form becomes a paper with legal standing if you are hired. After you have filled out the tenth application form in, say, three days, there is an understandable tendency to become careless and sloppy about it. People have written mistakes like these in response to questions on applications: "In accordance with your instructions I have given birth to twins in the enclosed envelope." "My baby was born two years old." "My son was branded as illiterate and that is a lie; I was married a week before he was born." Proofread the words you write. Approach the employer's application form as if it were a test—which it is. It is a test of your written expression, accuracy, honesty, neatness, spelling, ability to follow directions, and how well you represent yourself. Like the résumé, the application form by itself will not be enough to get you the job, but you must master it well enough to stay in the running.

After discussion and exercises pertaining to job application forms, the rest of this chapter considers several special problems that can emerge from a job search. Illegal questions on application forms (and in job interviews as well) present a dilemma. Opinions differ about how best to handle them. One idea is to ignore them if they do not personally bother you. Another strategy is to suggest politely that the inquiry is not relevant to the position being sought, thus protecting not only yourself, but also those whom the law is trying to protect.

This chapter concludes with two exercises on strengths and problems of the job application. Some job seekers have the problem of concentrating only on their weaknesses and ignoring their strengths. Exercise 4-3 may help you gain a better perspective on the strong points you already possess. Exercise 4-4 may help you cope with certain special problems that could arise on a job application form or during a job interview. Recognizing possible difficulties in advance allows you time to develop responses that could reduce or eliminate the negative impact of an unprepared answer.

COMPLETING AN EMPLOYER'S APPLICATION FORM

The application form is an innocuous-looking piece of paper, but it can be loaded with danger. There is a temptation to become careless when completing employers' application forms. Sometimes there are so many to fill out that you become punchy after a while. If you find yourself answering "Dad" for father's name or "womb" for place of birth, you have symptoms of "application apoplexy." Study the application form carefully. The employer may learn far more than you could ever imagine from this simple piece of paper.

If you make mistakes on the application blank, ask for another one. It is better to take time on it rather than leave a poor impression of yourself. Give the application form the same consideration you give any other part of your job search—that is, consider it very important. The application could become the most important link between you and the employer.

Here are some tips for filling out employers' applications. Some of these comments come from Michigan's Job Service (1988) program.

1. Read the entire application form carefully before you attempt to give information on any items or answer any questions.
2. Use your résumé as a source of dates and other information.
3. Fill out the form in black or blue ink with a fine-point pen. Print responses unless otherwise directed. Write your signature.
4. Answer all questions, even if you must print "not applicable" or "none" as a response. Unanswered items become conspicuous to some employers.
5. Follow directions carefully. This sounds trite, but not following directions trips up more people than you can imagine. Read each item before you respond to it.

6. Compose your answers on a blank or scrap sheet of paper first if you are not sure how to reply.

7. List two telephone numbers where you may be reached; usually these telephone numbers are from your home and work site. Include the area code.

8. If you answer an item about your marital status, list it as being married or single. Any other term may give the employer a negative impression (Job Service, 1988).

9. Report a health problem if it is obvious. Otherwise, indicate you would be willing to discuss any health problems in an interview.

10. In an "employment desired" inquiry, definitely give the exact title of the position for which you are applying. Also include the titles of similar or related positions you would be willing to accept. Do *not* write "anything" or "any job." Employers consider this response as a lack of focus. The author remembers a career services director telling job applicants to "jump off the roof" of a three-story building. When the astounded applicant asked why, the answer was "You said you could do anything."

11. Base a requested salary figure on your research of the organization. Avoid using a specific figure unless you have definite information from your research. Write "open to negotiation" if you are not sure of an appropriate amount.

12. Record your experience or work history data in such a way that they relate to the job position for which you are applying.

13. Use action verbs to begin each sentence, describing responsibilities and duties you carried out on previous jobs and volunteer work. (Use words from the list of Action Verbs for Résumé Writing in Table 3-1 of Chapter 3.)

14. Use numbers to describe accomplishments in your work experiences; for example, "Sold an average of 20 new products per day."

15. Use education, volunteer work, self-employment, and/or summer and part-time work to fill in employment gaps between full-time jobs.

16. Attach a separate page describing your work experience if there is not enough space to respond on the job application form.

17. Attach a copy of an honorable discharge from the military if you are a veteran. (Some employers give preference to veterans.)

18. List hobbies or interests if they relate to your job objective.

19. List names of professional associations of which you are a member, unless they are controversial organizations.

20. Indicate an availability date that will give your present employer sufficient notice of your acceptance of a new job.

21. Answer all questions honestly. If you are hired, your application form becomes a part of your permanent record.

22. Keep the application form clean and neat. You are giving a written impression of yourself to a prospective employer. Complete another application form if the first one is sloppy.

23. Check the accuracy of your spelling and punctuation.

24. Obtain the permission of your reference people before you use their names.

25. Don't forget to sign your name!

EXERCISE 4-1 APPLICATION FOR EMPLOYMENT

The application form in Exercise 4-1 on the next three pages is a composite of many employers' applications used in the past; use it for learning or teaching purposes only, because it contains several items that are now illegal to ask an applicant before he or she is hired. Fill out the sample Application for Employment, and circle the items you think are illegal. After the exercise, check your knowledge of legal and illegal questions asked before hiring takes place by consulting the Pre-employment Inquiry Guide included in this chapter.

APPLICATION FOR EMPLOYMENT

(To be completed in applicant's own handwriting in ink)
Not an actual application. To be used for teaching purposes only.

PERSONAL INFORMATION

Date _____   Social Security number _____

Name _____   Age _____   Sex _____
        Last   First   Middle (maiden name)

Present address _____
              Number and street   City   State   ZIP   Phone

Permanent address _____
              Number and street   City   State   ZIP   Phone

Birth _____   U.S. Citizen? _____   Height _____   Weight _____
    Date   Place

Married _____   Single _____   Widowed _____   Divorced _____   Separated _____

Number of children _____   Dependents (other than spouse and children) _____

Have you ever been   If yes,
convicted of a crime?   explain. _____

Do you own   If yes, give   License
a car? _____   details: _____   Make _____   Year _____   number _____

Do you have a   License   What   Date license
driver's license? _____   number _____   state? _____   expires _____

Driver's license ever   If yes, when
suspended or revoked? _____   and why? _____

Do you have any personal responsibilities or problems   If yes,
that might prevent you from coming to work at times?   explain. _____

EMPLOYMENT DESIRED

                        Date you   Salary
Position _____   can start: _____   expected: _____

Other job
interests _____

Are you willing   In what city or area
to relocate? _____   would you prefer work? _____

If related to anyone in our organization,
state name and department. _____

State reasons for preference
of work desired. _____

EDUCATION

	Name and location of school	Years attended	Graduation date and degree	Name of major or program
College				
High School				
Other				

Do you plan to further
your education? Explain.

Membership in professional, technical,
honorary associations

List any special skills
you have developed.

List hobbies, special interests,
and things you like to do.

MILITARY	Branch of service	Date of entrance	Date of discharge
Rank when discharged	Military Occupational Specialty		Type of discharge
Received disability payments?	Nature of disability		

EMPLOYMENT RECORD   (Start with your present or latest employer)

Date (month/year)	Name and address of employer (Include name of your supervisor.)	Title or position	Highest salary	Reason for leaving
From				
To				
From				
To				
From				
To				
From				
To				

Explain any periods of unemployment
or part-time work not listed.

_____

Attendance record: Average number
of days absent per month in last job.

_____

PHYSICAL RECORD: General health   Excellent ____   Good ____   Fair ____   Poor ____

Serious illness in the past five years?	If yes, state the nature of your illness.

Any physical handicaps or limitations?	If yes, explain.

Have you ever had a work injury for which you have received disability benefits?	If yes, when and for what reason?

Indicate whether you have had any of the following:

Diabetes ____	Heart condition ____	High blood pressure ____
Defective sight ____	Mental problems ____	Epilepsy ____
Back ailments ____	Hernia ____	Defective hearing ____
Frequent or serious headaches ____		

Other _____

Has any insurance company rejected your application for life insurance?	If yes, explain.

FINANCIAL

Have you ever been sued or had wages garnisheed or assigned?	If yes, explain.

List two businesses where you have established credit. (name, address, telephone).	1.
	2.

REFERENCES   Give names of three persons. (Do not list relatives or former employers.)

Name	Address	Telephone	Business or Occupation

I authorize investigation of all statements in this application. I understand that misrepresentation or omission of facts called for is cause for dismissal. All information I have given in this application for employment is true to the best of my knowledge.

What should you do if you encounter an illegal item on an application form? There is no simple answer to this question. Basically, you have four options:

1. You could write "not relevant to the qualifications required by the job" or "not an appropriate question before hiring" or (more directly) "This question is an illegal inquiry and I am not required to answer it." These responses are somewhat risky because they may make you appear uncooperative to the employer. You have the law on your side, but it may not help much. It takes time to prosecute repeated discrimination. Some employers know little about the legalities of hiring and thus may be unaware that a particular question is illegal. In a job interview, you could respond to a question you know is illegal by asking, "Can you explain to me how this relates to the job?"

2. Answer without answering. You must think quickly to use this strategy. Suppose you are asked (either on paper or, more likely, in a job interview), "Will your spouse be comfortable about your traveling?" You can respond with "Travel has never been a problem for me." Or, "Who will take care of your children when you are at work?" Your reply could be "I do not allow personal commitments to interfere with my work" (Hacker, 1999).

3. You can answer the question and ignore its illegality. Many job seekers answer questions they know to be illegal because they are desperate for a job or because the subject is of no great concern to them. Some people feel differently. They argue that job seekers should not aid and abet a clearly illegal procedure.

4. Tell the employer you will inform the nearest office of the Civil Rights Commission or the Equal Employment Opportunity Commission (EEOC). Of course, you can kiss the job good-bye, but ask yourself, "Would I want to work for this employer?" Before using this option, try the first one and give the employer a chance to comply with the law. The second option requires you to match wits with the employer in a kind of "cat and mouse" game. Successful prosecution of employers who illegally discriminate in their hiring practices is difficult. You must be able to show a repeated pattern of illegal job discrimination by the employer. Your best chance of winning your case is to get in touch with an advocacy group that has competent legal resources.

To become knowledgeable about the legality or illegality of items on employment application forms (and also in job interview situations), refer to the Pre-employment Inquiry Guide on pages 120–125.

Employers may apply for an exemption on the basis that religion, national origin, age, height, weight, or sex is a bona fide (legitimate) occupational qualification essential to the normal operation of the business or enterprise. If the employer shows sufficient evidence, an exemption may be granted.

The information given in the Pre-employment Inquiry Guide is drawn from a number of sources: *Pre-employment Inquiries: What (and What Not) to Ask* (NACE, 2000), *Job Hunting in the 21st Century* (Hacker, 1999), *Pre-employment Inquiries: What . . . and What Not . . . to Ask* (Kaplan, 1993), and civil rights departments, human rights commissions, and affirmative action offices from the states of Illinois, Michigan, Missouri, and Pennsylvania (see the References section for the names of these four sources). Relevant legislation on the national level includes the Equal Employment Opportunity Act (Title VII), the Higher Education Act (Title IX), the Age Discrimination Act, and the Americans with Disabilities Act of 1990. Some job discrimination precedents, particularly under the Americans with Disabilities Act, are still being decided in the courts on a case-by-case basis; however, legislation in the effort to combat discrimination has slowed in recent years. (There are trends in the antidiscrimination field just as in the occupational market.)

In the sections of the Pre-employment Inquiry Guide where you see a "BFOQ" designation, this means an exemption can be granted for a "bona fide occupational qualification."

Pre-employment Inquiry Guide

Subject	Lawful Pre-employment Inquiries	Unlawful Pre-employment Inquiries
1. Name	• Applicant's full name. • Have you ever worked for this company under a different name? • Is any additional information concerning a different name necessary to check your work record? If yes, explain.	• Original name of an applicant whose name has been changed by court order or otherwise. • Applicant's maiden name. • To ask if a woman is a Miss or Mrs.
2. Address or Duration of Residence/ Housing	• How long a resident of this state or city? • Place and length of current and previous address? • To ask for applicant's phone number or how he or she can be reached if a number is not available.	• To ask if applicant owns a home or rents. • To ask if applicant lives in an apartment or a house. • Who lives with you? • Do you live with your spouse (or parents)?
3. Age (BFOQ)	• Require proof of age by birth certificate *after hiring*. • Are you 18 years old or older? (This question may be asked for the purpose of determining whether applicants are of legal age for employment.)	• How old are you? • What is your date of birth? • Require applicant to produce proof by birth certificate or baptismal record. • Are you over the age of 50?
4. Birthplace		• Birthplace of applicant. • Birthplace of applicant's parents, spouse, or other close relatives. • To ask that applicant submit birth certificate or naturalization or baptismal record.
5. Religion or Creed (BFOQ)		• Inquiry into an applicant's religious denomination, religious affiliations, parish, pastor, religious holidays observed, or if attends a house of worship regularly. • To request recommendations from church officials.
6. Race or Color	• To ask about race, for affirmative action plan statistics, *after hiring*. • Ask for color of applicant's eyes or hair.	• Any inquiry that would indicate race, complexion, or color.

Pre-employment Inquiry Guide (continued)

Subject	Lawful Pre-employment Inquiries	Unlawful Pre-employment Inquiries
7. Photograph	• May be required *after hiring* for identification purposes.	• Requirement that an applicant for employment attach a photograph to an employment form. • Request that an applicant, at his or her option, submit a photograph. • Require a photograph after an interview but before hiring.
8. Height and Weight (BFOQ)	• Inquiry that is job related.	• Inquiry regarding applicant's height and weight.
9. Marital/ Parental Status	• Status (only married or single) *after hiring*, for insurance purposes. • Number and ages of dependents and/or spouse *after hiring*, for insurance purposes.	• Requirement that an applicant provide any information regarding marital status or children. • Are you single or married? ("Is that Miss or Mrs.?") • Do you have any children? • Is your spouse employed? • What is your spouse's name?
10. Gender		• Any inquiry that indicates gender, unless job related, such as for model and locker room or restroom attendant.
11. Sexual Orientation		• All inquiries into applicant's sexual orientation.
12. Pregnancy		• Inquiries into pregnancy, medical history, or family plans.
13. Child Care (BFOQ)	• Inquiry must be job-related and asked of all applicants.	• Inquiries about child care arrangements of *only* female applicants.
14. Health	• Do you have any impairments, physical, mental, or medical, *which would interfere with your ability to do the job for which you have applied?*	• Do you have a disability or handicap? • Have you ever been treated for the following diseases? • Do you use any adaptive device or aid?

(continued)

Pre-employment Inquiry Guide (continued)

Subject	Lawful Pre-employment Inquiries	Unlawful Pre-employment Inquiries
	• Inquiry into contagious or communicable diseases that may endanger others. If there are any positions for which you should not be considered or job duties you can't perform because of physical or mental handicap, please explain.	• Requirement that women be given pelvic examinations.
15. Citizenship	• Are you a citizen of the United States? • If not a citizen of the United States, do you intend to become a citizen of the United States? • If you are not a United States citizen, have you the legal right to remain permanently in the United States? • Do you intend to remain in the United States permanently? • Are you legally eligible to work in the United States?	• Of what country are you a citizen? • Whether an applicant is naturalized or a native-born U.S. citizen. • Requirement that an applicant produce naturalization papers or first papers. • Whether applicant's parents or spouse are naturalized or native-born citizens of the United States; the date when such parents or spouse acquired citizenship.
16. National Origin and Language (BFOQ)	• Inquiry into languages applicant speaks and writes fluently (only if this relates to the job position).	• Inquiry into applicant's lineage, ancestry, national origin, descent, parentage, and nationality. • Nationality of applicant's parents or spouse. • How did you acquire the ability to read, write, or speak a foreign language?
17. Education	• Inquiry into the academic, vocational, or professional education of an applicant and the public and private schools he or she attended. • Qualifications that require high school diplomas and college degrees must be job-related	
18. Experience	• Inquiry into work experience. • Inquiry into countries applicant has visited.	

Pre-employment Inquiry Guide (continued)

Subject	Lawful Pre-employment Inquiries	Unlawful Pre-employment Inquiries
19. Criminal Record	• Have you ever been convicted of a crime? If so, when, where, and nature of offense? • Are there any felony charges pending against you?	• Inquiry regarding arrests that did not result in conviction (except for law enforcement agencies).
20. Relatives	• Names of applicant's relatives, other than a spouse, currently employed by this company or a competitor company.	• Address of any relative of applicant, other than address (within the U.S.) of applicant's father and mother, husband or wife, and minor dependent children.
21. Notice in Case of Emergency	• Name, address, and relationship of person to be notified in case of emergency, *after hiring*.	• Name and address of nearest relative to be notified in case of accident or emergency.
22. Military Experience	• Inquiry into an applicant's military experience in the armed forces of the United States or in a state militia. • Inquiry into applicant's service in a particular branch of the U.S. armed forces.	• Inquiry into an applicant's general military experience. • Proof of honorable discharge. • Inquiries concerning experience in armed forces other than the United States.
23. Organizations	• Inquiry into job-related organizations of which an applicant is a member, excluding organizations the name or character of which indicates the race, color, religion, national origin, or ancestry of its members.	• List all non–job-related clubs societies, and lodges to which you belong.
24. References	• Who suggested that you apply for a position here? (Employers are advised not to require a reference from an applicant's current employer.)	• Name of applicant's pastor or religious leader. • Questions of acquaintances or former employers about applicant's race, color, religion, ancestry, age, disability, sex, or marital status.
25. Financial Status		• Inquiries concerning applicant's finances such as home or car ownership,

(continued)

Pre-employment Inquiry Guide (continued)

Subject	Lawful Pre-employment Inquiries	Unlawful Pre-employment Inquiries
		credit ratings, bankruptcy, arrangements for financing education, bank accounts, and past garnishment of wages.
26. Work Schedule	• To ask about willingness to work required work schedule. • To ask if applicant has military reservist obligations.	• To ask about willingness to work any particular religious holiday.
27. Disabilities	• Based on the job description, are you able to perform the essential functions of this job with or without reasonable accommodation? • As part of the hiring process, after a job offer has been made, you will be required to undergo a medical exam. (The results of the exam must be kept strictly confidential.) • Can you demonstrate how you would perform the following job-related function (but only if *every* applicant for the job is required to do so)?	• Do you have any disabilities? • Please complete the following medical history. • Have you had any recent or past illnesses or operations? If yes, list and give dates. • What was the date of your last physical exam? • How is your family's health? • When did you lose your eyesight? How? • Have you ever been hospitalized? For what? • Have you ever been treated by a psychologist or psychiatrist? For what? • Have you ever been treated for any mental condition? • Have you ever filed for workers' compensation?
28. Drug Tests	• For some job positions, drug tests are required by law.	
29. Lawful Product Use		• Inquiries regarding the use of lawful products such as tobacco during nonworking hours.
30. Driver's License	• Questions about whether applicant has a valid driver's license and/or owns a car *must be job related.*	• Asking for driver's license information for determining applicant's age, citizenship, or other personal information.

Pre-employment Inquiry Guide (continued)

Subject	Lawful Pre-employment Inquiries	Unlawful Pre-employment Inquiries
31. Availability	• Is applicant available for weekend or evening work? (only if asked of all applicants for the job) • How long do you expect to work here? • Would you require any lengthy absence in the near future?	
32. Miscellaneous	• Statement that any omissions of facts called for in the application may be cause for dismissal.	• Any non–job-related inquiry unnecessary to determine an applicant's abilities or qualifications for employment.

Restrictions on pre-employment inquiries vary somewhat from state to state. Your state's civil rights commission is the place to contact for answers to questions. You can also consult a lawyer if you have questions beyond this guide. One note of caution: If you unwittingly give out any information that would be illegal for the employer to ask for, it becomes fair game for discussion in an interview.

Medical examination forms, group insurance, census and enrollment cards, and surety bond application forms containing questions directly relating to race, color, religion, national origin, ancestry, or sexual orientation are unlawful *before* an applicant's hiring for employment, *but are permissible after hiring*. Where an employee is under contract with a government agency that requires information concerning applicable security regulations, it is proper for the agency to ask only such questions as are necessary to obtain the required security information (Regulations of the Commission on Human Relations, 2003).

As you can see, many legal principles are involved with pre-employment inquiries. We can mention only a few here. The *right of privacy* may come up under the U.S. Constitution, a state constitution, or common law. The idea behind a right to privacy is protection from unwarranted and unreasonable intrusions into a person's private affairs, particularly where the matter is not a legitimate concern to the public.

The federal government has determined that certain groups of people need *special protections from intentional discriminatory treatment*. Groups classified by race or color, gender, religion, disability, age, national origin, and citizenship receive this special protection.

Freedom from sexual harassment means protection against offensive sexual conduct that creates a "hostile environment" for the individual or requires sexual favors in exchange for a reward such as a job offer or promotion.

The concept of *reasonable accommodation* involves modifying recruitment processes, examinations, equipment, work schedules, and the job itself and making existing facilities readily accessible to persons with disabilities. More discussion of reasonable accommodation for people with disabilities comes later in this chapter. Reasonable accommodation also applies to specific religious needs of people in terms of modifying a job, work schedule, and work rules, at minimal cost to the employer, that enables the individual to practice his or her religion (NACE, 2000).

It is illegal to discriminate *on the basis of sexual orientation* in certain states of the United States. These states as of the year 2000 are California, Connecticut, the District of Columbia, Hawaii, Massachusetts, Minnesota, Nevada, New Hampshire, New Jersey, Rhode Island, Vermont, and Wisconsin (NACE, 2000). The situation may have changed in your state by the time you read this information.

APPLYING FOR A JOB OR RESEARCHING A COMPANY WHEN YOU HAVE NO RÉSUMÉ

Some job search experts suggest it may be helpful to revise and send your résumé to an interviewer *after* you have concluded the interview. The purpose of this strategy is (1) to help a busy employer remember you and (2) to highlight the skills the employer is seeking from the information you have obtained. Your résumé can be tailored to the particular company you have visited (Bolles, 2000). But what if you are asked for an indication of your seriousness by completing an application form before you can talk with anyone? A worksheet of basic information can prove to be useful. You are less likely to forget an important piece of information or make an error that you will need to correct later.

Therefore, if you are investigating a company in your job hunting and do not have a résumé prepared, complete the worksheet in Exercise 4-2 and take it with you when you apply for a job position in person. Another variation of this exercise is to write needed information on 3-by-5-inch or 4-by-6-inch cards. Smaller cards may be easier to handle.

EXERCISE 4-2 WORKSHEET FOR COMPLETING JOB APPLICATION FORMS

Name _____

Present address _____

Permanent address _____

Telephone _____   Business telephone _____   Social Security number _____

Person to contact in an emergency _____   Phone _____

OPTIONAL INFORMATION

Date of birth _____   Height _____   Weight _____

Marital Status _____   Maiden name _____   Number of children _____   Their ages _____

Child care arrangements_____

Driver's license no. _____   Make of car _____   Year _____   License no. (car) _____

Job Objective _____   Date you can start _____   Desired salary _____

Other job interests _____

Willing to relocate? _____   Area preferences _____

EDUCATION

	Name and location of school	Years attended	Degree	Program: major/minor
College	_____	_____	_____	_____
	_____	_____	_____	_____
	_____	_____	_____	_____
High school	_____	_____	_____	_____

Other (including conferences, workshops, seminars)

_____

_____

_____

Honors, achievements, extracurricular activities, hobbies, interests

_____

_____

_____

_____

EMPLOYMENT RECORD (in reverse chronological order)

Dates of employment	Name and address of organization	Title or position	Duties and responsibilities	Name of supervisor	Reason for leaving
_____	_____	_____	_____	_____	_____
_____	_____	_____	_____	_____	_____
_____	_____	_____	_____	_____	_____
_____	_____	_____	_____	_____	_____
_____	_____	_____	_____	_____	_____
_____					

Professional, union, social memberships _____

_____

Military Service Branch of service _____ Date of entrance _____ Date of discharge _____ Rank _____

Military assignments/ occupational specialty _____

Explain any special circumstances: _____

Personal responsibilities or health problems that might prevent you from coming to work; defects in hearing, vision, or speech.

_____

_____

_____

REFERENCES

Name	Address	Telephone number	Received permission?	Business/ Occupation

APPLICATIONS FOR JOBS IN THE FEDERAL GOVERNMENT

We will use the Optional Application for Federal Employment (OF 612) as the representative form for government job applications. The OF 612 has replaced the Standard Form (SF 171), and is probably the most extensively used form by applicants for federal jobs. It is called optional because you can also apply by using a *federal* résumé (Lipson and McKay, 2003). How you fill out an application for a federal job will have a bearing on the *rating* you receive. Your application's rating will be based on a numerical score that determines your eligibility or suitability for the job (McKinney, 2001). Following the advice given here will help you to maximize your numerical score if you intend to apply for a federal job.

Figure 4-1 is a blank Form OF 612. It looks quite quick and easy to complete, but there is more to the OF 612 than is revealed by your first glance. You will add more points to your score if you add attachments or "continuation pages" to the Work Experience and Education sections. Plan to expand these sections onto additional sheets of paper. The more detail you can provide on your attached sheets in the form of KSAs (knowledge, skills, and abilities), the better your chances are of landing the job you want. Answers to questions on the OF 612 should be typed onto the form.

Items 1 through 7 on Form OF 612 are direct requests for the job title given in the job announcement, the grade (usually, the General Schedule [GS] number), the announcement number, your full name, your mailing address, your Social Security number, and your daytime and evening telephone numbers.

Item 8 on Work Experience is often the most important part of the entire application. Do not scale down your account of what you did on a job so that it fits into the small space provided. To provide information for only your current and previous work experience is a mistake that could cost you points on your numerical rating score. Use additional pages to describe the duties, responsibilities, and accomplishments or additional jobs that relate to the position for which you are applying. When you run out of space on Form OF 612, indicate that more material will be "continued on a separate page" or type in "see attached page." On the separate page, put "Continuation Sheet" or "Attachment" at the top and indicate it is "for Item 8" (if continuing your work experience section), "for Item 11 or 12" (if adding material you have learned in your high school or college education), or "for Item 13" (if the subject is other qualifications). Include *all* of your work in your previous employment and volunteer history. Type in any KSA you have acquired. If you have the first book of this Career Planning Guide series (*Taking Charge of Your Career Direction*), consult the O*Net list of knowledges, skills, and abilities in Appendix H: *O*Net Skills, Abilities, and Knowledges* for help in writing about your KSAs.

Knowledge means you have learned an organized body of information that makes good performance on the job possible. Examples of knowledge might be the designs, uses, repair, and maintenance of machines and tools or familiarity with human behavior, motivation, and learning patterns. *Skill* deals with the correct uses of data, people, and/or things through physical, mental, or verbal methods. You use skills (as the O*Net define them) when you read, speak, write, actively listen, think critically, instruct, negotiate, and monitor. *Ability* refers to performing mental and physical activities to solve problems. Examples of abilities are remembering words, numbers, pictures, and procedures or responding quickly to a signal with your hands and feet. These examples of KSAs are among those defined by O*Net; they can be matched to many job requirements of private sector positions as well as government jobs. Of course, you must be completely honest in claiming a KSA and provide evidence of how you have learned and used it. That's why this application can easily expand into many pages.

The answers to Items 9–12 should be typed onto Form OF 612. Use an attachment page or continuation sheet for Numbers 11 and 12 if you have more information than will fit on the form. Item 13 can be handled in the same way. Anything you have

OPTIONAL APPLICATION FOR FEDERAL EMPLOYMENT – OF 612

Form Approved
OMB No. 3206-0219

Section A – Applicant Information

Use Standard State Postal Codes (abbreviations). If outside the United States of America, and you do not have a military address, type or print "OV" in the State field (Block 6c) and fill in the Country field (Block 6e) below, leaving the Zip Code field (Block 6d) blank.

1. Job title in announcement	2. Grade(s) applying for	3. Announcement number
4a. Last name	4b. First and middle names	5. Social Security Number

6a. Mailing address ★

7. Phone numbers (include area code if within the United States of America)

7a. Daytime

6b. City	6c. State	6d. Zip Code	7b. Evening

6e. Country (if not within the United States of America)

8. Email address (if available)

Section B – Work Experience

Describe your paid and nonpaid work experience related to this job for which you are applying. Do not attach job description.

1. Job title (if Federal, include series and grade)

2. From (mm/yyyy)	3. To (mm/yyyy)	4. Salary per $	5. Hours per week

6. Employer's name and address

7. Supervisor's name and phone number

7a. Name

7b. Phone

8. May we contact your current supervisor? Yes ☐ No ☐
If we need to contact your current supervisor before making an offer, we will contact you first.

9. Describe your duties and accomplishments

Section C – Additional Work Experience

1. Job title (if Federal, include series and grade)

2. From (mm/yyyy)	3. To (mm/yyyy)	4. Salary per $	5. Hours per week

6. Employer's name and address

7. Supervisor's name and phone number

7a. Name

7b. Phone

8. Describe your duties and accomplishments

U.S. Office of Personnel Management
Previous edition usable

NSN 7540-01-351-9178
50612-101

Page 1 of 2

Optional Form 612
Revised December 2002

(continued)

Figure 4-1 Optional Application for Federal Employment (OF 612)

Section D – Education

1. Last High School (HS)/GED school. Give the school's name, city, state, ZIP Code (if known), and year diploma or GED received:

2. Mark highest level completed: Some HS ☐   HS/GED ☐   Associate ☐   Bachelor ☐   Master ☐   Doctoral ☐

3. Colleges and universities attended. Do not attach a copy of your transcript unless requested.			Total Credits Earned		Major(s)	Degree (if any), Year Received
			Semester	Quarter		
3a. Name						
City	State	Zip Code				
3b. Name						
City	State	Zip Code				
3c. Name						
City	State	Zip Code				

Section E – Other Qualifiactions

Job-related training courses (give title and year). Job-related skills (other languages, computer software/hardware, tools, machinery, typing speed, etc.). Job-related certificates and licenses (current only). Job-related honors, awards, and special accomplishments (publications, memberships in professional/honor societies, leadership activities, public speaking, and performance awards). Give dates, but do **not** send documents unless requested.

Section F – General

1a. Are you a U.S. citizen?   Yes ☐   No ☐ →   1b. If no, give the Country of your citizenship

2a. Do you claim veterans' preference?   No ☐   Yes ☐ →   If yes, mark your claim of 5 or 10 points below.
2b.   5 points ☐ → Attach your *Report of Separation from Active Duty* (DD 214) or other proof.
2c. 10 points ☐ → Attach an *Application for 10-Point Veterans' Preference* (SF 15) and proof required.

3. Were you ever a Federal civilian employee?   No ☐   Yes ☐ →   If yes, list highest civilian grade for the following:

3a. Series	3b. Grade	3c. From *(mm/yyyy)*	3d. To *(mm/yyyy)*

4. Are you eligible for reinstatement based on career or career-conditional Federal status?   No ☐   Yes ☐
     If requested in the vacancy announcement, attach *Notification of Personnel Action* (SF 50), as proof.

Section G – Applicant Certification

I certify that, to the best of my knowledge and belief, all of the information on and attached to this application is true, correct, complete, and made in good faith. I understand that false or fraudulent information on or attached to this application may be grounds for not hiring me or for firing me after I begin work, and may be punishable by fine or imprisonment. I understand that any information I give may be investigated.

1a. Signature	1b. Date *(mm/dd/yyyy)*

Figure 4-1 Optional Application for Federal Employment (OF 612) *(continued)*

learned and applied can qualify as a KSA, but be sure each one matches the qualifications asked for by the hiring agency. Items 14–17 can be typed onto the form. Generally, you must be a citizen of the United States to qualify for a federal job. Veterans' preference grants extra points to qualified military veterans. If you are or were a federal civilian employee, give the job series number for the highest grade you held, the grade level, and the dates you held that grade. Previous federal employees eligible for reinstatement must attach a copy of their last Standard Form SF-50 as proof of employment (Damp, 2002).

Item 18: Read the entire certification and then be absolutely sure to sign and date it in ink. Your signature must be an original one, not a photocopy.

Note: The OF 612 form can be obtained online at this Web address: http://www.opm.gov/Forms/pdf_fill/of612.pdf.

JOB APPLICATION STRENGTHS AND PROBLEMS

Job application difficulties must be studied if you find yourself in situations that produce these problems, but it is your job application strengths and assets that can get you into an interview where you could be hired. Many people do a poor job of studying their strengths. If you get the most mileage possible from your strengths, you are more likely to win a higher-level job with higher pay and gain more personal satisfaction than if you give little attention to these critical factors.

EXERCISE 4-3 JOB APPLICATION STRENGTHS

Check any of the following statements that you think describe your situation.

_____ I can list a job objective that I am capable of doing well.

_____ I can list at least seven skills that I perform competently on the job.

_____ I can list at least seven values that lead to personal satisfaction expressed in the jobs I can do.

_____ I have completed my high school education or its equivalent (GED) and have received a diploma.

_____ I have pursued additional education in college (beyond high school).

_____ I have taken a trade school course, completed vocational/technical training, studied one or more correspondence courses, participated in a continuing educational program, or participated in some kind of special educational program.

_____ I have been given on-the-job training by a former employer for a specific task.

_____ I have been trained to operate some kind of special equipment.

_____ I plan to continue my education or training.

_____ I am a member of a technical or professional organization, association, or club.

_____ I have a technical or professional certificate or license.

_____ I have worked several years in one previous job.

_____ I have a good work record, and a former employer will recommend me as an excellent worker.

_____ My attendance record at school or in previous jobs is excellent.

_____ I can give positive reasons for leaving my previous job(s).

_____ My hobbies, interests, and things I like to do are related to the job I want to get.

_____ I have special military training and work experience that relates to the civilian job I would like to have.

_____ I have several excellent character references who know my work habits and who will give me a good recommendation for work attitude and competence.

EXERCISE 4-4 MAJOR JOB APPLICATION PROBLEMS

Check any of the following statements that you think describe your situation.

_____ It is difficult for me to name a job objective that I want to do and feel capable of doing.

_____ One of my major problems in obtaining a job is that I am young and have little work experience.

_____ One of my major problems in obtaining a job is that I am considered too old by employers, so no one will hire me.

_____ I am a member of a minority group, and this is one reason I believe I will have trouble finding employment.

_____ Getting a job is difficult for me because I am not a U.S. citizen.

_____ My recent separation or divorce seems to cause me difficulties when I apply for a job.

_____ A major problem in my getting a job is that I have a criminal record.

_____ I think employers will not hire me if they know I have an arrest record.

_____ My lack of transportation prevents me from finding or keeping a job.

_____ I don't have a driver's license, and this prevents me from getting a job.

_____ I don't have a high school diploma, and this makes it difficult to find a job.

_____ My attendance record at school or at previous jobs is poor.

_____ The reasons I left my previous job(s) are a big problem for me when I apply for a new job.

_____ One reason employers will not hire me is that I have poor health.

_____ I can't get a job because employers will see my physical handicap and will not hire me because of it.

_____ Employers will not hire me because of my past workers' compensation claims.

_____ Employers do not hire me because I have one of the following medical problems: diabetes, heart condition, high blood pressure, defective sight, mental or emotional problems, epilepsy, hernia, back ailments, defective hearing, frequent or serious headaches.

_____ My dishonorable discharge from the armed forces gives me problems when I look for a job.

_____ My past financial problems are a source of trouble when employers interview me for a job.

If you checked any of these statements, try to formulate the best response you could make if the subject arises. Possible answers are suggested in the next section.

HANDLING JOB APPLICATION PROBLEMS

How can you handle these or other problems should they require a response on a job application form (or in an interview)? The best thing to do is to be open and honest on the application form or with the interviewer—and with yourself. This isn't easy—you may be turned down sometimes—but the alternative is to lie or misrepresent yourself. Employers and interviewers have an uncanny ability to sense when something is wrong. Employers worry about many things concerning the hiring process. They will check your background very thoroughly, especially if they are both interested in you and suspicious of you.

Emphasize the positive aspects of your previous experiences and play down the negatives. If you have to mention something negative, indicate your desire to change and to be given the chance to prove yourself. For example:

Too young? Mention that you are looking for a job you can keep for some time. (Employers worry that young people are unsettled or have poor work habits.) Stress your skills, particularly if you think the employer regards you as inexperienced.

Too old? You will want to emphasize your experience and the abilities you have acquired over a long period of time. Your wisdom and experience may be well worth the higher benefit rates your employer may have to pay for you.

I'd hire you, dear, but that breaks our nepotism policy.

Divorced or separated? Indicate your ability to get along or cooperate with other people, particularly coworkers and supervisors. Some employers have negative feelings toward divorced people because they feel that home problems will become work problems.

Criminal record? The most important message you can give an employer is that you have changed. You realize you made a mistake and did a foolish thing, and now you want to work and go straight. Provide evidence of improved behavior since imprisonment or during probation. Get recommendations from probation or parole officers, a rehabilitation counselor, a chaplain, a caseworker, or some other person. If you were released early for good behavior, mention this. Don't make excuses for the behavior that got you into trouble; show that you take responsibility for your actions. You have to overcome the employer's natural fear that one misdeed will lead to another or that he or she will be ripped off. On the application form, answer this question with the statement that you are willing to discuss it during the interview.

Lack transportation? Possible solutions include riding with a person who works at the organization (offer to pay if necessary), asking a relative or friend for help, public transportation, or walking. Employers want to be reassured that your attendance record will be good. Have a back-up plan if your regular transportation fails.

Alcoholic? This problem must be under control, or else you will get no job. Offer to sign a statement that says you will keep your job only by staying away from alcoholic beverages. This would probably be a condition of employment, anyway.

Reason for leaving a previous job? If you were laid off, obtain a good recommendation from your former employer and include it with an explanation that the layoff was due to lack of seniority, a plant or office closure, or downsizing of the company, and had nothing to do with your work performance. If you quit, indicate a positive reason for leaving—for example, to accept a more challenging position, to complete your education, to fulfill a military obligation, to secure more steady employment, or to make better use of your skills. If you were fired, don't make excuses; state that you have changed whatever it was that caused you to be fired. Employers are afraid of hiring unmotivated employees, drifters, or people with poor work attitudes.

Avoid words or phrases such as "fired," "terminated," "personality conflict," "dissatisfied with employer," or "unhappy with coworkers or supervisors." If your reason for leaving was that you were not on good terms with the previous employer, it may be best to write, "Not enough space to explain here. Am willing to discuss during interview." You can then prepare a response that will explain the circumstances from your viewpoint. (Resist the temptation to say negative things about any previous employer, no matter how aggrieved you feel. A prospective employer is more likely to side with your former employer.)

Poor health? Indicate that you are taking steps to correct the problem. Employers worry that bad health will cause absences and constant complaining on the job. Seek help from a doctor, and tell the employer you are doing so.

Physically or mentally impaired? Explain to the interviewer or employer how any disability will not interfere with the performance of your work duties. Be sure, however, that you can do the job. A doctor's report and an assessment of your job abilities and goals from a rehabilitation counselor are valuable documents as you try to gain employment.

Employers cannot legally discriminate against people with physical or mental impairments if they are otherwise qualified to perform the essential functions of the job. The Americans with Disabilities Act (ADA) of 1990 bans such discrimination in businesses with more than 15 employees. The ADA applies to all employment practices—applications, testing, hiring, firing, advancement, compensation, and training—and all employment-related activities such as recruitment, advertising, tenure, layoff, leave, and benefits (U.S. Equal Employment Opportunity Commission, 1992). Employers must make "reasonable accommodation" to allow disabled people to do the job. Reasonable accommodation is any change in the way the job is usually done to allow equal employment opportunity for a person with a disability. For example, a blind person must be given an application like any other qualified person; reasonable accommodation means that the application must be in Braille or must be read to the blind applicant. The only exceptions to this principle are if the changed work arrangements would impose an "undue hardship" on the operation of an employer's business or if there would be a direct health or safety threat to the disabled worker or to other people. Undue hardship is determined on a case-by-case basis.

Medical problems? Mental problems, heart condition, epilepsy, back ailments, and more recently AIDS/HIV are probably the greatest obstacles to getting a job. Other medical problems include diabetes, bad eyesight, poor hearing, hernia, and serious or frequent headaches. If the problem is under control through medication or medical restoration, indicate this and state on the application form that you are willing to discuss it during the interview. Medical reports, doctors' recommendations, and rehabilitation counselors' reports can help you with these problems. Employers inquire about medical problems because employee medical expenses could increase their insurance costs or limit employees' ability to do the work.

Financial problems? Problems such as bankruptcy, garnishment of wages, or poor credit rating indicate poor planning and irresponsibility to the employer. Try to clear up any debts before you apply for a job. Paying your creditors may be the way to turn this liability into an asset; you can tell the employer that you have fulfilled your obligations.

These are but a few quick answers to complex problems, but they indicate what the nature of your responses could be.

SUMMARY

1. Completing employers' application forms is often an exercise in persistence, patience, and paying close attention to detail. Application forms are usually straightforward, but employers and personnel workers can glean a great deal of information from them. It is illegal for employers to ask applicants certain questions.

2. Inventory your job application strengths, because they will be your key to obtaining an interview and landing a job. Be knowledgeable about your problems, for that is the only way you can deal with them adequately. Preparing answers ahead of time for application forms and interviews will help you to handle difficult questions that develop in the job search.

REFERENCES

Affirmative Action Offices. 1996. *Guidelines for pre-employment inquiries*. Champaign: University of Illinois.

Bolles, R. N. 2000. *What color is your parachute?* (annual editions). Berkeley, CA: Ten Speed Press.

Commission on Human Rights. 2003. *Pre-employment inquiries*. Jefferson City: Missouri Department of Labor and Industrial Relations.

Damp, D. V. 2002. *The book of U.S. government jobs: Where they are, what's available, and how to get one*, 8th ed. McKees Rocks, PA: Brookhaven Press.

Hacker, C. C. 1999. *Job hunting in the 21st century: Exploding the myths, exploring the realities*. Boca Raton, FL: St. Lucie/CRC Press.

Job Service. 1988. *How to complete a job application*. Lansing: Michigan Employment Security Commission.

Kaplan, R. K. 1993. *Pre-employment inquiries: What . . . and what not . . . to ask*. Bethlehem, PA: College Placement Council.

Lipson, M., and McKay, D. R. 2003. *Federal civil service jobs*, 14th ed. Lawrenceville, NJ: Peterson's/Arco/Thomson.

McKinney, A., ed. 2001. *Government job applications and federal resumes*. Fayetteville, NC: PREP Publishing.

Michigan Department of Civil Rights. 1987. *Pre-employment inquiry guide*. Detroit: Michigan Department of Civil Rights.

NACE. 2000. *Pre-employment inquiries: What (and what not) to ask*. Bethlehem, PA: National Association of Colleges and Employers.

Regulations of the Commission on Human Relations. 2003. *Regulation 300: Lawful and unlawful pre-employment inquiries*. Philadelphia: City of Philadelphia. Available online at www.upenn.edu/affirm-action/preemp.htm. Accessed on July 15, 2003.

U.S. Equal Employment Opportunity Commission. 1992. *The Americans with Disabilities Act: Questions and answers*. Washington, DC: EEOC.

Chapter 5

Using Your Research Skills to Get a Job: Geographical Areas

Research is something you have become accustomed to doing in school and college. You have developed skills in gathering information, reading it, examining it critically, and compiling all your newly discovered knowledge into a term paper, complete with footnotes and references. This chapter invites you to use those same investigative skills on your own behalf to obtain information about geographical areas in which you could live and work. Many people allow their work to determine where they will live. Others, however, would rather determine for themselves where they want to live and then find their preferred work environments within those geographical areas.

RESEARCHING GEOGRAPHICAL AREAS OF INTEREST TO YOU

Where you live may have even more impact on your lifestyle than your choice of occupation or workplace. Some people work in a less desired occupation because it allows them to make a living in the geographical area they prefer. The assumption that your job determines where you spend your life does not apply to as many people as it once did. The conflict between job availability and choice of a place to live may not arise in occupations that are found in all parts of the country, unless local employment trends provide a higher supply than demand for workers in a certain occupation. Secretaries, mail carriers, nurses, and teachers, for example, find employment in all parts of the country. People in advertising, however, are concentrated mainly in big cities and are thinly scattered elsewhere. Television performers are centered mostly in New York City and Los Angeles. Oceanographers need to live near the ocean. Personal and family living preferences will also need to be considered, along with employment trends and the location of jobs in the occupation of your choice.

Whether you stay where you are or relocate to another community, weighing the costs and benefits calls for research. You might decide to stay put for a variety of reasons. Perhaps you are emotionally attached to your community and its familiar network of relatives, friends, services, schools, places of worship, neighborhoods, activities, and workplaces. Even if you would be willing to move, your spouse may be happily employed; you don't want to make him or her give up a good job. Whatever the reason, staying where you are located is your choice for now. Even so, you still need to research your home base, particularly the work organizations that employ people in your occupational preferences within reasonable commuting distance.

It is surprising how many people decide to relocate without first conducting any research on the place to which they will move. If you anticipate leaving your present job and moving to another community, start your investigation immediately. Lack of information about an area can be costly, both financially and emotionally. If a company is asking you to relocate, your research may turn up some compelling reason not to move. If you are offered choices, you have all the more reason to compare them through your own investigation. If unemployment is forcing you to look elsewhere, you should research target areas before you commit to another location. At one time, massive unemployment hit the author's home state; people pulled up stakes and took the family where the jobs were supposed to be. Many of those people returned bitterly disappointed, having encountered hostility (due to the competition they represented) and much lower pay rates for any jobs they were offered. The biggest problem for these people was their lack of adequate preparation. They did not assess their own skills or identify qualifications they could offer; they had neither developed contacts and referrals nor enlisted the help of job search resources; they never researched companies and employers in the area, nor did they check out living conditions and housing in the "promised land." They just threw themselves, unprepared and unorganized, into their search, and most of them returned sadder but wiser for the experience.

SOURCES OF AREA INFORMATION

Whether you are investigating a distant place or your hometown, most of the research principles are the same. How do you start? Where do you find information about a particular geographical location? Here are a few ideas:

1. The Internet. If you have access to a computer (home, school, or library), you can research any location in the nation, or the world, for that matter. Use any search engine (such as Google, Yahoo!, MSN, AltaVista), type the location's name into the "Search" box, click the Search button, and away you go. We'll list one Web site here (more follow in this chapter):

- *State and County QuickFacts (http://quickfacts.census.gov).* This is the U.S. Census Bureau's Web site for geographical information. Indicate the state and county, and hit the "go" button. Data on states and counties are compared with national data. You can learn about the makeup of the population, education, housing, income, business characteristics, government, employment figures, land area, and persons per square mile.

2. Local chambers of commerce. Lists of businesses and manufacturers are published by chambers of commerce in the areas they serve. These directories contain addresses, telephone numbers, names of officers, products made or services rendered, and the number of employees working for each company. The information you can obtain from these directories is worth the nominal fee you may pay for them. The local chamber usually publishes a free booklet describing the educational, cultural, religious, recreational, political, and economic life of the community. The chamber's job is to attract new people to the area, so ask them for all the information they can send. Write to the Chamber of Commerce of the United States, 1615 H Street N.W., Washington, DC 20062, for the address of the local chamber in your target city. The national chamber's toll-free phone number is 1-800-638-6582, the main phone number is (202) 659-6000, and the Web address is http://www.uschamber.com.

3. Local newspapers. Subscribe to the local newspaper of your target area for several weeks or months, or access it through its Web site. The newspaper office in your home city should have the name of the newspaper in your target area; its circulation department will mail copies to you. Sunday editions carry the most data about the market for advertised jobs. Newspapers can also give you important information about the community culture, lifestyle, housing, recreation, climate, politics, and education.

4. City, township, and county government offices. You can request information about an area from the office of the city manager or county executive; a city, township, or county clerk's office; or a regional planning office. Local governments may also have an economic agency to attract new business to the area. Ask for the same information they would send a prospective business. In addition, many areas have a consumer affairs department or a Better Business Bureau that can furnish information about the background of local businesses.

5. The Yellow Pages of the local telephone book. Most people look in the Yellow Pages to locate a product or service, so businesses make sure they are listed and advertise there. Headings and cross-references are listed alphabetically, from "Abattoirs—see Slaughter Houses" to "Zippers—Repairing." You will need to locate the telephone directory for your target area, often available at the local library.

6. The city directory. City directories are large volumes divided into major indexes that contain alphabetical lists of names of businesses, manufacturers, institutions, and residents and their occupations. A buyer's guide serves as a link between buyers and sellers in the community. A classified business directory arranges every business by type in alphabetical order, whether the business pays for it or not. A street directory of householders and businesses lists names, addresses, and telephone numbers. A numerical telephone directory is often provided, as well as a statistical and historical record of the city. Write to the local chamber of commerce, city government, or public library and ask how you can purchase a copy. Be warned, though, they are rather expensive, but for many people the expense is worth it.

7. The library in your target city. This is usually the public library, but it could also be a college or hospital library. Determine the information you need to know about the area you are researching, then politely ask the reference librarian in your hometown library to locate and obtain the material you need from the library in the community under consideration. This will involve mailing requests, interlibrary loans, and time. Offer to pay for photocopying and mailing this material.

8. Business and industrial directories. Commercial publishers print such directories on a statewide basis. State governments publish directories of public agencies. (National directories, covered in the next chapter, are not usually indexed by geographical area.) Your hometown library may have state directories in the reference section or may borrow them for you through an interlibrary loan. You can photocopy the geographical section that covers your target area. Usually, areas or cities are listed alphabetically. Each listing contains names of businesses and manufacturing industries, names of company officers, products made or services provided, addresses, and telephone numbers.

9. Local companies and corporations. As a public service, organizations in the community often publish promotional material about the area in which they do business or have a home office. Write to them or visit their headquarters to obtain these publications.

10. Personal contacts. When your target area is the community in which you live now, communicating with personal contacts is relatively easy. Researching a geographical area at a distance, however, requires more effort: making long-distance telephone calls or, better yet, visiting the target area. Some people may balk at the idea of visiting a potential place to live before making a commitment to the area: Why can't the Internet do my research for me? Yes, you can use the Internet to find some information, but think of your job search as being like buying property or a home site unseen in a faraway place. Some people who have done this have found that they invested their life savings in a section of swamp or desert. You don't get the "feel" of a place unless you go there. The costs of being uninformed can be great.

Do your homework on the target area. Before you visit the area, line up several informational interviews, starting with anyone you know. If you do not know anyone there, a personal contact in your hometown may know someone there. Ask for a referral. Have the person write a letter of introduction for you, or write one yourself if he or she is not willing. Your college alumni club, fund-raising office, and career services center keep track of former students; one of them may now be living in your target area. Your religious denomination may have a church, mosque, or synagogue in the area. The clergy are interested in helping people and enlarging their congregations. A group or association you belong to may have a branch in the community; this is a good place to develop additional personal contacts. The variety of groups is almost endless, including service clubs, labor unions, professional associations, political parties, veterans' organizations, ethnic groups, and special interest groups. Don't forget family groups; you may have relatives living in the target area who would be pleased to meet you.

As soon as you have several contacts lined up, set the dates for your visit and let people know you are coming. Consider visiting the area at a time of year when it is least attractive. In a southern state such as Florida, this means July or August. For a northern state such as Minnesota, visit in January or February. Can you or your family tolerate the heat or the snow (Kirkwood, 1993)?

When you get there, use the techniques of informational interviewing outlined in Chapter 7. Always ask your initial contacts to suggest more people for you to interview for information. The referral is the key to expanding your personal contacts. Remember to write thank-you letters to those who help you in your investigation.

In addition to the names of more personal contacts, what are you trying to learn about an area as you talk with people and read material? Subjects may include:

- Population figures
- Civic groups and service clubs
- Housing
- Police and fire protection
- Schools and colleges
- Banks and financial institutions
- Climate and weather
- Type of local government
- Churches, synagogues, mosques

- Cultural activities
- Utility services and costs
- Recreational facilities
- Library facilities
- Tax rates
- Transportation
- Human resources
- Health care

The preceding list provides plenty of topics for any informational interview. Notice that jobs, types of industries, employers, and work organizations haven't even been mentioned yet.

What are you looking for in a geographical area? Use Exercise 5-1, the Quality of Life Inventory, to review or identify features of geographical areas that are important to you. The inventory will help you consider some items you haven't thought of. Take the Cost of Living category, for example. Think of the amount taxes can take out of your budget. Federal income and Social Security taxes are the same wherever you live, but state and local taxes vary greatly. Some states (seven as of 2000) have no income tax; however, they could depend on a hefty state sales tax. Property taxes can differ greatly, too. Paying off a mortgage can be the largest single item in a family budget; the average is 20.1 percent. Savageau and Loftus (1997) found that food costs made up 15.8 percent, transportation costs 16.9 percent, utility costs 7.1 percent, and health care costs 7.36 percent of the average household budget.

The cost-of-living index often tops the list of concerns for people faced with a decision about where to locate. The numbers you see on an index are usually compared with a base rate of 100, which is the average when you take into account the entire country. Anything under 100 means the costs for expenses in that category are lower than average. The further the number is away from 100, the lower the costs. Any numerical index over 100 will indicate higher costs, and as the numbers increase above 100, the higher the costs. Table 5-1 gives the cost of living index for 45 cities in the United States. The composite index is a combination of the items listed before it: grocery items, housing, utilities, transportation, health care, and miscellaneous goods and services readily available across the country. At the top of the table, notice the percentage that each item contributes toward the composite index.

The Internet is a great source of comparative cost-of-living and other data among cities. At the following Web sites, you can enter the name of the city in which you live and the name of the city you want to research. To compare the cost of living, you enter your yearly earnings (or an estimate), click the "go" button, and wait several seconds while the program calculates the equivalent amount in your target city. A few of the many sites you can visit electronically are as follows:

- *ACCRA's Cost of Living Index (http://www.costofliving.org)*. Operated by the American Chamber of Commerce, you can get comparisons of total costs between urban areas. The data in Table 5-1 were drawn from ACCRA, which is an abbreviation for American Chamber of Commerce Researchers Association. There is a charge for this service.
- *BestPlaces (http://www.bestplaces.net)*. Compare two U.S. cities by housing, economic, education, health, crime, and climate factors.
- *Compare Cities (http://houseandhome.msn.com/pickaplace/comparecities.aspx)*. Operated by Microsoft, this site has the usual cost-of-living indexes between two cities. ("If you earn $50,000 in Columbus, Ohio, you will need $73,426 in Los Angeles, California."). However, there are also many data between cities on demographics, schools, crime figures, housing economy, health, and climate (and many variables within each group).
- *Job Star (http://jobstar.org/tools/salary)*. Click on "Salary Surveys," which connects you to more than 300 salary surveys on the Web.

Table 5-1 Cost-of-Living Index for Selected U.S. Cities

Index Weights	16%	28%	8%	10%	5%	33%	100%
City	Grocery Items	Housing	Utilities	Transportation	Health Care	Misc. Goods/Services	Composite Index
Montgomery, AL	92.4	83.2	103.6	97.3	87.0	92.1	90.8
Juneau, AK	126.9	137.2	139.0	128.5	178.5	112.1	128.6
Phoenix, AZ	102.0	84.6	96.8	107.2	111.2	97.5	96.2
Los Angeles, CA	109.6	199.1	110.6	112.9	111.1	109.6	135.2
San Diego, CA	125.4	194.8	79.8	121.9	133.3	115.1	137.8
San Francisco, CA	141.1	332.7	92.4	130.0	143.8	123.7	184.1
Colorado Springs, CO	99.1	103.5	80.5	102.1	113.7	94.0	98.2
Denver, CO	105.5	109.2	75.2	109.5	119.1	98.6	102.9
Washington, DC	116.4	173.3	114.1	123.8	123.9	116.2	133.2
Jacksonville, FL	107.4	85.8	88.3	94.9	88.6	102.4	96.0
Atlanta, GA	101.0	96.2	92.4	102.5	102.0	96.6	97.7
Honolulu, HI	157.6	170.8	167.0	125.4	116.9	120.2	144.5
Chicago, IL	119.7	185.5	116.6	120.7	135.4	110.3	135.7
Springfield, IL	92.5	101.8	88.9	92.6	101.0	90.7	94.6
Des Moines, IA	87.8	87.5	103.7	94.0	99.4	91.5	91.4
Topeka, KS	91.5	90.2	92.4	95.4	90.2	93.8	92.3
New Orleans, LA	98.3	121.3	109.5	102.7	90.6	102.6	107.1
Baltimore, MD	90.6	87.4	103.1	96.0	91.5	97.6	93.6
Boston, MA	114.8	177.3	153.9	106.4	134.8	114.6	135.5
Lansing, MI	97.5	89.0	78.7	96.2	84.9	104.3	95.1
Minneapolis, MN	98.9	103.7	114.1	119.0	121.2	103.5	106.1
Jackson, MS	90.1	94.3	95.4	90.0	80.9	97.3	93.6
St Louis, MO	108.0	93.8	107.2	103.0	97.6	101.2	100.7
Billings, MT	105.2	89.1	83.2	105.2	99.3	95.2	95.3
Omaha, NE	92.0	81.8	87.5	102.5	92.3	89.9	89.2
Las Vegas, NV	107.8	97.8	99.7	109.5	121.6	106.5	104.8
Albuquerque, NM	96.8	94.9	97.5	100.9	98.2	105.6	99.7
Buffalo, NY	122.0	91.0	138.6	107.0	91.6	93.7	102.3
New York, NY	146.8	415.7	155.9	120.2	165.6	138.2	218.3
Charlotte, NC	96.9	86.2	91.3	102.8	91.2	99.2	94.5
Cincinnati, OH	95.9	86.7	104.8	91.1	91.8	100.2	94.8
Cleveland, OH	111.5	96.2	130.9	110.9	106.2	98.6	104.2
Oklahoma City, OK	86.3	79.1	94.7	98.6	94.6	94.6	89.3
Portland, OR	103.5	121.5	109.5	112.4	119.5	106.6	111.7
Salem, OR	101.1	91.9	105.6	100.1	118.3	110.2	102.7
Philadelphia, PA	115.1	132.9	141.0	118.7	133.2	105.4	120.2
Memphis, TN	101.6	78.4	81.6	99.8	88.1	100.1	92.2
Dallas, TX	96.3	92.6	98.4	96.8	100.7	103.2	98.0
El Paso, TX	104.5	78.7	91.0	94.9	107.9	97.4	93.1
San Antonio, TX	76.7	77.8	81.0	85.4	89.7	96.0	85.3
Salt Lake City, UT	110.3	96.1	82.6	100.7	87.9	101.0	99.0
Richmond, VA	107.3	93.0	108.6	101.9	88.1	107.5	102.0
Seattle, WA	116.0	228.2	123.3	111.5	160.3	111.3	148.2
Milwaukee, WI	97.8	106.6	89.5	104.6	94.6	96.2	99.6
Cheyenne, WY	113.4	100.6	95.1	98.3	92.3	103.9	102.7

Notes:

1. The average composite index for the nation is 100 percent. Each city's index is read as a percentage of the overall percentage.

2. Data is from the third quarter of 2002.

3. Miscellaneous goods and services are those readily available across the United States.

Source: ACCRA Cost of Living Index, ACCRA, P.O. Box 407, Arlington, VA, 22210, www.costofliving.org. Retrieved December 22, 2003. Used by permission.

- *Realtor.com (http://www.homefair.com)*. Select "moving from" and "moving to" states. Compare U.S., Canadian, and international cities. Use the Salary Calculator, the Community Calculator, and the Lifestyle Organizer as well as the Moving Calculator, Relocation Wizard, and Military Relocation Wizard.
- *Salary.com (http://swz-hotjobs.salary.com)*. This is Yahoo!'s HotJobs site. Select a job category, enter your closest location or ZIP code, and hit the "calculate" button. You will receive a low, median, and high salary report for the occupation in that location. A second step is to select a more specific job title within the category you chose and then click "create salary report." You can then take the finding for that job and compare it with another city. Another option is to choose a related job and create a salary report for it.

There is more to geographical research than cost-of-living data. Transportation may be crucial to you, especially if you consider time more important than money. Traveling to and from the workplace could take up a significant portion of your life. Time spent in daily commuting generally increases with the size of the city and metropolitan area. Of course, the availability of jobs is an important item. The Department of Labor's electronic Occupational Information Network (O*Net, at http://www.onetcenter.org) and the current *Occupational Outlook Handbook* in book form or online (http://www.bls.gov/oco) will give you national trends. Of course, you want local and regional job trends, so you should go to America's Career Infonet (http://www.acinet.org) and click on "State Info." In Canada, try Canada Workinfonet (http://www.workinfonet.ca); this site will link you to hundreds of other sites in Canada. Chapter 4 in *Taking Charge of Your Career Direction* provides many sources of occupational information for you to use.

Climate affects the quality of life. Temperature differences tend to be reduced by bodies of water, whereas stretches of land such as the Great Plains of North America have great variations of temperature because of the distance from the moderating effects of water. Height above sea level lowers average temperatures. Climate usually has an influence on how we feel and behave, how much we work outside, and what we pay to be comfortable inside.

In addition to cost of living, transportation, and climate, six other categories make up the Quality of Life Inventory (jobs, education, crime, the arts, health care, and recreation), plus a miscellaneous set of characteristics (housing, government, organizations, and religion).

EXERCISE 5-1 QUALITY OF LIFE INVENTORY

Interesting work, earnings, and work environment are important considerations to people making decisions about occupations and workplaces. Another factor is location—the geographical area where a person lives and works. This inventory can help you determine what is important to you about a geographical area. Use the following key to rate each item in the inventory:

3 means the item is *very important* to you.

2 means the item is *of average importance* to you.

1 means the item is *of little importance* to you.

0 means the item is *of no importance*; it does not affect you.

1. *Cost of living.* I want to live in an area where the following costs are *affordable* and *below* the national average:

   ____ state and local income and sales taxes

   ____ local property taxes

   ____ the price of a well-built house

_____ mortgage and/or rent payments (under 15 percent of budget)

_____ utilities (gas, oil, electricity, water)

_____ food costs and restaurant prices (under 12 percent of budget)

_____ housing repairs, furniture, and appliances

_____ health care needs (medical insurance, nursing care, and so on)

_____ transportation (car prices, auto insurance, car repairs, and so on)

_____ education expenses and recreation costs

2. *Transportation.* I want to live in an area that has:

_____ an airport, airline service, and/or passenger rail service

_____ interstate highways close by

_____ uncongested roads, wide streets, and freeways

_____ public transit services (bus, rail, ferryboat, and commuter)

_____ a road system that is well planned and well maintained

_____ truck and rail lines routed away from heavily traveled roads

_____ strong traffic laws enforced against drunk or problem drivers

_____ easily accessible parking for vehicles

_____ longer-than-average life span for cars

_____ reasonable daily commutes to work (not over 20 minutes each way)

3. *Jobs.* I want to live in an area that has:

_____ rapid or above-average population growth (above 10 percent per decade)

_____ high rates of employment (or a low unemployment rate)

_____ high growth rates of employment

_____ a good business climate (lower taxes, fewer regulations, and so on)

_____ many new jobs being created or forecast to be created

_____ a strong manufacturing base and/or many jobs in service industries

_____ recession-resistant industries offering good job security

_____ many job search resources to help people find local employment

_____ salaries and earnings that are above the national average

_____ employers who emphasize the quality of work on the job

4. *Education.* I want to live an area where:

_____ the student–teacher ratio in schools is low; class sizes are small

_____ above-average amounts of money are spent per student

_____ teachers are paid well, even if it means higher taxes or tuition

_____ many opportunities for education are available in local colleges and schools

_____ teachers are accountable through good supervision and competency testing

_____ there is a selection of private schools and/or charter schools

_____ student absence rates are low; school attendance rates are high

_____ many adult, continuing, or lifelong education programs are available

_____ programs exist to involve parents in their children's education

_____ the quality of education is considered excellent and important

5. *Climate.* I want to live in an area that has:

_____ mild temperatures and few extremes of heat and cold

_____ low or moderate wind speeds; little chance of damaging wind

_____ low humidity; the air feels comfortable

_____ lots of clear days and sunshine

_____ moderate rainfall (and/or snow); little risk of flooding or dry spells

_____ changeable seasons (or weather that stays the same all year)

_____ little risk of severe thunderstorms, hail, hurricanes, and tornadoes

_____ small chance of earthquakes and volcano eruptions

_____ mountains and hills (or the terrain is mostly flat)

_____ adequate vegetation and forest growth

6. *Crime.* I want to live in an area where:

_____ people are not crowded together; the area is not densely populated

_____ the weather is mild or cold but not hot and humid

_____ the number of murders, assaults, and burglaries is low

_____ middle-class and well-to-do people predominate; few live in poverty

_____ strong ethnic neighborhoods exist and people know each other

_____ the population is stable and people stay basically the same

_____ rates of arson, alcoholism, drug abuse, divorce, and suicide are low

_____ the transient population is small

_____ the police force is considered strong, fair, and effective

_____ citizens and neighbors look out for each other's safety and property and offer information, identification, and testimony to help stop crime

7. *The arts.* I want to live in an area where:

_____ professional arts and theatrical performances are sponsored

_____ symphony orchestras and/or opera companies perform

_____ dance companies and ballet theaters perform and/or offer instruction

_____ acting companies offer productions and opportunities to perform on stage

_____ public television stations make quality TV programs available

_____ fine arts radio stations offer classical music and jazz programs

_____ art and natural history museums are available

_____ there is a library system with a large number of books and services

____ many artists, actors, writers, dancers, and musicians live

____ stores have quality books, magazines, and newspapers

8. *Health care and environment.* I want to live in an area that has:

____ an adequate supply of doctors in relation to the local population

____ sufficient numbers of hospital beds for the needs of the population

____ hospitals that are attached to medical schools or teaching hospitals

____ a good variety of medical specialists

____ cancer treatment, cardiac rehabilitation, and acute stroke centers

____ good family health and medical services

____ clean drinking water, free of chemical and organic pollutants

____ programs to encourage healthy lifestyles (nonsmoking, exercise centers, etc.)

____ clean air to breathe (air pollution and smog levels are low)

____ little or no ragweed pollen (or other allergens) in the air

9. *Recreation.* I want to live in an area that has:

____ many public or private golf courses

____ many fine restaurants

____ public parks; national or state parks and forests

____ many movie theaters, bowling alleys, and television stations

____ neighborhood eating places, bars, nightclubs, or other social gathering places

____ a zoo and/or an aquarium

____ an amusement or family theme park

____ many intercollegiate and/or professional sports events

____ horse or dog racetracks and/or automobile racetracks

____ skiing facilities, hiking trails, beaches, and/or boating opportunities

10. *Miscellaneous.*

A. *Housing.* I want to live in an area where:

____ most homes are single-family houses with sufficient yard space

____ most houses have three or more bedrooms, large living rooms and kitchens, basements, front porches, patios, more than one bathroom, and so on

____ places with adequate space are easily obtained

____ apartments, condominiums, and/or mobile homes are available

B. *Government.* I want to live in an area where:

____ there is good fire protection and quick response to fire alarms

____ the police provide good personal and property protection

____ responsible local governments provide services effectively and efficiently

____ people are civic-minded and take pride in their community

C. *Organizations.* I want to live in an area that has:

_____ a branch of my professional association, labor union, service club, lodge, and/or social group

_____ civic groups are interested in making improvements in the community

D. *Religion.* I want to live in an area where:

_____ there are churches, synagogues, or mosques of my religious affiliation

_____ religion and its commitments are taken seriously

E. *Other.* Add any item *not* on this inventory that is important to you.

_____ _____

SCORING THE QUALITY OF LIFE INVENTORY

Go back through the inventory and check or circle at least 10 items you consider most important. Save these for future use and thought. This exercise should help you determine which factors to research as you investigate an area. If you want to discover which category is most important to you, add the points you gave the 10 items in Categories 1–9 and record the totals below.

For Categories 10A and B, multiply your total by 2.5.

For Categories 10C and D, multiply your total by 5.

Multiply Category 10E by 10.

Totals in each category can range from 0 to 30.

Now indicate the rank order of each category. The category with the highest number of points should be ranked 1, the next-highest 2, and so on.

Category	Points	Rank
1. Cost of living	_____	_____
2. Transportation	_____	_____
3. Jobs	_____	_____
4. Education	_____	_____
5. Climate	_____	_____
6. Crime risk	_____	_____
7. The arts	_____	_____
8. Health	_____	_____
9. Recreation	_____	_____
10A. Housing (multiply total by 2.5)	_____	_____
10B. Government (multiply total by 2.5)	_____	_____
10C. Organizations (multiply total by 5)	_____	_____
10D. Religion (multiply total by 5)	_____	_____
10E. Other (if used): _____ × 10)	_____	_____

After you score the inventory, refer to the *Places Rated Almanac* (Savageau with D'Agostino, 2000), which rates metropolitan areas in the United States and Canada. A metropolitan area, as defined by the U.S. Bureau of the Census (2002), is a core area containing a large population center, together with bordering communities that have a high degree of social and economic integration with that core. An area qualifies as a metropolitan area if it has a central city of at least 50,000 people or it has an urbanized area of one or more towns of at least 50,000 located in one or more counties with at least 100,000 people (75,000 in New England). Metropolitan areas are usually found within single states, but some of them go across state boundaries. Metropolitan Cincinnati, for example, includes four counties in Ohio, six in Kentucky, and two in Indiana. A list of the U.S. metropolitan areas, arranged alphabetically, appears in Table 5-2.

Table 5-2   323 U.S. Metropolitan Areas, 1990 and 2001 Population (in thousands), and Number of Counties (parishes in Louisiana) Included in Whole or in Part (given in parentheses); Consolidated Metropolitan Areas Are Omitted

Metropolitan Area	Population 1990	2001	Metropolitan Area	Population 1990	2001
Abilene, TX (1)	120	124	Chico-Paradise, CA (1)	182	206
Akron, OH (2)	658	697	Cincinnati, OH-KY-IN (12)	1,526	1,658
Albany, GA (2)	113	121	Clarksville-Hopkinsville, TN-KY (2)	169	207
Albany-Schenectady-Troy, NY (6)	862	878	Cleveland-Lorain-Elyria, OH (6)	2,202	2,246
Albuquerque, NM (3)	589	723	Colorado Springs, CO (1)	397	533
Alexandria, LA (1)	132	127	Columbia, MO (1)	112	137
Allentown-Bethlehem-Easton, PA (3)	595	643	Columbia, SC (2)	454	544
Altoona, PA (3)	131	128	Columbus, GA-AL (4)	261	273
Amarillo, TX (2)	188	219	Columbus, OH (6)	1,345	1,560
Anchorage, AK (1)	226	265	Corpus Christi, TX (2)	350	380
Ann Arbor, MI (3)	490	591	Corvallis, OR (1)*		78
Anniston, AL (1)	116	111	Cumberland, MD-WV (2)	102	101
Appleton-Oshkosh-Neenah, WI (3)	315	363	Dallas, TX (8)	2,676	3,646
Asheville, NC (2)	192	229	Danville, VA (2)	109	110
Athens, GA (3)	126	156	Davenport-Moline-		
Atlanta, GA (20)	2,959	4,263	Rock Island, IA-IL (3)	351	358
Atlantic City-Cape May, NJ (2)	319	358	Dayton-Springfield, OH (4)	951	946
Auburn-Opelika, AL (1)*		117	Daytona Beach, FL (2)	399	510
Augusta-Aiken, GA-SC (5)	415	480	Decatur, AL (2)	132	146
Austin-San Marcos, TX (5)	846	1,313	Decatur, IL (1)	117	113
Bakersfield, CA (1)	545	676	Denver, CO (5)	1,623	2,161
Baltimore, MD (7)	2,382	2,573	Des Moines, IA (3)	393	463
Bangor, ME (1)	92	145	Detroit, MI (6)	4,267	4,448
Barnstable-Yarmouth, MA (1)	135	146	Dothan, AL (2)	131	138
Baton Rouge, LA (4)	528	608	Dover, DE (1)	111	129
Beaumont-Port Arthur, TX (3)	361	383	Dubuque, IA (1)	86	89
Bellingham, WA (1)	128	171	Duluth-Superior, MN-WI (2)	240	243
Benton Harbor, MI (1)	161	162	Dutchess County, NY (1)	259	284
Bergen-Passaic, NJ (2)	1,279	1,378	Eau Claire, WI (2)	138	149
Billings, MT (1)	113	130	El Paso, TX (1)	592	688
Biloxi-Gulfport-Pascagoula, MS (3)	312	366	Elkhart-Goshen, IN (1)	156	184
Binghamton, NY (2)	264	251	Elmira, NY (1)	95	91
Birmingham, AL (4)	840	928	Enid, OK (1)	57	57
Bismarck, ND (2)	83	95	Erie, PA (1)	276	280
Bloomington, IN (1)	109	120	Eugene-Springfield, OR (1)	283	324
Bloomington-Normal, IL (1)	129	152	Evansville-Henderson, IN-KY (4)	279	296
Boise City, ID (2)	296	452	Fargo-Moorhead, ND-MN (2)	153	176
Boston-Worcester-Lawrence-			Fayetteville, NC (1)	275	299
Lowell-Brockton, MA-NH (10)	4,576	6,099	Fayetteville-Springdale-Rogers, AR (2)	211	322
Boulder-Longmont, CO (1)	225	298	Fitchburg-Leominster, MA (2)	138	139
Brazoria, TX (1)	192	250	Flagstaff, AZ-UT (2)	102	124
Bremerton, WA (1)	190	233	Flint, MI (1)	430	439
Brownsville-Harlingen, TX (1)	260	345	Florence, AL (2)	131	143
Bryan-College Station, TX (1)	121	152	Florence, SC (1)	114	127
Buffalo-Niagara Falls, NY (2)	1,189	1,163	Fort Collins-Loveland, CO (1)	186	259
Burlington, VT (3)	152	201	Fort Lauderdale, FL (1)	1,256	1,669
Canton-Massillon, OH (2)	394	407	Fort Myers-Cape Coral, FL (1)	335	462
Casper, WY (1)	61	67	Fort Pierce-Port St. Lucie, FL (2)	251	330
Cedar Rapids, IA (1)	169	193	Fort Smith, AR-OK (3)	176	209
Champaign-Urbana, IL (1)	173	180	Fort Walton Beach, FL (1)	144	173
Charleston-North Charleston, SC (3)	507	555	Fort Wayne, IN (6)	456	504
Charleston, WV (2)	250	249	Fort Worth-Arlington, TX (4)	1,361	1,755
Charlotte-Gastonia-Rock Hill, NC-SC (7)	1,162	1,545	Fresno, CA (2)	756	942
Charlottesville, VA (3)	131	162	Gadsden, AL (1)	100	103
Chattanooga, TN-GA (5)	424	468	Gainesville, FL (1)	182	219
Cheyenne, WY (1)	73	82	Galveston-Texas City, TX (1)	217	256
Chicago, IL (9)	7,411	8,342	Gary, IN (2)	605	634

Metropolitan Area	Population 1990	2001	Metropolitan Area	Population 1990	2001
Glens Falls, NY (2)	119	125	Lewiston-Auburn, ME (1)	94	104
Goldsboro, NC (1)	105	113	Lexington, KY (7)	406	448
Grand Forks, ND-MN (2)	103	96	Lima, OH (2)	154	155
Grand Junction, CO (1)*	93	119	Lincoln, NE (1)	214	252
Grand Rapids-Muskegon-			Little Rock-North Little Rock, AR (4)	513	590
Holland, MI (4)	938	1,103	Longview-Marshall, TX (3)	194	210
Great Falls, MT (1)	78	79	Los Angeles-Long Beach, CA (1)	8,863	9,637
Greeley, CO (1)	132	195	Louisville, KY-IN (7)	949	1,031
Green Bay, WI (1)	195	229	Lubbock, TX (1)	223	244
Greensboro-Winston-Salem-			Lynchburg, VA (5)	194	215
High Point, NC (8)	1,050	1,269	Macon, GA (5)	291	326
Greenville, NC (1)	108	135	Madison, WI (1)	367	433
Greenville-Spartanburg-			Manchester, NH (3)	174	182
Anderson, SC (5)	831	978	Mansfield, OH (2)	174	175
Hagerstown, MD (1)	121	133	McAllen-Edinburg-Mission, TX (1)	384	590
Hamilton-Middletown, OH (1)	291	337	Medford-Ashland, OR (1)	146	185
Harrisburg-Lebanon-Carlisle, PA (4)	588	632	Melbourne-Titusville-Palm Bay, FL (1)	399	490
Hartford, CT (6)	1,158	1,158	Memphis, TN-AR-MS (5)	1,007	1,145
Hattiesburg, MS (2)*	99	113	Merced, CA (1)	178	219
Hickory-Morgantown-Lenoir, NC (4)	292	347	Miami, FL (1)	1,937	2,290
Honolulu, HI (1)	836	881	Middlesex-Somerset-		
Houma, LA (2)	183	195	Hunterdon, NJ (3)	1,020	1,184
Houston, TX (6)	3,322	4,290	Milwaukee-Waukesha, WI (4)	1,432	1,502
Huntington-Ashland, WV-KY-OH (6)	313	314	Minneapolis-St. Paul, MN-WI (13)	2,539	3,016
Huntsville, AL (2)	293	349	Missoula, MT (1)*		96
Indianapolis, IN (9)	1,380	1,632	Mobile, AL (2)	477	546
Iowa City, IA (1)	96	111	Modesto, CA (1)	371	469
Jackson, MI (1)	150	160	Monmouth-Ocean, NJ (2)	986	1,150
Jackson, MS (3)	395	445	Monroe, LA (1)	142	147
Jackson, TN (2)	91	108	Montgomery, AL (3)	293	334
Jacksonville, FL (4)	907	1,131	Muncie, IN (1)	120	119
Jacksonville, NC (1)	150	146	Myrtle Beach, SC (1)	144	202
Jamestown, NY (1)	142	139	Naples, FL (1)	152	266
Janesville-Beloit, WI (1)	140	153	Nashua, NH (1)	168	178
Jersey City, NJ (1)	553	608	Nashville, TN (8)	925	1,252
Johnson City-Kingsport-			Nassau-Suffolk, NY (2)	2,609	2,774
Bristol, TN-VA (7)	436	482	New Bedford, MA (2)	176	175
Johnstown, PA (2)	241	230	New Haven-Bridgeport-Stamford-		
Jonesboro, AR (1)*	69	83	Waterbury-Danbury, CT (2)	1,720	1,714
Joplin, MO (2)	135	159	New London-Norwich, CT-RI (4)	291	259
Kalamazoo-Battle Creek, MI (3)	429	453	New Orleans, LA (8)	1,285	1,333
Kankakee, IL (1)	96	104	New York, NY (8)	8,547	9,334
Kansas City, MO-KS (11)	1,583	1,803	Newark, NJ (5)	1,916	2,042
Kenosha, WI (1)	128	153	Newburgh, NY-PA (2)	336	397
Killeen-Temple, TX (2)	255	314	Norfolk-Virginia Beach-		
Knoxville, TN (6)	586	698	Newport News, VA-NC (15)	1,445	1,583
Kokomo, IN (2)	97	101	Oakland, CA (2)	2,080	2,434
La Crosse, WI-MN (2)	116	128	Ocala, FL (1)	195	268
Lafayette, IN (2)	162	183	Odessa-Midland, TX (2)	226	238
Lafayette, LA (4)	345	387	Oklahoma City, OK (6)	959	1,092
Lake Charles, LA (1)	168	183	Olympia, WA (1)	161	214
Lakeland-Winter Haven, FL (1)	405	493	Omaha, NE-IA (5)	640	723
Lancaster, PA (1)	423	475	Orange County, CA (1)	2,411	2,890
Lansing-East Lansing, MI (3)	433	449	Orlando, FL (4)	1,225	1,707
Laredo, TX (1)	133	201	Owensboro, KY (1)	87	92
Las Cruces, NM (1)	136	177	Panama City, FL (1)	127	150
Las Vegas, NV-AZ (3)	853	1,661	Parkersburg-Marietta, WV-OH (2)	149	151
Lawrence, KS (1)	82	100	Pensacola, FL (2)	344	416
Lawton, OK (1)	111	112	Peoria-Pekin, IL (3)	339	346

(continued)

Table 5-2   (continued)

Metropolitan Area	Population 1990	Population 2001	Metropolitan Area	Population 1990	Population 2001
Philadelphia, PA-NJ (9)	4,922	5,117	Sheboygan, WI (1)	104	113
Phoenix-Mesa, AZ (2)	2,238	3,384	Sherman-Denison, TX (1)	95	113
Pine Bluff, AR (1)	85	84	Shreveport-Bossier City, LA (3)	376	392
Pittsburgh, PA (6)	2,395	2,347	Sioux City, IA-NE (2)	115	123
Pittsfield, MA (1)	89	134	Sioux Falls, SD (2)	139	177
Pocatello, ID (1)*	66	75	South Bend, IN (1)	247	265
Portland, ME (2)	221	267	Spokane, WA (1)	361	423
Portland-Vancouver, OR-WA (6)	1,515	1,965	Springfield, IL (2)	190	202
Portsmouth-Rochester, NH-ME (3)	223	230	Springfield, MA (3)	588	609
Providence-Fall River-Warwick-			Springfield, MO (3)	264	331
Pawtucket, RI (4)	1,124	974	State College, PA (1)	125	136
Provo-Orem, UT (1)	264	377	Steubenville-Weirton, OH-WV (3)	143	130
Pueblo, CO (1)	123	145	Stockton-Lodi, CA (1)	481	595
Punta Gorda, FL (1)	111	147	Sumter, SC (1)	101	104
Racine, WI (1)	175	190	Syracuse, NY (4)	742	731
Raleigh-Durham-Chapel Hill, NC (6)	858	1,232	Tacoma, WA (1)	586	719
Rapid City, SD (1)	81	90	Tallahassee, FL (2)	234	285
Reading, PA (1)	337	378	Tampa-St. Petersburg-		
Redding, CA (1)	147	168	Clearwater, FL (4)	2,068	2,450
Reno, NV (1)	255	353	Terre Haute, IN (3)	148	148
Richland-Kennewick-Pasco, WA (2)	150	198	Texarkana, TX-Texarkana, AR (2)	120	131
Richmond-Petersburg, VA (13)	867	1,010	Toledo, OH (3)	614	618
Riverside-San Bernardino, CA (2)	2,589	3,402	Topeka, KS (1)	161	170
Roanoke, VA (2)	225	236	Trenton, NJ (1)	326	354
Rochester, MN (1)	106	126	Tucson, AZ (1)	667	863
Rochester, NY (6)	1,062	1,097	Tulsa, OK (5)	709	811
Rockford, IL (3)	330	375	Tuscaloosa, AL (1)	151	165
Rocky Mount, NC (2)	133	143	Tyler, TX (1)	151	179
Sacramento, CA (3)	1,340	1,700	Utica-Rome, NY (2)	317	298
Saginaw-Bay City-Midland, MI (3)	399	403	Vallejo-Fairfield-Napa, CA (2)	450	532
St. Cloud, MN (2)	150	170	Ventura, CA (1)	669	771
St. Joseph, MO (2)	98	102	Victoria, TX (1)	74	85
St. Louis, MO-IL (11)	2,492	2,618	Vineland-Millville-Bridgeton, NJ (1)	138	146
Salem, OR (2)	278	352	Visalia-Tulare-Porterville, CA (1)	312	374
Salinas, CA (1)	356	408	Waco, TX (1)	189	215
Salt Lake City-Ogden, UT (3)	1,072	1,349	Washington, DC-MD-VA-WV (25)	4,223	5,054
San Angelo, TX (1)	98	103	Waterloo-Cedar Falls, IA (1)	124	126
San Antonio, TX (4)	1,325	1,627	Wausau, WI (1)	115	126
San Diego, CA (1)	2,498	2,863	West Palm Beach-Boca Raton, FL (1)	864	1,165
San Francisco, CA (3)	1,604	1,720	Wheeling, WV-OH (3)	159	151
San Jose, CA (1)	1,498	1,668	Wichita, KS (3)	485	549
San Luis Obispo-Atascadero-			Wichita Falls, TX (2)	130	137
Paso Robles, CA (1)	217	251	Williamsport, PA (1)	119	119
Santa Barbara-Santa Maria-			Wilmington, NC (2)	171	241
Lompoc, CA (1)	370	400	Wilmington-Newark, DE-MD (2)	513	595
Santa Cruz-Watsonville, CA (1)	230	255	Yakima, WA (1)	189	224
Santa Fe, NM (2)	117	149	Yolo, CA (1)	141	175
Santa Rosa, CA (1)	388	464	York, PA (1)	340	386
Sarasota-Bradenton, FL (2)	489	610	Youngstown-Warren, OH (3)	601	591
Savannah, GA (3)	258	296	Yuba City, CA (2)	123	141
Scranton-Wilkes-Barre-Hazleton, PA (4)	639	620	Yuma, AZ (1)	107	165
Seattle-Bellevue-Everett, WA (3)	2,033	2,439			
Sharon, PA (1)	121	120	United States	248,718	281,422

*New metropolitan area

Note: A total of 323 U.S. metropolitan areas are listed here; 18 consolidated metropolitan areas have been omitted.

Source: U.S. Department of Commerce, 2002.

Places Rated Almanac provides detailed information and rankings of each of 354 metropolitan areas in the United States and Canada for the first nine categories of the Quality of Life Inventory. A cumulative score and an overall ranking for each area appear at the end of the book. About 75 to 80 percent of the U.S. and Canadian population live in these 354 areas.

As you might imagine, ratings such as these stir up quite a bit of controversy. Areas ranked near the top are pleased; those near the bottom think they have been handled unfairly and challenge the conclusions. Be cautious in using the information this or other almanacs provide. You should supplement the material in *Places Rated Almanac* with your own independent verification. In other words, the book contains a lot of good information, but you must confirm it through your own research (especially with personal contacts), as outlined in the first part of this chapter.

Other criticisms are made of this "ratings game." Detractors claim the factors used to rate areas are subjective in nature. You might consider putting more weight on leisure and recreational activities whereas the rater cares more about the availability of jobs in the area. Intangible factors resist being reduced to a numerical weight—natural beauty, for example. One critic suggests that simply watching where people migrate will give you the most accurate indication of the best place to live. In this "livability" ranking of 59 large metropolitan areas, Las Vegas came out well ahead of any other city, more than doubling the score of its nearest competitor, Atlanta (Wall, 1999). To really be accurate in your research using this method, however, you would need to ask the people who relocated to Las Vegas *why* they came there to live. Was it the dry desert air, the sun, the friendly people, gambling ("gaming" is now the preferred term), good food and entertainment, or what? If their reasons matched yours, then you would be onto something. Research, research—you can't get away from it, unless you want to decide life's decisions in ignorance.

Some people desire a certain ambience in the kind of environment in which they want to live. For example, if you like art, a good research book might be *The 100 Best Small Art Towns in America* (Villani, 1996). And although many readers of this book may be young students about to begin their job search, what about the other end of the cycle—retirement? Would you prefer to spend your retirement years in or near a college atmosphere with all of its cultural activities? Maybe you could spot one in *Choose a College Town for Retirement* (Lubow, 1999). In another book, *America's 100 Best Places to Retire* (Fox, 2000), the 10 best towns are picked in 10 categories—art, budget, lake, beach, college, mountain, small, undiscovered, four-season, and low-crime qualities.

Because the other 20 to 25 percent of the population live outside the nation's metropolitan areas, you can consult books on small towns and decide if they are more to your liking. *National Geographic's Guide to Small Town Escapes* (2000), *Making Your Move to One of America's Best Small Towns* (Crampton, 2002), and *America's Most Charming Towns and Villages*, 5th edition (Brown and Stein, 2003) are among those books available on the topic of living in smaller communities. The *National Geographic's* book covers 77 towns that feature bed and breakfast establishments (B&Bs), antique shops, inns, museums, annual events, and local and regional sites. The authors found 11 towns in New England, 12 in the Mid-Atlantic states, 12 in the Southeast, 10 in the Great Lakes area , 12 in the Plains, 12 in the Rockies and Southwest, and 8 in the West.

Is there any middle ground between large metropolitan cities and small towns or villages? The term *micropolitan area* (to contrast it with *metropolitan area*) was developed for 219 areas in *The Rating Guide to Life in America's Small Cities* (Thomas, 1990). Micropolitan areas consist of central cities with at least 15,000 residents in a county of at least 40,000 residents, or other population arrangements of surrounding territories. The features of the 219 micropolitan areas were a greater proportion of young people, friendliness, lack of stress, generally lower level of education, less racial diversity, lower incomes, closeness to nature, and closeness to metropolitan areas. Ratings were given on climate/environment, diversions, economics, education, sophistication, health care, housing, public safety, transportation, and urban proximity.

For many people who have just left college or who grew up in a big city, life in a small town may seem too isolated or just plain boring. They may feel that there is little or nothing to do after work and on weekends except drive to the nearest large city in search of social activities, shopping, and entertainment. Some people will have problems with the lack of privacy in rural areas; everyone knows everyone else, and newcomers are often the objects of great curiosity. Other people really like the more

Figure 5-1 U.S. Metropolitan Areas

Source: U.S. Department of Commerce, Economics and Statistics Administration, Bureau of the Census, 1999.

personalized, slower-paced atmosphere of the smaller community, where the commute to work is easier and living costs are usually lower. Because so many companies offer jobs located in small towns to new graduates each year, geographic location is definitely worth investigating. Figure 5-1 shows the location of the metropolitan areas in the United States; from the map, you can get an idea of where people are concentrated and where they are more spread out.

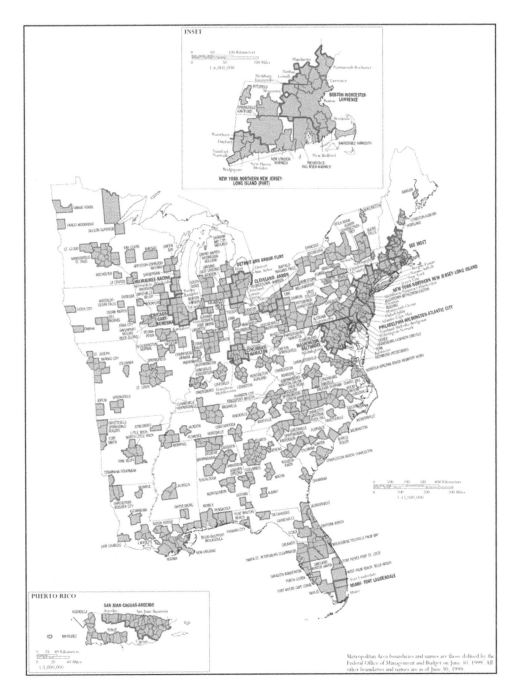

Figure 5-1   U.S. Metropolitan Areas *(continued)*

Table 5-3 Population (in thousands) by State in 1990 and 2000, Percentage Change Between 1990 and 2000, Rankings by State in 1990 and 2000, and Population per Square Mile of Land Area for Each State in 1990 and 2000

State	Population 1990	Population 2000	Percentage Change 1990–2000	Population Ranking 1990	Population Ranking 2000	Population per Square Mile of Land Area 1990	Population per Square Mile of Land Area 2000
Alabama	4,040	4,447	10.1	22	23	79.6	87.6
Alaska	550	627	14.0	49	48	1.0	1.1
Arizona	3,655	5,131	40.0	24	20	32.3	45.1
Arkansas	2,351	2,673	13.7	33	33	45.1	51.3
California	29,811	33,872	13.6	1	1	191.1	217.2
Colorado	3,294	4,301	30.6	26	24	31.8	41.5
Connecticut	3,287	3,406	3.6	27	29	678.5	702.9
Delaware	666	784	22.7	46	45	340.8	400.8
District of Columbia	607	572	–5.7	X	X	9884.4	9316.9
Florida	12,938	15,982	23.5	4	4	239.9	296.3
Georgia	6,478	8,186	26.4	11	10	111.8	141.3
Hawaii	1,108	1,212	9.3	41	42	172.5	186.6
Idaho	1,007	1,294	28.5	42	39	12.2	15.6
Illinois	11,431	12,419	8.6	6	5	205.6	223.4
Indiana	5,544	6,080	9.7	14	14	154.6	169.5
Iowa	2,777	2,926	5.4	30	30	49.7	52.4
Kansas	2,478	2,688	8.5	32	32	30.3	32.9
Kentucky	3,687	4,042	9.6	23	25	92.8	101.7
Louisiana	4,222	4,469	5.9	21	22	96.9	102.6
Maine	1,228	1,275	3.8	38	40	39.8	41.3
Maryland	4,781	5,296	10.8	19	19	489.1	541.8
Massachusetts	6,016	6,349	5.5	13	13	767.6	810.0
Michigan	9,295	9,938	6.9	8	8	163.6	174.9
Minnesota	4,376	4,919	12.4	20	21	55.0	61.8
Mississippi	2,575	2,845	10.5	31	31	54.9	60.6
Missouri	5,117	5,595	9.3	15	17	74.3	81.2
Montana	779	902	12.9	44	44	5.5	6.2
Nebraska	1,578	1,711	8.4	36	38	20.5	22.3
Nevada	1,202	1,998	66.3	39	35	10.9	18.2
New Hampshire	1,109	1,236	11.4	40	41	123.7	137.8
New Jersey	7,748	8,414	8.6	9	9	1044.3	1134.2
New Mexico	1,515	1,819	20.1	37	36	12.5	15.0
New York	17,991	18,976	5.5	2	3	381.0	401.8
North Carolina	6,632	8,049	21.4	10	11	136.1	165.2
North Dakota	639	642	0.5	47	47	9.3	9.3
Ohio	10,847	11,353	4.7	7	7	264.9	277.2
Oklahoma	3,146	3,451	9.7	28	27	45.8	50.2
Oregon	2,842	3,421	20.4	29	28	29.6	35.6
Pennsylvania	11,883	12,281	3.4	5	6	265.1	274.0
Rhode Island	1,003	1,048	4.5	43	43	960.3	1003.2
South Carolina	3,486	4,012	15.1	25	26	115.8	133.2
South Dakota	696	755	8.5	45	46	9.2	9.9
Tennessee	4,877	5,689	16.7	17	16	118.3	138.0
Texas	16,986	20,852	22.8	3	2	64.9	79.6
Utah	1,723	2,233	29.6	35	34	21.0	27.2
Vermont	563	609	8.2	48	49	60.8	65.8
Virginia	6,189	7,079	14.4	12	12	156.3	178.8
Washington	4,867	5,894	21.1	18	15	73.1	88.5
West Virginia	1,793	1,808	0.8	34	37	74.5	75.1
Wisconsin	4,892	5,364	9.6	16	18	90.1	98.8
Wyoming	454	494	8.9	50	50	4.7	5.1
United States	248,791	281,422	13.1	X	X	70.4	79.6

X = Not applicable

Source: U.S. Department of Commerce, 2001.

Concluding this chapter is Table 5-3, which presents 1990 and 2000 U.S. population figures by state, the percentage change from 1990 to 2000, the state's rank in 1990 and 2000, and the population per square mile of land for each state.

SUMMARY

1. Factors to consider about a geographical area that interests you include cost of living, transportation, jobs, education, climate and terrain, crime risk, the arts, health care and environment, recreation, housing, local government, social organizations, and religion.

2. Information about a specific geographical area can be obtained from the Internet, the local chamber of commerce, the local newspaper, government offices, the Yellow Pages of the telephone book, a city directory, libraries, business and industrial directories, local companies, and your personal contacts. If you are researching a distant location, you need to visit the area before making a commitment to move there.

3. The Quality of Life Inventory helps you to assess which of the factors mentioned in the first paragraph of this summary are of the greatest importance to you. A number of electronic and printed resources were given in this chapter to assist you in your research of geographical areas for determining where you want to live.

REFERENCES

ACCRA. 2003. *Cost of living index for selected U.S. cities.* Arlington, VA: U.S. Chamber of Commerce.

Brown, L., and Stein, J. (ed.). 2003. *America's most charming towns and villages,* 5th ed. Cold Spring Harbor, NY: Open Road Publishing.

Crampton, N. 2002. *Making your move to one of America's best small towns.* New York: M. Evans.

Fox, R. L., ed. 2000. *America's 100 best places to retire.* Houston, TX: Vacation Publications.

Kirkwood, C. 1993. *Your services are no longer required: The complete job-loss recovery book.* New York: Penguin Plume.

Lubow, J. M. 1999. *Choose a college town for retirement: Retirement discoveries for every budget.* Guilford, CT: Globe Pequot Press.

National Geographic. 2000. *National Geographic's guide to small town escapes.* Washington, DC: National Geographic Society.

Savageau, D., with D'Agostino, R. 2000. *Places rated almanac: Your guide to finding the best places to live in the United States and Canada,* 6th ed. (special millennium edition). New York: Wiley.

Savageau, D., and Loftus, G. 1997. *Places rated almanac: Your guide to finding the best places to live in North America,* 5th ed. New York: Macmillan Travel.

Thomas, G. S. 1990. *The rating guide to life in America's small cities.* Buffalo, NY: Prometheus.

U.S. Bureau of the Census. 1999. *Metropolitan areas of the United States and Puerto Rico, 1999.* Washington, DC: U.S. Department of Commerce. Available online at http://www. census.gov/geo/www/mapGallery/ma99_2pg.pdf. Accessed February 20, 2004.

U.S. Bureau of the Census. 2001. *Statistical abstract of the United States,* 121st ed. Washington, DC: U.S. Department of Commerce.

U.S. Bureau of the Census. 2002. *Statistical abstract of the United States,* 122nd ed. Washington, DC: U.S. Department of Commerce.

U.S. Bureau of Labor Statistics. 2002. *Occupational outlook handbook* (new editions every two years). Washington, DC: U.S. Department of Labor.

Villani, J. 1996. *The 100 best small art towns in America: Where to discover creative communities, fresh air, and affordable living.* Santa Fe, NM: John Muir Publications.

Wall, H. J. 1999, April. "Voting with your feet" and metro-area livability. *Regional Economist,* 7(2), 10–11.

Chapter 6

Using Your Research Skills to Get a Job: Work Organizations

The following is an adaptation of a story that has circulated on the Internet:

A manager died at a young age, and met St. Peter at the Pearly Gates. "Welcome," he said. "We usually don't expect managers to arrive here. However, we've decided to give you a choice. Heaven or Hell? You choose."

"I think I'd rather be in Heaven," said the manager. "But can you show me Hell first?"

"Yes, that can be arranged," replied St. Peter. "Come this way." He took the manager to a building and motioned to the descending steps. "I can't go with you any further," St. Peter explained. "Just walk down this long flight of stairs. In 12 hours, you must come back here, and we'll show you Heaven."

The manager walked and walked, finally reaching the bottom of the stairs. "Welcome to Hell," a sign announced. The manager saw a group of elegantly dressed people, some of whom had been companions in life. They took the manager to a table where all drank the finest wine and dined on steak and lobster, followed by a luscious dessert. After the meal, they enjoyed much animated conversation, funny jokes, lively dancing, and sparkling entertainment. The manager was having such a good time that the 12 hours were quickly spent.

The manager reluctantly had to be excused and slowly ascended the stairs back to Heaven's gateway and St. Peter. While in Heaven, the manager knelt in prayer, heard inspiring lectures, listened to a concert and a chorus of angels, and contemplated the decision.

At the end of 12 hours in Heaven, St. Peter asked the manager, "Well, have you made your decision?"

"I never thought I'd make this choice," came the reply, "but I think I would rather spend my time in Hell."

"As you wish," said St. Peter, indicating the stairs to Hell.

When reaching the bottom of the steps, the manager was met by the Devil. As far as the eye could see was a scene of desolation. Everyone looked haggard and was dressed in dirty clothes, shoveling piles of manure and picking up disgusting waste.

"I don't get this," cried the manager in alarm. "Twelve hours ago, everyone was well dressed and we had the most wonderful meal and entertainment. What happened?"

"Oh," explained the Devil. "You met our recruiters. Now you're an *employee*." (Adapted from Stitt, 1998.)

(Remember this story when we say, "Research the organization.")

To come back to earth, here's another story:

"Should I accept the offer from ABC Contracts?" a recent college graduate asked. "I really don't know if I should, although I think ABC is better than Design Concepts. It's smaller, not as far away, the salary is okay, and maybe I can move up faster in the organization." Four months later, the graduate was saying, "I wish I'd known then what I know now about this place! The company is close to going under. I don't know if I'll get another paycheck from them. Good people are leaving, and the boss is on cocaine. I've got to start looking again!" (This story is no fantasy; these events actually happened.)

Maybe this job seeker did everything right in the career decision-making and job search process, but one thing was lacking—the job hunter knew next to nothing about the companies she was considering for employment. Now this person is no better off than before, with only a painful learning experience to show for all the effort.

The more you know about work organizations, the better you will perform in a job interview with them. Also, your chances of winning a job offer from the most desirable ones are increased. Investigating companies, firms, corporations, businesses, and institutions is a vital but often neglected element of the job search process. These organizations are groups of people who work together to provide products and services to their customers and clients and to earn profits and rewards for themselves.

Great costumes . . . but this is radio.

All career counselors and job-hunting experts recommend researching the work organization *before* you have a job interview there—and no piece of advice is more often neglected than this one. Ignorance of the company may cost you a job offer if it becomes clear to the interviewer that you know nothing about the organization. Of all the qualities of a successful job seeker, none are more important than knowing about the companies that interest you (Crowther, 1993).

Consider the material in this chapter as essential to your job search. When you present your skills and qualifications to an employer, you know what you can give to the organization. What do you want *from* an organization, besides pay and benefits? As an employee, you will devote much time and energy to a company; therefore, you need to know which qualities of work environments are important to you. Satisfaction at work depends as much on your choice of a workplace as on your choice of an occupation.

You can identify various characteristics of specific companies by examining the companies' organizational charts, corporate cultures, annual reports, and other literature. You can also learn about companies by finding out what others say and write about them. Obtaining this information is a tall order, but you can do it. In fact, you *must* do it if you want to land an appropriate job and achieve satisfaction in your work. Gathering information about workplaces is something you can do even before you begin actively looking for a job, which will require you to do a thousand other things when the time comes.

An organization is a social structure designed for a purpose that a person cannot achieve alone. Civilization depends on organization. Society is organized into economic, political, geographic, and social units, which are subdivided into still smaller units. Thus, organizations exist within larger organizations (Schein, 1980). The purpose of work organizations is to manufacture products or provide services. One principle of company organization is the logical division of work. Similar functions are grouped together, bringing people into divisions or departments such as sales, accounting, personnel, or production units. If the organization grows larger, more responsibility and authority must be delegated and clear lines of organizational authority must be established.

In a bureaucratic work structure, you should know to whom you are responsible—from whom you take orders and to whom you report. Such lines of authority are most clearly indicated in a company's organizational chart, which is a good place to start investigating a work organization. An organizational chart shows lines of authority and responsibility that connect people, job positions, departments, and divisions; however, an organizational chart cannot show everything. An unwritten network of alliances, coalitions, and exchanges of favors develops within any human organization. Informal rules and internal politics give more authority to certain people and departments than to others. Over time, decision-making practices move toward centralization or decentralization and become more autocratic or more democratic. Not much of this will appear on a company's organizational chart.

Many companies today use more informal organizational models in which lines of authority are not as important, everyone deals directly on a person-to-person basis through a network of horizontal and vertical communication lines, and rewards are based more on your performance (Naisbitt and Aburdene, 1985). In a hierarchical company, people attempt to move their careers up the organizational ladder, where all too often (as the Peter principle puts it) they rise to the level of their incompetence (Peter and Hull, 1984). Good teachers, engineers, computer programmers, architects, scientists, artists, and so on, can change into poor or mediocre administrators and managers. Innovative models of work organizations encourage people to stay where they are and to be happy, creative, and productive, enabling them to achieve higher pay and status without having to climb the ladder of success into upper management. In such models, people are more likely to regard one another as equals instead of superiors or inferiors. When they need help, they can turn to their work associates rather than go it alone or call on a manager. A "lattice" or "LEGO" network (Pink, 2001) replaces the career "ladder." This network of people and teams works to complete projects. Few, if any, people hold positions of formal authority. The old organizational chart may be thrown out. Some people find this type of structure exciting and adventuresome, and their inventiveness and hard work are stimulated. Other people, however, may find the innovative work climate too nerve-wracking and stressful; they feel more secure in a bureaucratic workplace where everyone can be found on the organizational chart.

In what kind of an organization do you want to work? The only way you can find out from the outside is to research companies. You can start your investigations now. You don't have to wait until after graduation or when you are actively interviewing for a job, when you may not have sufficient time to do a thorough examination. Begin now and do a little research at a time; over a long period of time, you'll be surprised at how extensive your knowledge of companies has become. This chapter will teach you about characteristics of organizations to consider. This subject could very well be the single most important factor in making you a successful job seeker.

QUALITIES OF EXCELLENCE IN COMPANIES

What are you looking for in an organization? Leadership in a well-managed company is one of many important qualities. In a *Fortune* magazine article on the 10 greatest chief executive officers (CEOs) of all time, writer Jim Collins discovered this: ". . . if one thing defines these ten, it was their deep sense of connectedness to the organizations they ran. Unlike CEOs who see themselves principally as members of an executive elite—an increasingly mobile club whose members measure their pay and privileges against *other* CEOs—this group's ethos was a true corporate ethos, in the original, nonbusiness sense of the word *corporate:* 'united or combined into one'" (Collins, 2003, p. 56).

Managerial leadership has long been a topic of research. An *Economist* article entitled "How to Run a Company Well: Ten Commandments for Successful Leaders" highlighted the necessary qualities:

1. *A sound ethical compass.* If the boss's values are questionable, the company's values and mission are likely to be ambiguous and debatable.
2. *The ability to make unpleasant decisions.* Leadership is not always a matter of winning a popularity contest.
3. *Clarity and focus.* Leading a company often requires the ability to screen out the unnecessary and concentrate on what really matters.
4. *Creative ambition.* The best leaders are empire builders who want to create something that outlasts them; this is different from egotistical personal ambition.
5. *Effective communication skills.* These abilities call for a leader who can talk convincingly, conveying trust and authenticity.
6. *The ability to judge people.* One of the major tasks of leadership is assessing who will work best in which position.
7. *A knack for developing talent.* Learning from a good mentor, leaders must be teachers, transmitting their skills to those around them.
8. *Emotional self-confidence.* Leaders need an ability to work with people who may be better at their jobs than the leaders are at theirs.
9. *Adaptability.* Having the flexibility to change and to devise a completely different approach from a committed one.
10. *Charm.* Not taught, but few get to the top without it (Aisner et al., 2003).

A study of 62 highly regarded companies served as the foundation of a best-selling book, *In Search of Excellence* (Peters and Waterman, 1982). The authors identified eight attributes of excellent companies:

1. *Displaying a preference for action.* Being willing to experiment.
2. *Staying close to the customer.* Learning from the people served.
3. *Fostering autonomy and entrepreneurship.* Encouraging practical risk taking and tolerating failure.
4. *Developing productivity through people.* Respecting the individual by demonstrating trust and adult treatment.
5. *Being clear on those values the company stands for.* Maintaining a belief in being the best, emphasizing the importance of the details in doing the job well.
6. *Being able to "stick to the knitting."* That is, staying reasonably close to the business the company knows and understands.
7. *Maintaining a simple form of organization.* One in which everyone knows how the organization works and who reports to whom.
8. *Having simultaneous loose-tight properties.* A coexistence of firm central direction and maximum individual autonomy.

The qualities in the previous two lists may strike you as rather obvious, but unfortunately, they are all too rare in all too many organizations. Managers may pay lip service to these ideas, particularly in the area of employee relationships, without really believing in them. This attitude then spreads throughout the entire organization. Excellent companies live their commitment to action, customers, autonomy, risk taking, workers, and their values. In visits to the companies they were investigating, Peters and Waterman could sense the intensity of the organization's strongly held beliefs in the expressions of the people who worked there.

Business magazines often describe and rank companies for their qualities of excellence. Two books that began evaluating companies for the general public are *The 100 Best Companies to Work for in America* (Levering, Moskowitz, and Katz, 1994) and *A Great Place to Work* (Levering, 1988). More important than any specific policy is the building of a positive relationship between the company and its workers. Look for these qualities in a company:

- *Continuous two-way communication* between employers and employees (as opposed to secrecy and one-way decision making from the top down)

- *A friendly, informal atmosphere* where people trust each other (as opposed to a rigid social hierarchy and lack of respect)
- *Authentic teamwork* (as opposed to destructive internal politicking)
- *Fair treatment* (as opposed to favoritism, intimidation, and abuse)
- *Work designed to give purpose and meaning* (as opposed to an "it's just a job" attitude)
- A belief that *the company cares about and is committed to its employees* (as opposed to settling for an indifferent relationship)

A good workplace offers a genuine sense of community in a society where people have become increasingly isolated from one another. You look for a workplace in which you trust the people you work for, have pride in what you do, and enjoy the people you work with (Levering, 1988).

Beyond the nature of the relationship between employer and employees, great workplaces have all or most of these attributes:

- Wages and benefits that are considered fair and equitable
- Job security, meaning no layoffs or the organization tries not to lay off people without making an effort to place them in other jobs
- Commitment to a safe, healthy, and attractive work environment
- Procedures to provide workers with ways of taking on increasing responsibility for their own work
- Flexible working hours such as flextime, in which employees on eight-hour shifts can arrive at work from 7:00 to 9:00 A.M. and leave between 3:00 and 5:00 P.M.
- Opportunities for growth through promoting from within, in-house training programs, and tolerating mistakes as a part of learning
- Reduction of the social distance between managers and workers
- Rights of due process, meaning procedures exist by which decisions that employees consider unfair can be appealed
- Access to full and accurate information, not a whitewashed company line (exceptions might include other employees' personnel records and plans that could be used by competitors)
- Right of free speech without fear of retribution
- Right to confront those in authority
- Right of workers doing a good job to retain individual autonomy and not be socially pressured into conforming to a company image
- Sharing in company profits and rewards that result from the improved work of employees
- A share in the ownership of the company
- Recognition of work efforts; acknowledgment of a worker's contributions to the organization (Levering, 1988)

What should you watch out for and try to avoid in a workplace? Possible answers include:

- Arbitrary rule making by an authoritarian management.
- Abusive supervision that creates a master–slave relationship unless it is checked.
- Disregard for employee health, safety, and well-being. Work-related illnesses can reveal signs of a bad workplace for its employees.
- Higher priority for machines and systems than for people. A popular image of a rigid, mechanical approach to work is the factory assembly line of the industrial age, with its counterpart now firmly entrenched in the modern office. Jobs in this environment are likely to be monotonous, boring, repetitious, mindless, deadening, and dehumanizing. As a result, workers feel as though they are appendages to a machine, robots, or cogs in an endlessly revolving wheel.

- Manipulative methods of control over workers. One such technique is the "divide and conquer" strategy that pits workers against each other for political benefits gained by management. Another method is the subtle use of benefits and gifts to create a feeling of gratitude and indebtedness on the part of the worker toward the employer. Here, the gift is a bribe to secure influence over an employee. This contrasts starkly with the employer who gives rewards as a way of acknowledging and recognizing the employee's gift of work—something that makes the benefits possible. The motivation for the reward makes all the difference (Levering, 1988).

ORGANIZATIONAL CHARTS

Workplaces are organized around functions. As a company grows, it develops more functions, and the organizational chart becomes more complex. Typical functions are management, manufacturing or providing a service, marketing, maintenance of the physical plant, personnel, and accounting. In a one-person business, one person handles all functions, whereas in large companies hundreds of people can work on one function.

The growth of an organization creates additional jobs because the divisions of work become smaller and functions performed within the company expand. Engineers, researchers, technicians, and production workers are hired to design and make the product. Professionals, paraprofessionals, aides, and service workers are employed to perform the service the organization provides to the public. Advertising workers, salespeople, market researchers, and public relations staff are hired to promote and sell the product or service. Personnel workers are needed to interview, hire, and train employees, and a maintenance crew is required to keep the plant and offices operating efficiently. Management coordinates the efforts of the entire organization.

Large organizations will have a complex division of work. For example, hospitals have many occupations within their organizational structures, and some of those occupations you would not ordinarily associate with a hospital. To give you an idea of a hospital as a work organization, Table 6-1 shows occupational employment estimates made by the U.S. Bureau of Labor Statistics for major occupational categories and specific occupations (Wootton and Ross, 1995).

If you intend to work in an organization of any size, where will you fit in? Before you apply and interview at a company, examine its organizational chart and try to determine the division, department, or unit responsible for the work functions you can do and are interested in doing. Once you have identified your most appropriate workplace on the organizational chart, you can focus your attention on it and center your research around it. Doing your homework on an organization means reading whatever you can about it and talking with people who work within the department you have targeted.

The organizational chart shows the formal structure of the company. The oldest and simplest structure is the **line organizational structure**, where clear lines of authority are drawn and each person is directly responsible to one supervisor. Figure 6-1 illustrates the higher levels of a line structure. As an organization grows in size and diversity, a **line-and-staff organizational structure** emerges as line managers require the services of staff specialists to perform the increasingly complex functions of their departments. Line authority involves supervision, discretion, and disciplinary action if needed.

Staff authority does not have these responsibilities; rather, it involves assistance, advice, information, and expertise. Whatever authority a staff person or department possesses comes from the power of knowledge, persuasion, and reputation. A more interactive form of structure is the **matrix organization,** which has both vertical and horizontal lines of authority and communication. They serve to

(continued on page 166)

Divisions	Departments	Branches

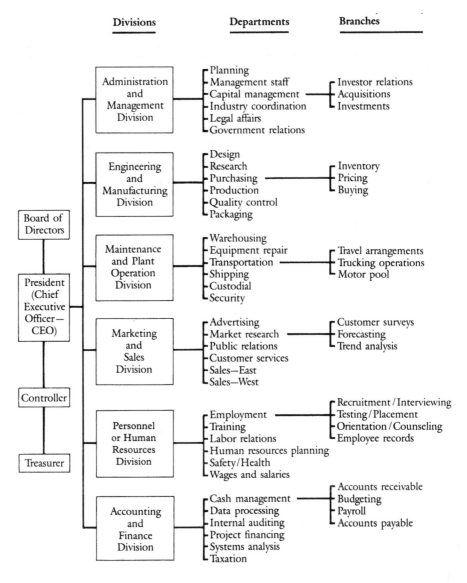

Figure 6-1 Organizational chart of a company

Table 6-1 Employment in U.S. Hospitals, 1992

Occupation	Employment*	Percentage of Total Employment
Total	**4,757,720**	**100.00**
Adjustment clerks	10,230	.22
Ambulance drivers and attendants	2,540	.05
Billing, cost, and rate clerks	43,820	.92
Boiler operators and tenders	5,240	.11
Bookkeeping, accounting, and auditing clerks	27,750	.58
Cardiology technologists	13,960	.29
Cleaning and building service workers (maids, janitors, cleaners)	177,520	3.73
Clergy	5,160	.11
Computer scientists, systems analysts, programmers, etc.	23,560	.50
Construction trades (carpenters, electricians, painters, paperhangers, plumbers, pipefitters, etc.)	21,340	.45

(continued)

Table 6-1   (continued)

Occupation	Employment*	Percentage of Total Employment
Corrective and manual arts therapists	950	.02
Dental assistants	2,210	.05
Dental hygienists	940	.02
Dentists	1,780	.04
Dietitians and nutritionists	15,980	.34
Dietetic technicians	11,200	.24
Electrocardiography technicians	13,790	.29
Electroencephalograph technologists	5,250	.11
Emergency medical technicians	28,300	.59
Engineering technicians and technologists	4,060	.09
Engineers (civil, mechanical, computer, electrical, electronic, industrial, and other)	7,900	.17
File clerks	18,720	.39
First-line supervisors (clerical and administrative)	46,800	.98
First-line supervisors (production, construction, maintenance)	8,830	.19
Food service workers (servers, bakers, cooks, etc.)	193,520	4.07
Gardeners, groundskeepers	6,390	.13
General office clerks	151,510	3.18
Guards	35,200	.74
Hand workers, including assemblers and fabricators	730	.02
Helpers, laborers, and material movers (hand)	10,000	.21
Home health aides	18,900	.40
Housekeepers	37,500	.79
Human service workers	9,050	.19
Interviewing clerks, except personnel and welfare	53,240	1.12
Librarians, professional	2,400	.05
Licensed practical nurses	256,960	5.40
Life scientists (biological and medical)	8,340	.18
Managerial and administrative (top executives, financial, labor relations, purchasing, marketing, public relations, health services, food services, lodging, and general managers)	217,650	4.57
Management support (accountants, auditors, budget analysts, etc.)	68,280	1.43
Material recording, scheduling, dispatching, and distributing workers (including ambulance dispatchers, stock clerks, and shipping-receiving)	47,000	.99
Mechanics, installers, and repairers	47,210	.99
Medical assistants	12,030	.25
Medical and clinical lab technicians	49,800	1.05
Medical and clinical lab technologists	97,380	2.05
Medical records technicians and technologists	34,730	.73
Medical secretaries	52,130	1.10
Motor vehicle operators	7,700	.16
Nuclear medicine technologists	10,900	.23
Nursing aides, orderlies, and attendants	299,850	6.30
Nursing instructors	10,310	.22
Occupational therapists	16,580	.35
Occupational therapy assistants and aides	6,060	.13
Office machine operators and data processing (billing, posting, calculating machine, computer, and data entry)	30,380	.64
Order clerks, material, merchandise, and service	5,290	.11
Other clerical and administrative support workers	47,010	.99
Other construction workers	3,180	.07

Occupation	Employment*	Percentage of Total Employment
Other health diagnosing and treating practitioners	2,330	.05
Other health professional and technical workers	91,190	1.92
Other health service workers	75,960	1.60
Other professional and technical workers	24,710	.52
Other service workers	10,720	.23
Other service supervisors	18,130	.38
Other therapists	7,760	.16
Other transportation and material moving workers	1,440	.03
Parking lot attendants	2,190	.05
Payroll and timekeeping clerks	8,080	.17
Personal service workers (child, home care)	10,550	.22
Personnel clerks, except payroll and timekeepers	7,000	.15
Pharmacists	44,920	.94
Pharmacy assistants	37,870	.80
Photographers	1,070	.02
Physical and corrective therapy assistants	18,970	.40
Physical and life science technicians and technologists	5,090	.11
Physical scientists	770	.02
Physical therapists	29,020	.61
Physicians and surgeons	97,050	2.04
Physicians' assistants	8,680	.18
Precision production workers	580	.01
Procurement clerks	4,560	.10
Psychiatric aides	55,240	1.16
Psychiatric technicians	58,520	1.23
Psychologists and other social scientists	13,470	.28
Public relations specialists and publicity workers	5,090	.11
Radiologic technicians	35,870	.75
Radiologic technologists	57,430	1.21
Receptionists and information clerks	37,540	.79
Recreational therapists	12,280	.26
Registered nurses	1,178,950	24.78
Respiratory therapists	66,300	1.39
Sales workers, including cashiers	16,920	.36
Secretaries, except legal and medical	93,550	1.97
Social workers, medical and psychiatric	54,020	1.14
Social workers, other	11,740	.25
Speech pathologists and audiologists	8,220	.17
Stationary engineers and other plant and systems workers	8,120	.17
Statistical clerks	19,800	.42
Stenographers	25,740	.54
Surgical technicians	40,220	.85
Switchboard operators	32,120	.68
Teachers and instructors, including vocational	20,130	.43
Technical assistants, library	1,720	.04
Textile workers (laundry, drycleaners, pressing machine operators, etc.)	19,960	.42
Typists, including word processing	31,900	.65

* Estimates for specific occupations with fewer than 50 workers or with less than 0.01 percent of industry employment have been counted in the appropriate "Other" or summary-level category.

Source: Based on U.S. Department of Labor, March 1995.

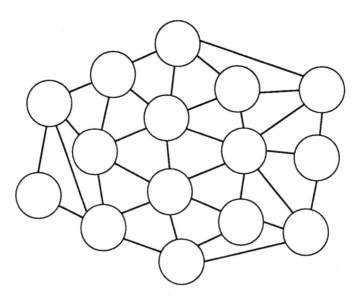

Figure 6-2 The committee form of organization

coordinate functions between departments and require teamwork and compromise in management. Finally, the **committee** form of organization (see Figure 6-2) furthers employee participation, communication, networking, and decision making. Committees can give workers a sense of partnership with the organization, implying a more democratic style of management. However, committees can be counterproductive if they require too much compromise for strong decisions, are perceived as wasting time, or continue to exist after their objective has been reached (Chruden and Sherman, 1980).

The committee form is similar to the *weblike* structure that characterizes many organizations today. Despite their appearance to people on the outside, these companies are very much in transition. They are converting their hierarchical, pyramid-shaped arrangements into new patterns that emerge more like a spider's web. At the center are idea people, with problem identifiers and problem solvers constantly spinning remodeled connections with each other. The newly designed work organizations may still have chief executive officers and managers, but power is decentralized and decisions are often distributed to teams or committees working on common tasks. Separate business units inside the work organization may have the authority to develop their own products and market them; however, the company may also contract with outside suppliers. Movie studios, for example, once produced the entire motion picture. Now the studio contracts on a project-by-project basis with independent producers, directors, actors, screenwriters, cinematographers, and crews using rented space and equipment; they also contract with independent distributors to get their films into appropriate theaters (Reich, 1992).

More than ever before, organizations are experimenting with novel approaches to cope with the increasing speed and complexity of the environment around them. Companies have gone through countless restructurings, redesigns, re-engineerings, and so on. One new corporate model for the new age is the **centerless corporation** (Pasternack and Viscio, 1998). Centerless doesn't mean leaderless, but it does mean getting away from the command-and-control model that has characterized the hierarchical nature of organizations during the industrial era. A core of functions, not a center, coordinates the mission of the organization.

Organizations other than businesses and corporations also have organizational charts. The school you attend is an organization. Perhaps your school's organizational chart looks somewhat like Figure 6-3, but maybe it is changing, or has changed, from this more traditional line-and-staff structure.

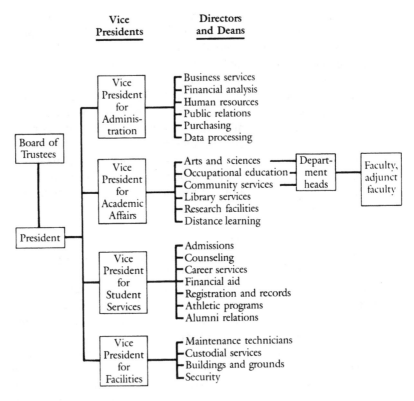

Figure 6-3 Organizational chart of an educational institution

When you have studied the official structure, your inquiry should turn to the informal social, political, and communication patterns that exist in the company. These are not revealed on an organizational chart. They are a set of invisible qualities, a way of getting things done—an organizational culture—which may be more influential than any formal system mapped out on paper.

ORGANIZATIONAL CULTURES

Every organization creates, maintains, and changes its culture and passes it on to succeeding generations. Companies develop their own assortment of values, beliefs, traditions, heroes, ceremonies, and histories. Strong corporate cultures create a set of informal rules that guide behavior, make people more productive, and enable employees to feel better about the work they do. They have provided the social energy for the successes of many organizations.

In your research of organizations, become knowledgeable about their cultures. Some of this information may not be apparent until you have read some material and talked with a number of people. Even then, you may not be certain what factors make the company tick. Corporate personalities are no less mysterious than individual human personalities. At times, you may wonder if learning about the organization's culture is worth all the effort. If you are dedicated to finding the work organization that matches your personality and will advance your career goals, you will persist in your investigations.

This is particularly true when you examine such an indefinite subject as corporate culture. Stick with your research; this is where you get close to the essential character and vital spirit of an organization.

What, exactly, is meant by *organizational culture*? Different people use the term to mean different things. Organizational culture has been described as observed behavioral regularities, or norms that develop in work groups (such as "a fair day's work for a fair day's pay"). The corporate culture may reflect the dominant values expressed by an organization, a philosophy that will guide policy toward employees and customers. Included are also "the rules of the game" for getting along (the ropes a newcomer must learn to become accepted), the feeling communicated by the physical layout, and the way in which members of the organization interact with customers and other outsiders. Schein (1985) advances a concept of organizational culture that involves a deep set of assumptions and beliefs the members of an organization share. Because these assumptions and beliefs have worked repeatedly, they are likely to be accepted uncritically and to recede from awareness. Without knowing the underlying assumptions on which an organization is based, much of the behavior that is observed cannot be understood. For example, workers may conflict with authority figures while at the same time they have intense loyalty to the organization. In this case, the underlying assumption could be: "We are one family who will take care of each other."

Deal and Kennedy (1982) specify several key elements of corporate culture. First are the *core values*; these form the bedrock of a company's philosophy for achieving success and are held by managers and employees alike. Shared values explain the fundamental character of the company. To outsiders, company values may appear to be platitudes, but to people within the organization they represent qualities that distinguish their company from all others. Values create a sense of identity for people in the organization, making them feel special.

Organizations often issue value statements. Some companies have attached a mystical, almost magical, quality to them. These declarations may be designated "mission" or "vision" statements that all employees are called upon to follow. Some corporate value statements are simply empty rhetoric; in other companies, however, they represent a sincere attempt to capture the essential character of the organization. A genuine value statement involves everyone within the company in its creation; it is clear, short, avoids phony exaggerations, and is actually put into practice consistently by the organization. If a sign on a wall says "People are our most precious asset" but the company has just laid off thousands, employees will be skeptical of anything the organization tries to do (Farnham, 1993). If a company proclaims "24-hour parts service anywhere in the world" or "productivity through people," these phrases cannot simply be advertising slogans; people belonging to the organization must deeply believe in them. Your research should identify the shared values and beliefs of the company and the actions that reinforce them. You should then ask yourself, "Are their values my values?" (Or, at least, "Are my values similar to theirs?")

One way to discover the values of an organization, according to Deal and Kennedy (1982), is to examine the organization's heroes, rituals, and ceremonies. Heroes represent the company's values and become models for workers to imitate. Rituals, or procedures to get jobs done, offer security to workers. Whereas rituals are commonplace, ceremonies are exceptional events by which the organization bestows awards and recognition. All heroes, rituals, and ceremonies possess great symbolic worth in upholding the values and philosophy of the organization.

Bridges (1992) prefers the term *organizational character* instead of *culture*, believing culture has too many meanings, can be misleading, and is useful only in describing patterns that have developed slowly and unconsciously. The idea of character is adapted from individual psychology and carried over to the organization.

Other elements of the corporate culture are the **communications network** and the **business environment.** Storytellers, gossips, spies, and interpreters of events form the hidden system for circulating information. Often called the grapevine, such word-of-mouth communication is the primary means of exchanging information within the company. Your research will be greatly enhanced if you can tap into this informal communications network. But above all else, the influence that most shapes a corporate culture is its business environment: the company's products, competitors, customers, and technologies and the marketplace and government regulations within which it operates. The business environment shapes what the company must do to achieve success.

TYPES OF CORPORATE CULTURE

In their quest for success, companies create several types of corporate culture. Deal and Kennedy (1982) propose four generic cultures: the tough-guy, macho culture; the work hard/play hard, or action culture; the bet-your-company culture; and the process culture. None of these types precisely describes a single company. A mix of all four cultures can be found in separate parts of an organization. Marketing divisions often develop a tough-guy culture of high risks and quick feedback on performance. Sales and manufacturing departments work hard and play hard in an active atmosphere of rapid feedback (either you make a sale or you don't), but of lower risks (no one product or sale is going to make or break you). Research-and-development people operate in an environment of high risk and slow feedback; the company bets its future on a new product, but it takes a long time to find out whether the product is a success. Accounting is process oriented and fits into a bureaucratic mold of low risk and low feedback. Figure 6-4 graphically summarizes the four corporate cultures in terms of risk and feedback.

Tough-guy, macho. The most nerve-wracking of all business cultures is the tough-guy, macho culture of high risks and high feedback. Construction, management consulting, venture capital, advertising, sports, and the entertainment industries fall into this category. Financial stakes are high. Advertising campaigns, expensive construction projects, and multimillion-dollar movies are typical enterprises of this culture. Their all-or-nothing nature makes for a fast-paced tempo rather than for endurance or persistence. Decisions must be made quickly, and the risk of failure dictates a tough attitude (at least on the surface) in order to survive in this culture.

Work hard/play hard, or action. This culture can be seen in most sales organizations—real estate, computers, automobiles, door-to-door operations, fast-food franchises, office equipment manufacturers, and retail stores. The primary values of this culture center on the needs of the customer. Success does not necessarily result from making and selling better products, but rather from creating a high volume of business. A team, not an individual, produces the volume. An action orientation permeates the culture; the worst thing you can do is stand still. "Try it, fix it, do it" is the prevailing ethic. Managers tell their workers that the race is to the swift. Develop initiative, they

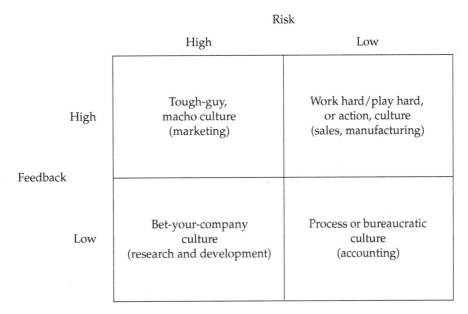

Figure 6-4 Risk and feedback in four corporate cultures

say, get moving, and stay in the race. The action culture is better than any other type at providing the mass-produced goods people want.

Bet-your-company. In this culture, a project takes years to develop before the organization knows whether it will succeed. Deal and Kennedy (1982) place capital goods companies, mining companies, large-systems businesses, oil companies, investment banks, architectural firms, computer design companies, and the actuarial part of insurance companies in this category. The values of this culture concentrate on investing in the future. People must develop the stamina to tolerate uncertainty, with no feedback over long periods. In this culture, careers, products, and profits are not developed quickly, but they last a long time when success is finally achieved.

Process. This culture includes banks, insurance companies, financial services, many government agencies, utilities, and heavily regulated industries such as pharmaceuticals. No one transaction is likely to bring boom or bust to the company. When feedback comes, attention often takes the form of blame. Government workers, for example, may receive recognition only when someone accuses them of inefficiency, corruption, or violating the public trust. These workers learn to be cautious and protect themselves as best they can. Process culture workers are seldom able to measure the results of their work, so they concentrate on how the job is done. The central values of this culture are attention to detail and systematic procedures.

Because the preceding classification of corporate culture may seem most appropriate to business firms, you might want to try other ways of classifying organizational cultures. The six types of work environments proposed by Holland (1997) come to mind. A **realistic** work environment is practical and mechanical, **investigative** is scientific and intellectual, **artistic** is expressive and intuitive, **social** is helpful and cooperative, **enterprising** is dynamic and competitive, and **conventional** is orderly and systematic. At least, that's the way the people see their work environments. Refer to Chapter 3 of the first book in the Career Planning Guide series for more complete descriptions of these types. No one type exists exclusively throughout entire organizations or even departments; a combination of cultures exists within structures. Production, maintenance, and custodial departments usually exhibit predominantly realistic qualities. Research and engineering divisions are likely to be investigative; advertising, artistic; public relations and human resources, social; executives and salespeople, enterprising; and accounting, data processing, and clerical areas are typically conventional. You can look for an appropriate match between your own personality and the cultural characteristics of a division within an organization.

The 16 personality types from the **Myers-Briggs Type Indicator (MBTI)** are used to describe organizational culture, or character. The 16 MBTI types come from two orientations that form four scales: extraversion–introversion (E–I), sensing–intuition (S–N), thinking–feeling (T–F), and judging–perceiving (J–P). These personal preferences, or orientations, are described in Chapter 3 of *Taking Charge of Your Career Direction*. Here, our focus is on organizations. Which preference among each of the four scales, described next, appeals to you? If you have taken the MBTI, are your preferences here similar to the ones on the inventory?

1. *E–I.* Extraverted organizations respond to external forces and look outward toward the market and customers, allowing more access and collaboration by others in their decision making. Introverted organizations look inward and draw energy from their own resources or leaders' visions, tending to rely on themselves when making decisions.
2. *S–N.* Sensing organizations are highly organized, handle masses of data and detail, trust actual experience and routine procedure, change slowly one step at a time, and are more at home in the present. Intuitive organizations are more loosely organized, look at the big picture, see possibilities, are more

likely to change by transforming things radically, and are more future oriented.

3. *T–F.* Thinking organizations apply principles logically in making decisions, are more concerned with products and services than the human element, expect employees to meet an objective standard, look at everything critically, and prize efficiency. Feeling organizations apply principles by what the organization values, emphasize the human dimension when making decisions, encourage their workers to do their best in a supportive way, and prize harmony as a social community.

4. *J–P.* Judging organizations prefer to reach firm decisions, spell things out clearly, and close out other options; they may run the risk of making decisions prematurely or on insufficient information. Perceiving organizations prefer to keep their options open, seek more information, and tolerate dissenting opinions—but risk avoiding a decision when one should be made.

Bridges (1992) describes the 16 types of organizations based on the preference developed from each of the four scales of the MBTI in his book, *The Character of Organizations.* The character of smaller departments or subdivisions may be quite different from that of the larger company. The smaller unit is likely to be more distinctive and have a more easily identifiable set of characteristics than the larger one.

Haberman (1983) writes of six cultures that define teacher and student roles in urban school settings: therapeutic, compensatory, business, intellectual, advocacy, and creative. As with Holland's types, each setting involves a combination of types, with the dominant type given as the title of the culture.

1. In a **therapeutic** setting, teachers act as therapists and view their students as clients, helping them to overcome handicaps. The therapeutic culture influences people to adjust and cope in their environment.

2. Teachers in a **compensatory** setting see students as learners who haven't learned as much as they should have. They aim to correct deficiencies with a test–teach–retest process. The teacher is coach, cheerleader, mentor, and instructor. This culture shapes people to strive and persist in their environment.

3. In a **business** setting, where school behavior is thought to be transferable to work behavior, people are influenced to produce. Schedules of production evaluate students. People are shaped to set goals and compete with others.

4. In an **intellectual** setting, the pursuit of ideas is the primary goal. Thoughtful analysis, reflection about the world, and basic insights are valued more than are their applications to the world. Teachers model the scholar and researcher; students follow in their footsteps on a more elementary level. The teaching process in this setting is one of hypothesizing, testing, thinking, and forming new hypotheses.

5. An **advocacy** setting brings the realities of direct life experiences into the school culture. The school is the society in miniature; teachers present real-life problems, conduct further discussion on them, and prod students to create solutions. This culture motivates people to become involved in a problem-solving process, take action, and promote change.

6. A **creative** setting encourages practice and mastery of skills considered essential to performing an art or a discipline. Once this is accomplished, people are free to express those skills. The teacher is judgmental in the learning phase but becomes almost entirely nonjudgmental and noninterfering in the creative stage.

You have probably experienced several of these school settings as a student. Reframe the teacher–student relationship of your school setting as the supervisor–worker relationship of an organizational culture. Which would you find most compatible with your personality?

There is one more classification scheme you can use to analyze organizational cultures. It is the simplest to use and the easiest to remember, which is why it was chosen. Your introduction to it will involve taking an inventory, the Work Organization Environment Survey (WOES), in Exercise 6-1. In this exercise, you will rate a series of characteristics according to their importance to you for your ideal work organization. If you are now working, you can rate your current workplace on the same characteristics. Types of organizational cultures will be identified for you after scoring so you can compare your ideal with your real work organization.

EXERCISE 6-1 WORK ORGANIZATION ENVIRONMENT SURVEY

Please read the instructions and complete the following survey before you read further. Before you begin, make several photocopies of the blank form for future use.

In the left column, circle the number that indicates the importance of each characteristic in your ideal work organization, using the following scale:

0 = not important

1 = somewhat important

2 = important

3 = very important

If you are now working or have recently worked in an organization, in the right column, circle the number that most accurately describes your current or recent work organization.

My Ideal Work Organization				Key: 0 = Not Important 1 = Somewhat Important 2 = Important 3 = Very Important	My Current or Recent Work Organization			
0	1	2	3	Has specific written procedures to follow	0	1	2	3
0	1	2	3	Promotes individual creativity and expression	0	1	2	3
0	1	2	3	Encourages close working relationships	0	1	2	3
0	1	2	3	Emphasizes systematic, efficient operation	0	1	2	3
0	1	2	3	Has spirited, active, dynamic people	0	1	2	3
0	1	2	3	Has friendly, warm, sociable people	0	1	2	3
0	1	2	3	Has clear lines of authority and responsibility	0	1	2	3
0	1	2	3	Develops a competitive, challenging environment	0	1	2	3
0	1	2	3	Has people who trust and help one another	0	1	2	3
0	1	2	3	Has rules that closely control people's behavior	0	1	2	3
0	1	2	3	Drives people toward excellence and success	0	1	2	3
0	1	2	3	Fosters cooperative behavior between people	0	1	2	3
0	1	2	3	Is well established, with a solid reputation	0	1	2	3
0	1	2	3	Is enterprising, adventurous, and entrepreneurial	0	1	2	3
0	1	2	3	Is safe, comfortable, and secure	0	1	2	3
0	1	2	3	Has a cautious, stable management style	0	1	2	3
0	1	2	3	Is forward-looking with a sense of optimism	0	1	2	3
0	1	2	3	Has supervisors who give encouragement and praise	0	1	2	3

0	1	2	3	Stresses position, titles, rank, and status	0	1	2	3
0	1	2	3	Encourages risk taking and high expectations	0	1	2	3
0	1	2	3	Emphasizes fair and equal treatment	0	1	2	3
0	1	2	3	Develops work roles that are well structured	0	1	2	3
0	1	2	3	Has an energized, stimulating work atmosphere	0	1	2	3
0	1	2	3	Has easygoing, harmonious work relationships	0	1	2	3
0	1	2	3	Is organized and businesslike in its performance	0	1	2	3
0	1	2	3	Puts pressure on people to get things done	0	1	2	3
0	1	2	3	Has a team or "family" approach toward everything	0	1	2	3
0	1	2	3	Has values oriented toward power and using influence	0	1	2	3
0	1	2	3	Is primarily concerned with results and goals	0	1	2	3
0	1	2	3	Cares about human and social relationships	0	1	2	3

Source: Based on Margerison, 1979.

Scoring. In each group of three characteristics, place a "B" next to the first characteristic, an "I" next to the second, and an "S" next to the third. Add all the B numbers for a total B score, the I numbers for an I score, and the S numbers for the S score. Scores for each type can range between 0 and 30.

The items in this survey will help you examine the degree to which you favor a bureaucratic (B score), an innovative (I score), or a supportive (S score) organizational culture. These dimensions come from the Organizational Style Index developed by Margerison (1979). If you are (or have been) associated with any organization, record the second set of scores and compare your current or recent organization with your ideal. Departments within organizations are likely to develop subcultures of their own. Therefore, you can photocopy the Work Organization Environment Survey and go through the 30 items as many times as you want. To analyze your ratings, record your raw scores and their percentile ranks (see Table 6-2) in the appropriate spaces of the following chart:

	Ideal Organizational Culture		Current or Recent Organizational Culture		Departmental Subculture		Departmental Subculture		Departmental Subculture	
	Score	Percentile	Score	Percentile	Score	Percentile	Score	Percentile	Score	Percentile
Bureaucratic Score										
Innovative Score										
Supportive Score										

After you have researched any organization's culture, you can rate it on the 30 items and record your results on the following chart for purposes of comparison:

	Name of Organization		Name of Organization		Name of Organization		Name of Organization		Name of Organization	
	Score	Percentile	Score	Percentile	Score	Percentile	Score	Percentile	Score	Percentile
Bureaucratic Score										
Innovative Score										
Supportive Score										

Table 6-2　Percentile Ranks for the Work Organization Environment Survey

	My Ideal Work Organization				My Current Work Organization		
Raw Score	B (Bureaucratic)	I (Innovative)	S (Supportive)	Raw Score	B (Bureaucratic)	I (Innovative)	S (Supportive)
30	99	99	96	30	99	99	99
29	99	99	88	29	99	99	97
28	97	96	79	28	98	99	93
27	96	92	70	27	97	98	90
26	93	87	61	26	95	97	87
25	90	81	51	25	92	95	83
24	83	74	43	24	87	94	78
23	80	67	36	23	81	92	74
22	73	60	30	22	76	89	69
21	66	53	25	21	72	85	65
20	59	46	19	20	66	80	62
19	52	39	14	19	61	74	57
18	45	33	11	18	55	69	52
17	37	26	8	17	49	64	48
16	31	20	7	16	44	57	44
15	25	16	6	15	37	51	40
14	20	12	5	14	32	42	36
13	16	9	5	13	27	38	32
12	13	8	4	12	21	32	28
11	11	6	3	11	16	27	24
10	9	5	3	10	13	22	21
9	8	3	2	9	10	18	17
8	7	2	2	8	9	15	14
7	6	2	2	7	8	12	12
6	5	1	1	6	7	9	8
5	4	1	1	5	5	7	5
4	3	1	1	4	4	5	4
3	2	1	1	3	3	3	3
2	1	1	1	2	1	2	1
0–1	1	1	1	0–1	1	1	1

Number of Ideal Work Organization respondents = 393
Number of Current Work Organization respondents = 272
Respondents were from career-planning and social issues classes at Jackson Community College (MI) between 1988 and 1994.

No organizational culture is good or bad in itself. A culture is good or effective if it carries out the purposes the organization intends to accomplish (Wallach, 1983). The organizational culture may be good or bad for you, depending on your goals and what is appropriate to the situation (Margerison, 1979).

Bureaucratic. Bureaucratic cultures are structured, ordered, impersonal, systematic, cautious, stable, and power oriented. They rely heavily on written rules and procedures. Behavior is carefully regulated, either alone by management or jointly by collective bargaining arrangements with unions. Seniority is likely to be important, and promotions come from within. Workers are expected to be dependable and committed to the organization's goals (Ayres, 2002). Work is controlled, with a fixed division of labor. The organization is hierarchical, with clear lines of authority and responsibility drawn on the organizational chart.

Bureaucratic organizations see themselves as mature and well established, with a solid, substantial standing in the business or governmental community. They somewhat resemble the process and bet-your-company cultures; the compensatory, business, and advocacy settings; the sensing, thinking, and judging characters; and the realistic and conventional types described in other classifications. Bureaucratic structures may be more appropriate for larger companies when the market for their products is stable and they have a large share of a particular market, a well-trained staff, and a strong organization. Creative and entrepreneurial people, however, may find this atmosphere stultifying and be frustrated in it.

Occupations have their own sets of beliefs, allowing members to make sense of the world in which they work. These beliefs can create a kind of knowledge base that separates one occupation from another, leading to subcultural differences within the larger organization. Tension and conflict can develop when a bureaucratic department tries to maintain order and stability in the organization as sales managers develop new orders and researchers introduce new ideas. Entire organizations may have to change their dominant work culture in order to survive. American Telephone and Telegraph (AT&T) appropriately developed a bureaucratic culture during most of the 20th century, but was forced to change when it was no longer a monopoly and had to compete with rivals, adapt to new communication technologies, and emphasize marketing and sales as never before. The old bureaucratic setting didn't operate as well in the new situation. International Business Machines (IBM), once a lumbering bureaucratic giant, had to restructure itself into a flexible, market-oriented company, which meant changing the corporate culture as well (McCarroll, 1992). IBM changed its slower, more careful pattern of decision making when some key market opportunities were lost to competitors (Cook, 1996). AT&T and IBM employees are now under pressure to perform in a manner better illustrated by the innovative work culture.

Innovative. Innovative cultures are spirited, challenging, creative, adventurous, competitive, entrepreneurial, and achievement oriented. People look ahead with optimism and are motivated to accomplish goals. People in innovative work cultures are willing to take risks and set high expectations for themselves. They are individualistic, ambitious, and driving. Pay is time related, increasing based on the time spent at work, or it is closely related to individual output, as in piecework or payment-by-results operations (Ayres, 2002). Hierarchy and lines of authority do not mean as much to people in innovative cultures as they do to people in bureaucratic cultures.

Innovative cultures correspond somewhat to the tough-guy, work hard/play hard, intellectual, and creative settings; the intuitive and perceiving characters; and the investigative, artistic, and enterprising cultures of other classifications. Innovative qualities are often more appropriate in smaller organizations, which can respond to market situations faster. There is an air of excitement and stimulation about them. However, such an atmosphere is intense, pressured, and stressful. Some people leave or avoid an innovative culture because their personal lifestyle doesn't fit the frantic pace demanded by the organization. Innovative and bureaucratic cultures appear to be at opposite poles, but organizations can blend certain aspects of both into a creative, reasonably stable system.

Supportive. Supportive cultures emphasize the values of harmony, trust, equality, security, warmth, and safety. People are more sociable, friendly, cooperative, encouraging of others, and relationship oriented than in other cultures. The organization is seen as a humanistic and psychologically healthful place to work. Supportive cultures are similar to the feeling character, the therapeutic setting, and the social environment of other classifications. A supportive culture provides an easier place in which to work, but there is little evidence that satisfaction with one's work environment makes for higher productivity (Margerison, 1979). Bureaucratic and innovative cultures can either exhibit or lack supportiveness. Managers can further a supportive atmosphere through their own personal relationships with workers. Managers cannot usually exert much influence on the amount of bureaucracy or innovation in an organizational culture, but they can affect its degree of supportiveness.

Table 6-3 shows the median scores for the bureaucratic, innovative, and supportive dimensions of organizations as measured by the Work Organization Environment Survey. Note that the median scores on all three measures for an *ideal* work organization are higher than those scores for *actual* work organizations. The distance between scores for ideal and actual supportive (7.3) and innovative (5.7) environments is greater than the distance between the scores for the ideal and actual bureaucratic environments (1.5). Overall, people place a higher priority in their ideal work organization on the characteristics designated supportive than on those labeled bureaucratic and innovative. If the survey results are an accurate representation, organizations do fulfill a considerable portion of those hopes and expectations. Although the word *bureaucratic* is a neutral descriptive term, it has become a negative word in our popular culture; as the survey shows, however, people want to find at least some bureaucratic qualities in their work organizations. The word *innovative* is used more positively, but according to the survey, people are less likely to experience innovative attributes than bureaucratic ones in typical work settings, despite the emphasis normally placed on dynamic change and exciting new challenges.

Although current information-based organizations are displacing the command-and-control model of management (Cetron and Davies, 2003), bureaucratic, innovative, and supportive cultures exist in all organizations to varying degrees. We have seen how production, engineering, advertising, personnel, managerial, and clerical departments can each create distinct subcultures, all within the same company. In the overall culture of a college, you might detect a bureaucratic subculture in the administration, an innovative subculture in the faculty, and a supportive subculture within the clerical and maintenance staff. A strong leadership might impress its own style on all elements of an organization; a more decentralized political style allows each unit to develop its separate subculture without intervention from a central authority.

These three types of organizational cultures resemble three major social motivators researched extensively by David McClelland: the need for power, achievement, and affiliation. People with a high need for power are motivated to influence others

Table 6-3   Median Scores on the Work Organization Environment Survey

	Ideal*	Current†
Bureaucratic	18.7	17.2
Innovative	20.5	14.8
Supportive	24.9	17.6

*393 respondents were students at Jackson Community College (MI) between 1988 and 1994.
†272 respondents were students at Jackson Community College (MI) between 1988 and 1994.

and actively seek positions more for the sake of prestige and leadership than for doing things well (achievement) or making friendships (affiliation). Many people will not admit or do not like to be told they have a high power motivation, yet power itself is neutral and can be an instrument for either good or bad (McClelland, 1972). Chapter 5 of the first book in this Career Planning Guide series explored the achievement motive. A person with a dominant achievement motive feels a need to complete tasks that are challenging and moderately difficult and to accomplish his or her goals with excellence, rather than to seek influence (power) or new companions (affiliation). Those with a high need for affiliation strongly desire to form work relationships and friendships, which are more important to them than attaining a leadership position (power) or completing a task with distinction (achievement). The strongest motive in your personality should be compatible with a corresponding organizational culture. If your principal motive is power, a bureaucratic culture would most likely suit your nature. A dominant achievement motive would be most productive in an innovative culture. A strong affiliation motive would most likely thrive in a supportive environment.

If you currently work in an organization, ask yourself how well its culture fits your personality. If there is considerable agreement, you are probably happy in your work environment. If there is a serious mismatch, the three options you have are (1) to adapt to your organizational culture, (2) to change or modify it, or (3) to withdraw from it. If you are embarking on an investigation of several organizations, you can now begin to appreciate the importance of researching and finding suitable organizational cultures in which to work.

The measurement and evaluation of organizational culture presented here is a modest attempt to analyze a complex subject. Perhaps you can use some of the items on the Work Organization Environment Survey as a basis for questions in informational interviews. Some organizations volunteer information about their company culture while you are researching them or during an orientation session if you are a new employee. If their self-analysis is accurate (you need to validate it), this is valuable information; beginning workers spend as much as six to nine months learning the way things are done in their new environment.

SOURCES OF INFORMATION ABOUT WORK ORGANIZATIONS

The two main sources of information about organizations are your personal contacts and written material, whether it is in publications or on the Internet. Inside information is usually more valuable than printed material. To obtain information, you can talk with people both inside and outside the organization. You may not know a soul inside an organization that interests you, which means you will need to start with your contacts outside—first of all, those who know something about the company you want to investigate. The key question to ask these people is the referral question: "Do you know the names of any people working within the organization who would be willing to talk with me?" If so, get their names and contact them for an informational interview (covered in the next chapter), or have your personal contact refer you by telephone or write a letter of introduction for you. With whom do you try to talk on the inside—the president of the company? Well, maybe. After all, this is the highest authority. Remember, however, that the boss and other top executives often put the best possible face on everything about the organization. It is better to start with secretaries, receptionists, middle managers, production workers, supervisors, custodians, or floor sweepers and move on to department heads and directors at a later time.

If the company, institution, or business is very small and doesn't publish anything about itself, personal contacts may comprise 100 percent of your information sources. Keep in mind, however, that even the smallest organization will have its name listed somewhere—in a business directory, telephone book, chamber of commerce publication, or city directory. The listing may also contain the organization's address and telephone number and the names of owners, top officials, and even a few employees. Before you start talking with people inside the target organization, read as much as you can about it. You will sound more serious and better informed when you do talk with people, and they won't feel that you are acting on a sudden whim or that they are wasting their time with you. In this phase of the job search, you are looking only for information, not a job, although you have your eyes open in case an attractive job opportunity develops. Your interviews can be conducted in a conversational manner with people you know. As you gain more skill in your interviews, people may not realize you are actually interviewing them. Even from casual conversations, you can obtain a lot of information about jobs and work organizations because people talk about these subjects all the time.

Written sources of information about organizations can be found in most public and college libraries, career resource centers, state employment agencies, chamber of commerce offices, government bureaus, and the organizations themselves. You can discover companies you never knew existed, names and titles of officers, locations, products manufactured and services provided, and the financial health of organizations. It bears repeating that you must investigate the company before you are hired. You don't want to be hired by a company that is about to go bankrupt, or find yourself in an organization that stands opposed to everything you believe in.

Electronic Sources of Information on Companies and Organizations

Electronic sources of information about potential employers are growing rapidly. An explosion of information is occurring on the World Wide Web, the most widely used feature of the Internet. Even small organizations have established Web sites. Online databases and compact disc indexes can also be used. The information in database files is often specialized and may exist in no other form. Electronic systems have speed and adaptability that make them valuable for any research. The information you get from electronic sources may be more up-to-date than the information you get from printed sources. A librarian trained as an online researcher can probably help you find information more quickly and accurately in your company research than you can on your own (Crowther, 1993). CD-ROM products are most often found in libraries and offices. A number of helpful Web sites can be found in Appendix D: *Web Sites for Company Information.* Keep in mind that more sites exist than those included in Appendix D, and new ones are being added constantly. If you are looking for information on the Web, but you don't know the URL of a specific company, try typing in an address like this generalized one: http://www.*[name of company]*.com.

Publications with Sources of Information on Companies and Organizations

Karmen Crowther (1998) suggests organizing your research of companies by determining whether the company is (1) publicly owned, (2) a subsidiary or a division, (3) privately owned, (4) foreign owned, or (5) local, regional, or otherwise small in scope. Of the directories and reference sources available, only a sampling can be mentioned here. These are among the most commonly used items normally found in the reference section of your library or in an electronic format.

1. **Publicly owned companies** make shares of stock available to the public and publish annual reports to shareholders. Information about these companies is more easily obtained because of their public nature. To determine whether stock is publicly traded, check price listings in the *Wall Street Journal* or another large-city newspaper. Online, you can check for a company's name at the New York Stock Exchange (http://www.nyse.com), the American Stock Exchange (http://www.amex.com), and NASDAQ (http://www.nasdaq.com).

   a. Annual reports from companies, colleges, corporations, foundations, hospitals, local governments, and the like. Call or write to their human resources or public relations offices for a copy. Help in reading annual reports can be found in Appendix E: *Reading Annual Reports* at the back of the book.

b. *Business Periodicals Index* (New York: H.W. Wilson Company). This is a biographic database that cites articles from leading business magazines and an array of trade and research journals. The articles, from periodicals published in the United States and elsewhere, discuss subjects ranging from accounting to transportation, and run at least one column in length.

c. *Million Dollar Directory* (New York: Dun and Bradstreet). This five-volume directory lists more than 166,000 public and private U.S. businesses and their subsidiaries that have more than $9 million in sales or a minimum of 180 employees. Companies are arranged by name, geographic location, ticker symbol, SIC (Standard Industrial Classification) code, or company size. Information includes addresses, telephone numbers, sales, and the names, titles, and short biographies of executives. A branch office will be given if there are 900 or more employees at that location.

d. *Moody's Complete Corporate Index* (New York: NY Mergent, Inc.). Now published annually, this index covers more than 20,000 corporations and organizations found in Moody's other business references.

e. *Moody's Industrial Manual,* three volumes (New York: Moody's Investor's Services). Presents detailed information on corporations, divisions, financial condition, officers, profit margin, stocks and bonds, and corporate history. Other Moody's manuals cover banks and finance, international business, public utilities, and transportation.

f. *Reference Book of Corporate Managements* (New York: Dun and Bradstreet). This reference lists companies in alphabetical order and gives brief biographies of their directors and officers. The first two volumes are arranged alphabetically by company, each with biographical material and a short portrayal of the organization. A cross-reference volume is composed of sections that list businesses geographically, by industry classification, by major officers and directors, by college and university ties of corporate officers, and by military connections of these officers.

g. *Register of Corporations, Directors, and Executives* (New York: Standard and Poor's). Volume 1 lists alphabetically over 55,000 corporations, with addresses, telephone numbers, names and functions of directors and officers, names of divisions, products made, sales volume, and numbers of employees. Volume 2 provides names of directors and officers alphabetically, their residences, dates and places of birth, and colleges attended. Volume 3 contains seven indexes, including industry arrangement and geographic location.

h. 10-K forms. Each publicly owned company must file an official annual report with the Securities and Exchange Commission (450 Fifth Street NW, Washington, DC 20549). Unlike a company's annual report to the shareholders, the 10-K has no glossy photos or hype (Crowther, 1993). The report contains audited financial statements and descriptions of company policies and operations, and is available from the SEC.

i. *Thomas Register of American Manufacturers* (New York: Thomas Publishing Company). This annual reference is a listing of about 173,000 manufacturers. In the 2003 edition, Volumes 1–24 index products and services alphabetically; Volumes 25–26 give company profiles in alphabetical order with addresses, ZIP codes, telephone and fax numbers, URLs, branch offices, asset rating, and company officials; and Volumes 27–29 contain a catalog file with thousands of company catalogs that tells you all you need to know about the company's products. The *Thomas Register* has long been an old standby of company information, "one of the most recognizable reference works in any business library," and "one of the most remarkable business directories ever devised," offering "a comprehensive, detailed guide to the full range of business products manufactured in the United States" (Lavin, 1992, 129).

j. *Who's Who in Finance and Industry* (Chicago: Marquis' Who's Who, Inc.). More than 18,000 business leaders are listed by name with their company name, title, and biographical data. Other volumes in this series include *Who's Who in America, Who's Who in American Politics,* and *Who's Who in American College and University Administration.*

2. **Subsidiaries and divisions of companies.** Because the parent company is not required to give facts about its separate divisions, it is harder to find and confirm information about subsidiaries than about publicly owned companies. Check the sources for publicly owned companies; those organizations may give information about their subsidiaries and divisions. Newspaper and magazine articles often publish articles about local and better-known subsidiaries. Two sources are:

a. *America's Corporate Families* (New York: Dun and Bradstreet). This annual publication lists more than 12,700 parent companies along with their branches, subsidiaries, and divisions. Descriptions of companies provide information on sales volume, number of employees, and names of chief executives.

b. *Directory of Corporate Affiliations* (New Providence, NJ: National Register Publishing Company). *Corporate Affiliations* contains business profiles and corporate linkage for 114,000 companies worldwide. Each listing includes the company name, address, telephone number, business description, executive names, and corporate family hierarchy. Additional data about the parent company includes sales, number of employees, or director names.

3. **Privately owned companies** do not sell shares of stock to the public. These organizations are owned by private individuals or families. Try to find out if key jobs are reserved for relatives, friends, or members of the family. If a privately owned company has large assets or sales, you may find it listed in a directory.

a. *America's Corporate Families* (New York: Dun and Bradstreet). Described in the previous section.

b. *Business Information Reports* (New York: Dun and Bradstreet). Rosen and Paul (1998) call this source the "most in-depth and comprehensive source of information about private companies."

c. *Directory of Corporate Affiliations* (New Providence, NJ: National Register Publishing Company). Refer to Volume 4 for privately owned companies.

d. *Hoover's Guide to Private Companies* (Austin, TX: Reference Press). 900 non-public enterprises in the United States are covered, including large industrial and service corporations, hospitals and health care organizations, charitable and membership organizations, mutual and cooperative organizations, joint ventures, government-owned corporations, and major university systems.

e. *Ward's Business Directory of U.S. Private and Public Companies* (Detroit: Gale Research Company). An annual four-volume directory containing more than 120,000 companies, 90 percent of which are private. Company descriptions are arranged alphabetically, geographically by state and ZIP code, and by sales within industry categories.

4. **Foreign-owned companies** are companies based in countries outside the United States that have established subsidiary or division within the United States. Foreign-owned companies are not subject to the same financial disclosure laws as U.S. companies; therefore, information on them may be harder to obtain.

a. *Directory of Corporate Affiliations* (New Providence, NJ: National Register Publishing Company). Volume 5 is the international file of public and private companies.

b. *Directory of Foreign Manufacturers in the United States* (Atlanta: Georgia State University Business Press). This directory provides data on 6,000 foreign-owned companies involved in manufacturing in the United States.

c. *Moody's International Manual* (New York: Moody's Investor Services). This three-volume manual covers company officers, products, financial data, and history in terms of worldwide business.

d. *Who Owns Whom: North American Edition* (New York: Dun and Bradstreet). Parent companies and their associate or subsidiary organizations are covered; includes U.S. and Canadian companies along with foreign organizations.

5. **Local, regional, or small companies** are usually not found in the first four groups. For these organizations, you may have to rely on chambers of commerce, state industrial directories, trade publications, local newspapers, business magazines, and members of your personal contact network. Electronically search for local chambers of commerce on the World Wide Web (http://www.uschamber.org) or write to the national office: Chamber of Commerce of the United States, 1615 H Street NW, Washington, DC 20062.

Other publications for company research. Other books and directories that can be found in the reference section of the library are in the following list. Again, keep in mind that these books are only a sampling; many other resources are available.

- The Better Business Bureau (BBB) reports on target companies. Contact the local BBB office or write to the Council of Better Business Bureaus, Inc., 4200 Wilson Blvd., Suite 800, Arlington, VA 22203. The BBB can tell you how honest and dependable a company has been or if it is having legal problems. The council may not have information about a company if no complaints about it have been filed. Local bureaus handle more than 11 million public contacts annually without charge. The BBB has a Web site (http://www.bbb.org) that lists addresses of local offices.

- Business periodicals such as *Barron's, Business Week, Dun's Review, Financial World, Forbes, Fortune, Inc.,* and *The Wall Street Journal;* the business pages of your local newspaper; and business sections in trade journals and popular news magazines such as *Time, Newsweek,* and *U.S. News & World Report* have articles on work organizations. The *Reader's Guide to Periodical Literature* in your library may help you find magazine articles that feature information on organizations.

- *Companies and Their Brands* (Farmington Hills, MI: Gale Group). This publication tracks over 20,000 manufacturers, importers, and distributors of more than 70,000 consumer products.

- *Encyclopedia of Associations: National Organizations of the U.S.* (Farmington Hills, MI: Gale Group). A source of information on nonprofit organizations, listing government, scientific, educational, health, religious, public affairs, business, labor, trade, legal, and other types of organizations. Association names, membership size, names of executive secretaries, addresses and phone numbers, division names, publications, and annual conventions are among the information given. An alphabetical name and keyword index is provided, so you can locate the name and address of the organization you need to contact.

- *Encyclopedia of Associations: Regional, State, and Local Organizations* (Farmington Hills, MI: Gale Group). A guide to more than 115,000 U.S. nonprofit organizations, this encyclopedia includes trade and professional associations, social welfare and public affairs organizations, and religious, sports, and hobby groups with voluntary members. Entries have the association name and complete contact information. Name and keyword indexes accompany each of the five volumes, which cover the Great Lakes, Northeastern, Southern and Middle Atlantic, South Central and Great Plains, and Western states.

- *Encyclopedia of Business Information Sources* (James Woy, editor, Farmington Hills, MI: Gale Group). One of the first places to look for what is available on companies and industries before selecting materials to read, this encyclopedia lists source books, periodicals, organizations, handbooks, and directories, organized by category, topic, and location.

- *Guide to American Directories* (Coral Gables, FL: B. Klein Publications, Inc.). This directory of specialized directories lists approximately 5,000 directories, arranged by type of business or professional association and providing publisher's name, cost, and contents of each directory. An alphabetical index appears at the end. This is also a helpful book to consult early in your research.

- *Harris Directories* (Twinsburg, OH: Harris Infosource). Annual directories are available for the entire United States as well as for every state and region. Companies are organized into alphabetic, geographic, and product/service categories. This resource is also available online and on CD-ROM.

- *Hoover's Handbook of American Business* (Austin, TX: Hoover's Business Press). Published annually, this two-volume set profiles 750 of the largest and most influential companies in the United States. Each profile includes an overview of the company; its history, names of officers, and location; its products and services; major competitors; sales volume; and stock performance.

- *Hoover's Handbook of Emerging Companies* (Hoover's Business Press). Six hundred small, rapidly growing U.S. companies are covered, with in-depth profiles provided for 200 of them.

- *Job Choices* series (Bethlehem, PA: National Association of Colleges and Employers). NACE produces four publications that are directed toward college students, particularly those about to graduate. Two of them are called *Planning Job Choices*. One edition is targeted for all students and the other, *Job Choices: Diversity Edition*, is aimed for minority students. A third publication, *Job Choices for Business and Liberal Arts Students*, features career opportunities in nontechnical disciplines: business majors in accounting, advertising, administration, retailing, finance, public relations, marketing, and the like, and careers for liberal arts majors. Finally, *Job Choices in Science, Engineering, & Technology* highlights career opportunities in the various branches of engineering, the sciences, the computer sciences, and health care. Employer listings in the last two publications include qualifications sought, benefits offered, and contact information. The *Job Choices* publications should be in your college career services office.

- *National Directory of State Agencies* (Washington, DC: Cambridge Information Group). This directory gives names, addresses, and telephone numbers of government agencies in every state. The first part of the book lists agencies by state, the second part by function.

- *National Trade and Professional Associations of the United States* (Washington, DC: Columbia Books, Inc.). Professional groups, trade associations, and labor unions are covered and indexed by organization, title, subject, and location.

- *Occupational Outlook Handbook* (Washington, DC: U.S. Bureau of Labor Statistics or Superintendent of Documents, U.S. Government Printing Office). This excellent and widely used reference covers future trends in more than 250 broad occupational groups, the nature of the work in these occupations, training and other qualifications needed, earnings, and employment prospects.

- *Researching Your Way to a Good Job* (K. N. T. Crowther; New York: Wiley, 1993). This book identifies factors to investigate about prospective employers and describes widely available information sources useful for researching various kinds of companies.

- *Wall Street Journal Index* (Ann Arbor, MI: University Microfilms). This monthly publication contains articles that have appeared recently in the *Wall Street Journal*. Part 1 provides company news reported by company name. Part 2 has general business news by subject.

Annual Reports

One hesitates a moment before writing about annual reports; recent corporate scandals have made people more wary of these documents. The dismantling of government regulations has had mixed results. Deregulated markets allowed corrupt traders to manipulate prices, pillaging both consumers and stockholders. Monitoring efforts by the government were hamstrung by the power of aggressive lobbying—for example, the attempt by the Securities and Exchange Commission to force corporations to count stock options for executives as expenses. Companies were allowed to artificially enlarge profits on paper, which in turn increased the price of stocks and the value of stock options (Kuttner, 2003). Accountants attest to the accuracy of annual reports; however, to get business from companies they audited, some catered to their corporate clients instead of serving the shareholders and the public, weakening the validity of annual reports. Governmental action was taken against those who helped cover up financial crises at Enron, WorldCom, and other corporations whose bankruptcies sparked demands for reform (*Economist*, 2003). For their part, to boost public confidence, companies are now providing more information in their annual reports. See Appendix E: *Reading Annual Reports* for assistance in reading and understanding annual reports.

TYPES AND NAMES OF WORK ORGANIZATIONS

As you begin your research of work organizations, the question you should first try to answer is: In what types of organizations would I enjoy doing the work I want to do? Use Exercise 6-2 to discover the types of work organizations that attract you. After that, you can begin to identify specific work organizations.

EXERCISE 6-2 TYPES AND NAMES OF WORK ORGANIZATIONS

The first part of this exercise concentrates on types, not specific names or organizations. Check those that appeal to you.

Would I want to work in:

____ a manufacturing company?	____ a factory (large or small)?
____ a business firm or office?	____ a corporation?
____ a hospital or nursing home?	____ a consumer cooperative?
____ a state or national government office?	____ a counseling/family service office?
____ an airplane/bus/train/taxi?	____ a fast-food restaurant?
____ a bank or financial institution?	____ an educational institution?
____ a church/religious organization?	____ a retail store?
____ the outdoors (most of the time)?	____ a building construction company?

_____ a business of my own?

_____ an information retrieval service?

_____ an airport/bus or train station?

_____ a professional association?

_____ a day care center?

_____ an animal-care hospital?

_____ a retirement community?

_____ a garden/farm?

_____ a newspaper/magazine office?

_____ a pharmacy?

_____ a department store?

_____ an architectural firm?

_____ a funeral home?

_____ a lumberyard?

_____ a long-distance truck?

_____ a short-distance route truck?

_____ a law office?

_____ a beauty salon or barber shop

_____ a clothing store?

_____ a publishing or printing office?

_____ a hardware store?

_____ a machine repair shop?

_____ a private or public foundation?

_____ a travel agency or bureau?

_____ a bakery?

_____ an advertising/public relations firm?

_____ a library or bookstore?

_____ a private home?

_____ a management consulting office?

_____ other: _____

_____ a museum/art gallery?

_____ a hotel or motel?

_____ a police or fire station?

_____ a government agency or bureau?

_____ a research laboratory?

_____ a department store?

_____ a theater/TV or radio station?

_____ a women's resource center?

_____ a boat/freighter/marina?

_____ a political organization?

_____ a recreational center?

_____ a restaurant?

_____ a military organization?

_____ a doctor's or dentist's office?

_____ an automobile service station?

_____ a supermarket?

_____ a youth or children's center?

_____ an employment agency?

_____ a machine and tool company?

_____ an appliance store?

_____ a dairy or dairy store?

_____ a community action agency?

_____ an insurance/real estate office?

_____ an auto dealership or garage?

_____ an amusement park?

_____ an engineering or design department?

_____ an industrial supply firm?

_____ a city or county government office?

_____ other: _____

After you have identified one or several types of work organizations that attract you, it will be easier to determine the names of specific work organizations you should investigate. The Yellow Pages of the telephone book is one place to start. You can also consult the National Association of Colleges and Employers' *Job Choices* publications (published yearly and found in a career resource center or college career services office). Look at a local city directory or an employer directory in your public library, chamber of commerce, or city hall. Resources covered in the previous sections may give you some leads. In the following spaces, list your potential places of employment.

Name of Work Organization	Name of Contact Person	Address/Telephone
1. _____	_____	_____
2. _____	_____	_____
3. _____	_____	_____
4. _____	_____	_____
5. _____	_____	_____
6. _____	_____	_____
7. _____	_____	_____
8. _____	_____	_____
9. _____	_____	_____
10. _____	_____	_____

THINGS YOU NEED TO KNOW ABOUT A WORK ORGANIZATION

In addition to the organization's structure and culture, you should research many other aspects of the company. The investigation can focus on an entire organization, if the organization is not too large. When the size of the company goes beyond 100 people, consider limiting yourself to a department where you could work within the organization or to a subunit within a department, if necessary. Keep the object of your investigation to a manageable size, with reasonable numbers of people involved. All the items in this section of the chapter can be turned into questions to ask while you read and interview for information.

1. Structure of the organization, division, department, or sub-unit. You want the name, address, telephone number, physical location, and number of employees in the organization. The physical location of a company—one location or several if there are divisions or subsidiaries—may generate questions you need to ask yourself. How important is geographic location to you? Is the company in a place acceptable to you? Are you willing to relocate if necessary? Size of the organization is another factor for your personal consideration. How large or small would you want it to be?

Secure a copy of the organization chart, if one is available, and determine your target department on the chart. This is where your investigation should concentrate, unless the organization is too small to have departments. Locate the industrial category into which the organization fits. Is it food growing or distribution, clothing, wood products, electronics, automotive, home construction, office equipment, chemicals, crude oil production, rubber or plastic products, education, financial services, paper products, aerospace, photographic equipment, pharmaceuticals, industrial or farm equipment, mining, petroleum refining, appliances, cosmetics, metal manufacturing, health care, social services, or some other category? Locate the person or committee with hiring authority in the target organization or department. If it is an individual, obtain that person's name and title. If it is a committee, get its name and the names of the people on it.

2. Products made or services provided by the organization or department. Why is the organization in business? Discover what it does to stay in business and make profits (or to keep appropriations coming, if it is a government agency). What is its volume of business and its market share in a certain area or in the country? This information might be available in the company's annual report, promotional material, or employment guide. Are the products or services good or inferior? Find out the opinions of the customers and general public. Always know what the company does before you interview there for a job. Ignorance of an organization's products and services is a real knockout factor in the minds of almost all personnel managers and employers.

3. The organizational culture or departmental subculture. An organization's or department's culture, or work environment, is expressed in its values, beliefs, assumptions, customs, procedures, leadership styles, and goals. Is the organizational culture bureaucratic, innovative, or supportive? Would you call it tough-guy, work hard/play hard, bet-your-company, or process? Is it realistic, investigative, artistic, social, enterprising, or conventional? Is the organization's character extraverted or introverted, sensing or intuitive, thinking or feeling, and judging or perceiving? You can ask questions about this subject in an interview. If you do, you may need to explain the meaning of the term *organizational culture*. You may also need to define the words, such as *bureaucratic* and *innovative*, that are used to describe different organizational cultures. Try out your assessment of the company atmosphere in nonjudgmental terms during an interview, and ask the person whether he or she agrees with your interpretation of the organization.

The values and beliefs of an organization or department are often indicated in the way people dress on the job, the physical setting, your first impressions, subjects highlighted in communication and publications, and the general appearance of the workplace. Do people dress formally or casually? Are buildings and offices functional, decorated artistically, or extravagant and lavish? Are the grounds attractively maintained? The physical characteristics of the reception areas and the degree of warmth with which you are received make up your first impressions of a workplace. Examine the organization's publications, such as a newsletter or annual report. These communications can give you an idea of which subjects an organization considers important. Do the places where people work appear clean and neat or sloppy and dirty? Are they standardized or personalized? These factors give clues to the characteristics of the corporate culture. Are the values and goals of the organization compatible with your personality pattern?

4. Types of people employed by the organization or in the department. What kind of people work there? Who gets ahead? Who are the "heroes"? Is there a predominant type of personality, almost to the exclusion of other types? Is there a mix of personalities? For example, try to analyze a work environment using Holland's personality types. Estimate the percentage of realistic, investigative, artistic, social, enterprising, and conventional types within the organization or a given department. Is your personality pattern compatible with the dominant types?

5. Needs and problems of the organization or department. If you cannot obtain information about the needs and problems of an organization from your personal contacts and people working on the inside, you may need to interview people in similar departments of organizations in the same field. Look for reasons why an organization is experiencing a problem or need. Typical causes of problems are declines or losses of sales; slow growth, no growth, or too much growth; low morale among staff; destructive political infighting; labor/management strife; high staff turnover; poor image in the community; obsolete equipment; stagnation; unnecessary expense; lack of communication; materials shortages; failure to find enough skilled people; questionable decision-making practices; unfavorable market forces; absenteeism; threats from competitors; lack of coordination between different segments of the overall organization; focusing inward when the perspective should be expanding; clashes between value systems; mediocre products or services; and inconsistent treatment of employees. Can your abilities help the organization solve its problems and provide for its needs? If so, a person with hiring authority may be willing to create a job that you would love to tackle because of the challenge it represents, the values that are expressed, and the skills you would use.

6. Decision-making patterns. What is the structure of the organization's decision-making authority? Is it centralized in the hands of one or a few, or is it decentralized, requiring the participation of many? Under what circumstances does the organization make its decisions? Some decisions may be made autocratically out of necessity whereas other decisions are made more slowly, allowing a democratic process to take place. Leadership can be authoritarian, democratic, or *laissez-faire*. In some companies, the conventional wisdom is to give all authority to a top official and get out of that person's way. In other organizations, that practice could cause an insurrection.

Do you want to be a part of an organization's decision-making process? Decisions take time: information must be gathered, committees meet and assign work, consensus is often slow to develop, leaders can reject the advice of an advisory group. These are the costs of a more democratic style, and you might become impatient with it. Authoritarian decision makers take the burden of decisions from you, but you suffer a corresponding loss of freedom. Determine your own decision-making preferences, and find out what the organization practices when it makes decisions.

7. Advancement and promotion opportunities. Find out how long it takes to move to a more desirable position. You expect to pay your dues in terms of time spent in an entry-level job, but you probably do not want to stay forever in the same job. What are the typical career ladders in an organization? Does a person or a committee make the decisions on promotions or increases in responsibility? Would you make your request for advancement through an interview, or is there an application process? Try to discover the kinds of people the organization is most likely to promote. A seniority principle may govern, or management may find a way to get around it. You can ask employees about the fairness of advancement policies, but be careful about the way you ask—it could be a sensitive area of inquiry. You could set in motion a lengthy account of past injustices, real or imagined, which would have to be confirmed or denied by others. Does the organization favor those who are the most productive, innovative, cooperative, enterprising, creative, cautious, or willing to take risks? Dissecting the organizational culture can go a long way in explaining why some people move quickly and others slowly on their career paths.

8. Wage structure and salary range. Look for beginning, average, and top wages and salaries offered by the organization in your chosen field of work. If the top pay rate is only 10 or 15 percent higher than the starting wage, this is not a good situation. Top pay rates should be at least twice as high as the beginning pay figures. A little research on this subject can put you in a stronger negotiating position if you decide to apply for a job with the organization. Obviously, you will compare this factor with the earnings offered by other organizations you investigate. Include fringe benefits in your research: bonuses, paid vacations, pensions and retirement programs, medical and dental benefits, sick days, personal days, stock purchase and profit-sharing plans, reimbursement of moving expenses, and conference and travel expenses.

9. Future prospects for the organization or department. What are the projections for the growth or decline of the entire organization or a separate division? What is the anticipated rate of change? Is the company increasing its sales or business activity and making a profit? What are its costs and liabilities (debts and obligations)? Learn the reasons for its expected progress or its downward course. Naturally, you want to associate with a growing company, but do not automatically reject an organization in trouble. Perhaps your abilities could help solve or lessen its problems and enable you to become one of its "heroes." Be alert for expansion plans or possible cutbacks. Where will they occur within the organization? Watch for new products and services being developed. Can you get in on the ground floor of these plans? There is also the hazard of products, services, and activities being phased out. Is there a current function to avoid because it may not exist in a few months or years?

. . . of course, this work environment also counts as a health plan . . .

10. History and past performance. An organization, like a nation, has a history. When did it start? Discover the significant past events and the names of leaders who affected its history. What have been its ups and downs over the years? Knowledge of the organization's past will score points for you in any interview situation. Review the company's business activity over several years to get a long-term perspective on its future prospects. Four or five previous years of consecutive annual reports may be helpful toward understanding the company's current financial status.

11. Standing or rank in the industry, field, profession, or region. Who are the competitors within the same industry or field? How does the organization rank in comparison with its competition? What perceptions do people have of the organization's image or reputation? (This is similar to people's rankings of colleges and universities.) What factors affect the reasoning and judgments that go into the ranking of an organization or one of its divisions? You may choose strictly quantitative criteria, dealing only with numbers and attempting to be completely objective. Sometimes, however, this kind of evaluation is too superficial and doesn't get to the heart of the matter. Many people make qualitative judgments that have more to do with character, nature, degree of excellence, and other subjective elements.

12. Staff morale. Do the workers consider their organization to be a pleasant or disagreeable place in which to work? Why? This has to do with working conditions and employee feelings. Workers motivated by the values and beliefs of the organization are enthusiastic about working there. Do the people you talk with see their workplace as beneficial to them, or is it just a place to make a living? Employees will not usually tell you that a company is a terrible place in which to work, but indifference and detachment could be a clue that all is not well. Check the turnover rate of the organization or your target department. Some turnover of staff is natural, but if the rate is high (one-third or more per year), it is a sign of trouble. A large proportion of people leaving a company could signal excessive stress, anxiety, and discontent. The organization's health and safety record may offer further indications of the disposition of employees. Good health and a low accident rate are often a sign of good morale; many illnesses and casualties could mean poor morale. Another feature to check is the manner in which rewards and recognition are given. Do they exist? When do they happen? How are they received?

13. Educational and training opportunities. Does the organization encourage its employees to further their education or training by offering to pay all or part of tuition and other educational expenses? Some companies provide educational facilities of their own, even multimillion-dollar campuses, to educate their workers. Check on the in-service and on-the-job training programs the organization offers. Are there workshops, conferences, and seminars you can attend? Does the company have a staff development fund set aside for the benefit of employees? Your ability to upgrade your skills will be a significant factor in staying employed and advancing on the job in the future.

14. Political environment within the organization or department. Office politics is an important part of corporate culture and an integral feature of every organization. Most people feel that politics is a nasty business and want no part of it; if it is ignored, maybe it will go away. However, ignorance of and indifference to politics will more likely make you a victim of some political struggle within the organization. Studying the political climate helps you make informed decisions about which organization to choose and how to survive when you get there. From interviews with over 1,000 people who have experienced job failures, Kennedy (1980) discovered that the great majority (75 percent) failed because they were unskilled in office politics. They possessed the technical skills but were unable to get along with their bosses, adjust to their coworkers, or be loyal to the values of the company.

Your political analysis should deal as much with your work associates as with your managers and administrators. You'll have to limit your analysis of management in large organizations, but you should reach at least two levels above and below where you would be on the organizational chart. Kennedy (1980) suggests several questions to answer in obtaining information for political analysis. To whom does each person report, and what is that person's position? Regarding managers, what is their leadership style (by default, dictatorial, somewhere in between)? Are there any major differences in style from that of others at the same level or above? Who reviews each person's decisions, and who has the power to veto those decisions? How much do each person's decisions affect the organization? Do they have line or staff positions? What has been each person's promotion record? How many and what kinds of people report to each person? Which people, and how many of them, consult with each person on their decisions? With whom does each person socialize? How astute is each one politically? What is each person's educational and socioeconomic background? Your personal contacts inside the organization must help you obtain this information; you cannot do it adequately by yourself from the outside. After answering these questions, rank these people in their order of importance, disregarding the titles they hold. Look for alliances and coalitions, if you can detect them during your research.

15. Special requirements. Would you have to meet any special qualifications or standards in order to join the organization or department? Some companies or institutions require that you obtain a license or certificate. You might need to provide your own tools or equipment in some organizations. Membership in a labor union is required in a closed shop; it might be desirable in some companies even though the employment contract does not require you to join. Similarly, some professional associations operate as if they were a closed shop.

16. Impact of employment in the organization on your family. How would your acceptance of a job in a new location affect the lifestyle of your spouse, children, or other relatives to whom you have responsibilities? What sacrifices would be necessary because of the working conditions of the organization? What benefits would result? Any change will have an emotional impact on your family and friends; this should be assessed. What cost-of-living increases or decreases would there be in housing, food, clothing, education, transportation, and cultural and recreational activities?

17. Other possible considerations. One additional consideration would be the stability of the company. In general, larger organizations tend to be more stable in their

This is an interview, sir! You can't keep "taking the Fifth"!

economic development. Public employment tends to be more secure than private jobs, if only because it is generally harder to terminate a government employee. All things being equal, an older company is usually safer than a newer one.

EXERCISE 6-3 WORK ORGANIZATION RESEARCH WORKSHEET

Choose an organization in your local area where you could conceivably seek a job in an occupation ranked high among your prospects. Your research could focus on an entire company or institution if it is small (say, under 50 or 100 employees). In the case of a large organization, you should concentrate on a division or department. In other words, limit the size of the unit you research; otherwise, your investigation will be too general and the scope too broad. Refer to the previous section for information on the subjects to research. This worksheet follows the format used in that section.

Photocopy this worksheet if you intend to investigate more than one work organization.

1. Name of organization _____

   Address _____

   Telephone _____ Other locations _____

   _____

   Approximate number of employees _____

   Industrial category _____

   Sources of information about the organization:

   Titles of written sources _____

   _____

   _____

   _____

People Contacted: Names	Address/Telephone	Dates Contacted	Interview Date
_____	_____	_____	_____
_____	_____	_____	_____
_____	_____	_____	_____
_____	_____	_____	_____

   Thank-you letters sent:

   Yes _____   When? _____   Will send _____   When? _____

   Yes _____   When? _____   Will send _____   When? _____

   Yes _____   When? _____   Will send _____   When? _____

   Yes _____   When? _____   Will send _____   When? _____

   Name and title of person with hiring authority _____

   _____

   Divisions/departments within organization _____

   _____

   _____

   Obtain or make an organizational chart. Indicate where you would fit in.

   In which department would I work? _____

   What could I do for this organization? _____

   _____

2. Goods produced/services provided _____

   _____

   Volume of business and share of market in area _____

   _____

3. Organizational culture or departmental subculture: Type(s) _____

   _____

Values/beliefs _____

_____

Clothing worn on the job _____

Customs/rituals/ceremonies _____

Physical setting _____

First impressions _____

Subjects highlighted in communications _____

General appearance of workplace _____

Are the values of the organization compatible with my personality? _____

Why? _____

4. Types of people in the organization _____

Compatible with my personality? _____ Why? _____

_____

5. Needs/problems identified _____

Could my skills help solve or reduce the problems or provide for those needs? _____

How? _____

_____

6. Decision-making patterns (describe them): _____

_____

How are decisions made? _____

_____

7. Advancement opportunities _____

_____

Next highest position on career ladder _____

8. Wage/salary structure: Pay in my intended job (starting, average, top)

_____

Benefits available _____

_____

9. Organizational growth prospects: Rapid? Slow? None? Decline? _____

Why? _____

_____

10. History: How old? _____ Significant events _____

_____

Past leaders _____

11. Rank or image in industrial category _____

Names of competitors _____

_____

12. Staff morale (good, bad, indifferent?) _____

    Why? _____

    _____

13. Educational/training opportunities _____

    _____

    _____

14. Political environment within organization _____

    _____

    Names of people (in rank order) studied in political analysis _____

    _____

    _____

15. Special requirements to be hired _____

    _____

    _____

16. Impact of employment in organization on my family _____

    _____

    _____

17. Other _____

    _____

    _____

    _____

SUMMARY

1. Characteristics of quality organizations are written about and discussed all the time. For example, books exist that could help you identify the features you are looking for in an organization. Four of the most influential in the past 25 years are Peters and Waterman's *In Search of Excellence*; Levering's *A Great Place to Work*; Levering, Moskowitz, and Katz's *The 100 Best Companies to Work for in America*; and Deal and Kennedy's *Corporate Cultures*.

2. Obtain a copy of an organizational chart when you research a company. It will give you an overview of the entire operation and help you locate the division or department that could best use your talents. Small businesses with few employees may not publish an organizational chart; in such cases, try to make one yourself.

3. Organizations develop their own unique sets of values, beliefs, customs, practices, rituals, ceremonies, heroes, communications networks, and ways of doing things. Companies operate in environments to which they must adapt if they are to succeed. Job seekers should study the culture of an organization ahead of becoming an employee there; you want your personality to be compatible with the atmosphere in which you work.

4. Several classifications of organizational cultures can help you analyze your attempt to match your characteristics with those of the organization. Deal and Kennedy (1982) classify corporate cultures into the tough guy, work hard/play hard, bet-your-company, and process types. Holland's realistic, investigative, artistic, social,

enterprising, and conventional types could be used to assess work environments. The Myers-Briggs Type Indicator identifies 16 types of people who create work cultures by preferences made from four scales: extraversion–introversion, sensing–intuition, thinking–feeling, and judging–perceiving. Haberman (1983) describes educational environments as therapeutic, compensatory, business, intellectual, advocacy, and creative settings. Margerison (1979) and Wallach (1983) analyze organizations in terms of their bureaucratic, innovative, and supportive cultures. This last classification can be linked to McClelland's (1972) power, achievement, and affiliation motives.

5. Information about work organizations can come from written resources, company Web sites, and interviews with personal contacts. Use a combination of all three. Written sources include annual reports, business sections of newspapers and trade journals, business magazines, the *Job Choices* series, and the many encyclopedic volumes on companies and their officials.

6. Annual reports can give you a lot of information. They contain statistical data, some of which are difficult to comprehend without help. A company's annual report usually includes sections that are featured in Appendix E: *Reading Annual Reports*.

7. Exercise 6-2 can help you identify types of workplaces that attract you and specific work organizations you could investigate.

8. After identifying a few places where you could conceivably work, you need to know a number of things about each organization in order to make a wise choice. Suggested features to investigate are (1) structure, (2) products made or services provided, (3) organizational culture or department subculture, (4) types of people, (5) needs and problems, (6) decision-making patterns, (7) advancement and promotion policies, (8) wage structure and salary range, (9) future prospects, (10) past history, (11) standing among competitors in the industry, (12) staff morale, (13) educational and training opportunities, (14) political environment, (15) special requirements, and (16) impact on your family. You should research all these factors for whatever work organizations you are seriously considering. Do it now; get in the habit of researching this subject all the time. When it comes to actively searching for a job, you may be too pressed for time to learn how to do it well.

REFERENCES

Aisner, J., Colao, V., Khurana, R., Martz, B., Minow, N, Owen, G., Poysti, K., and Teslk, S. 2003. How to run a company well. *The Economist*, 369(8347), 21–22.

Ayres, M. E. 2002. Work in the new economy. *Monthly Labor Review*, 125(4), 65–66.

Bridges, W. 1992. *The character of organizations: Using Jungian type in organizational development.* Palo Alto, CA: Consulting Psychologists Press.

Cetron, M. J., and Davies, O. 2003. Trends shaping the future: Technological, workplace, management, and institutional trends. *The Futurist*, 37(2), 30–43.

Chruden, H. J., and Sherman, A. W., Jr. 1980. *Personnel management: The utilization of human resources*, 6th ed. Cincinnati: South-Western.

Collins, J. 2003. The ten greatest CEOs of all time. *Fortune*, 148(2), 54–68.

Cook, W. J. 1996, June 17. The turnaround artist. *U.S. News & World Report*, 55–58.

Crowther, K. N. T. 1993. *Researching your way to a good job: How to find and use information on industries, companies, jobs, careers.* New York: Wiley.

Crowther, K. N. T. 1998. How to research companies. *Planning job choices*. Bethlehem, PA: National Association of Colleges and Employers.

Deal, T. E., and Kennedy, A. A. 1982. *Corporate cultures: The rites and rituals of corporate life.* Reading, MA: Addison-Wesley.

The Economist. 2003. American corporate reform: Sox it to them. *The Economist*, 368(8335), 13–14.

Farnham, A. 1993. State your values, hold the hot air. *Fortune*, 127(7), 117–124.

Haberman, M. 1983. Organizational cultures in school settings. *Education Digest*, 49, 47–49.

Holland, J. L. 1997. *Making vocational choices: A theory of vocational personalities and work environments*, 3rd ed. Odessa, FL: Psychological Assessment Resources.

Kennedy, M. M. 1980. *Office politics: Seizing power, wielding clout.* Chicago: Follett.

Kuttner, R. 2003. The great crash, Part II. *The American Prospect*, 14(6), 47–49.

Lavin, M. R. 1992. *Business information: How to find it, how to use it*, 2nd ed. Phoenix: Oryx Press.

Levering, R. 1988. *A great place to work: What makes some employers so good (and most so bad)*. New York: Random House.

Levering, R., Moskowitz, M., and Katz, M. 1994. *The 100 best companies to work for in America*, rev. ed. New York: Penguin Plume Books.

Margerison, C. J. 1979. *How to assess your managerial style*. New York: AMACOM (a division of American Management Association).

McCarroll, T. 1992, December 28. How IBM was left behind. *Time*, 26–28.

McClelland, D. C. 1972. The two faces of power. In D. C. McClelland and R. S. Steele, eds., *Human motivation: A book of readings* (pp. 300–316). Morristown, NJ: General Learning Press.

Naisbitt, J., and Aburdene, P. 1985. *Re-inventing the corporation: Transforming your job and your company for the new information society*. New York: Warner.

Pasternack, B. A., and Viscio, A. J. 1998. *The centerless corporation: A new model for transforming your organization for growth and prosperity*. New York: Simon & Schuster.

Peter, L. J., and Hull, R. 1984. *The Peter principle*. New York: Bantam.

Peters, T. J., and Waterman, R. H. 1982. *In search of excellence: Lessons from America's best-run companies*. New York: Harper & Row.

Pink, D. 2001. *Free agent nation*. New York: Warner.

Reich, R. B. 1992. *The work of nations*. New York: Vintage.

Rosen, S., and Paul, C. 1998. *Career renewal: Tools for scientists and technical professionals*. San Diego: Academic Press.

Schein, E. H. 1980. *Organizational psychology*, 3rd ed. Englewood Cliffs, NJ: Prentice Hall.

Schein, E. H. 1985. *Organizational culture and leadership*. San Francisco: Jossey-Bass.

Stitt, D. 1998. The executive. Available online at www.all-creatures.org. Accessed on August 5, 2003.

Wallach, E. J. 1983. Individual and organization: The cultural match. *Training and Development Journal*, 37(2), 29–36.

Wootton, B. H., and Ross, L. T. 1995. Hospital staffing patterns in urban and nonurban areas. *Monthly Labor Review*, 118(3), 23–33.

Chapter 7

Using Your Speaking Skills to Get a Job: Interviewing for Information

Interviewing is a subject that strikes terror into the hearts of job seekers everywhere. Writing résumés and researching companies, although time consuming, are parts of the job search that can be done in a relatively relaxed manner. But interviewing is something else. An interview is over almost in a flash, and a lot can happen in a short amount of time. The interviewer will ask you many questions, some of which you may not anticipate. You may be unsure whether you responded competently. Your voice may become shaky and unsteady, indicating your lack of composure. Your hands may be clammy when you first meet the interviewer; both of you will know how tense you are. You will probably be afraid that your mind won't work fast enough. You may trip over some words, again revealing your nervousness and lack of confidence. You know the interview is at the very center of the job search process, and this make-or-break atmosphere is what produces the strain of the situation. Interviewing is an activity you may have participated in only a few times, or it may be something you know you will have to do sometime to get a job but have never done before. Thus, most job hunters approach the interview with a sense of fear and apprehension.

Because of the tension surrounding the job interview, career counselors conceived the idea of first using interviewing as a means of obtaining information rather than a job. In doing this, a job seeker could improve interview techniques and obtain essential facts and knowledge about organizations and occupational opportunities at the same time. What could be better? If you made mistakes during the interview, disaster would not strike, because a job offer was not riding on the outcome. The risk of rejection was removed from the situation, and the pressure was considerably lessened. The people with whom job seekers talked would benefit, too. They could have the pleasure of reflecting on their work experiences and sharing their insights with another person who valued their knowledge. They could feel the satisfaction of helping someone else get started and possibly playing some part in their success.

Perhaps inevitably, some problems developed with the use of interviews for information. Some job hunters abused the ethics of this kind of interview when they found they could use it to get around the screening devices of the personnel or human resources department and move directly into the office of a person with hiring authority. The more those people with the power to hire were exposed to clever sales pitches for jobs rather than honest inquiries for new perceptions and understanding, the more suspicious they became of those who wanted to interview "for information only." Consequently, with some employers you may need to overcome an initial doubt concerning your motives. Tell them you are not asking them to consider you for a job at this time. Interviewing for information must be done sincerely and genuinely.

Informational interviewing is a powerful instrument in the job search. Used correctly and for the proper reasons, it can give you all kinds of new knowledge and widen your network of personal contacts. The nonjob survey—another name some people have given for the informational interview—will help you discover features about occupations, jobs, companies, and employers you cannot find any other way. And the more you interview for information, the more you become accustomed to interviewing itself. You begin to lose the anxieties and terrors you once felt about interviewing, and you become better equipped to handle the worries and pressures of job interviews when they arise.

PURPOSES AND ADVANTAGES OF INFORMATIONAL INTERVIEWING

An informational interview is just what the name suggests: an interview for information. It is a meeting between you and a person who has information that will help you in your job search. Your intent is to obtain advice and information about what the people you visit do in their positions and what their industry is like (Collins, 2002). This type of interview comes before job interviewing. Informational interviewing was recommended as a method of career exploration in the first book of this Career Planning Guide series. Now it is recommended as a way to discover jobs that are not publicly advertised. In fact, many job search authorities believe that informational interviewing is the only way to uncover at least 50 percent of all job openings, and particularly the hidden job market (Stoodley, 1997). As you talk with people about their jobs, you build a network of personal contacts from which you can gather information for a complete job search. Informational interviewing has been called the nonjob interview survey approach (Billingsley, 1978), because it involves making a survey of a company but not asking the employer for a job. Your purpose in a nonjob interview is to gain knowledge about work organizations and how they employ particular occupations of interest to you.

There are a number of advantages to using the informational interview technique. There may be gaps in the knowledge of occupations and organizations you have gained from your investigation of printed sources in publications and on the Internet, and the only way you can fill in those empty spaces is to talk with people. In some cases, occupations may be so new or organizations may be so small that they are not on the Internet, and no written material can be found about them; therefore, all of your information about them must come from people.

Informational interviewing gives you the freedom to hold more of the conversation in your own style (you are asking the questions) and to evaluate employers and their companies for yourself. There is less pressure or stress in this type of interview, because you are not discussing a specific job opening. Acceptance or rejection is not an issue; no such decision must be made. If you are talking with a person who is in a position to hire, that person doesn't have the pressure of such a decision either. You can relax more in this kind of interview, because you are screening the employer and the organization. You can focus on your needs more than those of the employer, although the needs of the employer are among the pieces of information you are trying to discover. The information you obtain is more likely to be up-to-date than the printed material you read. (Some printed information hangs around on the Internet for a long time.) Finally, by asking the referral question, you may add more personal contacts to your network of people who could help you later in your job search.

Typically, job seekers ask for employment instead of asking questions to determine whether the job and the employer are right for them. Interviewing only for career advice will set you apart from "the herd"—people whose first communication with an employer is to ask them for a job. "The best way to get a job is to ask for job information, advice, and referrals; never ask for a job" (Krannich and Krannich, 2003, p. 159).

Once in a while, the informational interview becomes an indirect route to a job offer. If you are talking with a person who has hiring authority, there is always the possibility you will impress that person enough that he or she will offer you a job. Remember, however, that the move to change the informational interview into a job interview must come from the employer. For the job seeker to switch an informational interview into a request for a job is dishonest and invades the employer's territory under false pretenses.

You may find that the greatest benefit of the informational interview technique is the loss of anxiety and fear of talking with people you do not know. The people you interview are generally very cordial when you ask them for facts and advice; in fact, they feel complimented. Students may approach an informational interview exercise with self-doubt and misgivings, only to emerge from it in high spirits, elated at their success, more knowledgeable, having made another contact or a friend, and ready to continue the process.

One cautionary note needs to be made, however. All information, particularly from interviewing, should be evaluated and verified. No one person represents everyone in the organization or the occupation. Find out whether the perceptions of the person you have interviewed are accurate, up-to-date, and objective. They should be relatively consistent with the data you obtain from other informational interviews and the material you read.

INFORMATIONAL INTERVIEW PROCEDURES

One formula for handling the problems associated with interviewing is the PIE method created by Daniel Porot (1996). PIE stands for *Pleasure* (or *Practice*), *Information*, and *Employment*. Because many people are shy when they talk with people for information and then for jobs, Porot suggests starting the interview process by talking with anyone who shares your enthusiasm about a topic not related to jobs. The subject could be a hobby, an interest, an admired person or object, or a cause that inspires your concern. The purpose of an interview for pleasure (or practice) is to develop confidence in your conversational skills and add people, even strangers, to your contact network. The interview for information is held with a worker in an occupation and/or organization in which you are interested. Although informational interviewing can be as simple as holding conversations with friends about their occupations, it usually requires a more methodical approach (Crosby, 2002), described fully in the following list. Interviewing for employment is covered in the next chapter.

Setting up and carrying out an informational interview generally proceeds along the following lines: (1) Identify and investigate a target organization. (2) Identify a person within the organization with whom to talk. (3) Understand and ethically use the informational interview approach. (4) Make an appointment by letter or telephone. (5) Prepare questions for the interview. (6) Conduct the informational interview. (7) Follow up the interview by writing a thank-you letter.

1. Identify and investigate a target organization. Read everything you can about the company and its industry *before* interviewing a person for information about it. Working people are busy people. However, they are generally willing to give you some of their time, especially when your questions are specifically tailored to their organization, industry, or occupation and the information they provide cannot be found anywhere else. They do not appreciate giving information you could have just as easily discovered for yourself, particularly when it is widely available in print (Bolles, 2003). For ideas on setting this beginning step in motion, refer to the previous chapter on researching work organizations.

2. Choose people to interview. Identify people within the organization likely to be available for informational interviews. They can be people who are working in a major occupational field you are interested in. They can have the authority to hire; however, it is better to start below top levels in the organization. You should *not* interview anyone who could become your boss (Porot, 1996). The people you interview can be important decision makers in the organization: a department head, a section chief, an administrative aide, or even an executive vice president. A middle manager, a staff worker, or a second-in-command in a department could also be appropriate, because these people may serve on committees that advise employers on hiring matters. Include all kinds of workers—secretaries, production workers, custodians, and so on. They know a lot about what goes on in an organization, even if they are not in a position of great authority.

With whom do you begin interviewing for information in an organization? Start with people who work in the occupational field you intend to pursue. In most cases, they should be people in lesser leadership roles. Then, if you need to, work up to people in top management (Bolles, 2003). The person you start with could be someone you already know or a person to whom you have been referred by a personal contact. If you or your contact do not know anyone inside your target organization, try interviewing someone in your occupational field from a similar organization or even a competing company.

Go over the names from the personal contact list you started building in the "Personal Contacts/Networking" section of Chapter 2. Perhaps you have a contact already working on the inside of your target organization. If not, does someone on your personal contact list know of a person within the organization? If that person is not working in your occupational field, talk with her or him anyway because there are plenty of questions you can ask about the organization. If you are in a career class or group, extend your contact list with Exercise 7-3, at the end of this chapter, which illustrates the reciprocal nature of networking. You may extend your list of contacts while at the same time helping others add to their contact lists.

Researching a company will help you identify people with whom you would like to talk. The second step in this list of procedures thus builds on the first.

3. Understand the purpose of the informational interview, and use it properly. If you have already decided to apply for a job at a workplace, you have gone beyond the purposes of the informational interview. The interview described here is not a job interview; that comes later in the job search. This is an interview for information and advice only.

Informational interviewing is like shopping before you buy a product. Shopping and buying are two separate activities. Shopping is gathering information that provides the basis for a later purchase. When you gather information about occupations and organizations from reading material and interviewing people, you are shopping for jobs (Greco, 1980).

Job seekers and people with hiring authority are analogous to salespeople and buyers, respectively. Sellers believe their product may meet some need of the buyer's. The seller proposes a survey to gather enough information to find out whether this is true. Then both buyer and seller are in a better position to discuss a possible sale. The job seeker, in effect, makes a similar proposal to an employer, asking for information in order to make a decision about whether to pursue a job with the organization (Billingsley, 1978).

Any talk about a job offer comes later, possibly as a result of the informational interview or at the discretion of the employer during the interview. The informational interview is simply a way of getting to talk with knowledgeable people, some of whom may be influential, important, and empowered to hire. Understandably, some employers may be suspicious of informational interviews, having been tricked by a job seeker posing as an information gatherer who suddenly puts the bite on them for a job. Informational interviews can lay the foundation for future job offers, but they were not designed to ask employers for jobs.

4. Write or telephone for an appointment. Have a definite purpose in mind for the interview. If you are in a career-planning class, you can say you are working on a class project to learn more about occupations, organizations, and jobs. An informational interview would help you with this project. Reassure the person that your purpose is not to ask for a job. The worst thing that can happen to you is that this person will say, "I'm too busy." However, most people are delighted when someone asks them for help and advice.

One way to ask for an interview is to write a **letter of introduction** or an **approach letter**. For a sample letter, see Figure 7-1. This type of letter is different from a cover letter or letter of application. The purpose of the cover letter is to obtain a job interview, whereas the approach letter or letter of introduction lets the employer know he or she will not have to make uncomfortable decisions about a job applicant. All you are asking for is an opportunity to obtain more information about an occupation, industry, or organization. No employment demands will be made. If you have been referred, say so by writing, "Your name was given to me by _____, who suggested she (or he) would be a good person to give you information about _____." If there has been no referral, you will have to flatly ask for 20 to 30 minutes of that person's time ("cold turkey" approach). Most people feel complimented by your request and interest in their work, particularly if they have the time to spend with you and you are genuine and sincere in your approach. Do not enclose your résumé with your letter (Krannich, 2002). You do not want to give the

91919 S. Jefferson Avenue
Anyville, Anystate 00000

April 30, 0000

Mr. John Doe
Vice President for Sales
XYZ Corporation
19191 N. Lincoln Street
Anytown, Anystate 00000

Dear Mr. Doe:

I am currently a member of a class (or group) at _____
and have been assigned a career-planning project to complete. The
project concerns an investigation of various occupations and organizations that are of interest to me. I would like to talk with you about a
career in selling and business management in a company such as
yours.

Sales and business management are the two occupations that interest me most at the present time. Interest inventories and work experiences indicate that I should seriously consider sales or management.
Right now, I need to talk with a person who is actually working in
these fields in order to gather information on which to base a decision
about my occupational future.

I will contact your office next Monday in the hope that I can set
up an interview with you. Please be assured I am not using this request for an interview as a way to ask you for a job. I need your advice
and more education before I start to seek a job. I will be most appre-
ciative of any information you can give me.

Respectfully,

Mary H. Dataseeker

Mary H. Dataseeker

Figure 7-1 Sample letter of introduction or approach letter

slightest hint that you might ask for a job at this time. The sample letter of introduction or approach letter should not be copied word for word; use it as a guide.

Your letter should answer the questions who? what? how? and when? Be clear
about *who* you are and *what* you want. Indicate *how* this person can help you. State
when you will call for the interview. If you have learned about the person you want to
interview through a personal contact, start your letter by mentioning that your mutual friend or acquaintance suggested talking with him or her. Always request permission before using a person's name as a referral source. The letter must be perfect
and typed on good-quality paper. Handwritten letters are fine if your handwriting
is good. Show your letter to a friend, counselor, parent, or spouse for proofreading before you send it.

Hello, Mr. Doe. My name is _____ from _____

_____.

I am working on a career-planning project that involves obtaining some

information about _____(name of occupation and/or organization)_____.

I'd like to meet with you for about 20 or 30 minutes to ask you a few questions.

May I suggest next _____ at _____ as a time

for the interview?

[If your request is accepted, make sure you know where and when the interview is to take place.]

Figure 7-2 Sample opening of a telephone request for an interview

You could begin a telephone request in the same way. Over the phone, you can explain that you are working on a career-planning project or contemplating a career change. You need to talk with a person who is currently working in an organization or an occupation that interests you. Ask for about 20 or 30 minutes of time so that you can get some questions answered and get some advice. You can also ask if the person could suggest any written sources of information for you to read before you come to the interview. You want to give the impression that you will not be wasting their time. If your target person says, "I'm busy," offer to schedule a more convenient time. If you hear "I really don't think I can help you," ask for a referral. If the person says they are not hiring, be sure to say you are not looking for a job at this time. Prepare a telephone script, especially when you are just beginning and feel nervous. Practice your script by yourself or with someone before your call. Figure 7-2 offers an idea for starting the telephone conversation.

Resist the suggestion of interviewing over the telephone if the opportunity is offered. Try to hold the interview where the person is employed so you can see the work environment for yourself.

Another way to obtain an informational interview is to have someone who knows the person you want to interview arrange the appointment for you. You could also appear directly at the organization without making a formal appointment. You may not be able to hold an interview right then and there, but you could try to arrange an appointment for a later time. If you cannot get by the front desk, try holding an impromptu informational interview with the receptionist. Ask this person some of your questions. Receptionists and other support staff know much more about their company than others often realize. They know how the organization works, the names of key people, job requirements, and so on (Quintessential Careers, 2003). Sometimes you can simply create an opportunity to interview for information on the spur of the moment. It can develop anytime or anywhere. You don't have to be in an office to hold an informational interview.

5. Prepare your questions. First, let's go over a few questions that should *not* be asked. "What does your company do?" heads the list (after "Is there a job here I could apply for?"). Even in an interview for information, employers and workers are likely to surmise you are just going through the motions or too lazy to find out the most elementary information about the organization. In this book, the subject of researching the organization came *ahead* of this chapter. The least you should know before interviewing are the products the company manufactures or the services it provides to "make its living." Do not ask about your interviewee's salary. Stay away from other sensitive information such as "What do you think of your boss?"

Before the interview, try to learn something about the person you will be interviewing. If this is not possible, don't worry—after all, you are the one seeking information. Write down your questions on sheets of paper or a notepad. Ask how the person became interested in the occupation and the organization and how your interviewee got there. Ask about the responsibilities of the job, the abilities and preparation needed, and what features of the work give personal satisfaction. Ask how she or he views the future of the job and workplace and what changes seem to be forthcoming. Avoid asking for information you could obtain in printed form elsewhere. A list of possible questions to ask in an informational interview follows in the next section. The last question to ask is for the names of any other people with whom you could talk. You want to expand your network of personal contacts. The referral question should always be asked before leaving the interview. If you obtain the names of more people from your interviewee, politely ask if you could use his or her name as an introduction to the referral. Most people will give you permission to do so.

You should have at least 15 questions for an interview of 20 or 30 minutes. Prepare a few extra questions in case your interviewee gives short, concise answers or asks you to stay longer. Frame your questions in an open-ended style to allow your interviewee to elaborate on answers. Avoid questions that encourage a simple yes/no response (Crosby, 2002). Concentrate on questions that have answers not easily found elsewhere, such as in company literature. Prioritize your questions in order of importance to be sure your greatest concerns are addressed. If you don't have time to ask all of them, at least you will have covered the most important ones (Hansen, 2000).

6. Conduct the interview. Plan to arrive 10 minutes early. By all means, get there on time. If you are unavoidably late (flat tire, traffic jam, detour), call and explain. In this situation, a cellular phone is very handy. When you arrive at the organization's work site, note the physical surroundings. Take into account characteristics such as the attractiveness of the workplace, where you would park, places for lunch, how people dress, whether the atmosphere is quiet or noisy, where you would work if hired there some day, and so on (Hansen, 2000).

When you meet the person you are interviewing, establish eye contact, give an impression of enthusiasm, smile, shake hands steadily, and introduce yourself after addressing her or him by name ("Hello, Mr. Smith; I'm Sally Miller.") Remind your interviewee of why you are there—to acquire more information about this person's job, occupational field, and/or company. In an informational interview, you are reversing the roles in a job interview. You become the interviewer. Begin by expressing your appreciation for this person spending time with you (Krannich and Krannich, 2003). Have your written questions with you, and use them as a framework for conducting the interview. Do the same things you would for a job interview: dress properly, have a neat appearance, know something about the company, show you are prepared from the questions you ask, listen carefully, maintain good eye contact, and so on. Refer to the next chapter (on job interviews) for more details. Have a clear purpose for your interview session. Limit yourself to goals that are achievable in the short amount of interview time you have. Carry notepaper (or this book with its informational interview exercise at the end of this chapter) and a pen or pencil with you to write responses to your questions in the form of notes or shorthand during the interview. Complete the answers from the words or phrases in your notes afterward. A tape recorder allows you to maintain better eye contact, but always ask permission of the person you are interviewing before you use one. Some people prefer to trust their memory and give the interviewee their full attention; however, have a notepad handy to write down everything you remember immediately after the interview (Hansen, 2000). The best strategy is to write questions on paper ahead of the interview and leave space for responses, as demonstrated in Exercise 7-1, the informational interview exercise. Also, you will need some paper on which to write in case you get the names of referrals.

Know when to end your interview. Adhere to the time limits you established when you set up the interview. You could say, "I want to stay within the 20 (or 30) minutes we agreed upon, so I have one final question for you." After the interviewee's response, be sure to thank the person for the time he or she spent with you. If the interview has gone well, it's all right to leave copies of your résumé with the person you have interviewed, as long as you make clear you are not asking for a job at this time. Just say that if he or she meets or hears of anyone who is looking for a job applicant with your career interests, abilities, and preparation, you would appreciate your résumé being passed on to that person. You will have expanded your opportunity to connect with employers who have jobs to offer.

7. Follow up by always writing a thank-you letter. Express your gratitude for the time, attention, and help given you. Send the thank-you note to the person interviewed so it is received no later than three days after the interview. Your thoughtfulness marks you as a courteous person and serves to activate the memory of the person you interviewed. If you did not leave your résumé after the interview, you could send several copies of it with your thank-you letter. Explain that you would be grateful, should the opportunity arise, to have your résumé passed on to an employer who may be looking for a person such as yourself. A separate thank-you note should go to the administrative assistant, if you arranged the appointment through one. Good impressions on assistants and receptionists might be very helpful later if you go back to their employer for a job interview. They could be asked for their opinions of job candidates. Also, consider sending follow-up notes to people in your contact network informing them of your progress in the job search.

SUGGESTED QUESTIONS FOR THE INFORMATIONAL INTERVIEW

Use the following list of questions as a guide. If the answer to any of these questions is available in print, read about the subject; don't ask a busy person to provide answers that could easily have been looked up (Bolles, 2003). People prefer to answer questions only they are able to answer. Compose questions of your own to fit the circumstances of the occupation or organization you are investigating. Be as specific as you can. Where you see "this occupation/organization" in the following list, substitute the name of the actual occupation or organization in your question. Restate your purpose for the interview. Make sure you have permission to ask questions about the person's occupation and work organization. In the following format, the topic of the question is stated first, followed by a number of questions you could use to open the subject you want to discuss.

1. *Job search techniques used.* How did you get into this occupation/organization? What steps did you take to get where you are now? What methods did you use to find work in the occupation you are in now?
2. *Occupational/organizational interests.* How did you become interested in this occupation/organization? What attracted you to this particular occupation or organization?
3. *Getting started in the occupation.* What entry-level jobs would you recommend to qualify a person for this occupational field? What is the likely progression of jobs, from the beginning to the top?
4. *Responsibilities in the work.* What does the company expect you to do on the job? What responsibilities and duties do you have in your work? What challenges do you (or, would I most likely) face in your job? What characteristics should a person like me look for in a job such as the one you have? How does the company evaluate an employee's work performance?
5. *Customers, competition.* Who are the company's customers? What is the company's relationship with its customers? Who are the company's competitors? What is your company's rank or standing compared with your competitors in the industry? How does your company differ from its competitors?

6. *Abilities and qualifications required.* What skills, aptitudes, or personal qualifications does a person need for this occupation (or to work in this organization)? What essential abilities are needed to do your job well?

7. *Preparation and background needed.* What preparation, education, training, or background do you recommend to enter this field of work? Are particular degrees or licenses required to enter the occupation?

8. *Values and personal satisfaction.* What aspects of this occupation/organization give you personal satisfaction? What values are expressed in your occupation or by the organization?

9. *The organizational culture.* What basic assumptions and beliefs are shared and supported by most people in your division or organization? What practices and ceremonies mean a lot to those working here and to the organization? Who are the "heroes" or exemplary figures in this organization, and what do they stand for? What is the guiding philosophy of your organization or department?

10. *Personality characteristics.* What personal traits, values, and interests do you believe are necessary or helpful to succeed and advance in your occupation or organization? What personal qualities do administrators and supervisors look for in their employees here?

11. *Causes of dissatisfaction.* What are the major frustrations, annoyances, or sources of dissatisfaction you face in the occupation or organization? What problems, both internal and external, can cause dissatisfaction in the job or workplace? What procedures are in place for resolving conflicts within the organization? How do you personally manage conflict among employees?

12. *Unique qualities or strengths.* What strengths set your occupation/organization apart from others? What are some of the best things you can say about your work (or company)?

13. *Working conditions.* How much time do you spend at work? Is the amount of time you spend on the job due more to the nature of the occupation or to the nature of your particular organization? Does your working time affect the amount of time you can spend with your family? How do people dress for work here? Is the work mostly indoors or outdoors? What is the noise level? Does the physical layout of the building(s) make the organization's work environment pleasant? Please describe the morale of the people who work for the organization. What are some of the reasons for their attitude?

14. *Salary ranges.* What are the beginning, average, and top salaries or wages in your occupation? How does your organization pay in comparison to other organizations in the same industry? What fringe benefits are offered? (Do *not* ask, What is your salary? Ask about salary in general terms only.)

15. *Decision-making patterns.* How would you describe the decision-making style of your organization? Who makes the decisions on how work will be done in your department?

16. *Organization of the organization.* What are the lines of authority in your company? (Ask for an organizational chart.) To whom do you report? Whom do you supervise?

17. *Advancement opportunities.* What are the opportunities for advancement, promotion, or change of jobs within the organization? Where could I expect to be in this organization after five years with a good work record?

18. *Typical day at work.* Describe a typical day at work in your occupation and in this organization. Can you leave your job behind after work, or is it the kind of job you take home with you, and how does this happen?

19. *Related occupations.* What other occupations are closely related to this one? Would one need the same skills and aptitudes for them? Are any related occupations represented in your organization?

20. *Temporary work and courses to take while in college.* Could you suggest any temporary, part-time, or summer work experience that would help a person

prepare for your occupation? What courses in school or college were especially helpful to you in preparing for this occupation?

21. *Professional associations.* Which professional journals and organizations would help me learn more about this occupational field? What advantages do you see in joining this occupation's professional (or trade) association?

22. *Future projections.* What do you see in the future for your occupation or organization? Will there be a continued demand for it (or its products and services)? Is the number of workers in the occupation or organization growing or declining? How secure will employment be in the occupation or organization?

23. *Changes.* What changes do you think are coming for your occupation or organization over the next few years? How can a person prepare for those changes? What are the latest developments in your field?

24. *Special problems and concerns.* Are there any special problems, concerns, situations, circumstances, or challenges of which a person like me should be aware when considering this occupation or organization? How would you try to solve these problems or face these challenges?

25. *Other information or advice.* What other advice or information can you give a person considering, preparing for, or entering this occupation or organization? Because you know this occupation (or organization) better than I do, what other questions should I be asking about it?

26. *The return visit.* Is it all right to contact you for another interview if I need more information and advice in the future? In case I need more advice and information in the future, could I make another appointment to talk with you?

27. *The referral question.* (Never conclude an informational interview without trying to obtain referrals to other people in the same or similar occupations/organizations.) Could you suggest the names of other people with whom I could talk in this occupation and/or organization? May I mention your name as the person who referred me? (Always get permission to use the name of the person you have interviewed to set up interviews with other people.)

You can also get ideas for questions from the 30 items of the Work Organization Environment Survey and the section on "Things You Need to Know About a Work Organization" in Chapter 6.

IF A JOB OFFER IS MADE . . .

Suppose you go to an informational interview sincerely and honestly seeking new knowledge and the employer is so impressed with you that he or she asks whether you would consider employment at the company. You have a decision to make on the spur of the moment, right in the middle of the interview. The employer is suggesting that the interview for information be changed into an interview for a job. This switch is perfectly legitimate, because the idea comes from the employer. What are your options?

One alternative is to continue interviewing for information. In fact, this is the option recommended by those who propose interviewing for information before interviewing for employment (Porot, 1996). You could say, "I am very honored by your proposal; however, I need more time to think about it. I have a few more companies that I want to look into before I decide which ones I am most serious about." (Then, assuming it is true, "I can assure you that I am greatly impressed by what I have seen here and I will be back to talk with you.")

The second option is to begin discussing the details of the job being offered and move right into the subject that constitutes the next chapter of this book. However, advocates of informational interviewing believe this is a mistake. Why? You have not prepared for a job interview, and you could be prematurely closing out the possibility of a better job offer from an employer you haven't contacted yet. It's better to stick to the original purpose of the informational interview and then decide which organizations you want to contact for an employment interview.

EXERCISE 7-1 INFORMATIONAL INTERVIEW EXERCISE

The directions for this exercise consist of following the informational interview technique outlined under "Informational Interview Procedures." For people in a career-planning group or class, there may be an eighth step: preparing a report for an instructor, counselor, or group to evaluate. You may also be asked to give a short account of your experience to your group or class. The informational interview report has three basic parts:

1. *Identification material.* Your name, the name and title of the person you interviewed, the organization that person works for, where the interview was held, and the date of the interview.

2. *Questions asked and answers received.* Your written list of questions composed before the informational interview took place and the answers you obtained in an abbreviated or shorthand form.

3. *Summary of subjects discussed and information obtained.* A short review of the topics covered and the knowledge gained from the interview.

These are working papers, so a polished essay is not a primary concern in the exercise. If you make a tape, include it. The purpose of the exercise is to experience the techniques of informational interviewing and to appreciate the potential benefits of this job search activity.

Informational Interview Exercise

A. *Identification Material*

1. Your name _____

2. Your major occupational interest(s) _____

3. Name of person interviewed _____

4. Title of person interviewed (or job duties) _____

5. Where interview was held _____ Date _____

6. Organization this person works for _____

7. Why did you select this person to interview? _____

   _____

8. Thank-you letter sent? ____ Date _____ Will send (date) _____

B. *Questions asked/answers received* (*Note:* Questions must be composed *before* the interview; answers can be briefly summarized *during* and *after* the interview.)

1. Question: _____

   Answer: _____

   _____

2. Q: _____

   A: _____

   _____

3. Q: _____

   A: _____

   _____

4. Q: _____

    A: _____

    _____

5. Q: _____

    A: _____

    _____

6. Q: _____

    A: _____

    _____

7. Q: _____

    A: _____

    _____

8. Q: _____

    A: _____

    _____

9. Q: _____

    A: _____

    _____

10. Q: _____

    A: _____

    _____

11. Q: _____

    A: _____

    _____

12. Q: _____

    A: _____

    _____

13. Q: _____

    A: _____

    _____

14. Q: _____

    A: _____

    _____

15. Q: _____

    A: _____

    _____

C. *Write a short summary.* Describe what you learned from this informational interview.

_____

_____

_____

_____

_____

_____

_____

_____

_____

_____

_____

_____

Informational Interview Report

Use this report form if you are asked to submit your informational interview exercise to your career class instructor, especially if your exercise form is scribbled with notes and abbreviations that are almost impossible for someone else to read. Yes, this will take a little more time, but it gives you the opportunity to make your report more neat and clean by writing or printing more legibly. You can also elaborate on the answers to your questions, which may help you remember more information you received from your interview.

If none of the above paragraph applies to you, use the report form for a second informational interview.

Are you planning further informational interviews beyond the second one? If so, photocopy this report form before using it.

A. *Identification Material*

1. Your name _____

2. Your major occupational interest(s) _____

3. Name of person interviewed _____

4. Title of person interviewed (or job duties) _____

   _____

5. Where interview was held _____ Date _____

6. Organization this person works for _____

7. Why did you select this person to interview? _____

   _____

8. Thank-you letter sent? _____ Date _____ Will send (date) _____

B. *Questions asked/answers received* (*Note:* Questions must be composed *before* the interview; answers can be briefly summarized or elaborated on *during* or *after* the interview.)

1. Question: _____

    Answer: _____

    _____

2. Q: _____

    A: _____

    _____

3. Q: _____

    A: _____

    _____

4. Q: _____

    A: _____

    _____

5. Q: _____

    A: _____

    _____

6. Q: _____

    A: _____

    _____

7. Q: _____

    A: _____

    _____

8. Q: _____

    A: _____

    _____

9. Q: _____

    A: _____

    _____

10. Q: _____

    A: _____

    _____

11. Q: _____

    A: _____

    _____

12. Q: _____

    A: _____

    _____

13. Q: _____

   A: _____

   _____

14. Q: _____

   A: _____

   _____

15. Q: _____

   A: _____

   _____

C. *Write a short summary.* Describe what you learned from this informational interview.

_____

_____

_____

_____

_____

_____

_____

_____

_____

_____

_____

_____

_____

_____

_____

_____

_____

_____

_____

_____

_____

_____

Oh, we have vacations! Two days a week . . . sometimes.

EXERCISE 7-2 FIRST IMPRESSIONS EXERCISE

First impressions, rightly or wrongly, carry a lot of weight when interviewers and employers evaluate you. Naturally, you want to create a positive first impression by appearing properly dressed, poised, and in control. Do you impress other people as you think you do? One way to find out is to conduct an experiment.

In the following list, circle five words that describe the impression you would most like to make when you meet another person for the first time. The word in parentheses after each item has the same or a similar meaning to the first word. If it expresses more clearly the impression you want, circle it instead.

Adventurous (daring)	Intelligent (bright)
Alert (observant)	Knowledgeable (well-informed)
Ambitious (aspiring)	Mature (grown-up)
Assertive (strong-willed)	Mild (placid)
Businesslike (efficient)	Modest (humble)
Capable (competent)	Optimistic (positive)
Caring (concerned)	Organized (disciplined)
Cautious (careful)	Outgoing (sociable)
Charming (appealing)	Pleasant (agreeable)
Cheerful (good-natured)	Polite (gracious)
Confident (self-assured)	Practical (down-to-earth)
Considerate (kind)	Progressive (forward-looking)
Decisive (firm)	Quiet (reticent)
Delicate (refined)	Radiant (sparkling)
Dominating (masterful)	Reliable (trustworthy)
Easygoing (relaxed)	Reserved (self-controlled)
Enterprising (energetic)	Sensitive (perceptive)
Enthusiastic (responsive)	Serious (resolute)
Forceful (aggressive)	Stylish (fashionable)
Friendly (amiable)	Tolerant (permissive)
Fun (playful)	Traditional (conservative)
Genuine (sincere)	Trusting (accepting)
Graceful (agile)	Unconventional (eccentric)
Hardworking (industrious)	Vivacious (lively)
Humorous (witty)	Warm (compassionate)

Next, have a conversation with someone you do not know. Talk for at least five minutes. Then, using the following form, ask the person with whom you have talked to select the five words that he or she believes best describe you. Cover the first list of words so the other person will not see the five words you have selected. If you are in a class, exchange lists with another person. Make sure you do not know each other well. This is a test of first impressions.

Please circle the five words you believe best describe the person with whom you have just talked. The word in parentheses has the same meaning as, or a similar meaning to, the first word. If it expresses more clearly the impression you want to describe, circle it instead.

Adventurous (daring)	Intelligent (bright)
Alert (observant)	Knowledgeable (well-informed)
Ambitious (aspiring)	Mature (grown-up)
Assertive (strong-willed)	Mild (placid)
Businesslike (efficient)	Modest (humble)
Capable (competent)	Optimistic (positive)
Caring (concerned)	Organized (disciplined)
Cautious (careful)	Outgoing (sociable)
Charming (appealing)	Pleasant (agreeable)
Cheerful (good-natured)	Polite (gracious)
Confident (self-assured)	Practical (down-to-earth)
Considerate (kind)	Progressive (forward-looking)
Decisive (firm)	Quiet (reticent)
Delicate (refined)	Radiant (sparkling)
Dominating (masterful)	Reliable (trustworthy)
Easygoing (relaxed)	Reserved (self-controlled)
Enterprising (energetic)	Sensitive (perceptive)
Enthusiastic (responsive)	Serious (resolute)
Forceful (aggressive)	Stylish (fashionable)
Friendly (amiable)	Tolerant (permissive)
Fun (playful)	Traditional (conservative)
Genuine (sincere)	Trusting (accepting)
Graceful (agile)	Unconventional (eccentric)
Hardworking (industrious)	Vivacious (lively)
Humorous (witty)	Warm (compassionate)

When you receive the other person's perceptions (or first impressions) of you, ask yourself whether this is the impression you want to make on other people. If so, congratulate yourself. If not, what changes can you make?

EXERCISE 7-3 PERSONAL CONTACTS SUGGESTED BY OTHER MEMBERS OF THE CLASS OR GROUP

Part One

Do you need more contacts in your networking efforts? If so, perhaps help could come from your career class or group (if you are in one). On the following form, give your name, major occupational choice, and the name or type of work organization that interests you or that you are researching. Pass your book around to each member of the class or group for suggestions of people you could contact. (They will be sending their books to you for your suggestions for personal contacts.) A follow-up session for this exercise will be needed to give and confirm addresses and telephone numbers—and, possibly, to add more names.

Part Two

Because this exercise illustrates the principle of sharing information in networking, you will need to copy the names of the class or group members you are helping and the names of people you have suggested to them. Before the next class or group session, obtain the addresses and telephone numbers of contacts you have suggested. Then you can share this information with your classmates or group members, while they share their information with you. (Some class/group members may be willing to write a letter of introduction for you, particularly if you are willing to do the same for them.)

Part One: Personal Contacts Suggested by Other Class/Group Members

Your Name _____

Your Major Occupational Choice _____

Name or Type of Work Organization You Are Researching _____

Name of Personal Contact	Address	Telephone	Suggested By
_____	_____	_____	_____
_____	_____	_____	_____
_____	_____	_____	_____
_____	_____	_____	_____
_____	_____	_____	_____
_____	_____	_____	_____
_____	_____	_____	_____
_____	_____	_____	_____
_____	_____	_____	_____
_____	_____	_____	_____
_____	_____	_____	_____

Part Two: Personal Contacts I Suggested to Other Class/Group Members

Name of Class/Group Member and Their Major Occupational Choice	Name or Type of Organization Interested In	Name of Person Who Could Be a Personal Contact (include address or telephone number)
Examples:		
Jane Coe Phys. Therapist	City Hospital	Ben Helpful (000-111-2222)
John Doe Drafter	XYZ Corp.	May I. Helpyou, 9999 S. Benevolent Rd., Anytown, TX
_____	_____	_____
_____	_____	_____
_____	_____	_____
_____	_____	_____

Name of Class/Group Member and Their Major Occupational Choice	Name or Type of Organization Interested In	Name of Person Who Could Be a Personal Contact (include address or telephone number)
_____	_____	_____
_____	_____	_____
_____	_____	_____
_____	_____	_____
_____	_____	_____
_____	_____	_____
_____	_____	_____
_____	_____	_____

SUMMARY

1. Two broad categories of interviews are informational interviews and job interviews. You never ask for a job in an informational interview; you request this type of interview to obtain facts and to evaluate returning for a job interview at a later time.

2. Informational interviews have several advantages. They can fill in the gaps of information you have collected from written publications about occupations and organizations. You can hold this kind of interview without the stress and worry of rejection. You can screen employers; they must pass your selection test. You can concentrate on your needs rather than those of the employer. Occasionally, an employer may be impressed enough with your potential to offer you a job on the spot. The initiative for changing an informational interview into a job interview, however, must always come from the employer. It is unethical to interview an employer on the pretense of a request for information when you are actually planning to ask for a job.

3. You need to follow several steps in conducting an informational interview: (1) Identify and research target organizations. (2) Identify people who are working in a major occupational prospect of yours or in an organization that would be attractive to you. (3) Understand the ethical issue that the request for information is not another way to ask an employer for a job. (4) Make the interview appointment. (5) Prepare questions. (6) Hold the interview. (7) Write a thank-you note expressing your appreciation for the time the person you interviewed spent with you. (If you are in a career class or group, an eighth step might be to prepare a report of an informational interview exercise.)

REFERENCES

Billingsley, E. 1978. *Career planning and job hunting for today's student: The nonjob interview approach.* Santa Monica, CA: Goodyear.

Bolles, R. N. 2003. *What color is your parachute?* Berkeley, CA: Ten Speed Press.

Collins, C. 2002. Finding the right fit in a changing workplace. *Career Planning and Adult Development Newsletter,* 18(4), 9.

Crosby, O. 2002. Informational interviewing: Get the inside scoop on careers. *Occupational Outlook Quarterly,* 46(2), 32–37.

Greco, B. 1980. *How to get the job that's right for you.* Homewood, IL: Dow Jones-Irwin.

Hansen, K. 2000. *A foot in the door: Networking your way into the hidden job market.* Berkeley, CA: Ten Speed Press.

Krannich, R. L. 2002. *Change your job, change your life,* 8th ed. Manassas Park, VA: Impact Publications.

Krannich, R. L., and Krannich, C. R. 2003. *The job hunting guide: Transitioning from college to career.* Manassas Park, VA: Impact Publications.

Porot, D. 1996. *The PIE method for career success: A unique way to find your ideal job.* Indianapolis, IN: JIST Works.

Quintessential Careers. 2003. Requesting an informational interview in person or by phone. Available online at www.quintcareers.com. Acccessed on May 16, 2003.

Stoodley, M. 1997. *Information interviewing: How to tap your hidden job market,* 2nd ed. Garrett Park, MD: Garrett Park Press.

Now let me ask you some questions, mister. Tell me your qualifications!

Chapter 8

Using Your Speaking Skills to Get a Job: Interviewing for Jobs

"This is it," you say to yourself. All your hard work in preparing a résumé and a cover letter, talking with personal contacts, registering at the college career services office, filling out application forms, scanning the newspaper want ads, researching companies, and talking to workers and employers comes down to this—going face-to-face with an interviewer for a job. Tension and anxiety mount as the time approaches. Your whole life, you think, is going to be decided in the short span of 30 to 45 minutes. Everything seems to depend on the interview.

Some job seekers worry themselves frantic. If you must torment yourself with anguish, Paul Hellman (1986) suggests that you imagine the worst. Really get into it.

> You walk into the interviewer's dimly lit office, which is painted dark gray and has narrow slits for windows. The interviewer, a beetle-like, spindly-legged creature, looks up and shrieks, "You dare come in here?" He proceeds to chase you around the room with a switchblade. "We went out of business a year ago, but we still wouldn't hire you even if you were the last person on earth." Television cameras zoom in to record your moment of humiliation. You go to pieces and babble incoherently. Wire services pick up the story; it is front-page news all over the world. People point at you as you walk down the street. An "R" for "Rejected" is emblazoned on your chest. Abandoned by family and friends, you wander aimlessly through life, a victim of the job interview!

When you are done with your worst-case scenario, come back to reality. Yes, the interview is important. It is where job offers are made, the culmination of your efforts to land a job. The "job interview world" is replete with stories of applicants stuck in an elevator, or with a price tag hanging on their interview suit, or with blouse buttons popping off, and other embarrassing episodes. Interviewers have their moments, too. One recruiter caught a thread in her skirt on a desk and the entire garment unraveled. She recovered, using a sense of humor. "Good thing I wore a slip today," she told the startled job candidate. And that's the point. Overcome these situations with humor. Don't dwell on the incident. Prepare and practice for the interview. Focus on the other person, and be yourself (Giventer, 1992). Keep in mind the world doesn't end if you are not offered a position. The important thing is to keep going, for many more job possibilities are out there. The more you work at interviewing, the easier it becomes.

Preparation and practice are the keys to effective performance in the job interview. Being prepared lessens the tension that can otherwise build up before such an occasion. Don't just wait for the interview to happen; do things to make it happen better. Research the company and its people. Thoroughly digest the ideas in Chapter 6, the chapter on work organizations. Look presentable, be well groomed, and wear appropriate clothing to make a good impression. The way people dress for the job is part of the information you collect in your visit before the interview. For practice, interview for information (the subject of the previous chapter) before you interview for a job. Also, before the job interview, have a friend, parent, or spouse help you rehearse answering anticipated questions. Questions interviewers typically ask are included in this chapter. Prepare several questions you can ask; write them on a card or piece of paper if you think you might forget them. Find out the interviewer's name so you can use it in your greeting. Figure out what you can do for the organization, what your value to it would be. Contact references for their permission in case you are asked to furnish names of people who will vouch for you. Choose your references carefully, making sure they know your work and will recommend you with sincere enthusiasm. Know the location of your appointment and how to get there, and plan to arrive a few minutes early. These ways of actively preparing and practicing for your job interview will help you approach it in a good spirit and with faith in yourself. You must prepare because job interviews can be negative in some ways. For example, from your job seeker's point of view, the purpose of an initial interview is to win a job offer or a second interview. However, there are employers and interviewers who regard it as a way of eliminating you as a candidate (Krannich, 2002).

Writing about job interviews would be a lot easier if hiring decisions were logical and straightforward. They're not. In the best of all worlds, the employer objectively offers the job to the best-qualified candidate. In the real world, the job is offered to a person who the employer likes best. This is why you must not give up if you are not selected. Sometimes people are hired or not hired for reasons that appear to make absolutely no sense. For example, in this chapter, you will read, "the basic, dark blue or charcoal gray business suit is preferred for most interview occasions." Notice we said "most," because there are always exceptions to a rule. The chief executive officer of one company is quoted as saying, "If they wear a suit, they're automatically out, because it means they don't know enough about us. The more tattoos and body piercings, the better I like you." (Take the hint: Research the organization!) Here's another anecdote about interviews and suits. After a job interview, the candidate was judged to be qualified but uninteresting. The employer invited the applicant and his wife to a San Jose Sharks hockey game that evening. They showed up in business suits, creating another bad impression in the employer's mind. During the game, the candidate suddenly jumped up and made a motion like shark jaws, taking the left hand, palm up, and the right hand, palm down, and clapping them together. That motion saved the day for the applicant; he was hired (Brown, 1998). All we can say is that landing a job is not as rational as we might like it to be.

Despite the subjectivity in job offers that seems to give employers the upper hand, interviewing for a job is a two-way street—it is a mutual exchange of information. You, the job seeker, and the employer are really interviewing each other. The employer is trying to determine whether you have the right qualifications for the job, and you are trying to decide whether this job is right for you.

TYPES OF QUESTIONS

The Job Interview Self-Test in Exercise 8-1 will introduce you to some questions commonly asked in job interviews.

EXERCISE 8-1 JOB INTERVIEW SELF-TEST

Suppose you are seeking employment in your number one occupational choice. To start the exercise, write your major occupational choice, the specific position you are seeking, and the type (or actual name) of the work organization where you are being interviewed. Assume you have the necessary qualifications and preparation for the position. The employer or personnel manager asks several questions, included in the following list. How would you answer these questions? For each interview question, write down the first thoughts that come to your mind. Either write the actual words you would use to respond, or indicate the substance of your response.

Job Interview Self-Test

Occupation _____

Position _____

Name or type of work organization _____

1. Why do you want to enter this occupation as a career?

_____

_____

_____

_____

2. Why are you interested in working for our company (or organization)?

    _____

    _____

    _____

    _____

3. Why should we hire you? What can you do for us?

    _____

    _____

    _____

    _____

4. What kind of people do you want to work with?

    _____

    _____

    _____

    _____

5. What salary range would you consider appropriate for this job?

    _____

    _____

    _____

    _____

6. What do you want to know about our organization? Do you have any questions you want to ask us?

    _____

    _____

    _____

    _____

After you have written your responses, review them and ask, "If I were the employer, would I hire myself? Why?" The six basic questions in Exercise 8-1 are likely to appear in one form or another in most job interviews. Our comments about each question will center on how you could respond, where you could find the information, and why employers ask the question.

Why do you want to enter this occupation as a career? Talk about your career interests, work values, and occupational goals. (Chapter 3 of *Taking Charge of Your Career Direction* identifies occupational interest areas, Chapter 7 prioritizes work values, and Chapter 9 helps you establish career goals.) Answering this question with a statement about your occupational goals and objectives and the values expressed in those goals demonstrates your motivation to achieve in your work. Employers like to hear that a job candidate is interested in a job being offered and values it because there are qualities about the job that make it important. A motivated employee simply makes a greater commitment to the job. To tailor your response to the organization in which you are seeking employment, Yate (2003) suggests calling another company in the field and making a request to speak with someone doing the same job you hope to get (the informational interview, again). Ask what the job is like, what this person does from day to day, how the job fits into the organization, and why she or he likes the work. With this information, you have a better idea of what you are getting into.

Why are you interested in working for our company (or organization)? To answer this question, you must have taken the time and effort to investigate the organization. You can say you have found the company has features that interest you. (Chapter 6 of this book contains information on researching work organizations.) Indicate where your values and interests coincide with those of the company. Employers are interested in finding out what you know about them. The fact that you have spent time researching the organization is a real compliment. Most employers will appreciate and be impressed with your knowledge of their company. Referring to a professional or trade publication article about the company is even more impressive, like putting "the icing on the cake."

Asking what the organization does is a "knockout" question; you could easily lose the chance of a job offer because you didn't do your homework. However, to show interest in the company, you can ask, "What products or services do you plan to introduce in the future?" Also, you can ask the interviewer, "What do you like best about the company? Why?" If the answer includes a lot of hemming and hawing, it may indicate the interviewer doesn't really like the company, whereas an enthusiastic response would mean just the opposite (Fry, 2000).

Why should we hire you? What can you do for us? This is the place to discuss your skills and aptitudes, and a job-related achievement or two. The company's job description may be helpful in uncovering the skills the organization is hoping to find. Emphasize how your abilities and background will fit the needs of the organization and the particular job you are seeking in it. Support your claim to an ability or skill with an achievement that proves it. The ability to substantiate your strengths will clearly separate you from your competition, and is one of the most important concepts in the job search process (LaFevre, 1992). (Chapters 5 and 6 of *Taking Charge of Your Career Direction* cover the subjects of achievements and abilities.) The employer has tasks to accomplish and wants to know how your skills and experience will help. Some job search experts consider this question the most fundamental of all.

What kind of people do you want to work with? This question may be another way of asking "What kind of a person are you?" You could think of a set of words that illustrate people, such as the ones you find in Holland's six basic personality types. Chapter 6 of this book gives a quick review of the six types in the section on corporate culture. You can find complete descriptions of the realistic, investigative, artistic, social, enterprising, and conventional types in Holland (1997) or in Chapter 3 of *Taking Charge of Your Career Direction*. Reviewing this material will help you find words that will describe you. You can explain that you are looking for a work environment that has these kinds of people. You want to be compatible with your fellow workers, and you hope your personality fits reasonably well with theirs. Who could argue with these sentiments? The employer has the same hope that you will fit in well. Neither of you wants to contend with personality clashes that are irritating, difficult, and frustrating.

What salary range would you consider appropriate for this job? If no other reason can convince you to explore companies before the job interview, the discussion of salary should. Employers often ask for salary figures because they want to know how much you may cost them and to gather data with which to screen candidates. Not doing your homework for this question can cost you money and even the job itself. Try to learn the salaries of the positions just above and below your target position on the organizational chart. You can begin salary negotiations at the top of this range without pricing yourself out of the market. You can also avoid underselling yourself, only to discover later that you could have settled for a higher figure. Quoting a salary figure that is too high could make you seem unreasonable and unrealistic. A low figure may give the impression that you lack a proper sense of self-worth. In other words, don't appear either greedy or needy.

If you cannot find the salary information you want from company sources, perhaps your personal contacts can provide it. Competing companies may furnish their pay scale for comparable positions. The Internet has a number of Web sites, such as Monster.com, Careerbuilder.com, and Salary.com, that give salary figures for thousands of jobs. You can look at average pay rates in such books as the *Occupational Outlook Handbook* or *The American Almanac of Jobs and Salaries* (Wright, 2000). The National Association of Colleges and Employers (62 Highland Ave., Bethlehem, PA 18017) publishes a quarterly *Salary Survey* for college graduates and maintains a Web site where articles on salaries are accessible (http://www.jobweb.com/SalaryInfo). Remember that salaries differ from region to region of the country.

In some organizations, salary schedules are published and become public knowledge. These wage figures are set by collective bargaining agreements between unions or associations and management. The salary question here is cut-and-dried; management must stick to the terms of the agreement. In some cases, however, the administration may have more flexibility; additional pay may be gained through supplemental job responsibilities. Keep in mind such benefits as paid leave days, medical insurance, pension plans, life insurance, and moving expenses. After you add benefits, a lower salary figure may be worth more than a higher figure.

What should you do if you cannot find definite salary numbers at all? If possible, do not give a dollar figure in the interview. You could state that, although you naturally desire a decent wage, your primary concern is to do the work you want to do. Ask for more time to think about salary. All things considered, it is better to delay salary negotiations until you have decided you want the job and the organization has decided it wants you, and this usually takes more than one interview. If you are the person a company wants, you are in a stronger bargaining position. The company is more likely to move toward the upper limits of a job position's salary range once they have decided to choose you (Half, 1994).

What do you want to know about our organization? Do you have any questions you want to ask us? An opening for you to ask questions is usually a sign the job interview is coming to a close. The further you investigate an organization, the more questions are likely to arise about it. These questions will become more specific and detailed with your increasing knowledge, revealing the extent to which you have researched the company. You should not start your questions inquiring about pay, benefits, expense accounts, vacations, and number of sick days. It is all right to ask about these matters but do so later, preferably after a job offer has been made (Yate, 1998). Combine them with other concerns such as responsibilities you would have on the job, how the job position came to be open, working conditions, the growth potential of the organization, the nature of the work in the position you are seeking, or how the organization employs your chosen occupation. Telephone or write to the human resources or personnel office before your interview, and ask the staff to send you pamphlets and brochures about the organization's products, services, and employee benefits. Ask for the company's annual report. Check with career resource centers, college career services offices, and chambers of commerce for this kind of information.

Employers often ask for your questions to find out whether you are curious about the organization and are motivated to learn more about it. Failure to ask questions may leave the impression that you are not all that interested in the company, a factor that will work against you in a job interview. Suggested questions you might want to ask as a job applicant are given in a later section of this chapter.

INTERVIEWERS

There are all kinds of interviewers. Good ones are able to turn a formal interview into a cordial discussion, make you feel at ease, and bring out a lot of information, all at the same time; however, you cannot assume that all interviewers will be proficient or professional in their work. Interviewing is a demanding job, far more difficult than job seekers realize. It is a real art, requiring extensive verbal and social skills. Some supervisors have been trained to do a different job, but wind up talking to job applicants. They may want to get the interview over as quickly as possible, creating the feeling that you are wasting their time. Other interviewers are pushed into talking with candidates because no one else is available to do the job. Many employers hire others to do the interviewing for them because they find it so burdensome. There are even a very few interviewers who probe where they shouldn't, deliberately create unnecessary stress, or don't take their responsibilities seriously.

Despite this, most interviewers will be competent and experienced. These interviewers will have prepared themselves by knowing some things about you. They will not allow constant interruptions such as a ringing telephone or other people walking into their office. They will display warmth, respect, and empathy for you, and they will be pleasant, practiced, and polite. They will ask you open-ended questions, giving you the opportunity to explain a subject such as a qualification or an experience. Open-ended questions allow a wide range of possible responses (Ivey with Simek-Downing, 1980). For example, which question would you prefer to answer: "What are some things you would like to tell me about your present job?" or "Do you like your current job?" The first question is open; it invites you to select any quality about your job that comes to mind. The second question is closed in that it calls for a yes or no response. Unless a follow-up question is asked or you are given a chance to volunteer an explanation, you may not be able to clarify your likes or dislikes. Not all closed questions are wrong. If a job seeker talks too much, an interviewer may use a closed question to limit the length of the response.

Because questions often put people on the defensive, capable interviewers create opportunities for job candidates to expand and elaborate on topics under discussion. Simple expressions such as "That's interesting," "I see," "Tell me more," or even "Uh-huh" or nods of the head indicate that the interviewer accepts your statements and encourages you to continue. Suppose you say, "I start rather slowly when I learn a new job, but when I know my work, I can do it without help from anyone else." The interviewer responds, "It takes a while for you to acquire new skills, but once you have, they stay with you for good." You feel accepted, listened to, and understood because the interviewer restated or paraphrased your thoughts. Suppose you describe an experience on a previous job by saying, "I appreciated my boss allowing me to try a new idea even though I did not foresee all the difficulties I would have." The interviewer replies, "You were grateful for your employer's support, particularly when the going got tough." Your emotional experience of gratitude is picked up and labeled by the interviewer, making you feel that you have been heard, acknowledged, and interpreted correctly.

In a comfortable atmosphere, you may need to practice restraining yourself from giving too much information. Interviews are not confessionals; you can usually control how much information you want to reveal. Most interviewers are not trying to trick you into making painful or embarrassing disclosures. They want to help you communicate, obtain certain facts about your abilities and preparation, determine your motivation and personality characteristics, stimulate your interest in their organization, and then close the interview courteously and efficiently.

Ron Fry (2000) categorizes three models of interviewers that predominate in organizations. The first type is the **telephone screener**, a busy person often found in small or mid-sized companies with no formal human resources or personnel departments. The main objective of the telephone screener is to discover reasons for removing you from active consideration before arranging a face-to-face meeting. Despite the ease of interviewing from your home, you should try to schedule an in-office meeting where you can establish eye contact and observe body language. If the interviewer insists on a telephone interview and you're not prepared for it, ask for a return call at a mutually agreeable time. When the call does come, try to project a positive picture through your voice and your answers.

The second type of interviewer Fry identifies is the **human screen**, often a human resources professional. These people are likely to be the most skilled interviewers because evaluating job applicants is a significant part of their job. Many job seekers are interviewed, but few are chosen because the major objective of the human screener is to send only the strongest candidates to a hiring manager (the third type of interviewer). Human screeners usually rely on job descriptions, meaning they do not possess the first-hand knowledge that the hiring manager has about the requirements of jobs to be filled. Unless you are applying for a position in human resources, your goal is to go beyond personnel screening and reach the person who has the power to hire.

Managers, the third type of interviewer, are generally supervisors who maneuver interviews into their busy schedules. Their interviews are mostly the result of referrals from the human resources department or from colleagues and personal contacts. The primary objective of the manager is to evaluate the skills, experience, and personal chemistry of the job applicant by means of a personal interview. Because managers could be working very closely with whomever they hire, they try to find out everything they can about an applicant. Managers may not have any formal training in the art of interviewing, but they often develop an intuitive sense of who will or won't be likely to perform the job well and be a good "fit" with others in the work group (Fry, 2000).

TYPES OF JOB INTERVIEWS

All job interviews involve evaluation of the applicant, but beyond this, they can be divided into several types. There are screening, structured, unstructured, group, board, stress, behavioral, serial, and secondary interviews. Two or more types can be combined into a single interview. Analyzing each kind of job interview separately can give you a greater appreciation of this complex form of interaction.

Screening interview. The initial interview is often a screening device; the interviewer does not intend to select anyone for a position at this time. The main purpose of a screening interview is to eliminate candidates who do not possess the necessary qualifications. Interviews conducted in a college career services office and over the telephone are almost always screening interviews. (The telephone is now increasingly being used as the first screening interview.) Your objective as a job candidate is to get invited to the subsequent (or selection) interview by competently presenting your abilities, preparation, and interests and by avoiding factors that can knock you out of the running. The screening interviewer will cover your qualifications and check the facts you have specified on your résumé and application form. Interviewers in this situation are under pressure. If they send unqualified job applicants to managers and supervisors, their own competence becomes suspect, and they could soon be out of a job. You can try to determine ahead of time the factors on which you will be judged. In your informational interviewing, perhaps you can ask for a list of factors by which job candidates are evaluated. Typical rating checklists include items such as enthusiasm, initiative, maturity, leadership potential, appearance, communication skills, experience, technical skills, and education. Many personality traits are difficult to assess with any degree of accuracy. In fact, studies have indicated that there is almost no correlation between the factors rated on a checklist after an initial interview and the ratings of the same factors after a year's observation of job performance (Drake, 1982).

Interviewers should evaluate only realistically observable behavior. Try to avoid the screening interview, if possible; however, for entry-level jobs there are probably few ways around this type of interview.

Structured (or directed) interview. The structured interview proceeds from a preselected list of questions that are asked of each job applicant. After all candidates have been interviewed, their answers are compared in an attempt to be as objective as possible. The interviewer makes notes about the applicant's responses or codes responses on a checklist. This type of interview can be impersonal, but it is the type that is used most often in screening interviews. The more directed or structured an interview becomes, the more difficult it is to introduce your own information to the interviewer. You may feel as if you are caught in a lockstep procedure that allows no variation. You could politely interrupt the schedule of questions by saying, "If I could break into your pattern of questions for just a moment, I'd like to give you some additional material on this point." This statement should be carefully timed and not be said in such a way as to make the interviewer think you are trying to take control of the interview. Most interviewers, no matter how structured their procedure, will give you an opportunity to add your own comments and ask questions.

Unstructured (or nondirected) interview. The questions in the unstructured interview are open-ended, allowing you to respond in many different ways. Open-ended questions give you the choice of how to respond; your answer is not directed by the way the question is asked. One favorite open-ended interview question is "Tell me about yourself." How do you respond? There are probably a half-million things you could say, but you must pick one of them. Even though the atmosphere is nonthreatening, an unstructured interview can cause considerable anxiety. The ambiguity of the situation augments the tension, especially to unprepared job seekers. The unstructured interview offers control of the interview to job applicants, some of whom do not want that responsibility. Interviewers may be more interested in the way you handle unstructured situations than in the content of your remarks. They use a nondirected approach because they believe it is possible to learn more about your personality this way. The more you are encouraged to talk in a job interview, the less structured the process is likely to be. Your goal, however, is no different from that in any other type of interview: You want to set forth your objectives, qualifications, and accomplishments as clearly as you can.

Group interview. When there are many job applicants, the group interview may be used. The technique of the group interview originated in the military as a way of selecting officer candidates. A group was brought together, given a task to accomplish, and carefully watched. From individual interactions within the group, a leader would eventually emerge (Medley, 1992). In a business situation, a group of people is told to hold a discussion on a given topic. Again, the group is observed. Candidates are presented with hypothetical situations that could conceivably occur on the job in order to estimate the degree to which they demonstrate the traits that will lead to success (Fry, 2000). Observers focus more on your behavior with other members of the group than on the actual words spoken. You may never experience this type of interview, but if you do, try to determine the characteristics the interviewers are looking for and direct your attention toward contributing to the functioning of the group.

Board interview. The board or "team" interview brings in one job applicant to face many interviewers. The interviewers have rehearsed their roles before you enter. Let's say seven people are on the board. Six may ask questions, each one concentrating on his or her own area of interest, whereas one person may watch only your nonverbal behavior. Nonverbal communication is body language, the way you express yourself without the use of words. The board interview is most likely to be used by an organization that is interviewing for a high-level position such as president or vice president. If you are ever in this interview situation, pretend you are talking to only one person, the one who is questioning you. In this way, you may forget the other eyes that are on you and mentally convince yourself that you are in a simple one-on-one interview. By concentrating on one person at a time, you may appear more relaxed and maintain your confidence, the two important factors for this type of interview (Medley, 1992).

Stress interview. Job interviews contain a certain amount of stress by their very nature. Some interviewers intentionally introduce stress into the interview to assess the candidate's reaction to pressure. Interviewers justify this approach when the job requires people who can cope with stress. They want to test an applicant's tolerance or resistance in high-pressure situations. The normal interview does not use artificially induced stress methods, so you are not likely to run into them. As for illegal questions, refer to the Pre-employment Inquiry Guide in Chapter 4.

One stress technique is silence. You are answering questions, and suddenly the interviewer becomes very quiet and simply stares at you without saying a word. A few seconds can seem like hours of silence. If you start displaying nervousness and become obviously uncomfortable, you are flunking the test. To pass the test, sit quietly, look up and smile pleasantly, and keep your composure. After a reasonable time, you could ask, "Is there anything more we haven't covered?" or "Would you want me to expand on anything I've mentioned so far?" Other stress techniques include speaking in a stern voice, being unfriendly, challenging everything you say, dwelling on the same subject much longer than necessary, returning to the same issue time after time, increasing the pace of questioning, and allowing progressively less time to compose answers. Some questions involving negative or sensitive issues may be intended to provoke a stressful reaction, as in the following examples:

- Tell me something about yourself that bothers you.
- Describe a time when an idea or a completed project of yours was criticized. What was your reaction?
- Why aren't you earning a higher salary at your age?
- You certainly change jobs a lot. Have you had problems with them?
- In what ways do you think your supervisor could have done a better job?
- Your grades in school are rather low. Are you really suitable for the job?
- Did you know the other applicants for this job have more experience than you?
- Where did you exaggerate or stretch the truth a bit on your résumé?

Try to imagine answering these questions when you are with friends. Request more time to answer. Reframe the question in such a way that you can introduce an ability you can prove you have. Whatever you do, maintain your composure and keep in mind that the interviewer may be pushing you to see how you react.

Behavioral interview. A type of interview that is being used more frequently, the behavioral interview is essentially an insistence on the part of the job interviewers for candidates to move away from vague, theoretical responses when answering questions and describe what they actually would *do* (or have *done*) in a situation. Questions are worded in a way to elicit a concrete reply. For example, instead of simply asking, "How would you deal with an angry person (as a customer, student, client, etc.)?" the question is stated, "Give me an example of when you had to deal with an angry person, and what was the problem and what was the result?" Your answer needs to be more than "I found what the problem was and offered assistance." The behavioral interviewer will consider this response only a half-answer; you need to tell what you actually *did* in offering assistance. When questions are negative, a behavioral interview may seem like a stress interview. The interviewer could say, "Tell me about an occasion when you made a mistake that cost your organization time and money" and press you for details that are embarrassing to admit. (Probably the best response in this situation is to give the details and say how painful the event was, but that it remains in your memory as a valuable learning experience and you are not about to repeat the mistake again.)

Serial or successive interviews. When you are invited to a company's home office after an initial screening interview, you may be given a series of interviews with several interviewers, each one usually on a one-to-one basis. Robert Half (1994) reports from a survey that an average of five people will interview a job candidate for a top management position, four people for a middle management position, and three people will interview a candidate for a staff position. Treat each interviewer as if he or she were the first, establishing a good relationship with each one and repeating any information you may have already given with as much enthusiasm as you can muster. A final decision about whether to offer you employment could be made by a committee composed of people you have met. The fact that you have gotten this far in the interviewing process indicates that you have been doing things right.

Secondary interview. The secondary interview is a follow-up to confirm impressions from the first interview. Any time you have more than one interview with the same person, it is important to be consistent in your responses. As with successive interviews, treat each one as if it were the first. You may grow tired of stating the same information several times, but don't let it show. Your most important interview will be with the person who would become your supervisor or manager in the event that you are hired (Rogers, 1982).

BEFORE THE INTERVIEW

1. *Learn as much as you can about the organization—its products, its services, how large it is, its record of growth, its problems, relationships with its employees, and so on.* Every professional job counselor and every piece of written material about interviewing gives this advice, but too many job seekers still go into the interview not knowing a thing about the company. If you are knowledgeable about the business and the concerns of the organization, you will be in a much better position to show how you can be of value to the employer.

Many companies prepare a fact sheet about their organization, print an annual report, and publish brochures about the kinds of job applicants they are seeking. They will send these publications to you at your request. Talk to insiders who work for the company or who know people working there. Most companies now have Web sites on the Internet. The library has business and industrial directories that give you names and data on organizations. Researching work organizations is thoroughly covered in Chapter 6 of this book.

Knowing some things about the organization will do wonders for your self-confidence as you approach the job interview. You will impress the employer or interviewer because you have taken the time to do your homework.

2. *Determine through your research of the organization and yourself what you can do for the employer and the organization.* Keep in mind that the employer's main interest is going to be what you can do for the organization, not what it can do for you. This is a time to review your past achievements and how they translate into present skills and abilities that could be of use to the employer. Answers may come in the form of increased production, a more efficient way of doing things, a better way of getting people to work together, increased sales, or higher profits. Prepare yourself for this ahead of time; your primary job in the interview is to convince the employer that it is in the organization's best interests to hire you.

3. *Role-play mock (or practice) interviews with a friend.* Rehearse what you want to say during the interview, but don't prepare a speech and memorize it. Practice in front of a mirror. Get a friend or relative to role-play a mock interview, casting yourself as the job applicant and your friend as the job interviewer. Use a video camera if possible, and then review the tape. The more practice you have, the more poise and self-confidence you will acquire for the interview. Anticipate questions the interviewer might ask you. Think of questions you don't want asked, and prepare answers for them. Work out your response to an illegal inquiry before the interview. (Return to Chapter 4 for the discussion on illegal questions.) Prepare questions you can ask at the interview on such subjects as the content of the work, hours, and working conditions.

4. *Make the appointment in a professional manner.* In the last chapter, your purpose in interviewing was for information only. Now you want not only information but also an offer of a job position. Setting up a job interview can be done properly through a written request such as a cover letter or a letter of introduction from a person in your contact network, or by a telephone call. If you have a home answering machine, be sure your message conveys the impression you would like to make on people calling for business. An introductory message that is humorous or cute to your friends may seem unprofessional or out of place to an employer.

When contacting an employer or personnel worker for the first time over the telephone, develop a script you can follow as you begin talking. In a sentence or two, state why you are calling and ask if you have reached them at a good time to talk for a minute. Usually, the answer will be "Yes." This gives you the opportunity to expand on your reason for calling (to schedule an interview). If you reach the employer's automatic answering machine, wait for the recorded voice to instruct you on pressing an extension number. You will probably hear the voice of an operator, receptionist, or secretary. Make a request for the name, title, and the extension number of the person or department you are trying to contact. "Hello. I'm trying to reach . . . (name or title)." If you have only a title, ask for the name of the person along with the extension number.

Almost all objections to arranging an interview can be converted into scheduling an interview, writes Martin Yate (2003), the job search author of the *Knock 'em Dead* series. You might run into objections or stalling tactics like these: "I don't have time to see you." "You'll have to talk with personnel." Or "Why don't you send me your résumé?" If the employer is too busy, offer to call back at a more convenient time, asking for the best time of day to do this. If you are told to contact the personnel or human resources office, comply with the request and be sure to ask for the name of the person you should talk with. For the résumé request, you could respond, "Of course. Would you give me your specific title and full address? . . . Thank you. To be certain my qualifications fit your needs, what skills are you looking for in this position?" You have agreed to send the résumé, shown consideration, and asked a question that could further the conversation (Yate, 2003).

5. *Know exactly where you are to go for your appointment so you can arrive on time.* As simple as this advice sounds, you'd be surprised how many job seekers get lost on their way to the interview. Obtain the exact address. Know how to get there, especially if you are coming from out of town. Know the location of the building and room where you are supposed to appear. Allow enough time for travel to the interview site so you won't be late. Call the employer's secretary or receptionist if you are unsure of any of these details. Give yourself extra time to get there in case of delays: traffic jams, a train, bad weather, you take a wrong turn. If you use public transportation, obtain the bus schedule and allow sufficient time for the trip. Arrive on time for your job interview; often, job seekers come 20 to 30 minutes early to take care of last-minute details (parking the car, combing hair, straightening clothes, and the like). Call to reschedule if a late arrival is unavoidable. Arriving late without a valid reason may end your chances of getting the job. Arriving excessively early will be annoying to the interviewer and could hurt your chances of making a favorable first impression.

6. *Take the following items with you to the job interview:*

a. *A pen.* You could be asked to fill out an employer's application form. You can ask to complete it at home (where you can take your time and respond more carefully to the items).

b. *A portfolio or file folder with achievements and copies of your résumé.* The portfolio of your achievements, written performance appraisals, transcripts, and so on will provide evidence of your qualifications and skills. And, even though you may have already submitted a résumé, take extra copies with you. The information on your résumé is accurate and can be easily transferred to an application form. You may be asked a question about some aspect of your life that appears on the résumé. (Don't say, "That's on my résumé!") Answer the question completely even though the answer is on the résumé.

c. *Some blank paper or a small notebook.* You may not use it, but the paper will be there if you need to write down important information the employer gives you.

d. *Your driver's license.*

e. *A reminder sheet* (if you don't have a résumé). This includes your social security number, your birth record, a list of previous places of employment (including locations, dates of employment, names of supervisors or employers, and duties performed), educational record (names of schools, locations, dates of attendance, and degrees obtained), and references. Refer to the worksheet in Exercise 4-2 of Chapter 4.

f. *A list of questions you want answered.* Looking at your written questions is acceptable so you can be sure to get the information you need to make a decision if a job is offered.

7. *Learn the name and title of your interviewer.* Ask for this information when you set up the interview. If you forgot to obtain the name and/or title of your interviewer when you made the appointment, call back to the company for it or check with anyone in your contact network who may know the interviewer. Although it's a small detail, this amount of research on your part will still impress the interviewer or employer. It's often said, "Nothing is more valuable to a person than his or her name." If you already know your interviewer or employer, you are one step ahead in the process. Any information you obtain about the interviewer or employer before the interview could be helpful. Also, try to discover the steps in the hiring process used by the organization. Is the procedure completed in one interview or will there be successive interviews? The interview that has been arranged may be only an initial screening one.

8. *Dress appropriately for the interview.* Wear neutral, professional clothing, and make sure it is clean and well pressed. Employers will assume they are seeing you at your best in terms of appearance. If you do not look your best, they will wonder, "How much worse can it get?" Your clothes say a lot about you before you open your mouth. The basic dark blue or traditional charcoal gray business suit is preferred for most interview occasions, although women have a little more flexibility with colors than men. Casual clothing is all right for some situations, as long as it is clean and neat; but when in doubt, stay on the side of formality. An option that is suitable for many jobs in business is a plain brown leather briefcase, which can provide a strong professional appearance in your favor. Shoes must be polished and shined; black or dark brown are preferred colors. To get an idea about clothing that is currently in style, watch how people dress for business programs on television.

Men must be shaved and have a neat haircut that conforms to current business standards. Men with a beard or a mustache need to have it neatly trimmed. A plain white, long-sleeved cotton shirt with a collar that fits comfortably is normally worn; a pale blue shirt is also acceptable. A good-quality tie, in colors that complement the suit and shirt, is recommended. The preferred material for a tie is silk. Width of the tie varies according to fashion, but a 2¾- to 3¾-inch width should be on the mark. Ties should reach the belt line. A safe choice for a belt is one that is leather, coordinates with the shoes, and has a small metal buckle (Cowan, 2002). Calf-length socks, reinforced by a top elastic band, that match or complement the suit, are advised. Short socks that expose hairy legs detract from a job seeker's appearance. Use very little jewelry; wedding rings are fine and so are cuff links if appropriate, but earrings, neck chains, and bracelets are not advised.

Women should avoid either flamboyant or ultrafeminine clothing as well as heavy makeup. Jewelry should not be overdone, but suitable for business; small earrings and a matching necklace are appropriate. Rings should be limited to one per hand (Alfaro, 1999). Perfume should be minimal. Be sparing in the use of eye makeup and lipstick (these can smudge). Blouses should be simple; low-cut necklines are out. A long-sleeved blouse looks more professional. Silk or cotton fabrics are recommended. Also preferred are solid colors in blue, white, pink, soft yellow, or cream. Skirts should be of moderate length. Hemlines change as fashions change, but skirts that fall about knee length are usually appropriate. The best choice for shoes is the closed-toe pump with heels of average height. As for the color of shoes, women have more leeway than men; blue, dark green, or burgundy colors can be used in addition to black or brown. Shoes should not be lighter in color than the skirt. Purses should coordinate with the outfit, and they should not be too large or overstuffed. Pants are still not preferred by some employers. In the case of successive interviews with the same company, think of ways to combine your clothes for the sake of variety.

People generally look their best by dressing conservatively and being neatly groomed. Personal hygiene is important. Think of a time when you were close to a person with bad breath, dirty fingernails, visible flakes of dandruff, and smelly body odor. You may have wanted to supply the person with toothpaste, mouthwash, soap, shampoo, and a deodorant! No employer is going to hire someone with hygiene and grooming problems. Leave political buttons at home; they may get votes, but they don't get jobs. Habits like gum chewing and smoking are completely out. Don't slouch in the chair if you have to wait a few minutes for the interviewer; you may be observed while you wait.

Some job seekers may regard the subject of interview dress as ridiculous, but keep in mind that appearance is important to most companies. In a survey conducted by John Molloy (1988), 93 percent of the executives in top corporations stated they would turn down—on that basis alone—people who showed up improperly dressed for a job interview. Companies take their image seriously, so the job interview is not the time to make a personal statement of independence and nonconformity. It is a compliment that you thought enough of the organization to dress professionally. As a job seeker you are also a product; package yourself well for the job market (LaFevre, 1992).

DURING THE INTERVIEW

1. *Give the impression of optimism and energy when you first meet the interviewer.* Introduce yourself to the interviewer and address him or her as Mr., Ms., or Dr. and last name. Shake hands firmly, but don't overpower the interviewer, crush bones, or jerk the arm out of the socket. Smile and indicate you are pleased to meet the interviewer; however, don't be gushy and come on too strong. Watch for a signal of where you are to sit. Sit down at the same time the interviewer does, not before. Be genuinely glad to meet this person; the interviewer could become a significant person in your life.

2. *Be aware of the importance of nonverbal communication.* Communication experts tell us that we transmit more information nonverbally than we do through words. (There is an old saying that talking sometimes gets in the way of genuine communication.) When interviewing, you need to adopt a posture of involvement with the interviewer. To teach this, Gerard Egan (1975), a counselor trainer, uses the acronym SOLER:

S = *Sit squarely,* facing the other person, your back against the back of the chair, both feet on the floor, maintaining good posture. (*S* is not for "slouch.")

O = *Open position*—crossed arms and crossed legs are often signs of lessened involvement. An open position is a nondefensive position.

L = *Lean slightly forward,* at about a 10-degree angle. Again, this is a sign of involvement.

E = *Eye contact*—look directly (but don't stare rigidly) at the interviewer most of the time. (*E* doesn't mean "evasiveness.")

R = *Remain relatively relaxed*—not fidgeting nervously or engaging in exaggerated facial expressions, but feeling natural with your body as an instrument of communication. Involvement has a kind of tension about it that is balanced with being comfortable in contact with other people. Relaxation gives you the space you need to listen adequately and respond fully.

The "SOLER rules" are not commandments to be rigidly applied in all cases; rather, they are guidelines to help you establish yourself physically with the interviewer (Egan, 1975).

Eye contact is an important element of nonverbal behavior. It should be established from the very beginning of the interview. Look directly at the interviewer whenever he or she is speaking. It's all right to look away for a short time while you are talking, but bring your vision back to the interviewer as you finish answering a question or making a point. People tend to draw conclusions based on eye contact or the lack of it. Looking away from a speaker indicates that you are concealing a reaction or are displeased with them; looking at a speaker conveys agreement with the words being expressed. Looking away while you are talking may mean you are uncertain of yourself; looking at the listener signals confidence in what you are saying (Medley, 1992). Eye contact should not be overdone, however. Staring at the interviewer is distracting, annoying, and unnatural. It is important to be aware of these features of nonverbal communication because of their potential to undercut the impression you want to make.

3. *Learn to control nervousness through preparation, good health, and an understanding that some nervousness is to be expected.* Everything you have done in your job search leads to the moment you face a person who can hire you. You realize all can be wasted if you don't handle things properly, and this knowledge creates the high tension often associated with the job interview. You may worry about the nervousness you're likely to exhibit. Four points about controlling nervousness can be mentioned here. First, interviewers accept applicants' nervousness as normal and as a sign of interest in the job. You wouldn't be nervous if you didn't care. As the interview goes on, nervousness tends to diminish or disappear entirely. Second, the more you prepare for the interview, the more you put yourself in control of things. Preparation is the key to self-confidence in this situation. Third, remember that interviewers and employers are under pressure, too. They must discover and hire good people, or else their business suffers. Fourth, get a good night's sleep before the interview. More important than this, though, is the long-term maintenance of good health habits. Exercise every day, eat right, and average seven or eight hours of sleep per night.

4. *Be sincere, brief, and truthful in your replies to the interviewer's questions.* If you are less than honest in your answers, you begin to create a fantasy world of fabrications that may come back to haunt you later. Bluffing is easily spotted by skilled interviewers, and it will destroy your chances of getting a good job. It indicates a lack of self-confidence. Don't say you can do something when you know you cannot. Claim a skill only when you can back it up with proof that you have used it to accomplish something. If you know yourself, you know what you can do and the kind of contribution you can make to the employer's organization. Stick to your purpose in the job interview.

Mention hobbies and personal interests only if they help to clarify a response or answer an employer's question. Being a champion tennis player may do wonders for your ego, but it doesn't say anything about your ability to be a secretary. Avoid talking too much; answer questions briefly and to the point. Focus attention on strengths and past successes. You don't have to volunteer information on weaknesses, but if you are asked a question about them, indicate what you are doing to overcome any shortcomings.

5. *Ask questions about the position and the organization.* They reflect an interest in the job and in the organization. Asking intelligent questions is one of the easiest ways to impress an employer. Some of your questions can relate to salary and benefits, but be sure to balance these concerns with other questions about the nature and content of the work itself and the responsibilities you will be expected to assume. That way you'll avoid the impression that you're interested only in what you take from the organization rather than what you can give. Don't overdo the number of questions you ask of an employer. Limit yourself to at most a dozen questions. Save some questions for subsequent interviews. Suggestions for questions to ask an employer appear later in this chapter.

6. *Anticipate a discussion about desired salary.* You are well into the final interview, the job interests you, and the employer seems interested in you, but there has been no discussion of pay. In this situation, you have every right to inquire about what salary to expect and to determine whether the money offered for the job is satisfactory. However, a discussion of salary is likely to occur without your bringing it up.

How would you handle the question "What salary do you expect?" You might start by saying, "Before discussing salary, let me find out if I fully understand the responsibilities of the job." Summarize the activities you will be expected to perform on the job, and do this in the most challenging and demanding way you can think of. After your review, ask, "Have I described the job accurately or is there something I have missed?" (Immediately clear up any misconceptions you may have.) Then ask, "What salary range has been approved or made available for this job position?" Another question could be "I would expect a salary that is appropriate to my experience and my ability to do the job successfully. What salary range do you have in mind?" When you are given a range, you can hook on to the upper part of those figures. For example, you are given a $32,000 to $36,000 range. You can come back with a minimum of $35,000 and an ideal of $38,000, giving yourself room to negotiate (Yate, 2003). If the interviewer simply will not give you a salary range, you must state specific dollar figures—and this is where your research really counts.

The "What salary do you expect?" inquiry can be a scary question if you haven't researched typical salaries in your occupational field, industry, and region of the country. Again, stating a figure that is too high may price yourself out of the job because the employer thinks you are unreasonable. A figure that is on the low end of the employer's range may be accepted, and later you may discover you have cost yourself money through your ignorance. A little research could have informed you about the high side of typical salaries for the occupation or even the employer's salary range. If you haven't done your homework on the organization, you'll have to say, "I'll take the going rate" and then hope for the best. That lethargic approach could cost you a considerable amount of money, when you think of the cumulative effects of starting at a lower salary. Finally, when you and the employer have settled on salary terms, get a copy of the agreement *in writing.*

7. *Know your etiquette. (Don't slurp the soup!)* Social skills are a factor in hiring decisions. Be courteous and polite; your nonverbal behavior will demonstrate much of this. You may be invited to lunch or dinner as part of the interview process. If you are uncertain about what to wear, ask the interviewer or company recruiter for advice. Play it safe in this situation. Don't order the most expensive item on the menu. Let your host take the lead. Wait for others to start eating before you do. Order food that is easy to eat. (Look out for spaghetti and sauce!) Take small amounts of food on your fork. Chew your food thoroughly and quietly, keeping your mouth closed while doing so. Avoid

smoking or the use of alcohol, even if your host does otherwise. Be courteous to people waiting on your table, and be sure to say "please" and "thank you." Contribute to the conversation, but don't dominate it. Be careful not to speak with your mouth full of food. Show you are a good listener. All of this advice may sound rather trivial, but remember, company representatives are probably judging your social poise.

8. *A few "don'ts" for the job interview:*

    a. Avoid the overly smooth, ultracool impression; interviewers don't appreciate con artists.

    b. Don't criticize previous employers or work associates. If you can't say anything good about them, say nothing. Employers are likely to assume you will give them the same treatment later on.

    c. Avoid running yourself down. Don't volunteer weaknesses or liabilities, but be prepared to discuss them if asked. Focus on your past accomplishments.

    d. Don't discuss controversial subjects; the job interview isn't the place for them.

    e. Avoid giving flat yes-or-no answers. Direct the conversation toward your goals, strengths, and achievements.

    f. Don't overdo your need for a new job. Anxiety may be interpreted as desperation.

    g. Don't be pressured into taking a job at a lower level than you want. Two weeks later, you could be looking for another job.

    h. Don't overstay your welcome. The interviewer will probably give you some cues when it's time to leave. Better to leave a couple of things unsaid than to put the interviewer seriously behind schedule. Thank the interviewer for the time spent with you. Reassure him or her that you really want the job.

9. *One thing to do before your interview ends: Establish a time frame that the employer expects to use in making a selection among the candidates for the job.* By setting an estimated date, you know the approximate length of time it will take for the employer to interview other applicants and to go through a selection process. (During that time, you will gain nothing by asking the employer whether you got the job.) Most importantly, you know when the proper time comes for you to contact the employer if you have not received any word about the decision. Then, you know that you have every right to inquire about the decision without being an annoyance. Sometimes employers have difficulty making up their minds, so they wait to discover who will call back. If that person is you, the employer is likely to think you are the one who wants the job the most and offer it to you.

Be sure to have the correct spelling of the names of the hiring manager or employer and your interviewer(s). You may need to contact one or several of them later, when you make your follow-up efforts. When nothing has been said about interviewing other candidates, you can inquire about this or ask for the next interview ("Is this a good time to schedule the next interview?").

AFTER THE INTERVIEW

1. *Evaluate the interview as soon as you can.* Before your impressions of the interview fade from memory, critically examine the process you have just experienced. Try to review your performance immediately after the interview, if possible. Consider the following factors:

    a. *Names.* Do I have the names and titles of the people I met?

    b. *The job.* What responsibilities does the job include? Will my skills and knowledge enable me to do the job successfully? What will be the main challenges?

c. *First impressions.* Did you greet the interviewer or employer with a sense of energy and a feeling of optimism? Were you dressed appropriately? Did you establish eye contact immediately? How relaxed did you feel?

d. *Preparation.* Were you adequately prepared for the interview? Did you know enough about the organization? Did you know the name and title of the interviewer? Were you able to anticipate some of the questions that were asked? Had you rehearsed answers to these questions?

e. *Communication.* Did you fail to communicate any information you wanted to tell the employer? Did you communicate your job objective, why you want the job, and your work values and abilities? Did you discover the nature of the work you would be expected to perform?

f. *Questions.* What questions did you ask? Did you leave out anything you wanted to ask?

g. *Responses.* Which questions from the employer did you answer well? With which questions did you have difficulty? How well did you handle questions that probed weaknesses or desired salary? Were you able to neutralize weaknesses or turn limitations into positive statements?

h. *Other impressions.* What kind of impression did you make on the employer? Identify the parts of the interview in which you believe you made your strongest impressions. When may you have given negative impressions? Did you thank the employer for taking time with you?

i. *Next steps.* Did you find out what happens next? How soon will the employer contact you? Is there anything you should do in the meantime?

j. *Improvement.* What would you do differently if you could interview again? How can you improve your interview style and presentation?

2. *Write a thank-you letter within a day of the interview.* Thank-you notes or letters have become increasingly important. The fact that you did *not* write a thank-you letter may be the one thing remembered about you (Mornell, 2000). State your appreciation for the interviewer's interest and time spent. This courtesy will lead the employer to think of you as a thoughtful and conscientious person. Restate your interest in the position and the organization. Remind the employer of the job for which you interviewed and the date and location of the interview. Clarify anything from the interview that will help persuade the employer of your worth. Add a new point of information about yourself if it is relevant or needed. If the job is one you really want, say so in your letter. Keep the thank-you letter brief; three or four lines are sufficient. If there was more than one interviewer, write to all of them. Include receptionists and anyone who helped you. Refer to Figure 3-11 in Chapter 3 for an example of a thank-you letter.

3. *Follow up.* As the thank-you letter indicates, your campaign for a job with an organization does not end with the employment interview. If the employer or personnel manager has promised to get in touch with you, it's easy to think, "I've done all I can do about the job opening, so now I'll wait and hope I get a job offer." Meanwhile, the employer is probably talking with other candidates and screening other résumés and applications. The hiring function is probably sandwiched in with a dozen other activities that make up the employer's working day. As the hours and days tick away, the memory of your interview fades in the employer's mind. Anything you can do to reinforce a favorable image or to correct any mistaken impressions will bring you back into awareness, if only for a moment. If you have not heard anything within the time frame established at the interview, get in contact with the employer by telephone, drop-in visit, or follow-up letter. Don't ask whether a decision has been made on the first follow-up; reaffirm your interest in the job, offer a new insight into a problem the employer is facing, or ask two or three more questions that have come to mind since the interview. Have a follow-up strategy because some employers use the lack of any follow-up as a screening device.

If you are truly interested in the organization, you will continue to learn about it, and your follow-up insights and questions to the employer will demonstrate this. Of course, no follow-up technique is a foolproof guarantee of a job offer. The employer may not have made a decision yet, or you could be turned down; however, you have strengthened your relationship with the employer and increased your chances of being offered a job. Persist without being a pest. A good follow-up strategy can increase your chances of receiving a job offer by 30 percent or more (Jackson, 1991). Many employers have stated they often hesitate when trying to decide between two or more equally qualified candidates. The only decision they can make at that point is to wait and see who calls them first.

4. *Accepting a job offer.* If the job is offered to you, notify the employer as soon as you have decided to accept. Assume that you don't have an offer until you get one in writing. Some offers contain a time limit for acceptance, after which the offer will be withdrawn. If no time limit is given, one or two weeks is usually considered sufficient time to decide whether to accept or reject an offer. If you can't make up your mind, ask the employer for an extension of time and state why you need more time to make a decision.

Your acceptance letter constitutes an employment agreement. Confirm the details of the job offer. Inform the employer when you intend to report for work, unless that date has already been established, and express your pleasure and enthusiasm for the opportunity. Refer to Figure 3-13 in Chapter 3 for an example of an acceptance letter. Also, write thank-you letters to those people who helped you by agreeing to act as a reference for you or providing information about employers and organizations.

5. *Declining a job offer.* If you decide not to accept a job offer, write a courteous letter informing the employer of your decision. Express appreciation of the employer's consideration, and give the reasons for your decision. You may want to apply to the same employer at some future date, so you will want to be remembered favorably. If you accept another job position before hearing from the employer, you should immediately inform the employer as well as the person who referred you. See Figure 3-14 in Chapter 3 for an example of a letter declining a job offer.

6. *If you did not get the job,* think through your interview and try to discover what you could have done better. Most job seekers experience plenty of rejections, so don't become discouraged. Stay open to all the techniques of the job search. The important thing is to keep trying.

QUESTIONS FREQUENTLY ASKED IN JOB INTERVIEWS

How would you answer the following questions in a job interview? Rehearse your responses with a friend. Assume you have the necessary qualifications and preparation.

Questions about Personal Characteristics and Opinions of Yourself

- Tell me about yourself. Describe yourself as a person.
- What kinds of people do you prefer to work with? Why?
- What kinds of people are the most difficult for you to work with? Why?
- What basic qualities of work motivate you most? Why?
- What aspects of work and life give you the greatest satisfaction? Why?
- What kinds of activities do you feel most confident in doing? Why?
- Describe an obstacle, either inside or outside yourself, that you have had to overcome. How did you do it?
- Describe an incident or a situation in which you fought or would fight for something you deeply believed and valued.
- How would a person who knows you well describe you?
- What motivates you to put forth your greatest effort? Illustrate your response using an occasion on which this happened.
- Which characteristics of yours do you think need to be strengthened? Why?

- Describe your greatest achievement.
- What two or three accomplishments have given you the greatest satisfaction? Why?
- Which historical or public figures do you admire most? Why?
- Which magazines do you read regularly? What do you like about them?
- Name a book you have read in the past year. Why did you read it?

Questions about Decisions, Goals, and the Future

- What motivated you to choose the career field for which you are preparing?
- Describe your long-term career goals and how you are preparing to achieve them.
- What do you see yourself doing five years from now?
- If you had complete freedom, would you choose a different occupation from the one you have chosen? What would it be? Why?
- What goals outside your career have you established for yourself?
- What would be your next step if we were to hire you for this job?
- What salary range would you consider appropriate for the job?
- What are your salary requirements or expectations?
- What do you expect to be earning in five years?
- Which is more important to you: the money or the nature of the work on the job? Why?
- What would you really most like to do with your life?

Questions about Abilities, Qualifications, and Skills

- Why should I hire you? What can you do for us?
- Tell me about any natural talents you have that other people, such as teachers, parents, relatives, or friends, have talked about.
- What do you believe are your strongest skills and aptitudes? How would they help you on the job you are seeking?
- In what ways do you think you can make a contribution to our company?
- How do your qualifications and preparation fit the requirements for this job?
- If you were hiring a person for this job, what qualities would you look for?
- What are the reasons for the successes you have experienced in your occupation?
- Describe a situation in which you worked under a lot of pressure.
- What kinds of activities or assignments have you felt most confident doing?
- What qualities or strengths do you have that would be helpful to our organization?
- Give the names of three people whom we can contact as references for you.

Questions about Education and Training Experiences

- What is the most important thing you have learned in your education?
- Tell me about any experiences in school or college of which you are particularly proud.
- How difficult was school/college for you? Which subjects were the easiest/hardest and why?
- Do your grades in school reflect your true ability? Why or why not?
- If you had an opportunity to live your school or college years again, what would you do differently? Why?
- What was your college major? Why did you choose it?
- What have you learned from your school or college experiences that will help you in your working or adult life?
- Describe your plans for continued study, degrees, or efforts to improve your skills.

- What did you learn from your extracurricular activities that you could carry over into your adult life?
- Do you believe your school and college experience has prepared you for your career? Why or why not?

Questions about Work Experiences

- Which full-time, part-time, or summer jobs have held the greatest interest for you? Why?
- Describe the biggest crisis in your work experience. How did you deal with it?
- What were the major difficulties and drawbacks in your last job?
- What kind of people do you prefer to work with? What about these people makes them easy to work with?
- What have you done in your previous jobs to become better accepted by your work associates?
- What accomplishments were recognized by your supervisors or managers in your previous work experiences?
- Give an example of a problem you encountered when working, and explain what you did about it.
- What are the most significant qualities you are looking for in an employer?
- What has been the most (or least) promising job you have ever held? How did it turn out? Explain your feelings about it.
- What were some aspects of your job performance that a supervisor believed you could improve on?
- (If you are now working) Why are you considering leaving your present job?
- What is there about this job that appears better than your current (or previous) job(s)?

Questions about Work Organizations, Job Positions, and Geographical Areas

- Why are you interested in joining our organization?
- What would you like to ask me about the organization?
- Will you relocate? Are you willing to go wherever the company sends you?
- Would you accept a temporary job with the company? Why?
- We are not able to pay you the salary you should have. Will you accept a lower pay rate and work up to the figure you believe you should have?
- Describe your ideal job.
- What would you do to improve the quality of work in this company?
- What kind of working conditions/atmosphere/culture/environment do you prefer? Why?
- When can you start work?
- How long do you plan to stay with our organization?
- I've asked you a lot of questions. Do you have any questions for me?

MORE RESPONSES TO INTERVIEW QUESTIONS

Answers to six basic interview questions were discussed at the beginning of this chapter. Here are several more questions, with ideas for responding.

Tell me about yourself. There it is—the granddaddy of all interview questions. Many interviewers consider this request a nice icebreaker, a way to acquire a little insight into your basic nature, and give you the burden of talking for a couple of minutes (Fry, 2000). What would you say? Do you talk about your favorite person, the weather, or your pet cockatoo? Before your interview, think about how you would respond to open-ended questions such as this one. The real question may be "Tell me something I can't get from your résumé" (Mornell, 2000). If you lack preparation, the open inquiry can throw you off balance. The interviewer is directing you to say something, but the subject is not specified. Of the thousands of topics you could bring up, the one you choose is assumed to be of great importance to you.

One strategy is to ask the interviewer to be more specific. You might ask, "What part of my background is of greatest interest to you?" If the interviewer still gives you nothing on which to focus, talk about a strength or qualification for the job. You can bring up an outstanding achievement experience, a list of skills you can deliver to the job, or how well your preparation fits the needs of the organization. Avoid giving personal information not related to your ability to do the work the job requires. Communicate your desire and enthusiasm for the work or how your values will motivate you to perform with excellence on the job. Practice a one- or two-minute summary about yourself before the interview. (Refer to the Two-Minute Spiel, Exercise A-1, in the Appendix of *Taking Charge of Your Career Direction*.) This question gives you a tremendous opportunity to steer the interview toward subjects you want to emphasize, so you definitely should prepare for it.

What are your weaknesses? There is no reason for you to volunteer negative points about yourself, but if you are asked to list any, accept responsibility for them, explain what you have learned from them, and indicate what you are trying to do about them. Do not dwell on excuses for a weakness; they will never help your performance in a job interview. If possible, discuss a weakness from a job that is not related to the job being considered (Krannich, 2002). When you can, turn a weakness into a statement an employer or interviewer can identify with. "I sometimes get impatient with others when a job needs to get done." What employer hasn't felt the same way? "I love the work in my occupation, so much so that I sometimes neglect a family obligation." Or "I usually show up at work when I have a bad cold and should have stayed at home." Although family responsibilities are important and others would rather not share your cold, what employer is going to consider your dedication to work a negative trait? Don't overdo these weaknesses-that-are-really-strengths strategies; most interviewers have heard them hundreds of times (Mornell, 2000).

Avoid the urge to say you have no weaknesses; you simply will be considered dishonest. If you must discuss a weakness, explain the steps you are taking to overcome it. "When I get frustrated by the lack of progress on a job, I remind myself to exercise patience with others so we can pull together and get the work done." If the interviewer keeps pressing for more limitations, you can say that every person has some weaknesses and you are no exception, but they are not so important that they get in the way of your performance on the job.

How did you get along with your former supervisor or boss? How did you respond to criticism of your work by a supervisor or employer? Such questions may be the interviewer's way of trying to discover faults or weaknesses, or how thin-skinned or teachable you are. Indicate that you listened carefully to the criticism, evaluated it, and resisted any temptation to defend yourself at the time. If the advice was constructive and reasonably presented, you could say that you appreciated the helpful concern of your supervisor. Emphasize your willingness to learn from your mistakes and to cooperate with your employer in doing your job better. Do not speak negatively about a former employer, even when you believe you have just cause. Employers tend to identify with other employers. While you are raking a previous boss over the coals and think you are scoring points with your righteous indignation, the interviewer may be thinking, "If you can say this about a former employer, you could do the same thing to us later." People who complain about previous work organizations are more likely to be perceived as potential troublemakers. Just mention that you respected your former boss as a professional and you appreciated your former supervisor's guidance, and let it go at that.

Why did you leave your last job (or any previous jobs)? An interviewer often probes with this type of question to find out whether you had any problem with a company or caused any trouble. There are plausible reasons for leaving a job. For example, another job offered a greater challenge, a higher salary, a more convenient location if the previous commute was too time consuming, or an opportunity more in line with your career goals. Other believable reasons to leave a job are to raise a family or return to school. Perhaps there was no possibility of further advancement; as long as you stayed in the old job, you weren't going anywhere. Your position might have been eliminated, or you might have been laid off due to the nature of the local economy, or perhaps the company was not generating new work. Basically, you want to reassure the interviewer that you left a job to improve yourself, to be happier, or to be more effective in your work—not because of something horrible that happened. Make every effort to be positive about leaving your current job.

Have you ever been fired from a job? If you haven't been fired, your answer is obviously no. If this happened to you, don't lie. It is an established fact, so stick to the truth. Cold, hard facts can be easily checked. Being fired is a common experience, and your interviewer may silently commiserate with you. Instead of using the words "I was fired," say, "I was let go," which means essentially the same thing but lessens the impact. If losing the job was your fault, be strong enough to admit it. Then, immediately indicate that you have matured and learned from your mistakes. You have taken steps to correct whatever the problem was, so the reason you were let go is no longer a concern. If you feel you were unfairly treated, refrain from telling your interviewer what a louse your ex-boss was. You could say you were interested in making some improvements or being more efficient on the old job, but not everyone saw it that way. The interviewer is likely to respect you for not bad-mouthing a previous employer with whom you have a grievance. If your company was bought out by another organization, perhaps you could explain that the new owners had completely different ideas on how to do things (Hellman, 1986).

Describe a difficult problem (or the most serious decision) you faced on a previous job (or in school). The interviewer is trying to determine *how* you dealt with the problem or decision as much as *what* you actually did about it. Take a cue from the decision-making model presented in Chapter 1 of the first book in this Career Planning Guide series, *Taking Charge of Your Career Direction*. First, you recognized there was a problem (awareness) and you committed yourself to its solution. Second, you studied the environment in which the problem existed. Third, using self-knowledge, you determined that you had the ability to solve the problem. Fourth, you generated several alternative solutions to the problem. Fifth, you gathered all the information you could find about the possible solutions to the problem, weighing the costs and consequences. Sixth, based on the information you obtained, you chose the best solution among the alternatives. Seventh, you implemented your decision and provided an actual solution to the problem. Last, you obtained feedback about how the solution was working and evaluated its effectiveness from what you discovered. You might even describe how you chose your occupational field and what you did to make that decision and put it into practice. The decision-making model just described is a standard one and can be used in many situations.

Why aren't you making a better salary, with your education and experience? This question may be one of those stress interview questions; nevertheless, it gives you the opportunity to indicate that money isn't the only thing that motivates you. Emphasize that nonfinancial values and interests energize your work, if it truly reflects what you believe. You could mention that you really liked your work and were willing to forgo high income for career satisfaction; however, one reason you are interviewing is because you want to balance your values with finances, something the interviewer's company might provide. Go on to briefly summarize your education and experience, and then ask, "What salary do you think I should be earning?" The interviewer's response could start a salary discussion, and so you need to be ready for it.

Describe something you wanted to accomplish but failed to do. Failure is a difficult subject for many people to deal with, but we have all experienced it. No one will believe that you have never failed at anything. Every interviewer knows these are common occurrences in life; they have had their share of failures, too. Part of living is acknowledging that we are vulnerable about some things. We are more likely to elicit empathy from an interviewer by calmly describing a failure than by becoming defensive about it. The important point here is to tell what we learned from a failure, what we did with it, how we improved from it, and what we did (or would do) differently next time. There are, after all, countless stories about how people have learned more from their failures than from their successes.

There is one exception to this advice. If the failure is so excruciatingly painful that you know you will dissolve into tears or rage even on discussing it with a stranger, avoid it. That's the only exception. Legitimate job interviewing is not designed or intended to break you down. Therefore, think of a failure that you have come to terms with and are willing to talk about—even with a stranger.

Where does your current boss think you are now? This question poses no problem if you are seeking your first full-time job or you have been given notice or laid off. Do not say, "He knows I'm interviewing with you so I can leave that hellhole behind. By the way, he'll be calling you tomorrow to find a job himself" (Fry, 2000, pp. 137–138). Knowing a potential employer will not like the impression you are sneaking out of a workday for the interview, there is a temptation to lie or say you are using a sick day. You can show a prospective employer your sense of responsibility to a current job by scheduling an interview before or after work hours, during your lunch hour, or on a nonworkday such as a Saturday or during a vacation period.

What kind of job are you seeking? What do you want to be doing five years from now? The interviewer wants to know whether you are just drifting aimlessly from one job to another or whether the job opening is a logical part of a larger career pattern. Your answer should demonstrate that you have definite career objectives and have well-planned long-term and short-term goals. Stating your career goals and objectives implies your desire to achieve and perform with excellence on the job. Employers are always looking for motivated employees. Emphasize your commitment to your occupational choice and your willingness to stay with the organization. One of the worst answers to this question is "Anything." Most employers interpret this as a sign of indecision, indifference, and instability.

Because each interviewer and interview is unique, there are no final or perfect answers to those questions. Many of your responses will be prompted by your research on the company and the people who work in it. Any questions about your private life are out of bounds. Some interviewers try to justify the invasion of your personal life on the grounds that they want to make sure your private life will not interfere with your work life. Your answer can indicate that you are applying for the job because it is work you want to do, and your personal life will not get in the way of your occupational life. Speak evenly, without getting angry. If the interviewer keeps asking personal questions, reconsider whether you are interested in working for the organization.

SUGGESTED QUESTIONS YOU CAN ASK AS A JOB APPLICANT

Even though you are being evaluated in the job interview, you should still make it an exchange of information. There is no reason to stop assessing the organization. Always be on the lookout for factors that would make the company a poor choice for you. In a structured interview, you may be asked to wait until the end to ask your questions. Specific inquiries should vary from one organization to another. Prepare some questions ahead of time; more will certainly come to mind during the interview. Focus your questions on the job and the nature of the work at first. The interviewer may feel you are narrow-minded and self-serving if you ask only about pay, benefits, and vacations.

A starter list of questions is printed below. Of course, you should add your own concerns to these suggested questions.

1. What are the characteristics of the people your organization or department usually hires?
2. What is the growth potential for the company? What new products or services are being planned?
3. Is there a job description of the available position? If so, may I see it? What are typical assignments or responsibilities in this job?
4. How long has this job position been a part of the company? Who held this job previously, and what is that person doing now?
5. What traits are you looking for in the person you expect to hire for this position?
6. What is management's policy or practice regarding promoting people from within the organization?
7. How will (the economy, a recent government action, a strike, the weather, a materials shortage, and so on) affect the operation of the organization (or department)?
8. What efforts are being made to improve (a situation you know about in production, construction, inventory, supply, accounting, management, technical details, and so on)?
9. How much responsibility would I have in (planning, budgeting, decision making, and so on)?
10. Will I be required to travel extensively on the job? How much time would I spend away from the home location?
11. How would you describe working conditions here? (Specific items could be hours, overtime, noise, work setting, company policies, and the like.)
12. Do you have an organizational chart for the company (or department)? Where would I fit in?
13. Who would be my immediate supervisor? Will I have an opportunity to speak with that person before a hiring decision is made?
14. What kind of formal training program does the organization operate? (If one exists, ask about its length and type.)
15. What is the schedule of salary increases in the company, assuming job performance is satisfactory?
16. How would my performance on the job be evaluated? How often are performance reviews given?
17. Where do people who work for the company live? What housing arrangements exist in the community?
18. Are internal candidates being considered for this job? (If so, are they thought to be in a stronger position than outside applicants?)
19. When could I expect you to contact me about your decision? (If a job offer is made: May I let you know by . . . ?) (Before you leave an interview, make certain you know what your next step will be.)

Keep going. Other questions can be asked at appropriate times. You should not ask, "Do I get the job?" Questions like this one put interviewers on the spot, and you will only hear that they have other job candidates to talk with. You will have made yourself look overly anxious and gained nothing in the process. Although you should avoid pressure tactics, you need to make it clear to the interviewer that you want the job. You could say, "I know you are talking with a number of fine candidates, but I want you to know I would very much like to work here. Everything I have learned about the company tells me this is a place where I would want to be employed. If you decide to hire me, I will do an excellent job for you."

INTERVIEW KNOCKOUT FACTORS: REASONS JOB APPLICANTS ARE REJECTED

- Job goals and objectives not well defined; lack of career planning
- Achievement motivation not evident; no record of achievement experiences to support skills claimed
- Not prepared for the interview; failure to research the organization
- No real interest in the job vacancy or in the work organization
- Interested only in the money and benefits; unrealistic salary demands
- Inadequate knowledge of the job position or the occupation
- Little or no social poise; inability to communicate clearly
- Disrespectful, rude, coarse; lack of tact, courtesy, and civility
- Poor personal appearance; poor posture; lack of eye contact
- No sense of humor; lack of enthusiasm; indifference, passive attitude
- Not able to take constructive or well-meant criticism
- No evidence of handling responsibility, leadership, or initiative
- Belittles and disparages previous employers and supervisors
- Expects too much too soon; job expectations are unrealistic
- Makes excuses for unfavorable comments on records, such as poor work habits
- Education or previous work experience has no relevance to job being sought
- Asks no questions or poor questions about the job or the organization
- Late to interview without plausible reason
- Displays nervous habits: chews gum, cracks knuckles, and so on
- Attitude of "What can you do for me?"

Here are some unusual interview knockouts gleaned from employer experiences reported in newspaper accounts. As silly as they sound, these interview incidents actually happened.

- Falling asleep: It became obvious when the candidate began to snore.
- Reason given for attending college: "To party and socialize."
- Using a word or phrase not understood: Candidate claimed to have graduated *cum laude* (with distinction) but went on to say she was very proud of her 2.1 grade point average.
- Inappropriate clothing: Applicant wore a bathing suit to the interview on a hot summer day.

In *Career Opportunities News*, Robert Calvert (1997) reports these interview experiences from an article in the *New York Times*:

- Bringing a cellular phone to the interview: When it rang, the candidate asked the interviewer to excuse him while he took the call.
- Bringing parents to the job interview: Not only were they present during the entire interview, they asked and answered all the questions.
- Coming to the interview without shoes: Applicant had left them on the plane after an overnight flight.
- Taking medications during the interview: A candidate popped 15 pills from 15 bottles arranged neatly on the interviewer's desk.
- Using mother as a reference: Curious to know what the applicant's mother would say, the employer got this reply: "I wouldn't hire him. He's not very dependable."

Interviewing for a job is not the time to chew gum, blow bubbles, phone your therapist, or bring your cat (or parents) into the interview room. Any of these knockout factors must be turned around for the interview to be successful.

TESTING, TESTING...

Before getting into aptitude and psychological tests, we need to mention drug testing. Tests for drug abuse are more common these days; in these cases, you want negative results. Sometimes a positive result from a drug test is inaccurate. For example, a pain reliever with ibuprofen can cause you to test positive for marijuana. Eating enough poppy seeds can cause a person's urine to test positive for opiates; three poppy seed bagels could generate a positive result. If this happens to you, ask for a more accurate means of testing than the traditional urinalysis, the most popular method of drug screening. The urine test examines a sample for five major controlled substances: cocaine, opiates, marijuana, PCP, and amphetamines. You could ask or be asked for a test of your blood, breath, or hair. A blood test measures the actual amount of alcohol or other drugs in your blood at the time of the test. A breath test shows how much alcohol is in the blood. Two inches of hair give a 128-day history of drug use (Nunes, 2003).

A positive drug test can stop you dead in your tracks on the way to a job offer. It takes from a day to more than a month for some drugs to clear your system, depending on the kind of drugs used and the type of test taken. If you receive a positive result from drug testing and have never used drugs, don't panic—speak to the medical review officer. People have different levels of sensitivity to certain prescription and over-the-counter medications. Ask that some research be done as to why you reacted positively. For drug testing to be considered thorough, an initial positive must be followed up with secondary tests to confirm results (Nunes, 2003).

Aptitude and psychological testing have become more common as a condition of employment. Although such testing is subject to error, employers are probing the honesty of potential employees to protect themselves against theft and being misled.

Aptitude tests are more straightforward than personality or psychological tests. Aptitude tests have one problem, though; they are timed, adding to the pressure you already feel knowing a job you want is at stake. For tests with a time limit, find out how much time you have and then pace yourself. You also should determine how the test will be scored. Aptitude tests are generally made up of multiple-choice questions. Usually, your total score is simply the number of questions answered correctly, meaning you are not penalized for wrong answers. Use all of your time and answer all questions. When you are not certain of the correct answer, go with your first impression. If you finish ahead of the time allotted, check to see if you made any careless mistakes.

Psychological tests are often called personality inventories. They try to measure various aspects of the human personality—with varying degrees of success. Some psychological tests are projective; this means you respond to a picture or abstract design such as an inkblot by making up a story about what's happening or what the picture or figure suggests to you. Incomplete sentences are also used as projective devices. You are given the first part of a sentence and then asked to complete it on your own. (Example: "When I think of work, I . . . .") Psychologists use your responses to projective tests to probe typically hidden parts of the mind and try to identify information that would be useful to an employer.

Psychological testing is a controversial issue. Some employers say the tests help them avoid making bad hiring decisions, and some acknowledge their own instincts are not an effective hiring process (Kaplan, 1997). Unfortunately, some employers use these tests to screen out applicants instead of taking the time and effort to make an honest appraisal. Critics of testing say that all a test administrator finds out is who is best at taking tests, not who is best (in this case) for the job. Defenders of testing respond by claiming employee selection is so subjective that some objective measure needs to be brought into the process, and tests fill that requirement better than anything else.

Next are some suggestions for you if you encounter testing in a company's interviewing and hiring procedure:

- Relax. You have been in this situation before. How many tests have you taken in school? Take a few deep breaths and get on with it.
- Take your time on psychological tests (they are almost always untimed). You may run into the same or very similar items that were used earlier. Answer these questions in the same way. Your consistency is being measured. Some employers may think a high number of inconsistent responses amounts to the same thing as untruthfulness, revealing a person who is prone to lie.
- Don't give false answers on a personality test, but do try to figure out what the employer could be looking for. For ideas on this subject, refer back to Thought Number 10 in Chapter 1 and Appendix A: *Characteristics Employers Want in Job Applicants* of this book.
- If the test is an objective test (multiple choice or true/false), ask how it is to be scored. Is your final test result the number of items answered correctly or will wrong answers detract from your score?
- Be careful when taking tests claiming to probe your integrity. Avoid answers that won't be believed. Probably the toughest question here is "Have you ever told a lie or shaded the truth?" If you answer no, the employer is likely to assume you have been caught in an outright lie, are faking an answer, or are being less than honest. Your best response in this case is yes, because these are things all of us have done at some point in our lives. If given the opportunity when discussing your test responses, you can express that you are trying to be honest now and you were not proud of what happened. Then, you could explain what you learned from the experience.
- Avoid taking a psychological test if you have an option and know that not taking a test won't count against you. You can explain that you would prefer to let your achievements speak for you. However, there may be times when you simply cannot avoid taking this type of test; it is a requirement of the company's hiring process. The most common psychological tests involve word checklists, usually adjectives, and you are forced to choose words you believe apply most directly to you. You could run into a list of positive words and a list of negative words, as in Exercise 8-2. (In this exercise, if you wish to do so, you can supplement the positive words with words from Exercise 7-2 of the last chapter.) Then move on to the negative words. This kind of test taking is a tough situation to be in, as you will see in Exercise 8-2.

EXERCISE 8-2 PSYCHOLOGICAL TEST EXERCISE

Using a pencil, circle all the words in the two lists you truly believe apply to you. The first list has 50 words with 50 more in parentheses that are usually thought to be *positive*. Circle any number of these words, including the ones in parentheses. The second list contains 111 words generally considered to be *negative*. *You must circle at least 10 words in the second list.*

List 1: Descriptive Words Usually Considered Positive

Circle all the words that describe you. The word in parentheses after the first word has the same or a similar meaning; if it is true of you, circle it also.

Accurate (precise)	Calm (self-controlled)
Active (energetic)	Careful (prudent)
Agreeable (personable)	Clear-headed (realistic)
Alert (observant)	Composed (poised)
Attractive (good-looking)	Confident (certain)
Bright (intelligent)	Consistent (steady)

Courageous (brave)   Obedient (devoted)
Courteous (respectful)   Optimistic (cheerful)
Creative (imaginative)   Orderly (neat)
Dependable (reliable)   Outgoing (sociable)
Determined (steadfast)   Patient (persistent)
Effective (capable)   Perceptive (insightful)
Efficient (competent)   Productive (useful)
Ethical (moral)   Punctual (on time)
Flexible (adaptable)   Quick-witted (keen)
Gentle (kind)   Rational (logical)
Gracious (cordial)   Relaxed (easygoing)
Healthy (strong)   Responsible (conscientious)
Helpful (practical)   Sense of humor (witty)
Independent (self-reliant)   Spiritual (reverent)
Inventive (original)   Studious (literate)
Just (fair)   Tactful (diplomatic)
Loyal (faithful)   Tenacious (resilient)
Mature (grown-up)   Truthful (honest)
Natural (spontaneous)   Wise (knowledgeable)

List 2: Descriptive Words Usually Considered Negative

(Circle at least 10 words that describe you.)

Abrasive	Difficult	Humorless	Out-of-date
Aimless	Disobedient	Ignorant	Passive
Arrogant	Disorderly	Impetuous	Plodding
Awkward	Domineering	Inaccurate	Pompous
Biased	Drab	Inarticulate	Prudish
Bitter	Dull	Inattentive	Quarrelsome
Bizarre	Egotistical	Inconsistent	Radical
Boastful	Extravagant	Indifferent	Rash
Boring	Faultfinding	Inefficient	Rigid
Brash	Fearful	Inflexible	Rude
Careless	Fickle	Inhibited	Secretive
Childish	Flaky	Insecure	Self-centered
Clumsy	Foolish	Insensitive	Self-satisfied
Conceited	Forgetful	Intolerant	Show-off
Controlling	Frustrated	Lethargic	Sickly
Corrupt	Furtive	Mean	Simpleminded
Cranky	Gloomy	Neglectful	Sloppy
Critical	Greedy	Nervous	Snobbish
Cruel	Grumpy	Oblivious	Sorrowful
Cynical	Hardhearted	Obnoxious	Spiteful
Deceptive	Hostile	Oversensitive	Stingy
Defensive	Hot-tempered	Overweight	Stubborn

Submissive	Tense	Unpredictable	Volatile
Sullen	Thoughtless	Unreliable	Vulgar
Superficial	Timid	Unsociable	Weak
Suspicious	Tricky	Unstable	Withdrawn
Tactless	Uncertain	Vague	Wooden
Temperamental	Unimaginative	Vindictive	

When you have completed Exercise 8-2, ask yourself how you would like to face an interviewer armed with the results of this "test." Would you want the same list of words, both positive and negative, to be sent to your references and former supervisors, asking them to circle the appropriate words, using the same rules that applied to you? The employer's reasoning for doing this is simple: They want a confirmation of your self-image (Gerberg, 1980).

The difficulty in taking these kinds of tests is the uncertainty over what to reveal about yourself. When you went through the words in Exercise 8-2, you probably said to yourself several times, "This word applies to me in some situations, but not in others." Then there is the problem of consistency, mentioned earlier. Almost all psychological tests check consistency by including words that are very similar to each other in meaning. The assumption is that when you identify one word as describing you, you should also check other words with similar meanings. The first list of (positive) words in Exercise 8-2 does this for you, but the second list with negative words does not. For example, if you circle "inflexible," you should also select "rigid." Circle "extravagant" and you should select "immoderate." If you don't select a word similar in meaning to one you did select, the assumption may be that you are not very bright or are faking and being dishonest.

Naturally, you want to project as good an image as you can, but this can be overdone. Portraying an image that is too perfect, you run the risk of not being believed. A person with no limitations really does not exist, so a less-than-perfect image will not knock you out of the competition. Of course, you don't want to overdo the negative side either. A balance has to be struck here. Keep in mind that some words generally perceived as negative in the culture may not be negative in the mind of an employer. A "stubborn" person may stick to a project an employer desperately wants done, after others have given up. Some negatives are far worse than other negatives (Gerberg, 1980). Being "difficult" can be irritating at times, but it is better than being "corrupt." Know the image you want to convey before choosing words to describe you, but keep your selections within the bounds of truthfulness. Descriptive words can help you remember your important characteristics. If you know yourself and the image you want others to have of you, you should not experience insurmountable difficulties in taking psychological tests. Remember, though, whatever self-descriptive words you select, you should be prepared to provide examples from your experiences that illustrate those choices.

DISCRIMINATION

Do you believe you have been discriminated against on the basis of your race, religion, gender, and so on? Did any psychological tests or items on them seem discriminatory to you? If you believe a potential employer has discriminated against you, consider the following points. Ask yourself if you are truly qualified for the job you sought in the company to which you applied. Put yourself in the employer's position and try to analyze as objectively as you can why you were not hired. Discuss the situation with people you trust and whose opinion you value. Ask them if they think the same as you do or if they believe the employer treated you fairly.

There are several actions you could take if you still think you have been discriminated against. One is to contact the director of the human resources or personnel division. Explain courteously, with specifics and details, how you believe you have been unfairly treated and ask to be evaluated a second time. If you think the discrimination still exists, contact your state's civil rights commission or attorney general's office or the state branch of the American Civil Liberties Union. On the national level, you can contact the Equal Employment Opportunity Commission in Washington, DC.

Mom! Get the axe! The interview didn't go well!

EXERCISE 8-3 ROLE-PLAYED JOB INTERVIEW

Work in groups of three. One person will be the job applicant, another person will be the interviewer or employer, and the third person will be the observer, who evaluates the interview on a rating form. The job interview in this role-playing exercise will probably last about 10 minutes. Then take about five minutes for the applicant and interviewer to discuss the interview and for the observer to evaluate it. When this process is completed, change roles and continue with the next two interviews.

Directions to the Job Applicant

1. You are applying for a job in your number one occupational prospect. Assume you have the necessary training and qualifications for the position. Give the interviewer your completed résumé and/or job application form from Chapters 3 and 4.
2. Answer questions asked by the interviewer honestly and sincerely. Say what needs to be said, but avoid talking too much. Think of reasons for the employer to hire you or for the interviewer to recommend you for another interview.
3. Ask questions of the interviewer. Determine the information you need to know about the organization and the position you are seeking.

Directions to the Interviewer

1. Determine what position the applicant is seeking and the name or type of organization you represent. Read the applicant's résumé and/or job application form and ask questions about them if you wish.
2. Ask questions of the job applicant from the list of questions found in an earlier section, "Questions Frequently Asked in Job Interviews." Ask at least two questions from each group; cover personal characteristics, decisions and goals, abilities and qualifications, education and training, work experiences, and work organizations and geographical areas, for a total of at least 12 questions. Feel free to improvise on these questions or to create your own questions if you prefer.
3. The job applicant should ask you some questions about the job and the organization. Because you are role-playing, simply make up your answers as best you can. Use any knowledge you have about the job or organization, or use your imagination to answer the applicant's questions.

Directions to the Observer

1. Make sure the job applicant identifies the title of the position or occupation and the name or type of organization before the interview begins. Record the names of the applicant and interviewer, as well as your own name as observer.
2. Observe the job interview. If the interview is recorded on videotape or audiotape, you will have the opportunity to replay the taped interview.
3. Evaluate the role-played job interview on one of the rating forms on the next two pages. Use the form in the applicant's book, or use a photocopied or mimeographed form and give it to the job applicant at the end of your evaluation. Because the role-played interview is for practice, be critical in your evaluation. You will do the applicant no favor if you ignore or overlook any mistakes he or she has made. Now is the time to correct them. In a real job interview, it will be too late to work on weak points of the job applicant's interviewing style.

JOB INTERVIEW RATING SHEET

	Name of Job Applicant	_____
Rating key for each item:	Name of Interviewer	_____

2 points = Excellent or Good on this subject; would not be a problem in a job interview.

1 point = Fair, but needs improvement; could be a problem in a job interview.

0 points = Poor, needs much improvement; will be a serious problem unless corrected.

Name of Interviewer _____

Name of Observer _____

Job Position Sought _____

Name or Type of Work Organization _____

First Impression/Dress/Clear Speech   **Points**

1. Applicant gives <u>feeling of optimism and energy</u> when first meeting the interviewer.   1. _____
2. Applicant has completed <u>résumé</u> or <u>job application form</u>.   2. _____
3. Applicant is <u>groomed well</u>; is neatly and <u>appropriately dressed</u>.   3. _____
4. Applicant <u>talks clearly and distinctly</u>; words are not mumbled.   4. _____

Nonverbal Behavior/Body Language

5. Applicant <u>sits squarely</u> in chair; has good posture.   5. _____
6. Applicant maintains <u>open position</u> (arms not crossed, and so on).   6. _____
7. Applicant <u>leans slightly forward</u> (about 10 degrees).   7. _____
8. Applicant establishes good <u>eye contact</u> throughout interview.   8. _____
9. Applicant appears <u>relatively relaxed</u>; maintains poise.   9. _____

Content of Job Interview

10. Applicant communicates <u>job objective</u> to interviewer or employer.   10. _____
11. Applicant expresses <u>work values</u> explaining why job is wanted.   11. _____
12. Applicant makes known <u>abilities</u> relevant to job being sought.   12. _____
13. Applicant relates past <u>achievements</u> to skills used on the job.   13. _____
14. Applicant demonstrates <u>interest and enthusiasm</u> for the job.   14. _____
15. Applicant <u>answers</u> interviewer's <u>questions with confidence</u>. 15. _____
16. Applicant <u>neutralizes weaknesses</u> or turns them into positives.   16. _____
17. Applicant <u>asks questions</u> about the job and work organization.   17. _____
18. Applicant <u>avoids flat yes or no answers</u> to questions.   18. _____

Closing the Interview

19. Applicant learns <u>when interviewer will contact him or her</u> about hiring decision.   19. _____
20. Applicant <u>thanks interviewer</u> by name for the job interview.   20. _____

Observer: Rate each item and add the points you gave the job applicant. Give this rating form to the applicant.   **Total Points** _____

36–40 points:	You're hired!
30–35 points:	You may get the job, but other candidates are in the running, too.
20–29 points:	Your getting the job is doubtful; you need more interview practice.
11–19 points:	Not likely to get the job; much more interview practice is needed.
0–10 points:	No job; you definitely need to do much more hard work on preparation and planning for job interviews and career planning in general.

Comments:

JOB INTERVIEW RATING SHEET
(modified for classroom use)

Rating key for each item:

2 points = Excellent or Good; this subject
would not be a problem in a job interview.

1 point = Fair or Average but needs improvement;
could be a problem in a job interview.

0 points = Poor, needs much improvement;
will be a serious problem unless corrected.

Name of Job
Applicant   _____

Name of
Interviewer   _____

Name of
Observer   _____

Job Position
Sought   _____

Name or Type
of Work
Organization   _____

Content of Job Interview   **Points**

1. Applicant communicates <u>job objective</u> to interviewer.   1. _____
2. Applicant expresses <u>work values</u> explaining why job is wanted.   2. _____
3. Applicant makes known <u>abilities</u> relevant to job being sought.   3. _____
4. Applicant relates past <u>achievements</u> to skills used on the job.   4. _____
5. Applicant <u>asks questions</u> about the job and work organization.   5. _____
6. Applicant <u>neutralizes weaknesses</u> or turns them into positives.   6. _____
7. Applicant <u>avoids flat yes or no answers</u> to questions.   7. _____

Nonverbal Behavior/Body Language

8. Applicant <u>sits squarely</u> in chair; has good posture.   8. _____
9. Applicant maintains <u>open position</u> (arms not crossed, and so on). 9. _____
10. Applicant <u>leans slightly forward</u> (about 10 degrees).   10. _____
11. Applicant establishes good <u>eye contact</u> throughout interview.   11. _____
12. Applicant appears <u>relatively relaxed</u>; maintains poise.   12. _____

Other Features of the Job Interview

13. Applicant demonstrates <u>interest and enthusiasm</u> for the job.   13. _____
14. Applicant <u>talks clearly and distinctly</u>; words are not mumbled. 14. _____
15. Applicant learns when interviewer will contact him or her about
    hiring decision and thanks interviewer for the job interview.   15. _____
    (Good grooming and appropriate dress are assumed in this exercise.)

Observer: Rate each item and add the points you gave the
job applicant. Give this rating form to the applicant.   **Total Points** _____

26–30 points:	You're hired!
21–25 points:	You may get the job, but other candidates are in the running, too.
16–20 points:	Your getting the job is doubtful; you need more interview practice.
11–15 points:	Not likely to get the job; much more interview practice is needed.
0–10 points:	No job; you definitely need to do much more hard work on preparation and planning for job interviews and career planning in general.

Comments:

SUMMARY

1. A job interview is different from an informational interview in that all parties know you are a candidate for a job opening. All kinds of questions will be asked of you: the reasons you are interested in a particular job in a particular organization, your qualifications and preparation, whether you will fit into the company's work environment, and desired salary or wages. In other words: Why are you here? What can you do for us? Will you fit in? What will you cost us? You should always ask questions of the interviewer for further information, demonstrating your interest in the organization. Of course, nothing should keep you from acquiring more information about the organization after the job interview or from continuing to evaluate that information.

2. There are many types of interviewers. Most are competent, courteous, and professional. Unfortunately, a few add needless stress to an already stressful situation. Skilled interviewers ask more open than closed questions, enabling job applicants to express themselves more freely. Capable interviewers encourage you to expand on your comments by listening carefully, rephrasing your statements, and reflecting your feelings accurately. These interview techniques aid communication, but you must be careful not to reveal more information than you intend to give.

3. There are several types of job interviews: screening, structured, unstructured, group, board, stress, behavioral, serial, and subsequent interviews. Some types can be combined with other types in a single interview. Job offers are unlikely to be made in the first interview, which is typically a screening session.

4. Before the job interview, you should learn all you can about the organization. Determine through your research what you can do for the employer. Anticipate questions and rehearse your answers. Schedule your appointment professionally by a written letter of introduction or over the telephone. Know exactly where the interview is to be held. Take pen and résumé with you. Learn the name and title of the interviewer. Dress appropriately.

5. During the interview, show energy and optimism to make a good first impression. Be aware of your nonverbal communication. Control nervousness through proper preparation. Respond to questions honestly and sincerely. Ask questions of the interviewer. Know proper etiquette. Handle salary and benefits from a base of researched information. Know when a decision regarding your application will be made.

6. After the interview, evaluate your experience as soon as possible and write a thank-you letter. Follow up with a telephone call, drop-in visit, or letter if you have not been notified of a decision within the time limit specified at the interview. If you don't get the job, persist in your efforts. Keep learning, and keep working to improve your job search skills.

7. Among the reasons job applicants are rejected after the interview are: vague explanations of career goals, no evidence of achievement motivation, lack of preparation for the interview, little or no knowledge of the organization or the job, and failure to support statements claiming skills with evidence of achievements. Other reasons include inadequate social poise, poor personal appearance, indifferent attitude, no record of handling responsibility, obnoxious or nervous habits, coming late to interviews with no excuse, and so on.

8. Psychological, aptitude, and drug testing have become a typical feature of many company interview and hiring procedures. Psychological tests present a number of problems, including forcing you to reveal more of yourself than you often care to and being consistent in your responses to items on the test.

REFERENCES

Alfaro, G. 1999. *Interview attire suggestions.* Jackson, MI: Jackson Community College Career Center.

Brown, E. 1998. The job interview. *Forbes,* 161(4), 18–20.

Calvert, R. 1997, December. Interviews with the truly weird. *Career Opportunities News*, 5.

Cowan, K. 2002, August 30. Suiting up for work. Jackson, MI: *Jackson Citizen Patriot*, B4.

Drake, J. D. 1982. *Interviewing for managers: A complete guide to employment interviewing*, rev. ed. New York: AMACOM (a division of American Management Association).

Egan, G. 1975. *The skilled helper*. Pacific Grove, CA: Brooks/Cole.

Fry, R. 2000. *101 great answers to the toughest interview questions*, 4th ed. Franklin Lakes, NJ: Career Press.

Gerberg, R. J. 1980. *The professional job changing system: World's fastest way to get a better job*. Parsippany, NJ: Performance Dynamics.

Giventer, K. 1992. Oops! Common interviewing gaffes. In *Wall Street Journal, Managing your career*. New York: Dow Jones & Co.

Half, R. 1994. *How to get a better job in this crazy world*. New York: Signet.

Hellman, P. 1986. *Ready, aim, you're hired! How to job-interview successfully anytime, anywhere, and with anyone*. New York: AMACOM (a division of American Management Association).

Holland, J. L. 1997. *Making vocational choices: A theory of vocational personalities and work environments*, 3rd ed. Odessa, FL: Psychological Assessment Resources.

Ivey, A. E., with Simek-Downing, L. 1980. *Counseling and psychotherapy: Skills, theories, and practice*. Englewood Cliffs, NJ: Prentice Hall.

Jackson, T. 1991. *Guerrilla tactics in the new job market*, 2nd ed. New York: Bantam.

Kaplan, R. 1997. Employers using pre-employment testing as a hiring tool. *Journal of Career Planning and Employment*, 58(1), 11–13.

Krannich, R. 2002. *Change your job, change your life: Careering and re-careering in the new boom/bust economy*. Manassas Park, VA: Impact Publications.

LaFevre, J. L. 1992. *How you really get hired: The inside story from a college recruiter*, 3rd ed. New York: Arco.

Medley, H. A. 1992. *Sweaty palms: The neglected art of being interviewed*, rev. ed. Berkeley, CA: Ten Speed Press.

Molloy, J. T. 1988. *John T. Molloy's new dress for success*. New York: Warner.

Mornell, P. 2000. *Games companies play: The job hunter's guide to playing smart and winning big in the high-stakes hiring game*. Berkeley, CA: Ten Speed Press.

Nunes, N. E. 2003. Drug testing: The "study-free" test. Available online at www.jobweb.com. Accessed on February 21, 2003.

Rogers, E. J. 1982. *Getting hired: Everything you need to know about resumes, interviews, and job-hunting strategies*. Englewood Cliffs, NJ: Prentice Hall.

Wright, J. W. 2000. *The American almanac of jobs and salaries, 2000–2001*, rev. ed. New York: Avon.

Yate, J. M. 1998. *Knock 'em dead: The ultimate job seeker's handbook*. Holbrook, MA: Adams Media.

Yate, M. 2003. *Knock 'em dead 2003*. Avon, MA: Adams Media.

Chapter 9

Into the Working World

You have learned a lot about job search strategies, sources of job leads, writing résumés and cover letters, completing applications, researching work organizations, and interviewing for information and jobs. What remains? In this chapter, we will answer two questions: When you have received several job offers, how do you evaluate them? After you have accepted an offer, how do you keep the job and cope with its problems? These questions deserve your attention. After a successful job search, some people fail to consider the equally important subjects of appraising job offers, keeping a job, and managing the problems of work. Reading this chapter will help you anticipate and prepare for situations you will encounter in the future.

EVALUATING JOB OFFERS

When your job search campaign succeeds in producing offers of new job positions, you have important decisions to make. In the case of a single job offer, the question is whether to take the job. With two or more job offers, the question becomes which one to choose. It's a nice problem to have, but a dilemma nonetheless. This situation actually may be quite rare because multiple job offers are not likely to occur at the same time. If you get a job offer you're not sure about, do not let your hesitation be too obvious. Express enthusiasm about the offer, and then ask for two or three days to consider it. Set a definite date on which you will contact the employer with a decision. This is a reasonable request most employers will honor. You are demonstrating your seriousness while also gaining a little more time to acquire more information both about the position being offered and about other job leads (Hermann and Sutherland, 1994).

Several circumstances must be considered as you seek further information. For example, benefits may turn a lower salary into a higher total compensation package in the long run. A lower beginning salary may be offset by a salary schedule offering more frequent salary increases. A growing organization is more likely to create advancement opportunities than a company that is standing relatively still. An organization that promotes from within is better for your advancement chances than one that relies on outsiders to fill higher-level positions. Consider the ages of your supervisors and coworkers; if they are close to retirement, advancement possibilities may be better. Lateral moves into related departments could hold greater opportunities for advancement. If you are thinking about job security, examine the layoff history of the company; some companies are quick to trim employees during economic downturns. Is the organization new or one that is well established? New businesses have a higher failure rate, but this possibility of job loss might be offset by the excitement of creating a company and the potential for sharing in its success. The important point is that you must persevere in your information-gathering activities in order to make proper evaluations of organizations that offer you jobs.

To help you evaluate job offers, we have prepared two lists of factors to consider—one for a single job offer, and the other for two or more job offers. It would take too much time to go into detail here about each factor in these lists, but as an example, consider the question of commuting distance. Suppose your commute to work takes only 5 minutes one-way. This translates into 10 minutes for a daily round trip, 50 minutes every week, and 2,400 minutes or 40 hours over the course of a year (assuming 48 workweeks)—the equivalent of one typical 40-hour workweek. A 20-minute commute one way means 160 hours of driving time per year—equivalent to 4 weeks of working time. A 60-minute commute to your workplace would be the equivalent of 12 weeks of working time over a year; 20 percent of your working time would be spent in the car or on other forms of transportation. The added travel time would make a 10-hour workday (assuming a normal 8 hours on the job). Now, how important is your daily commute to and from work? Only you can answer that question.

Examine these lists now to identify factors you should consider when you evaluate job positions. Then use the lists when actual job offers come your way.

Evaluating One Job Offer

Answer each question with a plus (+) when you feel positive, a minus (–) when you feel negative, and a zero (0) when your feelings are neutral or the question does not apply to you. No score can tell you exactly what decision to make, but avoid or beware of job offers that have a negative tally for a total score. Question and be cautious of those that total between 1 and 10 on the plus side, and carefully consider job offers that score more than 10 points. If you plan to use this exercise again and again, photocopy these questions before responding to them.

_____ 1. Will the position fit into my long-range occupational plans and career goals?

_____ 2. Does the job express my major work values and meet my basic needs in life?

_____ 3. Will my abilities and skills contribute to the progress of the organization offering the position?

_____ 4. Is the job itself intrinsically interesting and psychologically involving?

_____ 5. Are the salary being offered and the company's salary schedule for future years reasonable and satisfactory?

_____ 6. Does the organization offer an attractive benefits package, including insurance, paid vacations, income supplements, and the like?

_____ 7. Is the job an advancement over what I do now, and does it offer advancement opportunities for the future?

_____ 8. Does the organization have an excellent reputation in its field or industry?

_____ 9. Is the size of the organization or the department where I would work right for me?

_____ 10. Does the organization manufacture products or provide services with which I would be proud to be associated?

_____ 11. Are the people with whom I will be most closely associated in the organization compatible with me and possible for me to get along with?

_____ 12. Do the values, philosophy, and assumptions of the organizational culture fit my personality characteristics?

_____ 13. Can I easily commute to the workplace?

_____ 14. Will the work the job requires me to do bring out the best within me?

_____ 15. Is the management of the organization stable, responsible, and worthy of my respect?

_____ 16. Is my immediate supervisor a person who is competent, agreeable, and admired, with whom one can be friends?

_____ 17. Has the company experienced recent growth? Does the organization have growth potential for the future?

_____ 18. Does the company keep its employees even in hard times? Does the position have a reasonable degree of security or permanence?

_____ 19. Do the functions of the job have the support of the management of the organization?

_____ 20. Are the hours of work agreeable to me? Are other working conditions in the organization what I want them to be?

_____ 21. Is the company in an industry that is growing or that will be around for a long time?

_____ 22. Does the organization offer training programs or pay for continuing education?

_____ 23. Does the employer require the signing of arbitration, noncompetition, or nondisclosure agreements as a condition of being hired? (See the section after this exercise.)

_____ 24. Will the job in this particular organization allow adequate time for family and recreational interests?

_____ 25. Are desirable community, cultural, recreational, educational, social, and religious facilities available where the job is located?

_____ 26. Other (write in): _____

_____

_____

_____

_____

Evaluating Two or More Job Offers

The matrix that follows can be used to compare two or more positions. Completing the matrix involves six steps.

Step 1. The factors to be considered are listed vertically down the left side of the matrix. If you do not want a particular factor in your list, simply cross it out and don't use it. There are spaces for additional factors at the bottom of the matrix.

Step 2. List each job (position and organization) across the top of the matrix. The matrix contains spaces for up to four possible jobs.

Step 3. Weigh each factor on a scale of 1 to 5. Ask yourself how important each factor is to you, and give it a weight number in the weight column.

5 means the factor is very important to you.

4 means the factor is above average in importance to you.

3 means the factor is of average importance to you.

2 means the factor is below average in importance to you.

1 means the factor is of little importance to you.

Step 4. Use a code to show whether each job and organization is positive (+), neutral (0), or negative (–) with regard to each factor you are considering. Base your judgments on the information you have obtained from your research.

+ = Factor *is expressed* in the position/organization.

0 = *Neutral*; can't determine, don't know, or doesn't apply.

– = Factor *is not expressed* in the position/organization.

Place the code in the space just to the left of the parentheses.

Step 5. Multiply the weight by the code (W × C), and enter the product inside the parentheses. For example: $4 \times + = 4$, $3 \times 0 = 0$, and $2 \times - = -2$.

Step 6. Sum the products in each column, adding or subtracting as indicated. The total score gives you the rank of each job among the alternatives.

Comparison of Job Offers		Position/ Organization ___		Position/ Organization ___		Position/ Organization ___		Position/ Organization ___	
Factor	Weight	Code	W × C	Code	W × C	Code	W × C	Code	W × C
1. Job fits into career plans and goals.			( )		( )		( )		( )
2. Job expresses major values.			( )		( )		( )		( )
3. Abilities can be used on the job.			( )		( )		( )		( )
4. Work is interesting, involving.			( )		( )		( )		( )
5. Salary meets expectations.			( )		( )		( )		( )
6. Benefits are good, attractive.			( )		( )		( )		( )
7. Advancement potential exists.			( )		( )		( )		( )
8. Company has excellent reputation.			( )		( )		( )		( )
9. Size of organization is right.			( )		( )		( )		( )
10. Pride in quality of products/services.			( )		( )		( )		( )
11. Work associates will be compatible.			( )		( )		( )		( )
12. Organizational culture fits my personality.			( )		( )		( )		( )
13. Location of work is convenient.			( )		( )		( )		( )
14. Work will challenge my best efforts.			( )		( )		( )		( )
15. Management style is attractive.			( )		( )		( )		( )
16. Immediate supervisor is respected.			( )		( )		( )		( )
17. Company is growing/has growth potential.			( )		( )		( )		( )
18. Reasonable job security exists.			( )		( )		( )		( )
19. Job functions have management support.			( )		( )		( )		( )
20. Working hours/ conditions are agreeable.			( )		( )		( )		( )
21. Company is in a growing industry.			( )		( )		( )		( )

Comparison of Job Offers		Position/ Organization		Position/ Organization		Position/ Organization		Position/ Organization	
Factor	Weight	Code	W × C	Code	W × C	Code	W × C	Code	W × C
22. Training/paid education is available.			( )		( )		( )		( )
23. No restrictive agreements required.			( )		( )		( )		( )
24. Job allows adequate time off work.			( )		( )		( )		( )
25. Community is acceptable to family.			( )		( )		( )		( )
26. Other (write in)			( )		( )		( )		( )
			( )		( )		( )		( )
			( )		( )		( )		( )
			( )		( )		( )		( )
Total Scores									
Rank									

Factor	Weight	Job A		Job B	
		Code	(W × C)	Code	(W × C)
1. Job fits into career plans.	5	+	(+5)	−	(−5)
2. Job expresses major values.	3	0	(0)	0	(0)
3. Abilities can be used on job.	4	−	(−4)	+	(+4)
Total score			+1		−1

Figure 9-1 Job matrix using three factors

Figure 9-1 illustrates the use of the matrix with a simplified example that applies only three factors to two possible jobs.

Carefully Consider Agreements You Are Asked to Sign

Be aware of any agreements you are required to sign before the employer agrees to hire you for a job. You could be signing away rights that could later become very important to you. An **arbitration agreement** is a promise by the employee to pursue any legal claim against his or her employer through arbitration, rather than through a lawsuit. Arbitration is less formal than a court trial, and greater informality can make the process easier for all involved persons, especially employees who are not accustomed to legal matters. Arbitration cases can be resolved more quickly than court cases, which can take several years to complete. An arbitration is conducted by a private citizen (often a retired judge), paid by one or both sides to hear witnesses and evidence. Arbitration means there is no jury, and juries are thought to be usually more sympathetic than arbitrators to employees. The process often limits the amount of information each side can get from the other; this is generally unfavorable to the employee because employers usually possess the documents relating to the case. Arbitration awards are more final than court verdicts in that arbitration decisions usually cannot be appealed. There are obvious risks involved in refusing to sign an arbitration agreement; for example, the employer can rescind an employment offer. However, sometimes employers will negotiate this agreement and not require you to sign it, or they may make it more fair for you if they are more intent on gaining your skills and talents than they are on arbitration (Barnish, 2003).

Two other types of agreements are the noncompetition agreement and the nondisclosure agreement. A **noncompetition agreement** is a promise not to directly work for a competitor or compete against an employer with whom you have signed the agreement for a reasonable length of time. The agreement will probably be considered reasonable by the legal system if it lasts from one to five years, is confined to a specific geographic area such as a state, and is limited in the type of business it covers. In other words, you would be in violation of the agreement if you accepted a job at the only thingamabob producer in your area, learned all you could about making thingamabobs for six months, and then tried to start your own thingamabob company a block away.

A **nondisclosure agreement** means you agree not to reveal information the company considers confidential—new products, technology, business plans, financial notes, sketches, models, and so on. This agreement doesn't say you cannot work for a competitor; it simply means you can't use confidential information you have learned or obtained at one company with a new employer (Barada, 2003).

Accepting a Job Position

After accepting a job offer in an organization, you are ethically obligated to inform all employers with whom you have interviewed of the decision you have made. You should also thank all personal contacts who took the time to help you; this task is usually done by writing a brief letter. Offer to assist them in any way you can in the coming months and years. A sample acceptance letter appears in Figure 3-13 in Chapter 3. In the letter to all other employers, you can say you are writing to let them know you have accepted a position with another organization and you are withdrawing your application from further consideration at this time. You should not say to them you were offered a better job; simply write that the job you accepted seemed to be the most appropriate one for you now. Thank them for taking time to consider you. Tell them how much you learned in the interview with them, how attractive they appeared to you, and how tough the decision was to make, and wish them the best of luck in their future. You never know—you may want to apply for a job with them at some point in the future. A sample letter declining a job offer is shown in Figure 3-14 in Chapter 3.

WORKING ON THE JOB

The story is not over when you land a job. Working on the job, or job maintenance, is a whole new chapter. The first year on a full-time job is a transition from school to the workplace. Many beginning workers hope to connect with a mentor who will guide them in "learning the ropes" in an organization and advancing on the job. A mentor might offer advice similar to the guidelines for keeping a job presented later in this section. The employer has responsibilities, too, because the relationship between employer and employee is one of interdependence.

The Transitional First Year in a Full-Time Job

Just as you had to learn a new set of skills and attitudes when you first entered high school and college, the same is true for starting out at full-time work. Most new graduates feel somewhat insecure and worry about their ability to do the job; after all, your instructors focused on teaching you task-related knowledge and skills. Your employer, on the other hand, knows you have the ability to perform the basic tasks of the job—they wouldn't have hired you otherwise. What they are most concerned with are the many nontask aspects of the job: your willingness to learn new ways, fit into the company culture, become informed of the politics of the organization, and build effective working relationships.

Holton (1999) has a number of suggestions for first-year success, although only a few can be outlined here. As a new employee, try to find those people in the organization that are respected by others and model your behavior after theirs. Graduates can leave school with a false sense of their importance, so it's essential to demonstrate humility, readiness to learn, an open mind, respect for the organization, acceptance of assignments that may not be fun but provide good training, a work ethic, and a positive attitude. Keep your hopes about work realistic—your job may not be as exciting or significant as you thought. Expect to go through a "breaking in" period where you are an outsider, which means keeping your eyes and ears open and mouth shut to learn as much as you can about the organization and the people in it. It's okay for an insider to suggest changes, but when an outsider does the same or criticizes, it may be seen as an attack. You do not gain acceptance by challenging the system first. (You need to pay your dues to do that.) Leave college/student ways behind; those who carry them to the job are stamped as immature and in need of time to grow up. Build effective relationships with coworkers and managers, because much of what you need to know about getting things done will come from other people. You need as many skills to be a subordinate as you need to be a leader, and you need these skills to work productively with your boss. Develop an understanding of the organization's culture—its mission, guiding philosophy, social norms, ethical standards, accepted behaviors, and so on.

So far the focus has been on the nontask side of the first year of a new job. Now let's turn to the job itself. Learn how to apply your knowledge in the work setting. This may involve managing time, handling multiple projects, setting priorities, writing reports, making presentations, selling ideas, meeting deadlines, and so forth. Acquire the knowledge, skills, and abilities you need to master the tasks required in your job; take advantage of or ask for training programs offered by the employer. Remember, it's not the employer's obligation to make your transition to work a success—that's your responsibility (Holton, 1999).

Mentors

A mentor is a trusted guide or counselor who coaches a person in the art of career maintenance, development, and advancement in an organization. Mentoring is not systematic, planned action; it usually happens spontaneously. The mentor offers knowledge, support, encouragement, and wise advice, guiding a protégé through difficult situations or away from pitfalls. Mentoring is a very old concept; it comes from an ancient Greek mythological character named Mentor in Homer's *Odyssey*. Mentor, the wise old nobleman, had the responsibility of nurturing Telemachus while his father went off to fight in the Trojan War (Adams, 1998). However old they may be, formal and informal mentoring relationships are estimated to have quadrupled in the past 15 years (Zaslow, 2003).

Mentors are most likely to be found in managerial and professional work environments, although there is no reason that the same kind of relationship cannot develop in other types of work. The relationship can be compared to a good parent looking out for the interests of a son or daughter. In career mentoring, however, the relationship is professional rather than parental. For example, a junior executive identifies with a top manager, or a college student becomes aligned with a respected professor.

The protégé is not the only beneficiary of the mentoring relationship. Mentors often receive assistance in return from a willing associate, enhance a reputation for helpfulness, and gain satisfaction in contributing to the careers of others and to the success of the organization. The company may benefit from greater worker loyalty and better work adjustments made by new employees. Studies show that positive mentoring experiences increase productivity, worker retention, and job satisfaction.

However, because of today's greater competitive work environment, some employees, particularly those of the boomer generation, are struggling to shift from protégé to mentor. They claim mentoring is risky in that companies value mentors in good times and lay them off when times are bad, preferring younger, lower-paid workers who have been guided toward top performance. Some mentors may try to fine-tune their coaching by bringing a younger employee along just enough to get the job done, but not so much that they'll take the mentor's job (Zaslow, 2003).

Despite the problems sometimes encountered, many positives can be experienced in the mentoring relationship. Mentors teach their protégés the skills and abilities needed for successful job performance. With their accumulated wisdom and experience, mentors guide protégés through the unwritten rules of behavior. Advice, counsel, and support are provided when the protégé experiences difficult times. Mentors are role models from whom protégés can shape their own actions and style. A mentor may serve as a "safe harbor" or buffer for risk taking, someone with whom the protégé can explore ideas and experience failure without feeling defeated (Adams, 1998).

How do you attract and keep a mentor? Michael Zey (1990), in surveying executives, discovered eight methods by which an employee can attract the attention and interest of a potential mentor.

1. Show your competence by expressing your words clearly, performing your job capably, and perceiving the organization accurately.
2. Be visible by making presentations, writing reports, analyzing problems, and attending meetings.
3. Work on high-priority projects that involve senior managers.
4. Demonstrate a desire to learn in a student–teacher relationship. One way to do this is to signal to a prospective mentor that you believe there is much to learn from his or her years of experience.
5. Attend informal social gatherings and professional meetings where you can talk with prospective mentors on a more casual basis.
6. Indicate a willingness to help the mentor reach his or her goals, working on common projects and being available when needed.
7. Take the initiative when you want to become a protégé of a mentor. One approach is to ask for the mentor's advice about a problem or situation, which might lead to further discussions that could later develop into a mentoring relationship.
8. Be accessible beyond normal business hours, and be willing to go beyond the duties of your job description.

These methods not only are useful for creating a mentor relationship, but also are techniques for improving your chances for advancement within the organizational structure.

Before entering a mentor relationship, you should consider a number of questions and factors:

1. Does the mentor have strong political alliances throughout the organization? If so, this person is likely to be more helpful than others.
2. Does the mentor evoke respect in the organization? If so, this person inspires esteem and admiration and has earned high professional regard through excellent performance, achievement, and an ability to work well with others.

3. Is the mentor in a power position, having access to top management? Titles are not always an indication of power, and you need to be careful in estimating the influence a potential mentor may have.

4. Is the mentor a good teacher? Knowledge of basic job skills, company structure, and office politics must be communicated; a poor teacher is not likely to do this.

5. Does the mentor have the ability to motivate other people? Investigate the organization to learn who draws support through their leadership qualities.

6. Are your goals and needs similar to those of the mentor? If you and your prospective mentor have different work values and career paths, real problems could develop in the relationship over time.

7. Is the mentor secure in his or her own position? If your achievements are seen as a threat to the mentor's own position, that person could hinder your career advancement rather than help it. (Zey, 1990)

Marilyn Kennedy (1980) identifies five types of mentors: the information, peer, retiree, competitive, and godfather mentors. The information mentor tells you about customs and practices within an organization, communicating material that is not written in the company orientation manual. The peer mentor relates to you as an equal on subjects of mutual interest. Many companies connect you with this type of mentor after you are hired—an organizational buddy system. The retiree mentor, though no longer with the organization, can still provide a wealth of information about the history of the company. The competitive mentor is someone in your occupation that works for a company not on your target list. Finally, the godfather mentor is one who can make things happen for you. The "godfather" not only teaches and inspires, but also has power and clout. The relationship between you and this person is reciprocal. You may want to use the godfather's influence; the godfather wants to interact with a kindred soul who could become a sympathetic supporter in the organization. The relationship is based on a kind of chemistry that both recognize (Kennedy, 1980).

The Art of Keeping a Job

There seems to be nothing that one can say about keeping a job without sounding trite. Be on time for work, notify your employer ahead of time when you cannot avoid being absent, read the policy manual, follow directions—these are hardly unusual or controversial admonitions; however, such simple things cost people their jobs more often than anything else. Employees are rarely fired for lack of competence or ability to do the work. Usually the cause is some annoying habit, or poor interpersonal skills, or failure to communicate. The following 15 points are central to the art of keeping a job.

Punctuality. Come to work on time. Following this simple admonition can do more for you than an acre of promises. Employers see punctuality as a sign that you are responsible and dependable, and that is worth a lot of points in their books. When you first start a new job, plan to arrive 10 or 15 minutes early. This extra margin could save you from making a negative first impression by arriving late due to unfamiliarity with the route to work or the parking facilities, traffic jams, or the like. When lateness becomes a pattern, check your own attitudes toward your job.

Communication. Notify your employer (or manager) whenever you must be absent from work. The company policy manual will probably contain instructions on what to do whenever absence cannot be avoided. Workers sometimes need to leave work for doctor's appointments, to take care of legal matters, or to conduct other business they cannot do outside of work hours. Obtain your supervisor's permission in advance so there is no question about the legitimacy of your absence. Try to keep absences to a minimum. Employers want their workers to be physically present on the job in order to avoid delays or interruptions in production or service.

What's this obsession with reporting to work on time?

Know procedures. Read the organization's policies, which are usually printed in a manual or a pamphlet. Read the policies thoroughly before you start the job, or no later than the first few days of employment. Know what the policies are. You may disagree with some, and others may not make sense to you. Inquire politely about the rationale behind the policies you don't like; they may make more sense to you when you consider a different viewpoint. Some organizations have an orientation program to discuss company policies.

Listen to directions. Follow instructions, rules, and regulations. When you start a new job, contact your supervisor and find out exactly what you are expected to do. Ask questions, and keep asking them until you understand completely where you stand and how you should proceed. Directions are usually simple to comprehend, but many people stumble on this item because they failed to listen, were daydreaming, or were not paying attention.

Ethics. Do not take unfair advantage of your work organization by extending coffee breaks, lengthening lunch periods, arriving late for work, making frequent personal calls, reading newspapers or magazines, or stopping work a half-hour before quitting time. Sooner or later, this attitude will be noticed and will create a negative impression on your supervisor or employer. Give a few minutes of your own time to finish a task. Staying a few minutes overtime to complete something can't hurt you in the eyes of the employer and may make it easier to ask for a privilege later.

Stay occupied. Have something to do all the time at work. Offer to take on more duties if you don't have enough work to do. Learn the jobs of your work associates, even those of your supervisor. If a coworker could use some help in finishing a job after you're done with yours, volunteer your assistance. You may be repaid with interest some day.

Friendliness. Become acquainted with your fellow employees. Engage in friendly conversation with others on coffee breaks or during lunch periods. Get to know experienced employees. Your work associates can tell you of the informal procedures that operate at work. As a new employee, try to avoid becoming too closely associated with any one group, because work groups often have informal cliques. You might want to dissociate yourself from a group later, but this will be hard to do if you are closely connected to it from your first day on the job.

Recognize others. Give people credit when the occasion arises. You will increase your esteem among your work associates and supervisors if you can honestly compliment them or members of their families on their accomplishments. Learn the names of your coworkers and try to remember their interests and concerns. At social occasions, try to learn the names of your colleagues' spouses and children.

Anticipate accurately. Develop realistic expectations about work. Students who spend two or four years at college frequently experience an expectations gap—the difference between what a recent college graduate thinks the world should be like and what the world is really like. The campus is often quite different from the world of work; this can be quite a shock for the recent graduate. One of the great values of work experience during college is the lessening of this shock through actual contact with the world of work.

Teamwork. Learn to work cooperatively with your immediate supervisor and work associates. Your supervisor will generally make work assignments, evaluate your performance, and offer constructive criticism as needed. If you believe your supervisor is not meeting these responsibilities, try to discuss the matter courteously with the supervisor or obtain assistance from an appropriate person in the personnel or human resources office or a union representative.

Stay in style. Avoid extremes in dress, mannerisms, and hairstyles. It is better to remain on the conservative side, at least until you know more about the lay of the land. Even where no official dress policies exist, employers expect workers to maintain whatever standards of good taste or acceptability prevail in the organization.

Contribute. Show yourself to be a planner and a problem solver. Careful planning, combined with goal setting and frequent analysis of your efforts, will help you become a more valuable employee. When suggesting a solution to a problem at work, listen attentively to the ideas and suggestions offered by others. Consider why something is currently done; there may be perfectly valid reasons for it. Instead of criticizing current practice or another's suggestion, show how your idea could supplement or expand the value of their ideas. Positive ideas never run down other practices or suggestions; they have a greater chance of being accepted because they don't encourage negative reactions from others.

Excellence. Concentrate on the quality of your work on the job. You want your work to be accurate, well done, and neat. This will depend on the knowledge you have about the job and your ability to learn new responsibilities. You will gain greater acceptance from employers and work associates when your work carries a mark of excellence.

Faithfulness. Be loyal to the employer who is (or has been) loyal to you. This does not mean you must accept everything your employer does. When disagreements occur, bring them up with the supervisor or employer. Don't go to the outside and broadcast your complaint to the world; your employer will resent this, and it won't solve the problem. As long as you are a member of the organization, either speak well of it or don't speak of it at all.

Healthy self-confidence. Project a positive self-image at work. Acknowledge other people with good eye contact and a pleasant smile. Gracefully accept compliments for a job well done. Concede past mistakes, but don't dwell on them. Don't undersell your own ideas with phrases such as "There are probably better ways to do this, but . . .". Avoid putting yourself down with false modesty or boasting with misleading claims.

Obligations of the Employer

Workers are obligated to meet employers' expectations in order to keep their jobs or move up in the organization. On the other side of the coin, workers rely on employers to fulfill certain obligations to them.

Communication of expectations. Employers are responsible for letting employees know exactly what is expected of them on the job and for giving them the instructions, training, and guidance needed to meet these expectations. New workers usually receive much of this information from their immediate manager. This person is responsible for greeting new employees on their first day of work, introducing them to coworkers, showing them to their desks or workstations, and offering the information they need to learn their way around the workplace. In time, the supervisor is apt to explain exactly what the new worker is expected to do and to outline the work rules and procedures to be followed.

Pay. One of the employer's major responsibilities is to pay employees for their work. Forms of pay vary widely. Some workers receive annual salaries; others are paid a fixed amount per hour, day, or week. Some are paid on a piecework basis, according to the amount they produce. Salespeople are sometimes paid commissions, a certain proportion of the value of their sales. Commissions may either constitute a worker's total pay or supplement a fixed salary. Some workers (taxi drivers, waiters and waitresses, and cosmetologists, for example) count on customers' tips to boost regular wages or salaries. Pay schedules vary, too. Payday may occur weekly, biweekly, on specified days such as the 1st and 15th of every month, or according to some other schedule.

Regardless of how or how often workers are paid, however, they can expect their employers to withhold certain amounts from their earnings. The starting pay quoted to new workers is the base or **gross pay**—their earnings before deductions. Under the law, employers must withhold money from workers' base pay for federal income taxes, Social Security, and Medicare. Other withholdings are generally required for state and local income taxes. The amounts withheld depend on the amount a worker earns, his or her marital status, the number of people he or she supports (dependents), and various tax laws. To determine the amount withheld for taxes, new workers fill out tax-withholding forms, indicating their marital status, address, and number of dependents. The amount withheld each year should come close to the worker's annual tax bill. Payroll deductions are also made for retirement and disability programs, which provide retirement income or benefits to workers who are unable to work because of sickness or injury. By law, most workers must participate in these plans. Many workers may also elect to have their employers make deductions for health and hospitalization plans, savings bonds or other types of savings programs, union dues, or shares of stock in the employing company.

The amount a worker receives after all deductions are made—called **net pay** or **take-home pay**—can total less than two-thirds of your gross pay. New workers who are unprepared for these deductions may be disappointed to find that their first paycheck is less than they expected. However, many workers actually earn more than their paychecks indicate because of their benefits.

Benefits may include retirement income, disability pay, unemployment insurance, hospitalization coverage, paid vacations, paid holidays, sick leave, and other similar benefits paid for partly or wholly by employers. Because such benefits can significantly boost a worker's income, it is to a new worker's advantage to learn as much as possible about such plans and to participate in elective programs, such as insurance plans, that offer worthwhile benefits. A worker's immediate supervisor or a personnel office representative can usually provide detailed information about such plans.

While we are on the subject of money, how do you ask for a **pay raise**? First, you must be able to justify your request. Here is where a portfolio of your achievements will come in handy. All during your working life, keep a written (and where possible, a pictorial) record of the things you have accomplished. Document your successes. Keep any written commendations you have received, not just from supervisors and employers, but also from customers, clients, students, coworkers—in fact, just about anyone. While it is fresh in your mind, write an account of anything you have done well, whether you received any recognition for it or not. Keep work samples as evidence of your worth. You never know when records of this sort will save the day. Second, think about timing. Obviously, you want to make your request when times are good and/or when the organization is thriving and making a profit, not when the economy is in a deep recession and/or the company is downsizing or headed toward bankruptcy. Third, use any comparative data you can, especially when they show that others in the same occupation and with the same length of time in the job are more highly paid than you are. Make your appeal factual, not emotional. Information about pay rates is available on the Internet or in publications such as the *Occupational Outlook Handbook* (U.S. Department of Labor, 2004), updated every two years; the *American Almanac of Jobs and Salaries* (Wright, 2000), updated periodically; or the National Association of Colleges and Employer's annual *Salary Survey*. Finally, write a script and practice it with friends or business associates, asking them what they think of it. Don't show the script to the boss; rehearse it and try to memorize as much of your bid for a pay raise as you can. Much of this advice applies to *promotions* as well.

Adherence to laws protecting the rights of workers. Workers are guaranteed the **right to organize and to bargain collectively** through representatives of their own choosing under the National Labor Relations Act. The Fair Labor Standards Act sets hourly **minimum wages**, requires some workers to be paid **premium rates** for overtime pay when they work more than 40 hours in a week, and **prohibits oppressive and unsafe child labor**. Other laws require employers to give all persons **equal treatment**—regardless of race, color, religion, sex, or national origin—in all aspects of employment, including hiring, promotion, pay, firing, apprenticeship, job assignment, and training. The Occupational Safety and Health Act requires employers to provide workplaces that are **free of recognized health and safety hazards**. Other federal, state, and local laws that concern the rights and well-being of workers are too numerous to mention here. Many laws related to employment specify a minimum number of employees for a company to be subject to the law. For example, a company must have at least 15 employees to come under the provisions of the Americans with Disabilities Act, 20 for the Age Discrimination in Employment Act, 50 for the Family and Medical Leave Act, and 100 for the Plant Closing Act.

CONCERNS OF WORKERS

No work is without its issues and problems. In this section, anxieties and worries that affect certain groups of workers are discussed. Following that, the problem of job burnout is examined. Job burnout strikes many people after repeated disappointments and discouragements at work. The process often starts with unrealistic expectations of satisfaction on the job, followed by feelings of frustration and indifference toward the work when those expectations are not fulfilled.

Difficulties, Dilemmas, and Dissatisfactions of Selected Groups of Workers

Younger workers and autonomy on the job. Many young people start work with great expectations, sometimes beyond the capacity of any job to deliver. They expect a great amount of intrinsic reward from work—features such as opportunity for self-expression, challenge, interesting work, and freedom to make decisions. Young people are said to be more casual toward work, but they are less resistant to new learning. They tend to favor 12-hour shifts with more days off, whereas older workers usually stick with the traditional 8-hour day and standard weekly schedules. If new technology threatens their jobs, both youth and the elderly react with a somewhat indifferent attitude. The young are more likely to see their jobs as temporary, and the older workers can be unconcerned because they are nearing retirement. Those in middle age are the ones who are nervous about advancing technology (Aeppel, 2000).

Many young workers express an entrepreneurial spirit; they strive for independence and are willing to take risks. Some have already run their own small businesses while they were still in school or before they took on the responsibilities of marriage, when they had more time and freedom to experiment (Mariani, 1994). They are attracted more toward small, growing companies and less to large, bureaucratic organizations. They are bothered by authoritarianism at work and ask management to give them opportunities for self-motivation.

Younger workers may question basic assumptions such as the old expression "a fair day's work for a fair day's pay." Unions have traditionally been concerned with setting standards for a fair day's pay, whereas employers have asserted their right to determine a fair day's work. Younger workers challenge both union and management by demanding a voice in establishing their working conditions, as the following case illustrates. Three young workers in their early 20s were hired to clean offices at night. One evening the foreman caught one of the young janitors asleep with his feet on a desk, another reading a paper, and the third doing schoolwork. The foreman gave them a written warning, and the workers filed a grievance. By really hustling, they had cleaned all the offices in five hours instead of eight so they could use the other three hours for themselves. The union steward tried to understand their point of view but felt the company was justified in expecting eight hours work for eight hours pay. He explained to the young workers that if they continued to finish their work in five hours, the company would either give them more work or get rid of one of them. They slowed their pace. The union steward felt that he had settled the grievance within the understood rules and kept everyone happy, but the young workers were far from satisfied. They had wanted the union to establish the boundaries of work and the rate of pay, and then they wanted the freedom to manage their own work operations within the time frame and assignments given them (*Work in America*, 1973).

Questions to ponder and discuss:

- Should workers be given more freedom to determine how they will work on the job?
- Is increased freedom or autonomy on the job likely to be abused by younger workers?

Older workers and age discrimination. Acts of age discrimination are likely to grow as the American population grows older and more older people continue working or want to go back to work. According to an American Association for Retired Persons (AARP) survey, 69 percent plan to work in some capacity during their retirement years, not only for money, but also for unseen benefits such as enjoyment and a sense of purpose. Older people are generally optimistic about their own ability to find and keep a job, yet 67 percent of them have concerns about age discrimination being a major restriction to moving forward and being contented in the workplace (AARP, 2002).

By 2030, those age 65 and older will make up 20 percent of the population, up from 12 percent in 1995. In 2000, 32.3 percent of people age 55 and over were in the labor force, the highest participation rate since 1980 (Gill, 2001). The impact of the more than 80 million Americans now living who were born in the two decades after the end of World War II will be a significant force shaping the economy. The baby-boomer generation, as they are called, is far more numerous than any generation either preceding it or following it. In the years to come, this group will be the largest component of our increasingly older population (Judy and D'Amico, 1997). More than any identifiable group before them, boomers regard themselves as young. Yet nearly 84 percent of the work force retires before they reach age 65, the median age being 61. Corporate downsizings of recent years have prompted employers to offer early-retirement plans as a less painful yet distressing method of easing older workers out of the work force. A sizable number of these "young" retirees would like to continue working, but many of them believe no suitable work will be available to them or the business world will see them as "too old."

Even though the growing economy of the late 1990s drove unemployment rates to low levels, employer attitudes toward keeping older workers on the job have not basically changed. Unless many employers substantially change their perceptions and treatment of older workers, the number of age discrimination claims against them will greatly expand (Gregory, 2001). Since the 1980s, the number of people working or seeking work beyond age 65 has increased. Why? There are two reasons driving this trend, according to John Rother, director of legislation and public policy for AARP: (1) At the low end of the labor spectrum, more people are arriving at age 65 without pensions or without much in savings and must work, and (2) at the other end, people who are highly skilled and educated want to continue working because they have interesting jobs and they view work as part of their self-expression (Gill, 2001).

Age discrimination is rejecting an older worker because of false assumptions about the effect of age on the worker's ability to perform the job. Negative perceptions of aging derive from several common stereotypes. How many have you heard? Older workers are stubborn, inflexible, and oppose change. They are less productive and not as adaptable. As older workers slow down, learning new skills becomes more difficult for them. They are more difficult to retrain if their skills become obsolete. Employee benefits cost more for older workers. Older people want to retire at the earliest opportunity and will "coast" for the remainder of their careers. Investing in retraining older workers for new technologies makes no sense because they will remain with the company for only a short time (Gregory, 2001).

These assumptions have little evidence to back them up. Studies show no correlation between age and ability to perform on the job, except where strenuous physical labor is required. Older workers consistently have high evaluations regarding job skills, loyalty, and dependability and less turnover and absenteeism. Where people are continually challenged by their work, there is no resistance to change and no decline in interest and motivation. The performance of older workers is generally as good as and sometimes better than that of younger workers (Gregory, 2001).

The Age Discrimination in Employment Act of 1967 makes it unlawful for an employer to fire, to refuse to hire, or to take any other adverse action against a person concerning pay, terms, conditions, or privileges of employment because of that individual's age. Despite the research disproving the false stereotypes of aging and the legislation against age discrimination, the contributions of the older age group can easily be ignored or devalued in our youth-oriented culture. The elderly are viewed as a social problem, and our approach to social problems is to reduce their visibility (Slater, 1990).

Certain code words may be used in advertising job openings that indicate age bias. *Overqualified* is a term that might be used when an employer puts upper limits on the years of experience for a job. *Fast track* may indicate that the employer is looking for a younger worker, thinking an older candidate will be discouraged from applying for the position.

Forced or encouraged retirement occurs earlier for many people today. Retirement is the time-honored method of taking older people out of the labor force or out of the competition for jobs. Older workers find themselves fighting the impression that aging is linked with decreasing capabilities for work and training. Although a gradual slowing down can be associated with age for many people, this slowing can be more than compensated for by the wisdom and experience an older person brings to a work organization. Unfortunately, the labor market is generally unresponsive to the needs of older workers. If they need to find new work, older people often face a serious decline in their wages compared to their previous jobs. Only two choices are usually offered: either take a full-time job or accept total retirement. Alternative work arrangements, such as job sharing and gradual reductions in time schedules, are not options for many older workers (Rones, 1983).

Questions to ponder and discuss:

- Should companies and government offer part-time work at lower pay rates to older people? Or would this constitute age discrimination?
- Should programs of phased retirement be encouraged through a gradual decrease of hours for older workers?
- Is early retirement a subtle form of age discrimination?

Blue-collar blues and white-collar woes. Blue-collar workers are found mostly in production and maintenance occupations; they are often paid by the hour or according to the amount they produce. Historically, their major complaints about work stem from having little or no control over work assignments, lack of opportunity to advance, and the lower status conferred on them by the rest of society, which typically takes a skeptical view of manual labor. Furthermore, blue-collar workers compare themselves unfavorably to the white-collar group, seeing white-collar employees as having more job privileges than they do. Other negative views of blue-collar work include the lack of mental stimulation from repetitive work routines, physical exhaustion from working in a variety of weather conditions, and the loss of jobs to automation.

Of course, there are the positives voiced by blue-collar workers: less mental stress, the satisfaction of working with one's hands, being paid to learn with apprenticeships, and the better pay and benefits that come with union membership. Yes, automation takes away jobs; however, it also creates new kinds of work for blue-collar workers. "You may get your hands dirty on a blue-collar job," says one laborer, "but it sure beats sitting in a cubicle all day." Another despises the hypocrisy of social prejudice against workers in the trades: "Some people look down on our kind of work; however, if their car, appliance, or something in their house breaks down, the first person they call for help is a blue-collar worker" (Harrison, 2003).

The history of blue-collar work in the 20th century has been one of expansion followed by stagnation and decline. No, blue-collar workers express great anxiety about the loss of job security and the decline in the purchasing power of their earnings. Of the 2.7 million jobs that disappeared from early 2001 to the middle of 2003, 2.4 million were in manufacturing. The economic downturn in that period eliminated more than 1 in 10 factory jobs in the United States (Lindlaw, 2003). Global competition, corporate restructuring, improved technology, deregulation, automation, and outsourcing work overseas have shrunk the number of blue-collar jobs over the past several decades. Blue-collar wages have declined or stagnated, too. In all recessions since the early 1960s, the unemployment rate was at least twice as high for blue-collar workers as for white-collar workers. The blue-collar share of total employment dropped from 37 percent in 1960 to 26 percent in 1991; during the same period, the white-collar group increased from 43 to 57 percent.

White-collar workers is a term used to describe office, administrative, clerical, sales, technical, and professional employees. Much job dissatisfaction today is found among well-educated people in regimented, monotonous, low-paying clerical positions. White-collar workers complain about having to be accessible at all times, even on vacations, through cell phones, beepers, and laptop computers. When there is a layoff, they must take on more responsibilities (Frazer, 2002). Higher credentials are now demanded for white-collar work, but the pay, the status, and the amount of challenge of the jobs have not improved. The office is seen as the white-collar counterpart of the factory and its assembly-line methods. Computers have made white-collar work as vulnerable to automation as blue-collar work (Dent, 1995).

A growing number of U.S. companies are sending desired high-tech and service jobs to other countries where wages are lower in comparison. This trend has set off a debate in this age of globalization: Is outsourcing high-tech work offshore better for the U.S. economy, or does it mean pink slips for American workers? When blue-collar manufacturing jobs moved abroad, most white-collar workers thought, "It's not my problem." Now they are feeling the effects of globalization. Researchers predict that by 2015, 3.3 million U.S. high-tech and service jobs will be overseas, representing 2 percent of the work force and $136 billion in lost wages (Teicher, 2003).

The ranks of middle management have thinned considerably with recent corporate "downsizings," as top management gives more autonomy to self-managing work teams and individual workers. Middle managers sense that they lack influence in decision making but are still expected to carry out company policy. They worry about being out of touch with the values of younger workers and less competent with new technology. Feelings of insecurity and inadequacy may lead to damaged relationships with subordinates, colleagues, and those at home. Some managers want to change their career direction but think there is too high a price to pay or believe they must wait until their children are grown.

Questions to ponder and discuss:

- Do blue-collar workers suffer from a lack of status and regard from other people. If so, why?
- Do white-collar workers have more job security than blue-collar workers, or are they as vulnerable as blue-collar workers in today's labor market? Why?

African American workers and the effects of racial prejudice. How would you feel if you were a successful corporate lawyer who brought millions of dollars of business to your firm, but your partners balked at giving you just compensation for your efforts? Or, at your office building, as you got off the elevator with a younger associate who didn't know you, he stepped in front of you, blocked your way, and demanded to know why you were there? In both these situations, the only difference between you and the others is race: you are black, and they are white. These and other incidents are revealed in *The Rage of a Privileged Class* (excerpted in Cose, 1993). Because of his color, the younger associate believed he had the right to question an African American man's presence in a law firm. Because of his race, the black man's partners denied him the pay increase they would have given a white partner. As the author talked with African American professionals who have every attribute of success, he heard these melancholy words over and over again: "I have done everything I was supposed to do. I have stayed out of trouble with the law, gone to the right schools, and worked myself nearly to death. What more do they want? Why in God's name won't they accept me as a full human being?" (Cose, 1993, p. 57).

The anxieties faced by many African Americans and other minorities identified by Cose are these: (1) the assumption (made by whites) that African Americans will not fit into the company culture, (2) constantly having to prove they are worthy of respect, (3) racial obstacles to career advancement, (4) shattered hopes after years of trying to succeed, (5) presumption of inferiority, (6) fatigue from the stress of continually coping with stereotypes, (7) classification of jobs by color, (8) denial of one's own identity,

(9) enduring rudeness and affronts in silence, (10) living with white self-deception about the unpleasant reality of racism, (11) being blamed for the misbehavior of other African Americans and minorities, and (12) being excluded from social organizations to which other members of the same occupation belong.

The problems of African American and minority professionals may seem minor when compared to those of the underclass and the working poor. Over the years, many of them have remained unemployed or irregularly employed, or have given up looking for a job. Some have full-time jobs year round, but work mostly in manual labor or the service trades, which frequently pay less than a living wage.

> For many [minority] workers, . . . a quality job . . . is seen as a luxury that they cannot yet afford, and many look for jobs—the only ones they are likely to get—that they know beforehand they will hate. In effect, minority workers are the unwilling monopolists of the worst jobs that our society has to offer. (*Work in America*, 1973)

Then there are those trying to "make it in a white world." A society that frustrates those minority people struggling to work within the system may be undermining efforts to steer young minority people away from a life of hustling, burglary, and dope dealing. Solving America's racial difficulties involves much more than education and cleaning up urban ghettoes, important as these things are. Among other considerations, it takes understanding how minority people feel when, no matter what or how much they achieve in their life and work, their race will always be the most important thing about them (Cose, 1993).

African American white-collar workers often find themselves in a sort of no-man's land on the job. They have experienced the turnaround that has allowed them to enter occupations once reserved for white people, but they are still apprehensive about their security and survival in a work environment they perceive as hostile and threatening. Psychiatrists William Grier and Price Cobbs (1968) tell of an African American professional named John who competed in a training program that led to higher management positions. Although he was unnerved by the seeming confidence of his white, middle-class competitors, John performed with excellence in the classroom. His group went for specialized training in another city, staying in a sumptuous hotel. The inner conflict produced the first downward slide in his functioning. John wanted other African Americans in lower-level jobs to know that he was a "brother" and had not abandoned them even though he was in a management-training program. He felt uneasy with white employees below his job level, wanting friendly relationships with them but fearing that their prejudice could somehow undermine him. The essential skill to be mastered in his training program was supervision, but John began to have difficulty being firm with subordinates of both colors. African Americans would misunderstand, believing he was being tougher on them to impress whites. whites would complain that he was abusing his position of authority and acting out anti-white feelings. John coped with this problem, but other conflicts caused periods of depression. As his effectiveness declined, he was finally dropped from the training program. The inner strain John experienced when he had to exercise power over others sent him on a downward spiral toward failure. Anxieties such as those illustrated in this case can change only when social attitudes toward racial matters change as well.

Questions to ponder and discuss:

- Are most white employers biased against hiring African American job applicants, doing so only when required by government affirmative action regulations?
- Are African Americans who move up in a company with an 80 percent white work force likely to enter a no-man's land, as suggested by Grier and Cobbs's case study?

Hispanic/Latino expanding numbers, immigration, and jobs. Hispanics and Latinos outnumber African Americans as the largest minority group in the United States for the first time since the U.S. Census Bureau began counting the nation's population over two centuries ago. African Americans still claim to be the largest *racial* minority because they believe the Hispanic/Latino community is composed of different racial groups. The government considers "Hispanic" an *ethnic* classification, which means they can be black, white, Asian, or any race (El Nasser, 2003). The numbers may be difficult to assess because some Hispanic/Latinos may be unaccounted for when they are asked to identify themselves as "white," "African American," "Asian," or "Other." And, what about those who think of themselves as "Chicano" or "Puerto Rican"?

How many Hispanics and Latinos make up the U.S. population and in what sections of the United States do they live? The U.S. Census Bureau (2002) determined Hispanics to be 39 million in number and 13 percent of the population. Of these, 13.3 percent live in the Northeast, 7.7 percent in the Midwest, 34.8 percent in the South, and 44.2 percent in the West. About 34.8 percent are under age 18, 60.5 percent are between ages 18 and 64, and 5.1 percent are age 65 and older. These numbers testify to the growing importance of Hispanic/Latino voters, not only in certain states, but also nationwide.

Many non-Hispanic people express concern about illegal immigration, particularly in border states such as California, Arizona, New Mexico, and Texas. "We're not against Hispanics—just the illegals," they will say, and go on to point out that they resent undocumented immigrants using public services such as health care. Some even go so far as to say the immigrants are an alien invasion wishing to "reconquer" the Southwest. Those who are sympathetic to people trying to escape poverty and create opportunities for their children say the immigrants desire nothing more than what the ancestors of most Americans wanted—a chance for a better life. Because the situation is chaotic, over 90 percent of Hispanic/Latino adults want U.S. immigration laws to be reformed by promoting a system that increases the legal flow of workers into this country (Latino Coalition, 2003).

As for jobs, a CBS–*New York Times* poll reported that 8 in 10 Hispanics believe immigrants tend to take jobs no one else wants (Associated Press, 2003). The same poll revealed that most Hispanics and Latinos are optimistic about prospects for themselves and their children, and that economic opportunity is what makes life better in the United States than in the places they were born. In another survey, the Latino Coalition (2003) found jobs and the economy to be the most important issue facing Hispanic/Latino people and their families, outranking education, discrimination, and a host of other issues. Yet discrimination exists. One problem is the attitude of some employers who devalue certain jobs where Hispanic/Latino immigrants are overrepresented, such as farm labor, landscaping, construction, groundskeeping, and painting. The UCLA Chicano Studies Research Center analyzed census data from 1990 and discovered that both native and established immigrant men earned an average of 11 percent less than others in similar service and manual labor jobs when they worked with newly arrived Hispanics (Veiga, 2003). Here is evidence that exploitation of a vulnerable minority can mean lower wages, not only for a discriminated-against group, but for all.

Questions to ponder and discuss:

- Do newly arrived Hispanic/Latino immigrants face unique challenges or do they encounter the same difficulties all immigrant groups have faced in coming to the United States?
- Are Hispanics/Latinos more likely to be accepted in the dominant American culture than African Americans? Why or why not?

White males and affirmative action. *Affirmative action* means society must take positive steps to provide remedies for injustices caused by discrimination against minorities and women. The 14th Amendment of the U.S. Constitution proclaims "equal protection of the laws" for all citizens, but the achievement of equality seems to take forever. To bring about racial and gender equality requires more than putting an end to discrimination; it means giving special consideration to minorities and women. When weighing the merits of applicants for jobs, promotion, and admission to schools, affirmative action means race and gender can be taken into account in a positive manner.

At first, affirmative action policies seemed reasonable when measured against the cruel oppression of slavery and segregation for African Americans and the subjugation of women. Inevitably, however, a backlash occurred against affirmative action. The U.S. Supreme Court first dealt with it in 1978; in *Regents of the University of California v. Allan Bakke,* when a 5–4 majority ruled that a white applicant to a medical school had been wrongly denied admission in order to admit a less qualified black applicant. This case revealed a great ambivalence of thinking about affirmative action. The Court majority held that the school had a proper interest in increasing the number of minority students, which might justify the use of race as one among many other factors in deciding whether to admit a candidate. This ruling was reaffirmed in *Grutter v. Bollinger,* a 2003 decision involving the University of Michigan; however, the Court also ruled that the university could not award extra points on the basis of race in its admissions procedures (Kellogg, 2003).

Affirmative action employment practices have been criticized by a number of white males who have complained that they are the innocent victims of sins committed by others a long time ago. They believe a "reverse discrimination" is now depriving them of an equal opportunity in their occupations when there are fixed quotas or positions set aside for minorities and women. If discrimination against blacks and women was wrong, they say, then it is just as bad today to treat white males unfairly; injustice is not overcome and things are not set right by committing another wrong. Winning job offers, advancing in the workplace, and admission to schools should be based on ability and a true equality of opportunity. Others believe affirmative action becomes demeaning to blacks and women because it suggests that only racial and gender preferences can do for them what they cannot do for themselves (Steele, 1990). Requiring favored treatment in employment to make up for past discrimination simply reinforces the myth of black inferiority or that women "cannot make it in a man's world." All sides agree that everyone should have access to a level playing field, where all have an equal chance to succeed on the basis of merit. Those who believe affirmative action should continue state that the number of whites who have actually suffered from it is relatively small (Hacker, 1992). Some data have shown that white males have not lost ground in many occupations, despite efforts to open these fields to women and minorities.

To affirmative action advocates, ending discrimination is not adequate compensation for the ruthless brutality of previous discrimination. They feel the playing field is still tilted in favor of white males. The intentions of affirmative action policies are not racist or sexist, and they cannot be likened to the injustice of past discrimination, which was pursued as an end in itself (Fish, 1993).

A majority of voters in California and other states have approved state proposals to ban government affirmative action programs. Racial and gender preferences in public hiring were eliminated. Civil rights groups have filed lawsuits in an attempt to prevent these measures from becoming law.

Questions to ponder and discuss:

- Are complaints made by white males about "reverse discrimination" justified?
- Is affirmative action still needed, or has it outlived its usefulness?

Gays/lesbians and discrimination in the workplace. Most Americans believe discrimination because of a person's sexual orientation is not right. In a Harris poll of over 2,000 people nationwide, 77 percent said it should not be a factor when a person's job performance was being evaluated; 64 percent also replied that all employees, regardless of their sexual preference, were entitled to equal benefits such as health insurance for spouses or partners. However, the same poll discovered that when asked which groups of people were seen as encountering discrimination in the workplace, 73 percent answered "gays and lesbians"—just behind the highest group ("older adults aged 65 and over"). Other groups perceived as vulnerable to workplace discrimination included "people with disabilities" (68 percent), "women" (65 percent), "African Americans" (61 percent), "Hispanic Americans" (60 percent), "Muslims" (60 percent), "Asian Americans" (44 percent), and "Jews" (39 percent) (Harris Interactive, 2002).

Regarding the actual experiences of gay, lesbian, bisexual, and transgender people (GLBTs), 23 percent responded that they had been harassed on the job by coworkers, and 12 percent said they were denied promotion or job advancement because of their sexual orientation. Nine percent reported being fired or dismissed unfairly for the same reason. Eight percent were pressured to leave a job because of harassment or hostility against them in their workplace, while 22 percent reported "some other form of discrimination." Fifty-nine percent stated they had "never faced any form of discrimination because of sexual orientation or gender identity" (Harris Interactive, 2002).

Perceptions about discrimination can be deceiving. A majority of Americans mistakenly believe that workplace discrimination against gays and lesbians is already illegal. Although this is true in 12 states and numerous local jurisdictions, as of this writing there is no U.S. federal law, nor is there any law prohibiting discrimination on the basis of sexual orientation in 38 of the 50 states. The states that have enacted such laws are California, Connecticut, Hawaii, Maryland, Massachusetts, Minnesota, Nevada, New Hampshire, New Jersey, Rhode Island, Vermont, and Wisconsin, plus the District of Columbia (PFLAG, 2003).

In an attempt to avoid workplace discrimination, gays and lesbians need to carefully research the organization for clues that it is inclusive of all employees, whatever their sexual orientation. Alcorn (2003) suggests looking for a number of indicators of inclusion before interviewing for a job at a company, the first being a nondiscrimination statement. "If it doesn't include anything about sexual orientation," she writes, "it's a red flag" (p. 1). The organization's benefits plan should embrace everyone in its practices. Diversity initiatives need to be evident in its literature and the company should be free of discrimination lawsuits. Lists of the most employee-friendly companies or best companies for minorities are published in books and magazines. If your research has not uncovered any of this information, ask about it during the interview. Also, look for physical evidence when you walk around hallways before and after the interview.

Occupational strategies were covered in the first book of this series, *Taking Charge of Your Career Direction*. To briefly review them, they were self-employment, job tracking, and risk taking. Self-employment avoids the risk of being fired because of one's sexual orientation. Job tracking requires researching and finding work organizations that are nondiscriminatory to gays and lesbians. These first two strategies are relatively safe, but they do not completely eliminate the possibility of negative reactions from customers and coworkers. Risk taking means taking your chances; workplaces range from completely tolerant to homophobic (Chung, 2001).

The biggest fears about coming out at work are losing one's job, blatant hostility, and being passed over for promotions. Those who feel safe enough to come out on the job often experience a more integrated and honest identity. The stresses connected to living a dual life can take an emotional toll, but a gay or lesbian person must be prepared for possible negative reactions from some people (Bryant, 2003). Assess the nature of your workplace before coming out. Consider your personal safety. If you are in an extremely homophobic environment, finding a new job may make more sense than coming out in your current one (Signorile, 1995). If you decide to come out, determine how you will actually do it. Don't shout "I'm gay" with sudden announcements. Begin with a few trusted coworkers, or place a picture of you and your partner where you work. Mention an event you attended with your partner. Let the knowledge spread naturally, as it will. This new information about you will not be regarded as earth-shattering news, but simply another part of life (Bryant, 2003).

Questions to ponder and discuss:

- Why have so many state legislatures and the U.S. Congress not passed laws prohibiting discrimination in the workplace on the basis of sexual orientation?
- If you were counseling a gay or lesbian person, what advice would you give about how to deal with workplace discrimination?

Women and gender stereotyping of work. The gender shift in the American workplace may well be the most significant change in U.S. labor history. In 2002, 60 percent of all adult women were in the U.S. labor force (Spraggins, 2003), up from 33 percent in 1950. (The percentage of men in the labor force has dropped from 88 to 74 percent since 1950.) The 70.6 million women forecast to be working (and looking for work) in 2010 will comprise 47.9 percent of the labor force (Fullerton and Toosi, 2001), up from 29 percent in 1950. In the years immediately ahead, the number of women in the labor force is expected to come close to matching the number of men. Fifty-five percent of all bachelor's degrees, 53 percent of all master's degrees, and nearly 40 percent of all doctorates are now earned by women. In the future, women may be better prepared than men for professional careers in the information age (Judy and D'Amico, 1997). U.S. Department of Labor studies show that at least 9 of every 10 women will work outside the home at some point in their lives. Home, family, and the husband's job gave women their identity in the past, but an occupation other than housekeeping is increasingly the major source of identity for women.

Many half-truths have existed about women and work. One, less often heard now, was the idea that women need smaller amounts of income; they work just for "a little extra spending money." This idea was used to justify pressing women into low-paid occupations or paying them less for doing the same work as men. Actually, most women work because they must supplement an inadequate family income or support themselves and their children. Women are the sole earners in one-fifth of married-couple families. Both wife and husband work in 55 percent of all married-couple families. Women are the only earners in nearly two-thirds of families maintained by a single person (Judy and D'Amico, 1997).

Occupational segregation by sex can be explained by demonstrating how closely the characteristics of female-dominated occupations reflect the common stereotypes of women. Several illustrations provide examples. The caring nature of women is said to qualify them for occupations involving the care of children, sick people, and older people (nurse and teacher). Skills and experience in household-related work equip women to work in occupations that are home-based. Attractive physical appearance enables women to work as receptionists and other kinds of occupations where customers must be pleased. Another positive example is the presumed greater honesty of women, which helps qualify women for occupations where money is handled. Women are not inclined to supervise others, according to a negative stereotype; therefore, they are thought to be less qualified for supervisory and managerial positions. Less physical or muscular strength disqualifies them for work requiring heavy lifting. Other stereotypes hold that women have less ability in science and math and are not as willing to face physical danger and use physical force (Anker, 1998).

Another misconception is that women miss more days at work. The Labor Department reports that women accounted for slightly over a third of all work-related injuries and illnesses resulting in days away from work in 1992–1996 (U.S. Department of Labor, 1998). Other myths declare women are less involved in their work than men (studies show an equal concern with meaningful work); women are more content

Table 9-1 Female- and Male-Dominated Occupations, 2001 (numbers in thousands)

Female-Dominated Occupations	Number of Female Workers	Total Number of Workers	Percentage of Female Workers
Secretaries	1,821	1,846	98.6
Preschool and kindergarten teachers	487	495	98.4
Receptionists	697	712	97.9
Child care workers	132	135	97.8
Dental assistants	127	130	97.7
Early childhood children's assistants	229	239	95.8
Typists	370	388	95.4
Cleaners and servants, private household	197	207	95.2
Licensed practical nurses	271	287	94.4
Payroll and timekeeping clerks	139	150	92.7
Speech therapists	63	68	92.6
Teacher's aides	384	415	92.5
Eligibility clerks, social welfare	72	78	92.3
Bookkeepers, accounting, and auditing clerks	975	1,058	92.2
Billing, posting, calculating, and machine operators	100	109	91.7
Registered nurses	1,459	1,604	91.0
Hairdressers and cosmetologists	291	326	89.3
Bank tellers	270	303	89.1
Information clerks	1,220	1,384	88.2
Telephone operators	102	118	86.4
General office clerks	536	624	85.9
Data-entry keyers	462	546	84.6
Legal assistants	289	344	84.0
Special education teachers	261	314	83.1
Librarians	132	159	83.0
Elementary teachers	1,596	1,959	81.5

Male-Dominated Occupations	Number of Male workers	Total Number of Workers	Percentage of Male Workers
Automotive body repairers	174	175	99.4
Bus, truck, and stationary engine mechanics	306	309	99.0
Automobile mechanics	633	641	98.8
Carpenters	1,020	1,036	98.5
Heating, air-conditioning, and refrigeration mechanics	261	265	98.5
Electricians	739	752	98.3
Plumbers, pipefitters, and steamfitters	458	466	98.3
Brickmasons and stonemasons	179	183	97.8
Tool and die makers	109	106	97.2
Firefighters	235	242	97.1
Welders and cutters	485	500	97.0
Airplane pilots and navigators	98	101	97.0
Painters, construction and maintenance	347	358	96.7
Plant and systems operators	248	258	96.1
Industrial machinery repairers	403	420	96.0
Aircraft engine mechanics	121	127	95.3
Machinists	453	476	95.2
Sheet-metal workers	104	110	94.5
Groundskeepers and gardeners, except farm	574	609	94.3
Garage and service station–related occupations	118	127	92.9
Painting and paint spray-machine operators	139	152	91.4
Sales workers, motor vehicles and boats	267	294	90.8
Engineers (all kinds)	1,787	1,979	90.3
Surveying and mapping technicians	56	62	90.3
Electrical/electronic equipment repairers	789	884	89.3
Clergy	269	303	88.8

*Note: Two occupations were performed by 100 percent males: terrazzo and concrete finishers and excavating and loading machine operators.

Source: U.S. Department of Labor, 2002.

Table 9-2 Numbers and Percentages of Females and Males and Percentages of Women's Earnings Compared to Those of Men's in 11 Occupational Groups, 2001 (numbers in thousands)

Occupational Group	Total Number of Workers	Women		Men		Women's Earnings as Percentage of Men's
		Number	Percentage	Number	Percentage	
Executive, administrative, and managerial	15,795	7,446	47.1	8,349	52.9	66.6
Professional specialty	16,426	8,510	51.8	7,916	48.2	73.4
Technicians and related support	3,753	1,883	50.2	1,870	49.2	74.1
Sales	10,173	4,574	45.0	5,599	55.0	62.0
Administrative support	14,219	10,954	77.0	3,264	23.0	81.4
Service occupations	11,143	5,812	52.2	5,331	47.8	76.6
Precision production, craft, and repair	12,030	1,012	8.4	11,018	91.6	73.8
Operators, fabricators, and laborers	14,568	3,258	22.4	11,310	77.6	73.5
Transportation and material moving	4,505	356	7.9	4,149	92.1	74.8
Handlers, equipment cleaners, helpers, and laborers	3,990	783	19.6	3,207	80.4	85.4
Farming, forestry, and fishing	1,493	222	14.9	1,271	85.1	84.2

Source: U.S. Department of Labor, 2002.

with routine, undemanding jobs (there are no data to support this notion); and women are less concerned about advancement (women want promotions as much as men do). Stereotypes such as these help employers justify work-related discrimination.

The effects of these beliefs are visible. When an occupation is composed primarily of one sex, this is evidence of occupational gender typing. Women are excluded from occupations labeled "masculine." The same limitations in some occupations also can be imposed on men. Table 9-1 displays how sex stereotypes influence female–male ratios in occupations. Occupational gender typing usually has little reasoning behind it. "Men's work" in one age may become "women's work" in another. For example, telephone operating and secretarial work were once male-dominated occupations in the United States. Bank tellers were mostly males in the 1950s; in the 1980s, these jobs became dominated by females. When occupations shift their gender domination, the transformation usually results from changes in job structure, status, or wages that make them less attractive to men—and women are then allowed in. When an increase in female employment in an occupation reaches a critical point, men begin to move out, fearing a loss of status and earning power. An occupation once virtually all-male can become resegregated as nearly all-female.

As of 2001, women earned 76.1 percent as much pay as similarly employed men (U.S. Department of Labor, 2002). Although the existence of the gender pay gap is well documented and the factors that lead to it are debated, the largest contributor to the gap is the higher proportion of women in that occupation (Boraas and Rodgers, 2003).

Despite gains in managerial and professional kinds of work, women are still more frequently consigned to traditionally lower-status "female" jobs (Spraggins, 2003). Even in the higher-status occupational groups, women are paid only 66.6 percent of men's pay in executive and administrative occupations and 73.4 percent in professional specialty occupations (see Table 9-2). Advancement is harder for women to win, and much of the work assigned to women deflates their sense of self-worth. Women hold the majority of lower paying white-collar jobs, even though they derive the same satisfaction that men obtain from the intrinsic rewards of work. Two out of three poor adults in the United States are women. The "feminization of poverty" has long been a disturbing trend in American society. Hilda Scott (1984) writes "that it is impossible to attack the poverty in the industrialized or the developing world unless the extent to which poverty is a women's problem is recognized" (p. 14). Journalist Barbara Ehrenreich (2001) left her middle-class life and became a waitress, cleaning worker, nursing home assistant, and Wal-Mart clerk to report on how women in these jobs existed. Not very well, it turned out; at times she had to work two jobs to subsist on $6 or $7 an hour or minimum wage employment. The lack of affordable low-income housing means that many of the poor live in their cars, with relatives, and in homeless shelters even though they are working seven days a week. The earnings of the working poor on one job are not enough to support themselves and their families. With 12 million women having been pushed into the labor market by recent welfare-to-work legislation, many are trying to survive on the wages of the unskilled—at half the earnings that are considered to be a living wage.

Questions to ponder and discuss:

- What preconceived ideas about traits that men and women are presumed to possess might explain the rigid sex roles often found in the workplace?
- How would you explain lower pay scales for women, which average 76 percent of male pay for comparable work?

Workplace romances. From the perspective of the organization, it's hard to think of any positives coming from office romances. The company worries about a loss of productivity; those people involved have other things on their mind. Romance at work can create feelings of unfairness and jealousy, especially if it's a relationship between a boss and an employee. There is nothing illegal about a workplace romance, or a breakup. However, a breakup could lead to retaliation in the form of dismissal, demotion, or a lesser job assignment, which could in turn trigger a sexual harassment lawsuit. Twenty-five percent of workplaces expressly forbid office romances, and 81 percent of human resource managers believe these affairs are dangerous and likely to create conflict. Seventy-six percent of HR managers say they would avoid getting romantically involved with a person at their office (Bertagnoli, 2003).

But try telling all this to employees. Obviously, the best way to know someone else is through human interaction, and work is definitely personal interaction. You are likely to spend more time with your coworkers than with your family. Work gives you and your associates something in common. People usually look better at work than they do at home. And, people tend to be more comfortable with coworkers, whereas a first date is often filled with tension. So it's a dilemma: Work is a wonderful place to meet people, but not the best place to have a romantic relationship. Writer Lisa Bertagnoli (2003) asked management consultant Paul Hellman and dating coach Patti Feinstein for some ideas on keeping a romantic relationship from destroying your career (or vice versa). Their suggestions:

- Steer clear of married people. Your reputation is ruined if you break up a marriage.
- Use discretion at work. Avoid clandestine meetings, long lunches, excessive e-mailing, sharing private jokes, and other activities that feed the gossip mill.
- Expect other people to find out. There are many ways, from nonverbal communication to physical closeness, for others to know about an office romance.
- Focus on your job at work rather than your love interest.
- Separate work and home life.
- Consider finding a new job. If the romance is moving toward a deeper relationship, it is probably better for one of you to leave the company, however difficult this would be to do.

Questions to ponder and discuss:

- Because love cannot be willed or dictated, what would you do if you found yourself in a romantic relationship at work that was irresistible?
- Do office romances cause more trouble and unhappiness than they are worth?

Sexual harassment in the workplace. When you are working and interacting with a member (or members) of the opposite sex, is it sexual harassment to:

- Give compliments concerning his or her appearance?
- Tell jokes that have sexual content?
- Eye that person up and down in a suggestive manner?
- Make sexual remarks, innuendoes, or veiled allusions?
- Display seminude or pornographic pictures on a wall?
- Make insulting remarks of a sexual nature?
- Nonsexually or incidentally touch a person?
- Touch a person sexually?
- Ask for sexual favors?
- Require sex as a condition for work-related advantages?

Give this list of activities as a survey, and you will discover that there is no common agreement about what constitutes sexual harassment on the job (except, perhaps, the last item). As Barbara Gutek (1985) found in her study years ago, considerable differences in perception exist between men and women.

That survey covered eight items and dealt with complimentary and insulting comments, complimentary and insulting looks and gestures, nonsexual and sexual touching, and expected dating and sexual activity. In each case, more females than males saw a given behavior as sexual harassment. The fewest numbers (6 percent of men, 7 percent of women) considered nonsexual touching or incidental contact as sexual harassment. The highest numbers (94 percent of men, 98 percent of women) believed expected sexual activity as a job requirement to be sexual harassment. The greatest difference was found with regard to sexual touching, which 84 percent of women but only 59 percent of men saw as sexual harassment (Gutek, 1985).

A major problem in determining what is and what is not sexual harassment comes with trying to define it. Legally, it is any unwelcome sexual advance or conduct on the job that creates an intimidating, hostile, or offensive working environment. Worded more plainly, sexual harassment is any offensive conduct related to an employee's gender that a reasonable woman or man should not have to endure (Petrocelli and Repa, 1998). Another commonsense definition is "deliberate and/or repeated sexual or sex-based behavior that is not welcome, not asked for, and not returned" (Webb, 1991, pp. 25–26). Two kinds of sexual harassment have been outlined by the U.S. Equal Employment Opportunity Commission (EEOC). *Quid pro quo* sexual harassment occurs when sexual favors from an employee are required in exchange for a reward such as a promotion or pay increase, or a person is punished for withholding sexual favors. The precise meaning of *quid pro quo* is "this for that." **Hostile environment** harassment happens when a worker is repeatedly subjected to offensive, sexually oriented behavior (jokes, touching, name calling, and so on) that unreasonably interferes with the performance of job duties. *Quid pro quo* sexual harassment is usually quite blunt and easy to detect; a hostile environment is often subtle, because it doesn't promise or deny anything connected with employment. In lawsuits involving hostile environment, the courts require proof of psychological harm suffered by the employee, although the degree of proof varies among the federal courts and the courts of the 50 states (Domino, 1995).

The effects of sexual harassment are extensive and often devastating, ranging from being fired (for not submitting to sexual demands) to various kinds of mental and emotional anguish. Workers have suffered retaliation for reporting sexual misbehavior, including loss of pay raises, benefits, and promotions. Sometimes harassed workers have been the victims of physical attacks and demeaning pranks. Before the 1980s, there were no laws prohibiting sexual harassment; women were virtually invisible to the male legislators who wrote the laws. Sex discrimination became illegal with the Civil Rights Act of 1964. Sexual harassment became a form of sex discrimination under EEOC regulation in 1980, and in 1986 the U.S. Supreme Court concurred with that opinion. As a result of the uproar over Professor Anita Hill's charges against Supreme Court nominee Clarence Thomas at his Senate confirmation hearing in late 1991, public awareness of sexual harassment on the job greatly increased and Congress passed a bill allowing victims of sexual harassment to sue for monetary damages.

How widespread is sexual harassment in the workplace? Gutek (1985) reported that more than 20 percent of women had quit a job, been transferred, been fired, or quit applying for a job because of harassment. By 1993, several polls indicated that 50 to 80 percent of all female employees have experienced some form of harassment during their career and that 15 percent experience it in any given year (Domino, 1995).

What steps are suggested for a person who is being sexually harassed? Barbara Repa (2000) describes a series of five escalating alternatives. If a beginning tactic does not stop the offensive behavior, you can move to more legalistic strategies until you find one that is effective.

1. Confront the person creating the problem and try to persuade the harasser to stop. Make it clear that you regard the behavior as unwelcome, an important part of the definition of sexual harassment, that is also a crucial first step if you decide later to take legal action against the harasser. Tell the harasser to stop when the harassment occurs. However, if your harasser caught you off guard, you may have been too surprised to respond directly or you may not have expressed yourself clearly, in which case, you should talk to this person the next day. Offer no excuses nor use humor to make your point. Be direct and brief. This strategy is not realistic in every case, particularly when you have suffered injuries or would be in danger. Put your communication in writing if the harassment persists, stating exactly the behavior you find obnoxious, why it is, and that you will take action if it does not stop. Enclose the company's written policy against sexual harassment if it has one. Before you send this letter, make a copy of it and show it to a person you trust. Ask this person's opinion of what you have written to make sure you have clearly stated the behavior that is bothering you. Because retaliation is possible, try to document the harassment by appealing to witnesses both inside and outside the company.

2. Use the company complaint or grievance procedure. Get help from the human resources department. Many companies have adopted sexual harassment policies on their own or by court order if there has been a history of these kinds of problems. This usually involves filling out a complaint form, followed by an investigation. If the company does not have a sexual harassment policy, lobby to get one.

3. File a complaint with the EEOC under the U.S. Civil Rights Act or with a state or local fair-employment practices (FEP) agency under a similar state or local law. Contacting these agencies starts an investigation by the EEOC or state agency and is a necessary requirement if you begin a lawsuit with the help of an attorney.

4. If the EEOC or state FEP agency investigation and conciliation does not bring acceptable results, file a private lawsuit for damages under the U.S. Civil Rights Act or state FEP law. Going to court in these kinds of lawsuits requires getting legal advice from an attorney.

5. File a common-law tort (civil wrong) suit like any other lawsuit based on personal injury. Here you will need an attorney, because you must prove that the harasser's conduct was truly outrageous. Often the last legal course for sexually harassed workers, tort actions provide a wider range of possible remedies

than those under the Civil Rights Act. If you are employed by an organization with fewer that 15 employees, a tort lawsuit is the only legal remedy you have, because you are not covered by the U.S. Civil Rights Act.

If the harassment continues after you have made it clear that it is unwanted, collect all the evidence you can—notes, photos, or letters you receive; cartoons, messages, or pinups posted on walls. Keep a journal of events. Write down the details of who, what, where, and when. Discreetly tell friends and coworkers you trust and can rely on for support. Keep a copy of your work evaluations and anything you have written at home where it is safe. Assuming they are not in league with the perpetrator, consider contacting your supervisor and the harasser's supervisor or, if the harassment does not stop, the next higher official in the company. Consider taking formal action, such as requesting transfer of the harasser to a distant site, using the company's complaint process, or filing a lawsuit. Enlist the help of the company, if you can, because sexual harassment has an impact on its business and profits from lost productivity, missed work days, and the flight of good employees who quit their job (Petrocelli and Repa, 1998). For more information, contact a local office of the EEOC and your state FEP agency, a union, or a law school clinic; many of them will provide you with legal advice, written materials, training programs, support groups, and attorneys (Repa, 2000). Finally, realize that the essential basis of sexual harassment has little to do with physical attraction; like rape, it has more to do with hostility, power, and control.

Questions to ponder and discuss:

- Who should decide what is sexually objectionable behavior in the workplace?
- Do most men accused of sexual harassment really intend to offend women?

Job Burnout

A social worker, burdened with a heavy caseload and too much paperwork, complains, "The job has become just a job. I must have 20 forms to fill out in triplicate every time I see a client." A psychiatric nurse reveals, "Lately, my first reaction to patients has been 'Now what do they want?' If things keep going this way, *I'll* be the patient." A teacher admits, "At one time, I really cared for my kids. I've simply lost interest in them. It doesn't matter to me what they learn." A corrections officer says, "I've seen it all. Now, I just go through the motions. Every day is just another day on the job." Every kind of work has boring aspects, and everyone experiences a bad day periodically, but when long-term feelings of alienation and exhaustion result in statements like these, the person may well be on the road to burnout.

Burnout appears to be especially common in the helping professions, but it may affect all types of work to some extent. Although burnout has undoubtedly existed for a long time, psychologists have only recently studied burnout seriously. Herbert Freudenberger (1980) compares a burned-out person to a burned-out building.

What had once been a throbbing, vital structure is now deserted. Where there had been activity, there are now only crumbling reminders of energy and life. Some bricks or concrete may be left; some outlines of windows. Indeed, the outer shell may seem almost intact. Only if you venture inside will you be struck by the full force of the desolation. . . . people, as well as buildings, sometimes burn-out. Under the strain of living in our complex world, their inner resources are consumed as if by fire, leaving a great emptiness inside, although their outer shells may be more or less unchanged. (Freudenberger, 1980, p. xv)

Christina Maslach (1982) identifies burnout on the job as a reaction to stress. It is a response to constant emotional strain from interaction with people, particularly with troubled people. Burnout runs in a cycle of emotional exhaustion, depersonalization, and a reduced feeling of personal accomplishment. For example, people in helping professions may try to do too much, get overinvolved, or become overwhelmed by the emotional demands made by others. Such people feel drained of physical and mental resources. They lose energy, drive, and spirit until they cannot give any more of themselves to their clients. Cynicism replaces idealism. People experiencing burnout detach themselves emotionally from the needs of other people. Some detachment is necessary to function well on the job, but too much can lead to indifference. Burned-out people exhibit less caring and a negative feeling toward others. Finally, they turn their negative attitudes inward, and burnout culminates with a sense of inadequacy on the job. As self-esteem and a belief in personal competence crumble, the burnout victim may turn to counseling and therapy or change jobs to find work that doesn't involve stressful contact with people.

Some work environments seem to be breeding grounds for burnout. These are workplaces where workers feel they have little or no control over their work, no influence on decisions affecting them, no opportunity to get away from stressful situations, and more responsibility than they can handle. There are too many demands made on them, too many people to serve, too much information to digest, and too little reward for making the effort. Workers may even be ordered to check out after an eight-hour shift, and then continue working for no pay or "donate" blocks of their time free of charge (Ehrenreich, 2002). Workers are thrown into situations more competitive than they can bear, such as competing for bonuses, promotions, or recognition. They are evaluated according to the number of products made or people served rather than by the quality of their work. A counselor, for example, may be judged by the number of clients seen, not by what was done for them. Some institutional policies may be damaging to psychological health. Workers are asked to follow procedures they don't believe in. Endless paperwork, red tape, writing reports, and filling out forms hold back the achievement of doing the job a person was hired to do. Employees complain about lack of support and inconsistent application of the rules. All workplaces may have one or a few of these characteristics, but too many of them in extreme forms can precipitate burnout over time.

Some people are more vulnerable to burnout than others. They may be overachievers with unrealistic expectations. Some people envision work as an everlasting adventure, filled with challenge, excitement, pleasure, and productive activity. When these expectations are not fulfilled, they are unable to adjust to reality. They try even harder and throw all their time and energy into the job, but this devotion is rarely rewarded. After the initial period of enthusiasm wears off, stagnation, frustration, and apathy are likely to follow (Edelwich with Brodsky, 1980). Burnout candidates often have low self-esteem and self-confidence. They feel at the mercy of their environment and do nothing to shape or improve it, passively allowing things to happen to them. A definite factor in burnout is the need for approval. When appreciation from others is not forthcoming, candidates for burnout feel betrayed and may begin to belittle those around them. People who do not have control of emotions such as hostility, anger, impatience, and intolerance toward others appear to run greater risks of burnout. For example, a person who constantly puts others down may be using hostility to prop up a weak ego (Maslach, 1982).

The job itself may contain built-in dissatisfactions that lead to burnout. Jerry Edelwich and Archie Brodsky (1980) catalog frustrations that can eventually add up to burnout:

- *Not enough money.* Choices are limited, and life is constricted.
- *Too many hours.* The working day has excessive hours with little chance to get away from the job; inadequate vacation time is offered.
- *Career dead end.* People feel blocked or caught in a rut, and little or no opportunity exists for advancement to a higher position.
- *Too much paperwork.* Filling out forms and writing numerous reports rather than doing the job described at the time of hiring makes people think they are serving only the organization's needs, not those of people.

- *Not sufficiently trained for the job.* For example, paraprofessionals may have to do the work a professional should do. Sometimes, however, the opposite is heard: "I am overtrained for this work."
- *Not appreciated by clients.* This occurs most commonly when working with people who don't want help in the first place or who demand more than a helper can give.
- *Not appreciated by supervisor.* Workers are not given responsibility equal to their skills, not consulted about decisions, overlooked by supervisors, and evaluated unfairly or by irrelevant criteria.
- *Lack of support for important decisions.* A worker is held responsible for a superior's failure to support or implement recommendations.
- *Powerlessness.* A worker has little or no chance to make an impact on other people or to influence decisions; recommendations are ignored.
- *System not responsive to client's needs.* The organization exists for its own sake and places a low priority on meeting the needs of the clients and customers it is meant to serve.
- *Bad office politics.* Internal power politics get nasty; polarization occurs among superiors and subordinates; too much petty infighting, jealousy, and undermining of reputations occur.
- *Other frustrations.* These might include instances of sexism, racism, ageism; being caught in the crossfire of bureaucratic decisions and nondecisions; too many demands made by too many people; a suspicious public constituency; lack of community awareness or support; poor personal image; or disappointment with one's fellow workers.

Apathy takes the form of a progressive emotional detachment in the face of frustration. The starting point is the idealism and enthusiasm of the beginner. If an employee is to come out of the clouds and work effectively, some detachment is desirable and inevitable. In the burned-out person, however, the detachment that develops out of frustration is a kind of numbness. A psychiatric ward aide expressed apathy as follows:

> At the beginning, like everybody else, I was gung-ho. I'd wake up thinking, "Here's another day. What can I get done today?" I spent a lot of time with the patients, gathered as much information as I could, and tried to work as a team with the rest of the staff. After five or six months, as I found the results I had expected not happening, I got to be indifferent. I'd wake up in the morning and not care about going to work. It was just another day, just a job. I spent less time with patients and did what was necessary only to get by. It was unpleasant having to do things that way, and I got away from it by spending time socializing with the staff instead of working with patients. (Edelwich with Brodsky, 1980, pp. 165–166)

"Indifferent," "just another day," "just a job," "did what was necessary to get by," "going through the motions," "putting in time"—involvement and enthusiasm have turned to apathy. The worker has decided to stop trying, hoping only to avoid future letdowns.

Apathy results in alienation and estrangement not only from others, but also from oneself. Many burnout victims feel removed from the rest of society, unable to connect their own lives to the lives of other people. Symptoms of depression may appear; listlessness and despair may surround one's personal life as well as life on the job. Apathy is a defense mechanism the burned-out person uses. It separates the person from the painful situation, but it also cuts that person off from things that might be of help: other people, meaningful work, and a feeling of belonging. For this reason, this numb, alienated stage of burnout is the most dangerous (Mangano, 1982).

What can a person do to counteract burnout? The following strategies will help neutralize the effects of burnout or reduce its likelihood:

1. *Adjust expectations and set realistic goals.* This does not mean giving up your ideals. It does mean setting achievable goals based on an honest appraisal of your abilities and values.

2. *Do your job differently; vary your work routines.* Determine which parts of the job can be changed and which cannot. Analyze the consequences of a change in work procedures. Talking to coworkers or taking a workshop may give you some new ideas about doing your job. Taking action may not be easy, but constant frustration is worse.

3. *Get away from the job for a while.* Getting away can range from a 15-minute coffee break or a 1-hour lunch period to a day, a week, or a month. Use a sick day or a vacation period if necessary. Avoid working through lunch hours or coming back at night to catch up on work.

4. *Get enough rest and relaxation.* Get sufficient sleep. Use relaxation techniques such as stress management, biofeedback, and imagery exercises. Change pace and wind down after work. Listen to music or meditate. Engage in a vigorous physical activity or become absorbed in a hobby. Leave the strains of the job behind.

5. *Seek satisfactions outside work.* Open up your life beyond the boundaries of your work environment. Family and friends can offer encouragement when work problems threaten. Outside activities and relationships provide outlets for creativity and challenge.

6. *Seek counseling or other professional help.* There is no reason to feel isolated or alone. Take advantage of any counseling services offered by your work organization or community.

7. *Leave the job or even the occupation itself.* Such a decision is personal. It should be made after you have tried all other strategies and have determined that the difficulties on the job have simply become overwhelming. Make a self-analysis: Assess your goals, values, skills, abilities, temperament, and attitudes. Recycling the career decision-making process and sharpening your job-hunting skills may be necessary.

Work organizations can take steps to counteract job burnout. The following strategies to alleviate the conditions that lead to burnout are adapted from Mangano (1982):

1. *Divide or rotate the work.* Organize work so employees can take turns at various job functions and no one person is overexposed to high-stress situations. Variety gives workers relief from monotonous tasks.

2. *Plan regular breaks in the work routine.* Coffee breaks during the workday and adequate vacations allow employees to avoid stress. Companies can provide memberships in recreational clubs and gyms and encourage their workers to use them during lunch hours or after work.

3. *Hire more workers when the workload becomes too heavy.* Despite the additional expense involved, this option should be considered when relatively inexpensive kinds of extra help are available.

4. *Provide adequate job preparation.* Burnout is linked to unrealistic expectations. A good orientation program can help put the demands of job performance into proper perspective. Training cannot anticipate all the situations that may occur on the job, but it is better than nothing.

5. *Provide opportunities for staff development.* People need to continue learning throughout their careers. Training should go beyond the first few days on the job. Staff development programs can contribute positively to professional and personal growth. Such programs can take various forms: workshops on special topics of interest, regular staff meetings, brainstorming and problem-solving sessions, courses at a university or a local community college, and even social occasions among staff members. Burnout victims feel isolated and insignificant, and these programs can prevent such feelings from becoming overwhelming.

6. *Give constructive feedback about performance on the job.* Burnout victims often have no idea of how they are doing on the job. It is important that workers receive praise and recognition when they have earned it. Too often, workers get attention from management only when they make a mistake or threaten a grievance. Constructive criticism can be presented in a nonthreatening manner, letting a worker know he or she is a valued member of the company. Praise and constructive criticism should not come only at formal evaluations, when promotions and pay raises are discussed, but should also be offered spontaneously and informally.

7. *Clarify organizational goals and the role each worker plays in achieving those goals.* People want and need to know what is required of them on the job. Job responsibilities that are reasonable, well-defined, clear, and consistent help workers identify themselves in a large structure and create a shared purpose between individual and company. Vague job descriptions can generate as much frustration as rigid, overdemanding requirements.

8. *Provide preventive counseling.* Intervention by skilled counselors can help prevent job burnout. Counselors should not be viewed as a part of the company; workers need to express their feelings and thoughts freely when they talk with a counselor.

EXERCISE 9-1 ON-THE-JOB PROBLEMS

Working will bring its share of problems. The problems presented in this exercise may help you anticipate situations that could develop at some time in your working life because all of them have happened before. Some problems concern ethics; according to recent surveys, 25 to 30 percent of workers have been asked to do or have seen unethical behavior on the job (Pink, 2001). In each case, you are asked, "What would you do?" and the response "Nothing" is an option. You can do this exercise alone, but if you are in a class or a group, it is often instructive to hear how others would handle the same problem. Teachers or group leaders may want to divide people into small groups and assign each one a situation for 10 or 15 minutes. Then spokespersons can report their conclusions to the entire group.

Situation A: Unused Talents

You have just been hired as an administrative assistant at a major state university after graduating with a master's degree in educational administration. For the first month, most of your time is spent in various "gofer" assignments: running errands for senior administrators, getting coffee for the rest of the office, operating the copy machine, picking up mail at the post office, collecting catalogs from other colleges, and other routine tasks. You feel you've been trained for higher responsibilities than these. What would you do?

Situation B: Idealism Versus Materialism

You are a college graduate who majored in humanities and have now worked at a business firm for about two years. While you were in college, you became very idealistic and learned to despise status symbols, conspicuous consumption, worship of money and physical objects, planned obsolescence, useless gadgets, and all the trappings of a materialistic society. The company where you now work, however, is very materialistic. It is absorbed in selling and making a profit on its products; profit is the bottom line that resolves all questions. The company advertises its products with average or sometimes substandard taste. It gives cash bonuses for new ideas, and its executive offices are decorated lavishly with expensive carpeting and furniture. Your critical, humanistic background leads you to comment freely on the company's obsession with materialism and its lack of human and spiritual values. Some of this criticism gets back to your supervisor, who tells you that you should keep your opinions to yourself if you have any hopes of promotions and greater responsibility within the company. What would you do?

Situation C: The Productive Employee

You have been working at a parts assembly plant for only a couple of weeks. Your rate of production has been consistently higher than that of your work associates. You enjoy the work and want to impress your employer and supervisor with your skill and hard work. Your coworkers, however, are beginning to harass you because they feel threatened by your high production rate. You want to have a good relationship with your work associates, yet you believe you should do your best and maintain high standards at work. What would you do?

Situation D: No Raise, No Promotion

You have been working for your employer for nearly two years, going all out and doing high-quality work. You get along well with your supervisor and bosses. Even with your excellent work record and good relationships, you have not received a pay raise or a promotion. You bring this problem to the attention of your supervisor, who tells you that management is aware of the situation, but the company hasn't made a profit for a year and the state of the economy is poor. The company hopes things will improve, but there is no guarantee. What would you do?

Situation E: The Pink Slip and Re-employment

You and two other employees have been working in a public organization for three years when the three of you receive "pink slips" saying that you are being laid off work in three months. You are told that budget cuts have made this move necessary. The administration regrets the layoffs very much, because they are happening through no fault of the employees involved. Then you discover that several people who were hired after you will still be employed. You are furious because the seniority principle has not been followed, but the administration claims that these people are working in more crucial positions. About two months later, you and your two coworkers are recalled to your old jobs. Your colleagues state that they will now work as little as possible because of the shabby treatment they received. What would you do?

Situation F: Taking Advantage of an Employer

You have been working in an office for about four months when you notice that a coworker and friend of yours is taking advantage of your employer. Your friend has been taking a few office supplies, making personal long-distance telephone calls on the company phone during office hours, allowing others who don't work for your employer to use an employee discount privilege, padding expense accounts, wasting time on the Web, and so on. These offenses start small, but they build steadily to a larger scale. What would you do?

Situation G: Blowing the Whistle on Your Employer

You have been working at a chemical company for six months as a toxicologist, researching the effects of various chemical poisons the company produces. Inadvertently, you discover that the company is dumping unacceptable levels of toxic chemical wastes into a nearby river. You discuss this problem with another research scientist, who tells you that the costs of properly storing and disposing of the chemical wastes are prohibitive and might even put the company out of business. What would you do?

Situation H: Perceived Preferential Treatment

You are a new employee and want to make friends with your work associates, but they are cool toward you; they believe you have been given some kind of preferred treatment in the hiring process (due to your sex, race, relationship to the employer, or social group membership). You feel they are judging you unfairly. What would you do?

Situation I: The Mistake

You have been working in the advertising department of a local television station for three months. Your job is to prepare copy for a device that projects lettering on the TV screen. Unfortunately, you misspell the name of an advertiser, and the error shows up in the next commercial displayed live for the viewing audience. The advertiser is angry and calls the station manager. At this time, no one is aware of who made the mistake. What would you do?

Situation J: The Difficult Supervisor

You have been working for a good organization in a job that you like very much, but you find it hard to talk with your immediate supervisor. This supervisor is reserved, distant, constantly finds fault, and has a negative attitude toward others. Your coworkers regard the supervisor as unfair and have as little to do with him (or her) as possible. You want to improve your relationship with this supervisor because you like all the other aspects of the job so much. What would you do?

Situation K: On-the-Job Training That Failed

You have been working for three months in the company's sales and marketing division. The manager was eager to hire you—your outstanding college record was very attractive. From almost the first day, you were turned over to the company's star salesperson, a 16-year veteran, for guidance and development. Your mentor took you on sales calls to help you learn the ropes, but the "star" knew the customers so well and had such an easy relationship with them that no product details were discussed and sales techniques were not needed. Now you believe your on-the-job training has not helped at all. You learned nothing new. Soon you will be on your own, but you really won't know what to do. What would you do?

Situation L: The Performance Review

You have been working at XYZ Company for over 25 years, coming in early on many days and receiving good performance reviews. At the end of your latest evaluation, you are shocked when your boss says, "This time, I'll have to rate you below average." You ask for reasons. You are told you've never stayed after official work hours and you are resistant to change because you sometimes ask for explanations of work duties. The review doesn't include the 10 half-day Saturdays you've worked in the past year. In conversations with others, you discover that almost all workers over 45 in your department have received low performance ratings. The younger, less-experienced coworkers are all rated higher than you. What would you do?

Situation M: The Invitation

You believe you have been the object of sexual attention by your supervisor. You've been on the receiving end of long looks, occasional winks, and comments such as "How's your love life?" and "You really look wonderful today" accompanied by soft touches on the arm, elbow, and shoulder. Your supervisor invites you to dinner alone, mentioning that a promotion you have applied for will be discussed. What would you do?

EXERCISE 9-2 THE JOB PROMOTION EXERCISE

A top administrative position has become vacant in the sales division of your company. You are on a committee responsible for recommending one person for the position. Six people have emerged as finalists. Read the description given for each person. Who would you choose, and why? If you are in a class, make an individual decision first and then come to a group decision after discussing your choice with the other members of the group.

The Candidates

1. *Frederick:* Male, age 48, white, married, two children in college; master's degree in business administration, undergraduate degree in engineering; Air Force veteran; has been with the company for 18 years, 10 as an engineer and 8 in various management positions; good performance reviews; considered an effective manager; successfully ran a friend's political campaign for state senator a few years ago; takes his religion seriously and is currently the head of his church's governing board.

2. *Robert:* Male, age 41, black, married, three children in middle and high school; associate degree in business management from a local community college, bachelor's degree in economics from a nearby college after six years of evening and Saturday classes; has been with the company for seven years, starting on the production line and becoming a foreman after three years; has risen steadily in management ranks; very articulate, expresses himself effectively in meetings; good evaluations; active in supporting minority causes; considered a political liberal.

3. *Ruth:* Female, age 44, white, married, two children in high school; master's degree in counseling and guidance, undergraduate degree in English; spent two years in Israel as an English teacher, worked seven years as a high school counselor before joining the company's personnel department; noted for her cooperation with people; is currently head of the parent–teacher association at the local high school; independent and moderate in politics; devoted to her synagogue and quietly but firmly supports various Jewish activities.

4. *Jeffrey:* Male, age 34, white, single; scholastic aptitude tests placed him in the top 1 percent of his college class; master's and bachelor's degrees in political science; student government president in college; supported antiestablishment causes in college, but has mellowed considerably, and friends claim he is becoming a staunch conservative; joined the company after graduation and has worked for 10 years in the public relations department; has won admiration for the way he represents the company in public; recently promoted to assistant director of customer services.

5. *Marcia:* Female, age 38, white, divorced, one child (not living with her); majored in secretarial studies at the local community college, transferred to the state university for an undergraduate degree in finance and now has a master's degree in business administration; worked as a secretary in a local bank's loan department, sold real estate part time; obtained a sales job in the company after her divorce, has been in the sales department for three years and is now an assistant sales manager; quick to learn, good evaluations; active in women's support groups.

6. *Carlos:* Male, age 37, Hispanic, married, three children in elementary and middle school; dropped out of high school, graduated from night school; worked in father's store for three years; won a tuition grant at an area college, where he majored in art and design with a minor in business; loves to paint and make pottery, began to achieve recognition as an artist while in college, has sold his work at art fairs; joined the company's advertising department six

years ago, several ideas for advertising campaigns boosted company sales dramatically over the short run; became interested in sales and has nearly completed a master's degree in marketing.

Make a preliminary choice based on the information you now have. If you are in a group, discuss your choice with the other members, and then come to a group consensus. Do not read further until you (and your committee) have made an initial decision.

Additional Information about the Candidates

Further evidence is now available from a psychological consulting team hired to provide a profile and evaluation of each candidate.

1. *Frederick* has some concerns about his physical condition and worries about a future heart attack (his family has a history of heart problems). His own medical checkups have shown that his health is good. He is very committed to his administrative work. Family relations have been strained at times because he spends so much time away from home on job-related activities. Intellectually, he is very capable; however, he may need counseling help if he becomes upset over health and personal affairs.

2. *Robert* is strongly attached to his family and seems to be an excellent husband and father. His high school record and aptitude test scores are average. Teachers remember him as someone who had a problem in getting things done at times. Although his college record was slightly above average, several instructors commented that he often did just enough to get by. (Robert acknowledges these comments and explains that his family and work obligations usually left him without enough time and energy to pursue his studies as intensively as he would have liked.)

3. *Ruth* is very dedicated to Jewish principles and goals and to solving problems at the school concerning the education of her children. She is active in her synagogue. Friends say she dislikes small talk and seems absorbed in her religion, schools and education, and her children. Ruth is considered capable of performing important administrative duties, but the consulting team wonders if her outside activities could detract from her work responsibilities.

4. *Jeffrey's* friends remember him as being firm about his liberal and radical political views. They all liked him as a person, however, despite his persistent pursuit of these views. Current companions say he is now becoming just as persistent about conservative causes. Jeff is viewed as a rising star in the company. Although he appears to be on an upward track, he seems quite anxious at times about life in general.

5. *Marcia* is described as a model career woman by some of her administrators. Several friends have expressed the opinion that her natural aggressiveness and competitiveness may have contributed to the breakup of her marriage; nevertheless, these traits have served her well in the business world. She is rumored to have friends in high places, and some coworkers expressed some resentment toward the favors she seems to have gained. Marcia has become a heavy smoker, and several people who work with her have complained about this habit.

6. *Carlos* is widely admired for his artistic talent. He is regarded as a free spirit with a flamboyant, energetic personality. His family tolerates his absorption in his work, saying they became accustomed to it when he worked long hours in the store and traveled to art shows. Although some colleagues think he is a near genius about knowing what the public wants, others feel he might get carried away on a project that could end in disaster, and thus needs to be restrained.

Either individually or as a group, make a final choice among these six candidates, and explain the reasoning behind your decision. (Note: Normally, more information would be presented about each candidate for a top administrative position; however, in this exercise we are operating under certain limitations of time and space.)

SUMMARY

1. Evaluating job offers involves the appraisal of many factors. Some of them deal with how well the job will fit into your long-range career planning, work values expressed, abilities used, salary offered, advancement potential, reputation and size of the organization, products made or services provided, and characteristics of people in the company or department. Other factors have to do with organizational culture, commuting distance, management style, prospects for company or industry growth, working conditions, location of workplace, and training and development.

2. Working on the job means living up to your responsibilities as an employee and knowing the obligations of the employer. You may connect with a mentor, a trusted counselor who helps you make your way around the organization. This chapter presents 15 points to keep in mind when fulfilling your mission of keeping a job. Employers have the responsibilities of letting you know what is expected of you, paying you for your work, and complying with the rules that govern employer/employee relations.

3. Various types of workers have special concerns and problems regarding employment. Younger workers want more freedom and autonomy on the job. Older workers experience feelings of obsolescence and worry about age discrimination. Blue-collar workers express anxiety over the lack of job security. White-collar workers feel they are now just as insecure and powerless as blue-collar employees. Minority workers cope with perceptions that race is all that matters, whatever their accomplishments might be. White males believe they are discriminated against when minorities and women are given preferences in employment or admissions to schools to redress the injustices of past discrimination. Women struggle to overcome myths and stereotypes about their presence in full-time careers once reserved for men. Personnel experts urge caution about office romances. Now that sexual harassment has been brought out into the open and is widely discussed, it is apparent that the problem is more pervasive in the workplace than most people once thought.

4. Job burnout afflicts many workers, notably in the helping professions. Burnout is a feeling of emotional exhaustion on the job. The cycle seems to start with great enthusiasm followed by stages of stagnation, frustration, and apathy. Individuals and organizations can use several strategies to counteract the effects of burnout. These strategies range from adjusting expectations and applying relaxation techniques to varying job functions and staff development measures.

REFERENCES

Adams, H. G. 1998. *Mentoring for professional development: Mentor/protégé handbook.* Notre Dame, IN: National Consortium for Graduate Degrees for Minorities in Engineering and Science.

Aeppel, T. 2000, April 7. Young and old see technology sparking friction on shop floor. *Wall Street Journal,* 1.

Alcorn, E. 2003. Avoid discrimination based on sexual orientation. Available online at www.monster.com. Accessed December 9, 2003.

American Association of Retired Persons. 2002. *Beyond 50: A report to the nation on economic security.* Washington, DC: AARP.

Anker, R. 1998. *Gender and jobs: Sex segregation of occupations in the world.* Washington, DC: International Labor Organization.

Associated Press. 2003, August 6. Hispanics enjoy life in U.S., poll finds. Available online at www.miami.com/mld/miamiherald/newsnation. Accessed September 9, 2003.

Barada, P. W. 2003. Before you sign a noncompete agreement. . . . Available online at http://www.content.salary.monster.com/articles. Accessed July 4, 2003.

Barnish, B. 2003. Arbitration agreements with your employer. Berkeley, CA: Nolo Press. Available online at www.nolo.com/lawcenter/. Accessed July 14, 2003.

Bertagnoli, L. 2003, June 11. When Cupid comes to work: Experts say office romances are trouble—but try telling that to employees. *Chicago Tribune*, 6-1, 6-4.

Boraas, S., and Rodgers, W. M. 2003. How does gender play a role in the earnings gap? An update. *Monthly Labor Review*, 126(3), 9–15.

Boyett, J. H., with Boyett, J. T. 1995. *Beyond workplace 2000: Essential strategies for the American corporation*. New York: Dutton.

Bryant, S. 2003. Coming out at work. Availalbe online at http://featuredreports.monster.com/gayandlesbian/comingout/. Accessed December 9, 2003.

Chung, Y. B. 2001. Work discrimination and coping strategies: Conceptual frameworks for counseling lesbian, gay, and bisexual clients. *The Career Development Quarterly*, 50(1), 33–44.

Cose, E. 1993, November 15. Rage of the privileged. *Newsweek*, 56–63.

Dent, H. S. 1995. *Job shock: Four new principles transforming our work and business*. New York: St. Martin's Press.

Domino, J. C. 1995. *Sexual harassment and the courts*. New York: HarperCollins.

Edelwich, J., with Brodsky, A. 1980. *Burn-out: Stages of disillusionment in the helping professions*. New York: Human Sciences Press.

Ehrenreich, B. 2001. *Nickel and dimed: On (not) getting by in America*. New York: Metropolitan/Henry Holt.

Ehrenreich, B. 2002, June 30. Another day, another indignity. *New York Times*, 4-15.

El Nasser, H. 2003, June 19. 39 million make Hispanics largest U.S. minority group. *USA Today*, A-1.

Fish, S. 1993. Reverse racism, or how the pot got to call the kettle black. *The Atlantic Monthly*, 128(5), 128–136.

Frazer, J. A. 2002. *White-collar sweatshop: The deterioration of work and its reward in corporate America*. New York: Norton.

Freudenberger, H. J. 1980. *Burn-out: The high cost of high achievement*. Garden City, NJ: Doubleday/Anchor.

Fullerton, H. N., and Toosi, M. 2001. Labor force projections to 2010: Steady growth and changing composition. *Monthly Labor Review*, 124(11), 21–38.

Gill, J. 2001, June 28. As the workforce ages . . . . *Business Week Online*. New York: McGraw-Hill. Available online at www.businessweek.com/print/careers/content/jun2001/ca20010628_993.htm?ca. Accessed September 2, 2003.

Gregory, R. F. 2001. *Age discrimination in the American workplace: Old at a young age*. New Brunswick, NJ: Rutgers University Press.

Grier, W. H., and Cobbs, P. M. 1968. *Black rage*. New York: Basic Books.

Gutek, B. A. 1985. *Sex and the workplace*. San Francisco: Jossey-Bass.

Hacker, A. (1992). *Two nations: Black and white, separate, hostile, unequal*. New York: Charles Scribner's Sons.

Harris Interactive and Witech-Combs Communications. 2002. *Gays and lesbians face persistent workplace discrimination and hostility despite improved policies and attitudes in corporate America*. Rochester, NY: Harris Interactive.

Harrison, I. 2003. The pros and cons of a blue-collar career. Available online at www.askmen.com. Accessed September 3, 2003.

Hermann, R. L., and Sutherland, L. P. 1994. *The 110 biggest mistakes job hunters make (and how to avoid them)*, 2nd ed. Washington, DC: Federal Reports.

Holton, E. 1999. Managing the transition to work. *Journal of Career Planning & Employment*, 59(3), 28–31, 49–56.

Judy, R. W., and D'Amico, C. 1997. *Workforce 2020: Work and workers in the 21st century*. Indianapolis, IN: Hudson Institute.

Kellogg, S. 2003, June 29. Relatively few feel impact of affirmative action ruling. *Jackson Citizen Patriot*, A-2.

Kennedy, M. M. 1980. *Office politics: Seizing power, wielding clout*. Chicago: Follett.

Latino Coalition. 2003. *2003 national survey of Hispanic adults*. Washington, DC: The Latino Coalition Foundation.

Lindlaw, S. 2003, September 2. Bush to appoint manufacturing czar. *Jackson Citizen Patriot*, A-6.

Mangano, C. A. 1982. *Teacher's guide to burnout on the job*. Pleasantville, NY: Human Relations Media.

Mariani, M. 1994. The young and the entrepreneurial. *Occupational Outlook Quarterly*, 38(3), 2–9.

Maslach, C. 1982. *Burnout: The cost of caring*. Englewood Cliffs, NJ: Prentice Hall.

Petrocelli, W., and Repa, B. K. 1998. *Sexual harassment on the job: What it is and how to stop it*, 4th ed. Berkeley, CA: Nolo Press.

PFLAG. 2003. *Civil rights: Workplace fairness*. Washington, DC: Parents, Families, and Friends of Lesbians and Gays.

Pink, D. H. 2001. *Free agent nation: How America's new independent workers are transforming the way we live*. New York: Warner.

Repa, B. K. 2000. *Your rights in the workplace*, 5th ed. Berkeley, CA: Nolo Press.

Rones, P. L. 1983. The labor market problems of older workers. *Monthly Labor Review,* 106(5), 3–12.

Scott, H. 1984. *Working your way to the bottom: The feminization of poverty*. Boston: Pandora Press.

Signorile, M. 1995. *Outing yourself: How to come out as a lesbian or gay to your family, friends, and co-workers*. New York: Fireside.

Slater, P. 1990. *The pursuit of loneliness*, 3rd ed. Boston: Beacon Press.

Spraggins, R. E. 2003. *Women and men in the United States: March 2002*. Washington, DC: U.S. Department of Commerce, Census Bureau.

Steele, S. 1990. *The content of our character*. New York: St. Martin's Press.

Teicher, S. A. 2003, July 29. White-collar jobs moving abroad. *Christian Science Monitor,* 1, 3.

U.S. Census Bureau. 2002, March. *The Hispanic population in the United States*. Washington, DC: U.S. Department of Commerce.

U.S. Department of Labor. 1998, July. Women experience fewer job-related injuries and deaths than men. *Issues in Labor Statistics,* 1.

U.S. Department of Labor. 2002, May. *Highlights of women's earnings in 2001*. Washington, DC: Bureau of Labor Statistics (Report 960).

U.S. Department of Labor. 2004. *Occupational Outlook Handbook, 2004–05 Edition*. Washington, DC: U.S. Government Printing Office.

Veiga, A. 2003, August 19. Hispanics, men, low wages linked: Study: Those who work with newly arrived Latinos make less. Available online at www.msbnc.com. Accessed September 9, 2003.

Webb, S. L. 1991. *Step forward: Sexual harassment in the workplace: What you need to know*. New York: Mastermedia.

Work in America: Report of a special task force to the Secretary of Health, Education, and Welfare. 1973. Cambridge, MA: MIT Press.

Wright, J. W. 2000. *American Almanac of Jobs and Salaries*, rev. ed. New York: Avon.

Zaslow, J. 2003, June 5. Don't trust anyone under 30: Boomers struggle with their new role as mentors. *Wall Street Journal,* D-1.

Zey, M. G. 1990. *The mentor connection: Strategic alliances within corporate life*. New Brunswick, NJ: Transaction.

Chapter 10

The Bigger Picture of Work

Career-planning books are written for the individual making an occupational choice and entering the job market. However, we don't live in isolation from other people; the bigger, broader picture of work must be considered, if only briefly. One of the many definitions of work is "an activity that produces something of value for *other people*" (*Work in America*, 1973, p. 3). Because we depend on other people to first produce and then purchase goods and services, and because we work with and for other people, we will devote some space here to issues resulting from the human interaction of working.

This chapter is organized in terms of where we have been, where we are now, and where we are going. Consideration of such topics as the role of work in our lives, the work ethic, labor relations, job satisfaction, and changing management styles will give you a brief historical perspective on work in the 20th century. Also discussed are the attempts of pioneering individuals and companies to improve work and working conditions. Finally, what will the future of work be? Forces and trends that influence occupations and organizations are identified and briefly analyzed. To close this book, the last exercise engages your thinking about the social, psychological, economic, and political trends that will influence your life and work in the days and years to come.

THE ROLE OF WORK IN HUMAN AFFAIRS

A hundred years ago, work and the "work ethic" were as important as they are today; however, certain features of life such as family, religion, and community were often regarded as more significant than one's job. Now, the meaning of work has become central to the way we live, going well beyond making money to have food, clothing, and shelter. Work more than anything else defines who we are to others and how we see ourselves. Perhaps for most people, it is the essential core of their identity—you are what you do, as a popular notion puts it. Our job influences many of the nonwork parts of our lives, having a great impact on our socioeconomic status and the roles we play in our communities. We are more likely to put together a social network around our coworkers than our neighbors and relatives. Doing a job well provides many satisfactions—self-esteem along with respect and recognition from others are highly valued rewards.

With the potential of jobs to give us so many good things, many people have allowed work to become the center of their lives. Stress is rampant as workers find it increasingly difficult to leave the job behind. We may ask more of work than it can provide, especially when the job moves into so much of one's personal life. Our labor can bring frustration and disillusionment. Fed on "rags-to-riches" stories, people born poor have often experienced the bitter reality of dying poor after a lifetime of hard work. Objections are given about "turning (financial) success into a god" and making wealth a sign of divine favor or calling poverty the result of punishment for one's sins, a response to the belief that prosperity was a sign of God's grace and poverty was evidence of eternal damnation. The magnitude of misery and joblessness during the Great Depression of the 1930s helped to break down the notion that moral and material misfortune came only to those who deserved it (Piven and Cloward, 1982). Many middle- and upper-class people went from riches-to-rags overnight, so the cause had to be outside of people, and not character flaws within the poor (Scott, 1984). A current definition of the term *work ethic* leaves out morality and makes its focus strictly economic: The work ethic is "a view of life that promotes hard work and self-discipline as a means to material prosperity" (Hirsch, Kett, and Trefil, 2002). Another definition is more inclusive: The work ethic is the idea that diligent labor, thrift, and deferred gratification constitute the most moral, patriotic, productive, and healthy way to live (Work in America, 1973).

Work in the Ancient and Medieval World

How did we get to where we are now, with the views we hold of jobs and working? A look at the long history of work may give us some help. According to the Judeo-Christian tradition, work may have been a pleasant activity in the Garden of Eden; however, when sin entered the world from man's disobedience to God, humans were cast out of this paradise with this grim message in Genesis 3:19. "By the sweat of your brow you will eat your food until you return to the ground, since from it you were taken; for dust you are and to dust you will return" (Holy Bible, New International Version, 1984). This was a somber statement, yet a realistic one, because most of humankind has lived on the edge of survival throughout their earthly existence. Thus, work became a curse and a punishment. With the Greeks and the Romans, manual labor was also regarded as a curse, fit mainly for slaves.

The status of work improved to some degree in Europe during the Middle Ages. St. Thomas Aquinas developed a hierarchy of professions and trades. The ideal occupation was a monastic life of prayer and contemplation of God. Agriculture, handicrafts, and commerce followed in the human world of work. Each person set out on a particular course of work as a result of a calling from God. Martin Luther gave all work a religious basis, declaring that even manual labor served the purposes of God. When John Calvin introduced the idea of the Elect being predestined for eternal life and the damned being condemned to Hell, a distinct new attitude was formed toward work. No one could know for sure who was one of the Elect, but surely the way a person conducted his or her affairs in life provided proof. If you were idle and unconcerned, this was a sign that you were one of the damned. If you were a strict, industrious, hard-working soul, you displayed the traits of those who were God's chosen. From concepts such as these, the groundwork for the Protestant work ethic was laid. As the Protestant Reformation spread, theology ordained the right to choose one's work, giving a divine dignity to all occupations and paving the way for the emerging economic systems of mercantilism and capitalism (Hill, 1996).

Industrialization and the Modern Age

As national wealth became more important than individual welfare under mercantilism, work became a patriotic duty. The pioneering economist Adam Smith saw competition as an "invisible hand" that required people to work efficiently in order to compete successfully with others and for nations to prosper. The enormous productivity of capitalism would bring high-quality goods and low prices to all. Sigmund Freud emphasized that love and work developed a healthy personality. People believed that not working was somehow immoral and unpatriotic and made a person into a useless, mentally disturbed social misfit (Macarov, 1983). Children learned from their readers and spelling books that idleness was shameful and dishonorable. If people failed to work hard, the nation would fall into economic ruin. All people had a moral duty to be productive for the good of themselves as well as the state.

The Industrial Revolution brought far-reaching change to the way people lived. In the early days of the United States, work did not take on the steady, incessant nature that it has today. The work of 90 percent of the American population was agricultural, which meant it was seasonal—frantic and feverish during planting and harvesting but more relaxed during the winter months. The same was true for those who worked in the stores, homes, and workshops in town where most manufacturing was done by hand (Hill, 1996). Industrialization and the factory system changed all that. Starting in the textile industries of New England, factory mass production replaced the handicraft trades of the home and workshop. Hand-made goods simply could not compete against the enormous output of factories. People left farm labor and the hand trades to take jobs in the factory, and their work lives were transformed forever. Jobs became routine and structured as people submitted to the discipline of

... and so, the Association of Buggywhip Manufacturers
will continue to fight change ...

the workplace. A strict, authoritarian style of management was justified by the fierce competition of capitalism that forced factory owners to keep their prices low and their labor costs even lower.

FROM SCIENTIFIC MANAGEMENT TO HUMAN RELATIONS AND HUMAN RESOURCES

One outcome of the Industrial Revolution was the formation of managerial groups to plan and direct the activities of workers in manufacturing goods. Frederick Winslow Taylor, famous for his time-and-motion studies, changed management into a science in the early days of the 20th century. At the Bethlehem Steel Company, Taylor observed workers shoveling coal; the weight of a full shovel varied from $3\frac{1}{2}$ to 38 pounds. Differences like these were inefficient. Which load weight was best? Under **scientific management**, the answer to this question would not be someone's opinion; it was a matter settled through precise investigation. Taylor and his assistants experimented with the capacity of the shovel until they found $21\frac{1}{2}$ pounds to be the optimal amount of coal per shovel load. Having a specialized tool for each job became a principle of scientific management. Small shovels were designed for heavy material such as ore, and large shovels were made for light material such as ashes. Supervisors were required to study each worker carefully so that the workers could be given the work to which they were best suited. In time, only 140 shovelers were needed to do the work previously done by 500—clearly a gain in efficiency and a reduction in labor costs. No one remembers what happened to the other 360 men who became unemployed. Taylor himself lost his job at Bethlehem Steel when a new management group took control and discovered that Taylor expected the workers to be paid more for their increased productivity.

Perhaps some, or even all, of such employment losses were compensated for by the new managerial and clerical tasks that had to be done, although each new job had to be filled by a different kind of worker. Management was no longer simply a matter of giving orders to workers. It had become a science, with its own theories, research, and literature dedicated to the task of organizing and planning work. Workers had to be carefully selected and correctly trained; clerks kept records of each worker's productivity and pay; instructions were given for each day's work. Everything was done according to exact measurement; nothing was left to chance. Pure science is neutral, and scientific management had no political ideology or economic doctrine. Henry Ford adopted Taylor's methods for automobile manufacturing in the United States. Joseph Stalin did the same for the collectivized heavy industries of the Soviet Union. As for Taylor, the justification for scientific management was always "the bottom line."

> It is a very proper question to ask whether it pays or whether it doesn't pay . . . scientific management has nothing in it that is philanthropic; I am not objecting to philanthropy, but any scheme of management which has philanthropy as one of its elements ought to fail; philanthropy has no part in any scheme of management. No self-respecting workman wants to be given things, and scientific management is no scheme for giving people something they do not earn. So, if the principles of scientific management do not pay, then this is a miserable system. The final test of any system is, does it pay? (Taylor, 1947, p. 171)

As industry adopted Taylor's ideas, work was divided into smaller, simpler tasks and placed under constant supervision. More efficiency brought spectacular increases in productivity, and profits soared. Principles of scientific management were extended into the office. Workers benefited from higher wages, but at a price. The costs were a prevailing authoritarianism in the workplace and a standardization of job procedures that counteracted some of the psychological benefits of work. Work became more productive, but workers also felt more powerless and alienated in their monotonous jobs. The legacy of scientific management was the assembly line and its robotlike jobs.

In their zeal for profits, many employers focused only on the efficiency side of Taylor's message and forgot human and social values. The work force (and the individual worker) was considered only a cog in the gigantic machinery of industry. Machines were often more highly regarded than human beings; after all, they did not tire or break down as often as human laborers would. "Taylorism" is now considered outmoded, although it is still widely used today, especially in mass-production industries (Odiorne, 1987), and in other companies we seldom, if ever, hear anything about. Workers are better educated today than they were in the early 1900s, and good pay is no longer the only motive for working. To offset the cold impersonality of scientific management, the **human relations** movement was born.

Human Relations Management

Industrial human relations dates from the period 1927–1932, when sociologist Elton Mayo and his associates studied the Hawthorne Works of the Western Electric Company in Illinois. When the Mayo-led team cast aside the scientific management set of assumptions about people at work, "the groundwork was laid for . . . the field of organizational behavior—a perspective with its own set of assumptions" (Ott, Parkes, and Simpson, 2003, p. 134). **Organizational behavior** has four basic propositions:

1. Organizations exist to serve human needs; humans do not exist to serve organizational needs.
2. Organizations and people need each other. Organizations must have the ideas, energy, and talent of their people. People need the work opportunities and salaries that organizations provide.
3. When the fit between individual and organization is poor, both will suffer. The individual will be exploited or will seek to exploit the organization or both.
4. When the fit between the individual and the organization is good, humans can do meaningful, satisfying work while providing the resources for the organization to accomplish its mission (Bolman and Deal, 1997).

Mayo's team of social scientists examined the human factor in work. No matter what they did, productivity went up. If the researchers increased the lighting, the work output went up. If the lighting was decreased, production still went up.

Changes in work schedules and rest periods had the same effect. The results of these experiments were perplexing. Mayo finally concluded that the rises in productivity and morale came from paying attention to the workers in the experiment, not from changes in the lighting or the working hours. His recommendations for management included methods for helping workers believe they were part of a team on the job. Communication between labor and management improved so that each could better understand the other. Employee benefits were made better, and supervisors expressed more concern for workers. These ideas brought warmth and a sense of compassion that had previously been lacking. The human relations movement prepared the way for a shortened workweek, minimum-wage laws, the prohibition of child labor, collective bargaining, and a variety of employee services that are generally standard in the workplace today (Dickson, 1975).

The human relations movement was a step toward a more humane work environment, but it was not a complete answer to the problems of working. Some human relations advocates went overboard with their message and forgot to balance their concerns with the technology and workmanship needed to make a profit and stay in business. Also, some workers believed the human relations approach was just another management technique to manipulate them into higher production. Human relations supervision was more decent than the old authoritarian supervision, but the job was still the same, dull kind of work.

Human Resources Management

Gradually, a shift occurred to a style of management that has come to be called the **human resources** approach. This model deals extensively with assumptions about human nature, human motivation, and the nature of the work actually performed. The human resources approach is perhaps best illustrated by the work of three theorists: Douglas McGregor, Chris Argyris, and Frederick Herzberg.

Douglas McGregor argues that every managerial decision is based on a set of assumptions about human behavior. He describes two basic styles of management, rooted in opposite views of human nature, which he labels Theory X and Theory Y.

Theory X managers assume that people dislike work and will avoid it whenever possible; management must somehow counteract people's inherent tendency to avoid work. Thus, most people must be forced, directed, controlled, and threatened to direct them toward the achievement of the manager's goals. Furthermore, the average person prefers to be directed, tries to avoid responsibility, lacks ambition, and wants security more than anything else.

Theory Y calls for a blending of individual and organizational goals, and operates on a completely different set of assumptions. The physical and mental effort expended in work is as natural to people as play or rest. People freely seek work when it is a source of satisfaction. If work is considered a form of punishment, people will avoid it whenever they can. When workers are committed to values and objectives, including those of the organization, they will demonstrate self-direction and self-control in the service of the shared objectives. Given suitable conditions and experiences, people learn not only to accept, but also to seek responsibility in work. If they avoid responsibility and lack ambition, it is because they have learned those responses, not because of any inborn human tendency to do so. Workers possess a relatively high degree of imagination, resourcefulness, and creativity in solving organizational problems. However, work is often organized in such a way that the abilities of the average person are only partially used.

Theory Y assumptions are dynamic, carry the potential for human growth, and emphasize the obligation of managers to achieve the promise of human resources. Theory X gives management an easy way out. If the organization fails, that is because its workers are stupid, lazy, indifferent, uncooperative, and unwilling to take responsibility. Theory Y implies that those undesirable worker traits are caused by management's own methods of organization and control (McGregor, 1960).

For purposes of clarity, both Theory X and Theory Y have been described here in extreme terms. Actually, most managers fall somewhere between these two extremes, and many are fairly close to the middle. Nevertheless, McGregor suggests employers and supervisors have a basic tendency to adopt either Theory X or Theory Y, because both theories can be proved rather easily. A Theory X boss can show you stupid, indifferent, lazy, dull workers who do not care about their performance on the job. A Theory Y boss can show you bright, motivated, hardworking people who are willing to take on the responsibilities of work. McGregor concluded that workers are molded according to management's perception of them, resulting in a self-fulfilling prophecy; in time, people become the type of workers bosses and supervisors expect them to become. The assumptions of Theory X result in rigidity and authoritarianism in management. Workers learn to work hard and follow orders in order to protect their jobs and standard of living. The Theory X company wants the worker to know that much has been achieved by its way of running things and that much more could be accomplished if employees would adapt themselves to management's idea of what is required. The worker thus learns that the organization comes ahead of the individual. By contrast, the assumptions of Theory Y encourage flexibility, willingness to experiment, innovation, openness, and the creative resources the worker can contribute to the success of the organization.

Chris Argyris also writes of two basic styles of organizational management. One approach emphasizes the needs of the organization; the other stresses the needs of the individual. People have basic needs for self-esteem, achievement, creativity, and a feeling of participation. When management ignores these needs, workers become frustrated, and problems result. People will use their human energy in beneficial, creative ways when their aims and the goals of the organization are similar. Workers lapse into apathy and destructiveness when their goals and those of the organization are widely dissimilar and when organizational goals receive attention at the expense of the personal goals of individuals.

Management can go a long way toward improving the workplace when it begins to serve human needs as well as organizational needs. The organization should move away from a centralized, hierarchical power structure to a more equalized, democratic power arrangement; develop a greater feeling of trust and openness among people who work in the organization; and carefully redesign jobs and work for individual employees (Argyris, 1957). Roadblocks are in the way of democratizing the workplace, however. For instance, sometimes a real need exists for uniformity in work procedures. Another obstacle is the power needs of some managers and administrators, who may want to keep authority in their own hands rather than share it with the work force.

Thus, in organizations where scientific management has evolved into human relations and human resources approaches, a manager tends to be less of a boss and more of a catalyst, a facilitator, or a developer of the abilities and resources of those workers for whom he or she is responsible. The way each considers the use of information demonstrates the difference in the two humanistic approaches. The human relations method prescribes that workers be given selected information about the company through newsletters and other communications, whereas the human resources approach allows the work group to determine for itself the information it needs in order to carry out its job and reach its goals (Dickson, 1975). The human relations approach is thoughtful and treats workers decently; the human resources approach emphasizes individual autonomy and responsibility.

Frederick Herzberg has examined the issue of improving jobs from the perspective of the workers themselves. His study revolved around the central question "What do people want from their jobs?" (Herzberg, Mauser, and Snyderman, 1959). The results of the study extended Abraham Maslow's concept of a hierarchy of needs to include the problems of job motivation. Maslow proposed that a person's basic needs arise in a sequence, beginning with physiological needs, followed by safety needs, and then by the higher levels of relationship, esteem, and self-actualization needs. Initially, the physiological needs are the most powerful. Whenever they become basically satisfied, the next need level gradually presses into awareness. As each need level emerges, the individual must find ways to satisfy those needs and continue growth toward self-actualization.

Herzberg found a distinction between factors that make workers satisfied with their jobs and those that merely keep them from being dissatisfied with their work. Job satisfaction and job dissatisfaction are two separate dimensions; they are not opposite ends of a scale. When workers say they are happy and satisfied with their jobs, they usually describe factors related to the work itself, experiences that involve successful performance, and increased opportunities for further professional growth. When people say they are unhappy and dissatisfied with their jobs, the reasons they give have more to do with the conditions that surround their work than with the job itself.

Factors external to the work itself that can cause dissatisfaction with the job include salary, benefits, company policy and administration, supervision, interpersonal relations, and working conditions. These factors relate to the context of the job, not to the work itself. When working conditions, supervision, pay, and company policies and administration deteriorate to a point that workers find unacceptable, the result is job dissatisfaction. A positive trend in these external factors, however, does not lead to positive job attitudes. Herzberg calls such improvements **hygienic measures**. They are similar to the principles of medical hygiene. "Hygiene operates to remove health hazards from the environment of man. It is not a curative; it is, rather, a preventive" (Herzberg, Mauser, and Snyderman, 1959, p. 113). Such measures help satisfy physiological and safety needs, but they may not have much to do with the needs for affiliation, esteem, and self-actualization.

Hygienic measures with respect to work are not to be discounted. Without them, life would be much more difficult. They do alleviate unhappiness with the job—for a while. But workers, having met their physical and security needs, next press for changes in the intrinsic nature of the work itself. Lack of adequate salary, for example, causes so much dissatisfaction that a period of good feelings follows when salary is increased. This period, however, is short-lived. With the passage of time from the last pay raise, workers want a raise again, and if it is not granted, job dissatisfaction sets in again.

Hygienic measures are needed to make the job acceptable, but to make it excellent, qualities that Herzberg calls **work motivators** are also required. Work motivators involve the nature of the work itself, a sense of achievement, recognition for accomplishments at work, responsibility on the job, and genuine opportunities for advancement. These factors provide the "psychic income" of working and create the real satisfaction people seek from their jobs. These internal qualities are more closely related to esteem and self-actualization needs than to hygienic measures. The idea of personal growth in one's working life is a far cry from the old notion of work as punishment. It comes much closer to the self-realization motive that many psychologists, including Carl Jung, Carl Rogers, and Abraham Maslow, have considered the ultimate goal of human beings.

You can "grade" jobs using Herzberg's concepts, as depicted in Figure 10-1. Work motivators and the lack of them are placed on one baseline and hygienic measures and the lack of them are on the other. In jobs where work motivators exist *and* hygienic measures are practiced, work is very rewarding and the job is rated very high; the grade is, say, an A+. The job rates a B if work motivators are present but hygienic measures are absent; the work is good although dissatisfactions over pay and working conditions exist. Where work motivators do not exist although hygienic measures are practiced, the job is only bearable for a while, giving it a C– grade. The job lacking both work motivators and hygienic measures flunks on all counts; it gets a failing grade.

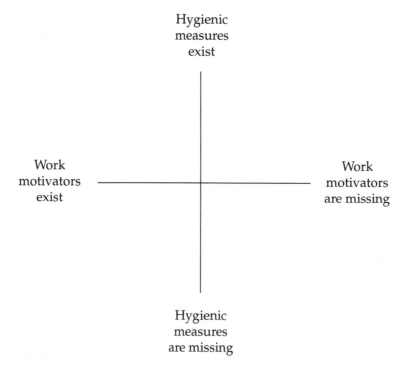

Figure 10-1   Work motivators and hygienic measures in jobs

WORKER ALIENATION/WORKER SATISFACTION

With all of the attempts to improve the atmosphere of the workplace in the preceding century, are workers more alienated from their jobs today or are they more satisfied with their jobs than they were in the past? Is the human resources approach really practiced in most organizations today, or does it exist just to put a new title on the personnel department and conceal a resurgence of scientific management principles? Some historians and social scientists view the 1980s, 1990s, and into the 2000s as a partial rollback to the earlier doctrines of *laissez-faire* and Social Darwinism that featured the ruthless competition and inhumane working conditions of over a hundred years ago. Old assumptions have been brought forth as new ideas; for example, people are motivated first and foremost by greed and the drive to acquire things, but this will lead to social progress. Government has increasingly abandoned the duties of regulation and relied on market forces to control the economy. The internal governance of many corporations is still viewed as authoritarian. The "bottom line" is the ultimate priority in any decision making, just as it was with scientific management. Corporate practices of downsizing, mergers, acquisitions, automation, and outsourcing are so overwhelming that the individual usually has no choice but to go along with employers' needs and demands. Our economic future appears to be headed toward domination, not by small businesses, but by networks of large companies forming strategic alliances, acting almost like single firms and spanning many different industries and countries (Korten, 1995).

Surveys show that people profess belief in the virtues of hard work, but their behavior can send a different message. The work ethic is being questioned by many people and abandoned by some. In the 1980s, the percentage of Americans who believed in the value of hard work fell from 60 to 44 percent (Thurow, 1996). Automation makes some workers feel useless. A majority of people, when offered attractive pay and benefits, choose early retirement over continuing to work. The incidence of industrial sabotage, absenteeism, and turnover is disturbing. Efforts to humanize work often succeed in reducing dissatisfaction but still do not provide positive satisfaction in work.

Job dissatisfaction appears despite improvements in pay and working conditions. The sweatshops are gone in most places. Extreme dangers at work have been reduced. Laws, company policies, and labor unions protect workers. Living standards, real income, health standards, and life expectancy have risen. Workers' personal possessions and bank accounts have increased. Unemployment compensation helps people weather tough times. Workers' compensation provides for those injured on the job, and Social Security benefits are available at retirement.

However, adequate pay and good working conditions do not necessarily make people feel satisfied with their work. Such external factors help diminish dissatisfaction, but they may not promote actual satisfaction with the job. As Herzberg discovered, intrinsic rewards of working, such as having an opportunity to perform well, to grow in competence, to be recognized for contributing, and to develop self-regard, contribute more to feeling good about work. When these needs and values are not realized on the job, alienation toward work can develop. **Alienation** is reflected in a person's attitude toward self, others, work, and those in authority. A worker feels separated from the organization, does not identify with the work, and becomes increasingly estranged from others and self. Yearly polls conducted by the Louis Harris survey organization show that levels of alienation rose from slightly more than 25 percent of the U.S. population in the late 1960s to more than 50 percent in the 1970s, and those levels rose further in the 1980s and early 1990s (Morrison and Schmid, 1994). In his classic book, *Working,* Studs Terkel (1972) writes of work as a search "for daily meaning as well as daily bread, for recognition as well as cash, for astonishment rather than torpor; in short, for a sort of life rather than a Monday through Friday sort of dying" (p. xi). He quotes a steelworker on how frustrated assembly-line workers handle aggressions generated at work:

> When I was single, I used to go into hillbilly bars, get in a lot of brawls . . . Just to explode. . . . When I come home, know what I do for the first 20 minutes? Fake it. I put on a smile. I don't feel like it. I got a kid three years old. Sometimes, she says, "Daddy, where've you been?" I say, work. I could have told her I'd been to Disneyland. What's work to a three-year-old kid? If I feel bad, I can't take it out on the kids. Kids are born innocent of everything but birth. You can't take it out on your wife either. This is why you go to the tavern. You want to release it there rather than do it at home. What does an actor do when he's got a bad movie? I got a bad movie every day." (Terkel, 1972, p. xxxv)

Despite alienation, poverty, unemployment, and broken hopes, more optimistic views of the economy are voiced. They say we are at the beginning of a powerful explosion of creativity, innovation, and entrepreneurial vigor that will result in strong economic gains lasting well into the 21st century. From the Internet to biotechnology and beyond, we are acquiring knowledge in several fields that will be unprecedented and truly exceptional. The information revolution will foster an upsurge in productivity across the economy and will transform information-dependent industries such as finance, the media, and wholesale and retail trade. Major breakthroughs in technology will create new industries in the days ahead. There will be times of dislocations and uncertainty for workers and businesses as new technologies are adopted. Economic and financial volatility will be with us and may increase, but in the long run the price we pay will be worth it (Mandel, 1998).

Enter the "Free Agent"

Beyond the scrutiny of many "industrial era" outlooks comes the development of a growing number of independent workers or "free agents" determined to find or create meaningful work for themselves, on their own. Some are tired of working for someone else; they want to be their own boss. Others are tired of authoritarian workplaces, layoffs, top-down management, constant corporate restructuring, outsourcing, and so on. The old tradeoff of worker loyalty to the company for security from that same company is slipping away. Smaller enterprises are creating more jobs in the economy than large organizations. Another shift in employment is occurring, one that is more conducive to work in the Information Age. The independent free agent may very well be the new representative of this change. Free from the controls of a large institution, free agents are the directors of their own futures and are the prime examples of the new models of work in the United States today (Pink, 2001).

New technology has provided individuals with machines and capabilities once held only by large companies. Individual workers can now own the means of production, long a goal of utopian dreamers. Innovative technologies, often involving the computer and the Internet, have opened up opportunities for self-employment on a scale that was thought impossible a half-century ago. These changes in work are described in Daniel Pink's book, *Free Agent Nation* (2001). Of course, not all workers are independent. Pink estimates he is writing about one in four of the entire American workforce, but their numbers have enlarged greatly in the past two decades and will continue to increase.

With this short discussion of the free agent and independent worker, we have, in a sense, come full circle. Thus far, we have gone from Taylorism (methods of work for mass production organizations) to *tailorism,* where free agents design their work lives independently to match their own needs and goals. The endless discussion over work, workers, and organizations goes on.

ATTEMPTS TO IMPROVE THE QUALITY OF WORK

Of course, some work organizations make sincere efforts to upgrade the jobs of their employees. Job seekers are urged to take notice of companies that care about employee morale, redesign jobs to fit the needs of their workers, share decision-making authority and profits, and experiment with flexible working hours. In addition to the ideas mentioned in connection with job burnout in the last chapter, some ideas for improving the quality of work are briefly covered here.

Job enrichment. The major purpose of job enrichment is to focus on the nature of the job itself and endow it with the characteristics that Frederick Herzberg identified as work motivators. Some jobs need to be redesigned to become worthy of the people who fill them. Company objectives must give the goal of good jobs for their workers equal status with shareholder and customer satisfaction. Changing routine jobs to give workers more control over their work and trusting them with greater responsibility requires commitment by management to the idea of enrichment. Some employers say they want workers to accept responsibility on the job but do not delegate real power, preferring instead to keep authority in their own hands.

Job enrichment or job redesign has certain characteristics. Workers are given opportunities to analyze their own jobs and make changes in them. Work functions are designed with more variety and less repetition. Workers have more control over their jobs. Workers can take on challenging assignments that give a sense of achievement. Management allows employees more opportunities for self-management, personal interaction with others, and freedom at work. Rules and procedures come from the entire group of workers, not only from management. The company gives rewards and recognition for achievements and learning new skills. There is a greater emphasis on teamwork. Differences and status symbols between management and workers are reduced. Workers can set their own production goals, assemble entire units, and achieve the satisfaction of completing a whole product. Job enrichment proposals involve changes that cannot be forced on workers by a well-meaning employer. Because workers may be suspicious of the motives for change, employees are brought together with management to plan new ways of working.

Organizational democracy. Living in a society with a political climate that values individual rights does not ensure that democracy will be practiced where you work. Companies can maintain or adopt an authoritarian style of management patterned essentially on a military model. The disparity between political ideals in the culture and the power realities within organizations often leads to labor–management conflicts.

The essential idea of democratizing the workplace is to give workers the opportunity to share power with their employers. Beyond power, another concern is communication. In a democratic company, workers have full and free communication, no matter what their rank or status may be. Among the ways organizational democracy can be implemented are electing employees to the board of directors, giving workers real power to regulate their own work processes on the job through autonomous work teams, and having workers participate in the selection of supervisors. Employees can be allowed to influence the formation of personnel policies, participate in long-range planning projects, and have membership on committees evaluating new job applicants. Dickson (1975) reports on a rating scale developed in Sweden, listing five levels of worker influence designed to measure the extent of worker democracy.

1. Control over the job itself.
2. Control extended to personnel policy, such as hiring and the division of work.
3. Control over technical matters, such as production planning.
4. Control over product problems, such as quality control and specifications.
5. Sharing managerial control in such areas as long-range planning, budgeting, and the design and planning of new plants. (When a work environment has reached the fifth level, it is presumed to be in a state of full democracy.)

Profit sharing and responsibility sharing. Profit sharing means that, as well as their regular salaries, employees receive an agreed-upon percentage of the company's profits. When jobs have been enriched or redesigned without profit sharing, workers may suspect that they are being manipulated, and productivity may slip back to former levels. When increases in productivity are tied to profit sharing, workers feel that they have a stake in the success of the organization. Personal needs (such as esteem and relationships with others) and economic goals (such as increased productivity) can be fulfilled by sharing in both the responsibilities of production and the profits earned from production. Responsibility sharing implies that workers have decision-making power in their jobs *and* that they are accountable for the outcome of those decisions. Most workers are willing to take on responsibility for decisions if they are also allowed to share in the results. The *Work in America* (1973) project reported that profit-sharing arrangements or responsibility-sharing arrangements by themselves are not likely to make significant differences in productivity and profits; these measures work best when they are connected to each other. Profit sharing alone does not increase the size of the profits to be distributed. Responsibility sharing without profit sharing is likely to be regarded by workers as manipulation and to be rejected for this reason.

Employee ownership plans. Surveys have indicated that a majority of Americans would rather work in an employee-owned company than in one owned by private investors or the government. Worker-controlled organizations occur throughout the world; in the United States, the most common form of worker ownership is the Employee Stock Ownership Plan (ESOP). Advocates believe ESOPs boost morale and productivity by giving workers a stake in the company's success. Workers have often saved their jobs by banding together to purchase the company when it appeared to be going out of business. In many cases, they have made sacrifices by accepting wage concessions in return for stock certificates and by borrowing money to complete the buyout. Conceived by Louis Kelso in the 1950s, ESOPs became a way of changing the pattern of capital ownership from a few wealthy individuals to a vast array of employees. The

ESOP concept is primarily a form of economic democracy that gives workers the experience of ownership and control of their means of livelihood.

Examples of creating employee-owned companies involve assigning places for employees on the board of directors, greater job security, and an equity stake in the organization in exchange for work-rule changes and wage cuts (Alexander and Baker, 1994). Workers make concessions, but they gain by investing in their own company, keeping jobs that would otherwise be lost, and reaping benefits when their efforts result in success for their organization.

Self-managing work groups. Instead of a mile-long assembly line or a huge office filled with cubicles where each of hundreds of workers perform simple and monotonous work functions, a team of several workers follows a product or project from its beginning to its completion. The groups are large enough to perform a number of tasks, yet small enough to allow for face-to-face meetings for decision making and coordination. Work teams decide among themselves who will do what tasks. Most members learn each other's work, rotating jobs and sharing the work equally, and are able to cover for a sick or absent worker.

Can employees plan, direct, and control their work—typically the role of the supervisor? When changing from traditional methods of management to a self-managing team concept, workers may have misgivings and feel apprehensive about their new responsibilities. They wonder if they will be knowledgeable or skilled enough to do the new tasks acceptably. Some workers would rather stay with the certainty of familiar work they have performed. Self-managing work teams are challenging to workers and managers alike, because they go beyond what is comfortable and ask people to take on new and different work roles. When self-managing groups are successful, employees who may have been skeptical at first come to realize that they now are truly owners of their work. They set high standards for themselves, demonstrating that Herzberg's work motivator concept really does allow workers to experience personal growth in their jobs and that Douglas McGregor's Theory Y does lead employees to use their resourcefulness and creativity and to willingly accept responsibility for their work.

Compressed workweeks. When most people worked a 6-day week, spending 10 or 12 hours a day on the job, a 5-day, 40-hour week would have seemed like the dawning of the Golden Age. Now you hear of 4-day weeks, with 40, 36, or 32 hours per week, as the desired standard. One experiment that has already been tried was a 3-day, 36-hour week, working 12 hours per day. A workweek of fewer than five days will lower employees' gasoline consumption, and may cut heat and electricity bills at company buildings. It can reduce absenteeism, improve efficiency, reduce costs, and give employees a more satisfying work schedule. Some labor unions have opposed compressing the 40-hour workweek into 4 days or fewer. They want to shorten the workweek to 35 or 32 hours in their own way, and the 4-day week would require people to work more than 8 hours a day without receiving overtime pay. Another objection is the possibility of replacing one inflexible work schedule with another.

Flextime. This term, a contraction of "flexible time," reflects the concept of floating work hours. For example, the official workday could extend from 7:00 A.M. to 6:00 P.M. An employee could arrive at work any time between 7:00 and 10:00 A.M. and leave any time after 3:00 P.M. The worker would still need to complete a 40-hour workweek, but would have a certain amount of leeway each month. Workers could make up missing hours later, and extra hours could be "banked" as credit for a day off at a later time. Recent studies reveal that employers are beginning to acknowledge that many workers want schedules allowing greater flexibility in choosing the time they start and end their workday (Beers, 2000). The Bureau of Labor Statistics (2002) reported that in May 2001 about 29 million or 28.8 percent of full-time wage and salary workers had flexible work schedules, nearly doubling the proportion from 10 years earlier.

Job sharing and splitting jobs. The advantage of job sharing and splitting is that they allow time for both family and a career. The first three of the following five concepts involve two (or more) workers sharing the duties of one full-time job; the last two arrangements involve one person.

1. *Paired or partnership work.* Two people fill one full-time job, sharing responsibility equally. One person could work mornings, with the other coming in for the afternoon. An elementary teaching job could be shared, for example. Two employees could offer the suggestion to divide a job to their employer.
2. *Shared work.* Two people divide a job, each taking responsibility for half the total work. Unlike paired work, the two do not necessarily have to split the day; rather, they split the total workload of a single job.
3. *Split-level work.* One full-time job is broken down into its functional skills and split along different levels of training and ability. (A job in which a person is required to compose letters and then word-process or type them in final form could be split into two jobs: a part-time writer and a part-time secretary.)
4. *Split-location work.* Work is done at home as well as at the office by one person. Assignments that can be done on computer have enhanced this idea. The work schedule can be worked out in advance so that appointments can be met at the office.
5. *Specialist.* A person takes a job that requires less than full-time employment, such as teaching a specialized subject not in heavy demand.

Other time arrangements. Options include sabbaticals—taking a year or part of a year off from job duties. Released time off may be given to do social or political work. People have tried tailor-made workweeks divided into two- or four-hour modules. Time bonuses can be given such as paying workers for 40 hours of work even though they work only 36 hours during certain periods, such as between Thanksgiving and Christmas. Varied shifts could consist of four 9-hour shifts and a 4-hour shift for a four-and-a-half day week. Another time arrangement involves "banking" vacation time.

Telecommuting. The term *telecommuting* means linking a worker to a main office by a computer, fax machine, or pager. The employee works at a location other than the home office, headquarters, or main work site; this usually means working at home or in a branch office. Commuting time for the worker is saved and the organization may save on office space.

WHERE ARE WE HEADED?

Making forecasts of future trends is always risky. Social scientists, futurists, business leaders, and historians try to identify trends that will influence the organizations in which we work. With the advantages of hindsight, we can poke fun at some predictions about technological and cultural changes that were definitely off the mark. The chairman of International Business Machines (IBM) in 1943 was quoted as saying, "I think there is a world market for maybe five computers." An IBM engineer, commenting on the microchip in 1968 asked, "But what . . . is it good for?" The founder of Digital Equipment in the mid-1970s said, "There is no reason anyone would want a computer in their home." A recording company in 1962 rejected the Beatles declaring, "We don't like their sound, and guitar music is on the way out." Responding to a student's paper proposing a reliable overnight delivery service, a business management professor wrote, "The concept is interesting and well-formed, but in order to earn better than a C, the idea must be feasible." (The student went on to create the Federal Express Corporation.) One of the owners of Warner Brothers movie studio in the 1920s asked, "Who wants to hear actors talk?" An 1876 memo within a communications company stated, "This 'telephone' has too many shortcomings to be seriously considered as a means of communication. The device is inherently of no value to us." All of that having been said and quoted, we now turn to a sampling of projections you may find interesting:

1. *The "job" as we have known it throughout the industrial era is disappearing* (Bridges, 1994). In the future, workers will use a variety of flexible skills to perform multiple jobs within the organization or for a number of different companies, rather than being confined by the boundaries of a traditional job description. Your chances of survival will be better in the emerging job market if you develop portable skills—abilities that can be transferred to other work-places if the need arises. Another key to job survival is to become the kind of worker who can function on several projects at the same time. (The title of this book may have to change from *Job Search* to *Work Search*.)

2. *Workers will need to become more cross-functional.* In the past, workers performed more specific tasks and functions on the job. Today, many employees are being asked to work across functions and areas of expertise. A new work environment will have "a core of main functions and positions, supported by temporary functions and positions that come into being (and disintegrate) on an as-needed basis" (Schecter, 1993, p. 12). You will make yourself more valuable by thinking of yourself as a ceaseless learner, constantly taking advantage of on-the-job training opportunities, workshops, college courses, seminars, conferences, professional conventions, and anything that will increase your knowledge and skills.

3. *Compiling a portfolio of achievements and skills will be more important to career planners than a résumé.* A portfolio is a collection of papers that substantiate your educational and work experiences. Keep all records, letters of commendation, work samples, school projects, and the like so you can support the achievements and skills you claim to have. Include personal accounts of how you used your knowledge to get things done. Refer to Exercise 5-5 in Chapter 5 of *Taking Charge of Your Career Direction* for ideas about the kinds of material that can go into a portfolio. With the features of a portfolio of your accomplishments in mind, you are as likely to find opportunities within your work organization as outside it.

4. *Lateral moves in one's career development will occur just as often as, if not more often than, promotions and advancement within work organizations.* Moving to a position across rather than higher in an organization was once considered a career dead end, but now a lateral move may be necessary in order to learn new skills and prepare for a new challenge or advancement later on. "Free agent" writer Daniel Pink refers to lateral moves as part of a "LEGO career" (remember your LEGO set from childhood?).

5. *The excellence of your work will be a key contributor to your survival on the job.* Okay quality and pretty good job performance aren't good enough anymore, as the Big Three Detroit auto makers found out in the 1970s and 1980s (Boyett with Boyett, 1995). "Excellence" and "zero defects" are not simply buzzwords for company motivational sessions and advertising slogans; they are attributes that are now essential to survival in the highly competitive world of work.

6. *Entrepreneurs and small firms will spark much of the economy.* Web sites are free, easy to create, and a useful device to attract customers, investors, and new employees with ideas. The World Wide Web has changed many business landscapes. The used book business, for example, was once a strictly local enterprise. Now, many small book businesses are selling books worldwide, thanks to the Web and the Internet. Entrepreneurs are often naïve innovators who think their ideas cannot fail to attract investment and survive, grow, and prosper. Only a fraction of new businesses make it past five years, but this statistic doesn't keep people from trying new ideas. Smaller companies can often adapt faster to changing market conditions. For many small businesses to suc-

ceed takes patience on the part of venture capitalists who can be in too much of a hurry for profitable results.

7. *Workers will need to learn how to cope effectively with new work methods inspired by new technology.* People can deal with the introduction of new ways to work. The computer revolution is a mixed blessing; it also has a negative side. The widespread use of computers has made many people too sedentary because the computer can do so many things one once had to move around to do. Computers can add to worker stress as supervisors are able to watch employees by the minute instead of by the day. The computer is able to automate many work functions, thus throwing some people out of work. Not enough attention is being paid to **ergonomics**, the study of fitting work to the individual. However, people will become more flexible in adjusting to the new demands of work, as they have in the past. Technological change has always been with us. When workplace changes occur, it takes time for people to become comfortable with the new technology. There was resistance to the use of the telephone over a hundred years ago, but now no one thinks twice about using the phone and its several adaptations as a way of communicating.

8. *The liberal arts in one's education will still be viable.* If you have a major in history, English, philosophy, sociology, or some other liberal arts discipline, you have probably heard someone say, "What do you plan to do with a degree in *that*?" With so many people fascinated with technology, science, and computers, you can feel you have made a wrong choice of academic major from which you'll never recover. Liberal arts graduates often do have a harder time translating their college major into a career goal, but don't lose hope; graduates in the liberal arts have been found to keep pace with graduates in science, engineering, allied health, and technical studies in getting jobs (National Association of Colleges and Employers, 1997). Students with technical degrees run a greater risk of finding their skills becoming obsolete after several years, whereas liberal arts graduates have a broader, more wide-ranging approach that allows them the flexibility to stay with their chosen occupational field over a longer period of time.

9. *Traditional worker loyalty to the employer and the company will be replaced by worker self-reliance.* The social contract that forged so many productive relationships between employers and employees for so long has been scrapped. Layoffs, downsizing, outsourcing, privatization, automation, divestitures, and mergers have been explained or excused (depending on your point of view) as necessary to remain competitive, but they have all taken their toll. Worker–employer loyalty is being replaced by an ethic of career self-reliance in many workplaces.

10. *Career self-reliance, although understandable, will develop its own set of limitations and deficiencies.* Career self-reliance is thinking of one's self as a business or acquiring a frame of mind that today's workers are self-employed even when working inside an organization. The concept of career self-reliance is controversial. Management now expects individuals to take personal responsibility for managing their own work as well as their private lives. Because so many employers no longer provide job security, workers must provide their own. Typical career advice to young people is to treat every job as though you are self-employed and look out for yourself because no one else will. Self-reliance, then, becomes important and useful in today's workplace, encouraging people to take charge of their own lives. It emphasizes flexibility and constant learning, helping workers to survive and thrive in a changing workplace. In one sense, self-reliance has always been a factor in work life. However, without a balance of interest between self and community, an overemphasis on career self-reliance has serious flaws (Byster, 1998). Individuals may blame themselves for difficulties in managing their careers rather than considering the possibility that these problems might be larger than a single person and

should be viewed within a larger social context. The idea that "I'm in this alone" increases a feeling of isolation and misses opportunities to connect with others for support. Loyalty is dismissed as a value when workers and organizations both feel the other is only looking out for its own self-interest. Tremendous stress is put on people who come to believe we live in a dog-eat-dog world where only top performers will survive. The current over-emphasis on self-reliance in managing careers often asks people to deny who they are and adapt themselves strictly to the needs of employers.

11. *Redesigning and restructuring work organizations will continue.* Work organizations will employ fewer people who will be expected to attain higher rates of productivity. (These practices have damaged loyalty to the organization and added stress to those workers who remain.) But companies have found that decreasing the number of workers doesn't change the basic ways business gets done. The organizational architecture of many companies is undergoing a complete redesign in an effort to create a central core surrounded by a number of specialty units. Technological advances make fluid, shifting design possible. The pyramid structure that once characterized the pattern of companies, as a result, will be shaped flatter (less hierarchical) and leaner (Boyett with Boyett, 1995).

12. *Performance reviews will become more important (and controversial).* Traditionally, your immediate supervisor made the evaluation, which could depend on the mood your boss was in that day. Studies showed that managers' subconscious stereotypes about race, age, and physical attractiveness could affect employee ratings. In trying to bring about greater fairness in performance reviews, employers began to build "360-degree" appraisals with comments from customers, coworkers, and subordinates as well as bosses. The evaluations are more frequent than the old yearly reviews, as computer programs have developed the ability to track daily performance. The most debatable change is a "forced ranking system" where the top 10 or 20 percent workers or managers are identified and marked for advancement. However, the bottom 10 percent are also identified, who would have to improve or leave. Many employers like this system, thinking it is the fairest and easiest way to downsize. Workers, certainly those receiving low ratings, allege the tough new systems are designed to weed out employees of a specific race, age, or gender rather than only poor performers. It is very unfair, they contend, to begin with the assumption that a certain percentage of your workers are unsatisfactory (Clark, 2003).

13. *Incentive pay will be used more as a major reward.* Growth in base pay rates will slow, and annual salary increases will no longer be automatic (Thurow, 1996). Instead, incentive pay will increasingly account for a sizable portion of many workers' total earnings. Bonuses will be tied to individual and group performance on the job.

14. *The national economy will become even more global.* Manufacturing has improved the quality of its products and its ability to export them as international trade has become increasingly important for the economy. In 1969, fewer than 4 percent of all manufacturing workers held export-related jobs; by 1991, this figure had climbed to 18.6 percent. It was expected to go beyond 25 percent in 2000 and approach 50 percent by 2010 if current trends continued. This trend will benefit highly skilled workers. Less-skilled workers, however, are likely to find their jobs increasingly at risk and pay rates lowered because of growing competition from workers in developing countries who produce goods for the American market (Judy and D'Amico, 1997).

15. *"9/11" has strengthened some job areas and diminished others.* The reaction to the 9/11 terrorist attack in New York and Washington has resulted in an expansion of security-related jobs as Americans become more safety conscious than at any time in their history. The new Transportation Security Administration

has deployed nearly 60,000 people throughout the country to scan air passengers and their luggage (Levine, 2003). The nation's infrastructure (water systems, electrical installations, roads, bridges, tunnels, airports, railways, chemical and nuclear plants, and so on) needs greater protection, which creates jobs for security guards, air marshals, airport screeners, cargo monitors, border and immigration agents, and the like (Roane, 2003). Workers such as firefighters, police officers, emergency medical technicians, and hospital workers would be "first responders" in urgent situations (Glasser, 2003). The airline and tourist industries are examples of fields and the occupations allied with them that have thus far been adversely impacted by 9/11. Responding to terrorism is a subject shrouded with uncertainty. For example, debate over the proper balance between security and liberty is an issue that divides Americans.

16. *Life will be a continuous series of job (or work) searches.* The average worker will be employed in at least 10 different types of jobs and 5 different companies before he or she retires (Boyett and Conn, 1991). Make a prediction as to how many times you will need and use this book (or one like it) in your life.

Next, we turn to analyses of 13 broad social and economic trends and their implications for work. A question or two is posed about each one. Another discussion of economic forces and labor trends can be found in Chapter 2 of *Taking Charge of Your Career Direction.*

1. *Economically, the United States is the most important nation in the world, but it is only one player in a competitive global economy.* Americans are immersed in the realities of international trade. The North American Free Trade Agreement (NAFTA) is a treaty promoting tariff reductions on manufactured goods among the United States, Canada, and Mexico. Other Latin American countries may be included by the time you read this page. China and Asia's Pacific Rim nations—Japan, South Korea, Taiwan, Singapore, and Malaysia—manufacture attractive, high-quality goods and sell them on the world market, often at lower prices made possible by their lower labor costs. Another major player in the world economy is the European Union (EU), an organization that seeks to remove the trade barriers that were once raised to protect these nations from each other. Foreign competition causes anger among workers who believe their jobs are threatened by workers in other countries or by adjustments due to trade agreements. Some domestic companies call for government protection against foreign rivals. Foreign trade works both ways, however. The United States exports many goods and services that create jobs at home. The world economy is credited with giving Americans a wider range of excellent, competitively priced products. How will the global economy affect your future work?

2. *An explosion of information produced by the computer will drive our economy.* The great majority of jobs now involve gathering and using information in one form or another. Widespread data collection, analysis, and circulation are uniquely suited to the computer's capabilities. Communications technology shortens the time involved in sending and receiving information. Transmitting electronic data takes seconds, and important news is delivered instantly. The Internet is a great tool for learning, but some people say we will drown in the flood of data and the result will be "information pollution." Are we accumulating so much information that people will be tempted to simply tune it out?

3. *Job opportunities will continue to increase for women.* Today, women make up 47 percent of the labor force. Women are hired to fill two-thirds of all new jobs created. Women may be better adapted than men to establish themselves in the professional and leadership positions of the Information Age. New leaders will tend to function as teachers or facilitators, roles traditionally associated with "feminine" traits. Despite the "glass ceiling" in some organizations, the number of women in administrative and managerial jobs is increasing. As

more women move into the workplace, changes occur in people's personal lives as well. Fewer women are choosing to marry, and those who marry do so at a later age. More children have working mothers than in the past. Only about 20 percent of American families now have a father who works outside the home and a mother who is a full-time homemaker. Child care is a major concern, and companies are pressured to provide this service. There is evidence that women are generally healthier and happier than 30 years ago, even though problems develop from assuming the dual role of wage earner and parent. Feminists applaud increasing opportunities and new lifestyles, but are these developments good for children, for women themselves, and for society in general?

4. *The population will keep moving south and west and into the newer suburbs.* The U.S. population has been continuing its shift to the south and the west, with California, Texas, and Florida leading the way in terms of numbers. Between 1990 and 2000, smaller states such as Nevada, Arizona, Colorado, Utah, and Idaho had population increases in the 28 to 66 percent range. With this migration of people, economic and political influence has shifted southward and westward as well. Almost as dramatic as this population shift is the movement from cities to the suburbs and into the nonmetropolitan areas beyond the suburbs. Older suburbs now face many of the same problems as cities, with traffic jams, air and water pollution, strained sewage systems, and rising crime rates. Could there be a population shift back to our cities and to the north and east— and why? Can our large cities be made more livable?

5. *Minorities will become a larger element in the U.S. population.* Most members of minority groups have been treated as second-class citizens at one time or another; still, they have made their mark on the American culture. African Americans are about 13 percent of the U.S. population, but Hispanic/Latino Americans have overtaken them to become the largest minority group. In terms of percentage, Asian Americans are the fastest-growing group. A major challenge confronts American society in trying to help minority groups, who are growing at a faster rate than the American population as a whole. How will the white middle class accept a minority status at some time in the future?

6. *Education and the arts will occupy center stage.* Our nation is increasingly concerned with education. Concerns are expressed about the effects of television, the Internet, and popular culture on scholastic test results, especially when the performance of American students is compared with that of students in other countries. Attention is being directed to improving elementary and secondary education. American colleges and universities rank among the best in the world, and foreign students flock to them for educational opportunities that do not exist in their home countries. Large numbers of students are attracted not only to regular degree programs, but also to continuing education courses, workshops, and seminars. Because knowledge becomes obsolete so quickly or is incorporated into computers so readily, many workers will return to the classroom for training several times during their careers. As for the arts, how do more Americans spend their Sunday afternoons: watching football on television or visiting a museum? You are correct if you chose the latter. The rebirth of the visual arts, poetry, dance, theater, and music will have tremendous economic implications. New careers and business opportunities in the arts will flourish. However, questions continually arise about the value of education and the arts. In a pragmatic culture, are the arts an essential for the good life, or are they only luxuries made possible by an affluent leisure society?

7. *A maturing society will keep on growing older.* Despite the emphasis on youth culture in modern advertising , the United States is experiencing a change in which middle-aged and older people will dominate society by their sheer numbers. The proportion of older citizens is greater now than during any previous period in American history. In this first decade of the 21st century, the

"baby boomers" (those born between 1946 and 1964) are in middle age and approaching elderly status. The maturing of America profoundly affects the economic values and occupational trends of the future. Sales and marketing workers are likely to focus on the needs of middle-aged and older people. Long-term health care will become more important. As people live longer, chronic illnesses will have to be increasingly cared for. Disagreements between the young and the old are bound to occur, such as the issue of paying for social security. Workers aged 60 and over who are in good health may want to delay retirement, believing their occupations give their lives meaning, purpose, and an identity they find nowhere else. When older people stay in the workforce, will they take job opportunities from young people? Will the ever-present conflict between the generations intensify?

8. *Powerful advances will continue to take place in biology and medicine.* Just as information technology supports today's economy, biology may drive tomorrow's, particularly in medicine and agriculture (Carey, 1998). Health services are among the fastest-growing groups of occupations, but high health costs could present real problems for jobs in the long run. Illnesses that once killed people are now less of a threat because of advances in medical treatment. The childhood scourges of polio, measles, and mumps have almost disappeared with the advent of new vaccines. Patients survive diseases that at one time were considered incurable. Transplant surgery offers new hearts, kidneys, and lungs to people once condemned to a sickbed or death. Where human organs are not available, surgeons use artificial devices. Heart disease can be combated through open-heart surgery, pacemakers, exercise and diet, and new drugs. New instruments have been developed to help doctors and allied health personnel diagnose and treat health problems, from ultrasound, CAT scanners, radioscopes, and fiber optics to laser technology. Biotechnology changes the genetic composition of plants and animals, and we use their altered forms to produce more fertile soil, bigger crop yields, leaner meat, and

So the technology is a bit old. . . .
It's the BEST of its line!

more milk. Gene therapy, by manipulating or replacing defective genetic structures, offers hope and cures to patients with inherited diseases. All these medical and biological advances create new occupational opportunities; however, they also create financial and ethical problems. Modern medical miracles and additional health care practitioners cause runaway health costs that often go beyond an ordinary person's capacity to pay for them. Will soaring health payments mean that fewer people can afford adequate health care? Could this eventually reduce job opportunities in the medical field?

9. *Technological change and progress will continue to drive much of our economy.* Think of the expansion of jobs taking place in telecommunications, fiber optics, robotics, biotechnology, computer graphics, energy, electronics, and medical technology, just to name a few industries. Throughout history, whenever technological advances have occurred, the nature of work has changed. The microchip downgrades skills in one job and upgrades them in another. Fewer people are needed to do the work in microchip technology, so the total number of jobs declines. Yet the overall effect of microchip technology has long been considered uncertain because it creates other jobs for workers to design, manufacture, transport, sell, and service the new machines (Wegmann, Chapman, and Johnson, 1985). The impact of robotics on manufacturing has also been regarded as mixed. Some labor analysts describe factories without workers, filled with robots that can measure, cut, drill, assemble, spot-weld, and paint. Robots will become more complex, requiring talented people to construct and market them. Robotics engineers will be needed to design the software that instructs the computer-controlled robots in their tasks. In the short term, new technology appears to cost jobs, but its long-term influences are unclear. Your job may be either eliminated or created by high technology. What will be the impact of technological development on society: more jobs eliminated or more jobs created?

10. *Unemployment worries will afflict many people even with a record number of jobs.* Many jobs have been added to the American economy in the past half-century, yet the unemployment rate has stayed steady at about 4 to 6 percent for almost all that time. A 4 to 6 percent official unemployment rate figures out to about 9 to 15 million unemployed people, when you add the discouraged workers who have given up on finding a job. With such enormous job growth, why are job security and unemployment a problem? Among the answers are the effects of new technology, increased numbers of job seekers, deregulation, and foreign competition. Technological changes have meant worse jobs or no jobs for some people because they lack the skills and the means to acquire new ones. The poverty-stricken people who huddle in urban ghettoes and rural areas go unnoticed by suburbanites as they travel the highways above. Unprecedented numbers of people seek jobs in the American labor force. The high birthrates that created the baby boom ultimately strained the labor market to such a degree that it could not absorb the supply of workers. Birthrates have lowered since then, but that decline may be offset by large groups of women and immigrants entering the labor force. Deregulation policies have increased competitive pressures, and many companies have reduced the number of their employees in order to survive. The bankruptcy of large companies is front-page news, but many small firms go out of business almost unnoticed. Whether a business decreases the size of its workforce or closes its doors, the effect is a loss of jobs. Foreign competitors acquire new technology, have lower labor costs, produce efficiently, and can transport their goods inexpensively; this enables them to offer Americans attractive prices for their products. As the number of foreign-made products Americans buy exceeds the number of American-made products sold abroad, the foreign trade imbalance costs jobs—although how many jobs is controversial. After

the latest recession, we hear of a "jobless recovery." What can we do to ensure a job to everyone who wants one?

11. *Underemployment, misemployment, and displacement of workers will persist.* For the college educated, *underemployment* is more of a problem than unemployment. Underemployment occurs when a well-trained, highly skilled person works at a job that requires neither the training nor the skills possessed by the worker. A college degree today does not necessarily guarantee a job in the occupation for which the graduate is trained. However, college graduates earn more income than noncollege graduates do over the course of their careers, and eventually obtain jobs in their chosen occupations. Nonetheless, it is often a great source of dissatisfaction for a highly educated person to work in a low-paying, low-status job. Then there is the tragedy of *misemployment*. The claim is made from a number of surveys that a majority of American workers are in jobs for which they are not well suited. People can "fall into" jobs without much thought about their interests, abilities, and values or finding an organization appropriate for them. When they accumulate seniority and benefits, they are reluctant to risk the gains of employment, so they stay in the old job instead of changing to one in which they might have more interest and natural aptitude. One of the recurring problems of the American economy is the plight of worker *displacement* by company restructuring and plant closings. Even when the displaced worker gets a new job, it may mean fewer hours and lower pay than before. Mental depression is likely to occur. Health problems, from headaches to high blood pressure, are common among displaced workers. Economic problems, such as trying to sell a house, often make moving to a new location extremely difficult. How can we diminish the anguish caused by underemployment, misemployment, and displacement of workers?

12. *"Wild cards"—earth-shaking events—will occur in the future.* This is an easy statement to make; the real surprise would be if the future brought us no surprises at all, especially because the future has astounded us so often in the past. Futurists have a special term for these startling events—*wild cards*. On September 10, 2001, who would have predicted the destruction of the World Trade Center (WTC) by terrorists steering hijacked airliners into the famous twin towers? Yet, the warning clues were all there; in fact, the WTC had been specifically identified as a choice target by Marvin Cetron in a 1994 *Futurist* magazine article. Over the past century, the most memorable year for wild cards was 1941: Germany invaded the Soviet Union, and Japan attacked the United States. The Soviets and Americans were caught by surprise, and both were tragically unprepared, but warnings had been ignored by leaders and their advisers (Cornish, 2003). What wild cards await us in the future? Futurist John Petersen (2000) suggests some 80 of them, including faster-than-light travel, energy advances that will make fossil fuels obsolete, the secession of a western state from the United States, the collapse of the world economic system, the arrival of extraterrestrial life, and a rapid spread of altruism throughout the world.

13. *The world's population will go beyond 6.3 billion to 9.1 billion by 2050.* The number of people on Earth is 6.3 billion as of 2003 (Haub, 2004) and will grow to 9.1 billion around the middle of the 21st century (U.S. Bureau of the Census, 2003). With moderate projections from the U.S. Census Bureau (2001), America's population will overtake Europe's falling numbers around 2030 and, given high projections about fertility rates, will reach a half billion around 2050. At least 10 million people will live in each of 25 cities around the globe. Although industries will continue to increase the amount of material goods in most countries, some forecasters say that the world's people will be poorer in many ways in the years ahead. You can see it now; around the periphery of most large cities in underdeveloped countries are slums and squatter communities, teeming with jobless, poverty-stricken people.

In 1972, the Club of Rome published a report, *The Limits to Growth*, which warned that Earth's resources are not likely to support current rates of economic and population growth much beyond the year 2100, even with advanced technology (Meadows et al., 1972). More recently, the book *Juggernaut: Growth on a Finite Planet* (Grant, 1996) warns that endless physical growth and relentless population advances will be a catastrophe for human society. A world of scarcity, disease, crime, chaos, and anarchy is foreseen as our future; sketches of it are already present in West Africa. Imagine a stretch limo cruising down a pot-holed street where homeless beggars live. Riding in this air-conditioned carrier are the modern regions of North America, Europe, and the emerging Pacific Rim. Out in the street is the rest of humanity, going in a different direction (Kaplan, 1994). This doomsday scenario is contrasted by more confident assertions that technological advances and proper environmental planning can bring a future of rising affluence, energy, and food for virtually everyone. Information and knowledge is accessible to all people, as illustrated by the telecommunications revolution. The optimists, with their faith in science, technology, and the free market, see open-ended possibilities for humankind. The most extreme pessimists forecast global impoverishment, environmental destruction, and economic collapse. Both futures are possible (Moffett, 1994). Which vision will prevail?

EXERCISE 10-1 LIVING IN THE 21ST CENTURY

The last exercise in this book is a series of paired, opposing statements about the future of work. Which statement will be more accurate during the 21st century? The future is difficult to predict, but everyone loves to do it anyway. You might as well join the crowd. Try to explain or illustrate the reasons for your responses. If you are in a group or class, these are good discussion topics.

In the 21st century, there will be . . .

_____ more personal satisfaction in working.

_____ less personal satisfaction in working.

_____ more occupations from which to choose.

_____ fewer occupations from which to choose.

_____ increased competition for highly skilled jobs.

_____ less competition for highly skilled jobs.

_____ lower unemployment.

_____ higher unemployment.

_____ more jobs that require greater ability.

_____ more jobs that require less ability.

_____ greater job security; more protections for keeping your job.

_____ less job security; fewer protections for keeping your job.

In the 21st century, there will be . . .

_____ more democratic work environments; workers will make more decisions on the job.

_____ more authoritarian work environments; workers will make fewer decisions on the job.

_____ more work that is interesting and challenging.

_____ less work that is interesting and challenging.

_____ more jobs where people operate machines and have less to do with people.

_____ more jobs that are involved with people and have less to do with machines.

_____ more men than women in the U.S. labor force.

_____ more women than men in the U.S. labor force.

_____ more trust of those who have power in business, labor, and government.

_____ more distrust of those who have power in business, labor, and government.

_____ more flexibility for workers in determining their hours on the job.

_____ less flexibility for workers in determining their hours on the job.

_____ more leisure time or greater amounts of time spent away from work.

_____ less leisure time or more time spent at work.

_____ more identification by work role than by other social roles.

_____ less identification by work role than by other social roles.

_____ fewer barriers in work opportunities because of sex and race factors.

_____ more barriers in work opportunities because of sex and race factors.

_____ more workers over age 65 in the labor force.

_____ fewer workers over age 65 in the labor force.

_____ more high-paying manufacturing jobs.

_____ more low-paying service jobs.

_____ more white-collar jobs in the United States than now.

_____ more blue-collar jobs in the United States than now.

_____ more goods-producing jobs in the United States than now.

_____ more service-providing jobs in the United States than now.

_____ more emphasis on the work ethic.

_____ less emphasis on the work ethic.

In the 21st century, there will be . . .

_____ greater choices in personal lifestyles.

_____ more restrictions on choices of personal lifestyles.

_____ a stronger economy than now.

_____ a weaker economy than now.

_____ an increased need for training and education throughout life.

_____ a reduced need for training and education throughout life.

_____ increased severity in social problems (pollution, crime, and so on).

_____ social problems remaining, but they will be less severe than they are today.

_____ more emphasis on individuality and personal expression.

_____ greater pressure toward conformity to organizational or social goals.

_____ fewer marriages that end in separation or divorce because of work.

_____ more marriages that end in separation or divorce because of work.

_____ increased social distance and wider income gaps among people.

_____ greater equality in social status and personal incomes among people.

_____ closer family ties and greater social support for the family.

_____ increased separation between parents and children.

_____ higher percentages of income spent on the necessities of life.

_____ lower percentages of income spent on the necessities of life.

_____ greater emphasis on self-interest and "looking out for number one."

_____ increased emphasis on social welfare and cooperation with others.

_____ greater respect for religion and increased emphasis on belief in God.

_____ less respect for religion and decreased emphasis on belief in God.

_____ a rebirth of culture and learning.

_____ a new Dark Age, with little culture and learning.

_____ a more humane way of life.

_____ a less humane way of life.

SUMMARY

1. The role of work has always been central to the lives of people, whether or not it was recognized as such. At first, work and manual labor was considered as a curse and punishment for human sins. Gradually, the concept of work was elevated

to a status where, if one worked hard and prospered, it was a sign of God's grace. The "work ethic" became a belief that the best way to live involved hard work, saving, and delaying present satisfactions for future gains. It is now being questioned as never before because of such factors as automation, early retirement, welfare benefits, alienation, and changing attitudes. The work ethic is certainly not dead, but it has changed; people expect more psychological and economic benefits from their work.

2. Three movements have influenced management styles and employer–employee relationships in the 20th century: scientific management, human relations, and human resources. Scientific management organizes work rationally to create the greatest possible efficiency. This promotes productivity but often has harmful psychological effects on workers. In response to the cold, mechanical efficiency of scientific management, human relations and human resources gained prominence. The human relations approach brought a more personal touch to management, and the human resources approach emphasized improving the nature of the work itself. Important as these workplace developments have been in the 20th century, some people believe these gains have been rolled back recently in order to meet the challenges of increased competition in a supercharged global economy.

3. Many attempts to improve jobs and working conditions have been and continue to be made: job enrichment and redesign, organizational democracy, profit sharing and responsibility sharing, employee ownership plans, self-managing work teams, telecommuting, compressed workweeks, flextime, job sharing, and other time arrangements.

4. Historians, futurists, and social scientists identify trends in today's world that influence the occupations and organizations in which we work. This chapter has presented some of them. The traditional, industrial-age idea of the job is disappearing. Workers will be more cross-functional. Portfolios will be used more by job seekers. Lateral moves will occur more often within organizations. Excellence in work is a key to survival on the job. Entrepreneurs and small companies will continue to stimulate much of the economy. Workers will need more training to cope effectively with new technology. The liberal arts in one's education will still be practical and usable. Worker loyalty to the company is being replaced by a concept of career self-reliance on the part of the individual. Career self-reliance, however, has its own limitations. Organizational restructuring will continue. A new emphasis on performance reviews is developing. Incentive pay will be used more than annual pay increases. The national economy will be influenced increasingly by international trade. The 9/11 tragedy has caused increases in security-oriented jobs and decreases in other work, but the far-reaching effects are still ambiguous. A lifetime job at one workplace will be almost a thing of the past, as life becomes a series of work searches.

5. Thirteen forces and trends are also influencing the way we work and live. (1) The United States no longer dominates the global economy. (2) The Age of Information is upon us. (3) Increasing opportunities exist for women. (4) The population continues to move south and west and into the suburbs. (5) Minority groups are becoming a larger proportion of the society. (6) Education and the arts are growing more important. (7) The nation keeps on maturing, and the elderly are becoming more numerous. (8) Advances in medicine and biology are miraculous but create rising concerns about health costs. (9) Technological developments continue to drive our economy. (10) Unemployment is painful even while there is record job growth. (11) Underemployment, misemployment, and displacement of workers persist. (12) Wild card or spectacular events such as 9/11 are surprising when they happen, but they have been a rather constant feature of life throughout history. (13) Planet Earth now supports more than 6 billion people, and huge population gains are accompanied by predictions of prosperity or disaster.

REFERENCES

Alexander, K. L., and Baker, S. 1994, October 24. If you can't beat 'em, buy 'em. *Business Week,* 3394, 80–81.

Argyris, C. 1957. *Personality and organization: The conflict between system and the individual.* New York: Harper.

Beers, T. M. 2000. Flexible schedules and shift work: Replacing the "9-to-5" workday? *Monthly Labor Review,* 123(6), 33–40.

Bolman, L. G., and Deal, T. E. 1997. *Reframing organizations,* 2nd ed. San Francisco: Jossey-Bass.

Boyett, J. H., with Boyett, J. T. 1995. *Beyond workplace 2000: Essential strategies for the new American corporation.* New York: Dutton.

Boyett, J. H., and Conn, H. P. 1991. *Workplace 2000: The revolution shaping American business.* New York: Penguin/Plume.

Bridges, W. 1994. *Job shift: How to prosper in a workplace without jobs.* Reading, MA: Addison-Wesley.

Bureau of Labor Statistics. 2002, April 18. *Workers on flexible and shift schedules in 2001, summary.* Washington, DC: U.S. Department of Labor.

Byster, D. 1998. A critique of career self-reliance. *Career Planning and Adult Development Journal,* 14(2), 17–28.

Carey, J. 1998, August 31. We are now starting the century of biology. *Business Week,* 3594, 86–87.

Clark, K. 2003. Judgment day: It's survival of the fittest as companies tighten the screws on employee performance reviews. *U.S. News & World Report,* 134(2), 31–32.

Cornish, E. 2003. The wild cards in our future. *The Futurist,* 37(4), 18–22.

Dickson, P. 1975. *The future of the workplace: The coming revolution in jobs.* New York: Weybright and Talley.

Glasser, J. 2003. Improving emergency response. *U.S. News & World Report,* 135(8), 29–30.

Grant, L. 1996. *Juggernaut: Growth on a finite planet.* Santa Ana, CA: Seven Locks Press.

Haub, C. 2004. *2003 world population data sheet.* Washington, DC: Population Reference Bureau.

Herzberg, F., Mauser, B., and Snyderman, B. B. 1959. *The motivation to work,* 2nd ed. New York: Wiley.

Hill, R. B. 1996. Historical context of the work ethic. Athens, GA: University of Georgia. Available online at http://www.coe.uga.edu/%7Erhill/workethic/hist.htm. Accessed September 10, 2003.

Hirsch, E. D., Jr., Kett, J. F., and Trefil, J., eds. 2002. *The new dictionary of cultural literacy,* 3rd ed. Boston: Houghton Mifflin.

Holy Bible, New International Version. 1984. Grand Rapids, MI: Zondervan.

Judy, R. W., and D'Amico, C. 1997. *Workforce 2020: Work and workers in the 21st century.* Indianapolis, IN: Hudson Institute.

Kaplan, R. D. 1994, February. The coming anarchy. *The Atlantic Monthly,* 44–76.

Korten, D. C. 1995. *When corporations rule the world.* West Hartford, CT: Kumarian Press and San Francisco: Berrett-Koehler (copublishers).

Levine, S. 2003. Airline and port security. *U.S. News & World Report,* 135(8), 26.

Macarov, D. 1983. Changes in the world of work: Some implications for the future. In H. F. Didsbury, Jr., ed., *The world of work: Careers and the future* (pp. 3–24). Bethesda, MD: World Future Society.

Mandel, M. J. 1998, August 31. Innovation: You ain't seen nothing yet. *Business Week,* 3594, 60–63.

McGregor, D. 1960. *The human side of enterprise.* New York: McGraw-Hill.

Meadows, D. H., Meadows, D. L., Randers, J., and Behrens, W. W. 1972. *The limits to growth: A report for the Club of Rome's project on the predicament of mankind.* New York: Universe.

Moffett, G. D. 1994. *Global population growth: 21st century challenges.* New York: Foreign Policy Association.

Morrison, J. I., and Schmid, G. 1994. *Future tense: The business realities of the next ten years.* New York: Morrow.

National Association of Colleges and Employers. 1997. Careers and the liberal arts grad. in *Planning job choices: 1998* (p. E22). Bethlehem, PA: National Association of Colleges and Employers.

Odiorne, G. S. 1987. *The human side of management.* Lexington, MA: D.C. Heath.

Ott, J. S., Parkes, S. J., and Simpson, R. B. 2003. *Classic readings in organizational behavior,* 3rd ed. Belmont, CA: Wadsworth.

Petersen, J. L. 2000. *Out of the blue: How to anticipate big future surprises.* Lanham, MD: Rowman and Littlefield.

Pink, D. H. 2001. *Free agent nation: How America's new independent workers are transforming the way we live.* New York: Warner.

Piven, F. F., and Cloward, R. S. 1982. *The new class war: Reagan's attack on the welfare state and its consequences.* New York: Pantheon.

Roane, K. R. 2003. Protecting our infrastructure. *U.S. News & World Report,* 135(8), 26, 29.

Schecter, E. 1993. Managing careers in changing organizations. *Career Planning and Adult Development Journal,* 9(1), 11–14.

Scott, H. 1984. *Working your way to the bottom: The feminization of poverty.* Boston: Pandora Press.

Taylor, F. W. 1947. Scientific management. In D. S. Pugh, ed., *Organizational theory: Selected readings.* Harmondsworth, Middlesex, England: Penguin Books.

Terkel, S. 1972. *Working: People talk about what they do all day and how they feel about what they do.* New York: Pantheon.

Thurow, L. C. 1996. *The future of capitalism: How today's economic forces shape tomorrow's world.* New York: Penguin Books.

U.S. Census Bureau. 2001. *Old world and new.* Washington, DC: U.S. Department of Commerce.

U.S. Census Bureau. 2003. *Total midyear population for the world: 1950–2050.* Available online at www.census.gov/ipc/www/worldpop.html. Accessed March 4, 2004.

Wegmann, R., Chapman, R., and Johnson, M. 1985. *Looking for work in the new economy.* Salt Lake City: Olympus.

Work in America: Report of a special task force to the Secretary of Health, Education, and Welfare. 1973. Cambridge, MA: MIT Press.

Characteristics Employers Want in Job Applicants

The Conference Board of Canada (2002) divides the skills employers are trying to find in job candidates for positions in their organizations into three groups: fundamental, personal management, and teamwork skills.*

1. *Fundamental skills.* Needed as a base for further development. You will be better prepared to progress in the world of work when you can:

   a. *Communicate*

      - Read and understand information presented in a variety of forms (e.g., words, graphs, charts, and diagrams).
      - Write and speak so others pay attention and understand.
      - Listen and ask questions to understand and appreciate the points of view of others.
      - Share information using a range of information and communications technologies (e.g., voice, e-mail, and computers).
      - Use relevant scientific, technological, and mathematical knowledge and skills to explain or clarify ideas.

   b. *Manage information*

      - Locate, gather, and organize information using appropriate technology and information systems.
      - Access, analyze, and apply knowledge and skills from various disciplines (e.g., the arts, languages, science, technology, mathematics, social sciences, and the humanities).

   c. *Use numbers*

      - Decide what needs to be measured or calculated.
      - Observe and record data using appropriate methods, tools, and technology.
      - Make estimates and verify calculations.

   d. *Think and solve problems*

      - Assess situations and identify problems.
      - Seek different points of view and evaluate them based on facts.
      - Recognize the human, interpersonal, technical, scientific, and mathematical dimensions of a problem.
      - Identify the cause of a problem.
      - Be creative and innovative in exploring possible solutions.
      - Readily use science, technology, and mathematics as ways to think, gain and share knowledge, solve problems, and make decisions.

*From the Conference Board of Canada, 2002. Used by permission.

- Evaluate solutions to make recommendations or decisions.
- Implement solutions.
- Check to see if a solution works, and act on opportunities for improvement.

2. *Personal management skills.* The personal skills, attitudes, and behaviors that drive one's potential for growth. You will be able to offer yourself greater possibilities for achievement when you can:

   a. *Demonstrate positive attitudes and behaviors*
      - Feel good about yourself and be confident.
      - Deal with people, problems, and situations with honesty, integrity, and personal ethics.
      - Recognize your own and other people's good efforts.
      - Take care of your personal health.
      - Show interest, initiative, and effort.

   b. *Be responsible*
      - Set goals and priorities balancing work and personal life.
      - Plan and manage time, money, and other resources to achieve goals.
      - Assess, weigh, and manage risk.
      - Be accountable for your actions and the actions of your group.
      - Be socially responsible and contribute to your community.

   c. *Be adaptable*
      - Work independently or as part of a team.
      - Carry out multiple tasks or projects.
      - Be innovative and resourceful: Identify and suggest alternative ways to achieve goals and get the job done.
      - Be open and respond constructively to change.
      - Learn from your mistakes and accept feedback.
      - Cope with uncertainty.

   d. *Learn continuously*
      - Be willing to learn continuously and grow.
      - Assess personal strengths and areas for development.
      - Set your own learning goals.
      - Identify and access learning sources and opportunities.
      - Plan for and achieve your learning goals.

   e. *Work safely*
      - Be aware of personal and group health and safety practices and procedures, and act in accordance with these.

3. *Teamwork skills.* Attributes needed to contribute productively. You will be better prepared to add value to the outcomes of a task, project, or team when you can:

   a. *Work with others*
      - Understand and work within the dynamics of a group.
      - Ensure that a team's purpose and objectives are clear.
      - Be flexible: Respect, be open to, and be supportive of the thoughts, opinions, and contributions of others in a group.
      - Recognize and respect people's diversity, individual differences, and perspectives.
      - Accept and provide feedback in a constructive and considerate manner.
      - Contribute to a team by sharing information and expertise.
      - Lead or support when appropriate, motivating a group for high performance.

- Understand the role of conflict in a group to reach solutions.
- Manage and resolve conflict when appropriate.

b. *Participate in projects and tasks*
- Plan, design, or carry out a project or task from start to finish with well-defined objectives and outcomes.
- Develop a plan, seek feedback, test, revise, and implement.
- Work to agreed-upon quality standards and specifications.
- Select and use appropriate tools and technology for a task or project.
- Adapt to changing requirements and information.
- Continuously monitor the success of a project or task and identify ways to improve.

The particular employers you deal with in your job search may not rank all of these characteristics as highly as did the Conference Board of Canada (2002), nor may you as a job hunter, but now you have an idea of the attributes many employers are looking for.

Another survey (Kretovics and McCambridge, 1998) identifies three areas employers want in new hires: technical skills, communication skills, and personality characteristics.

1. *Technical skills* include business functions/academic discipline skills and personal computer skills such as word processing, spreadsheet applications, database management, and graphic design. These competencies are measured by work experiences, involvement in internships, specific courses, and grades.
2. Three subgroups comprise *communication skills*. Social effectiveness skills—needed to work effectively with coworkers, clients, and customers—include team skills, coaching, leadership, sales skills, solving problems, organization skills, and crisis management ability. Presentation skills involve writing and public speaking. Other communication skills are knowledge of the global economy, languages, and different cultures.
3. *Personality characteristics* are being responsible, a self-starter, flexible/adaptable, imaginative/creative, a change agent, trainable, motivated, a motivator, self-confident, street-smart, quick thinking, a risk taker, and mobile (willing to relocate).

Hawk (1998) gives much the same answer in *What Employers Really Want*: technical competence, distinguishing personality qualities, and five critical traits. *Technical competence* includes education, work experience, computer proficiency, and demonstrated accomplishments. *Distinguishing qualities* include excellence, discipline, enthusiasm, goal orientation, handling priorities, problem solver, self-analytical, and willingness to listen and learn. The *five critical traits* are being a clear communicator, self-motivated, a team player, honest, and a hard worker.

REFERENCES

Conference Board of Canada. 2002. *Employability skills 2000+*. Ottawa, Ontario: Conference Board. Available online at http://www.conferenceboard.ca/education/learning-tools/employability-skills.htm. Accessed May 16, 2002.

Hawk, B. S. 1998. *What employers really want: The insider's guide to getting a job*. Lincolnwood, IL: VGM Career Horizons.

Kretovics, M. A., and McCambridge, J. A. 1998. Determining what employers really want: Conducting stakeholder focus groups. *Journal of Career Planning and Employment*, 58(2), 25–31.

Electronic Job Banks: Questions to Ask and Web Sites

QUESTIONS TO ASK

In his book, *Guide to Employment Web Sites,* Peter Weddle (2002) asks the following questions about organizing Web site information. After the question, he gives the reason for the question. You can ask the same questions when considering on which job bank to post your résumé.*

- *When did the site first appear on the Internet or World Wide Web?* Although not always the case, the longer a site has been in operation, the more established its methods and the more reliable its service. Less than a year in business may be risky.
- *What is the name of the organization that owns the site?* (It may be different from the organization that operates it.) This information can help you assess the quality of the information given and become aware of organizations providing the resources you are using online.
- *What is the number of people visiting the site each month?* (Also ask: Is each person counted *only once,* regardless of the number of times that person visits the site?) You can estimate the reputation of the site as well as how much competition you may encounter when applying for a listed opening. However, a small number—say, less than 10,000—means employers are not likely to use the site for recruiting purposes.
- *What is the approximate total number of jobs posted on the site at any given time? Are full-time jobs posted?* This indicates the extent of the opportunity available to you so you can determine whether the site is worth your time to visit it
- *What are the types of occupational fields appearing most frequently among the jobs posted at the site?* Find out how good the site's database is for your field of interest or specific career objective.
- *What are the top two salary ranges that appear most frequently in the site's job listings?* You should discover whether the posted jobs have the right salary range for you.
- *Where is the geographic focus of the site's posted job ads?* Find out whether the site's employment opportunities are where you currently live or want to live.
- *How are the job postings acquired?* Are they from employers, search firms, headhunters, and other job boards or copied from other sites? How many employers use the site to recruit applicants? It helps to know who will be screening your credentials and postings. If the job bank simply copies its openings from other sites, its job postings are not likely to be as current as listings from other sources. The job bank should be able to give the names of some or all of its clients from the past year.

*Adapted with permission from Weddle, 2002.

- *Will the site store applicant résumés or profiles in a public or private database?* You need to know whether your résumé or profile is open to anyone (or anyone who pays a fee) or in a database that notifies applicants privately when it matches a posted opening.
- *How long can you store your résumé in a site's database without reposting or updating it?* You should know how frequently you must return to the site to repost your résumé or whether you should return to delete your résumé because you have found a job.
- *What are the restrictions, if any, on the use of the Web site?* The site may require users to be members of an association, registered with a site, or in a certain career field or industry.
- *Is there a fee to store a résumé or profile?* You should expect to pay a reasonable fee for the services of a commercially owned Web site. Find out the cost for the length of time your résumé or profile will be posted; this will help determine the extent of the visibility you are likely to get when you want to connect with the kinds of recruiters you want to reach. Government and association Web sites are free (however, your taxes or dues pay for it).
- *Does the site offer an automated job agent?* A "job agent" automatically compares your job objective with all of the jobs posted on the site and will contact you privately whenever a match occurs. This service is typically provided at no cost to the job seeker. Using a site's job agent will save time; while the agent is checking openings for you at the site, you can be using other sources of job leads.
- *Is career and job search information provided and are links to other sites made available?* Job banks that do this enhance their value to you.
- *Does the site protect your privacy?* It can do so by blocking out contact information from your résumé or by keeping employers from accessing the résumé database, thus serving as an intermediary between you and the recruiter until you decide to reveal your identity. When a job bank protects your privacy, you can search for a new job and remain in charge of your job search. If you are employed, you don't want your résumé sent to your current employer!

In his *Guide to Employment Web Sites* Peter Weddle (2002) includes 350 sites that use the format just described, which admittedly is only a fraction of the thousands of job search Web sites out there. However, these 350 sites are re-evaluated by him each year and are considered to be the best resources. In an earlier book on the same subject, Weddle (1995) posed some other questions you might want to ask a job bank:

- *How many people were actually matched with employers in the past year?* If the figure is less than 25 percent of those in the site's database, then its value is reduced to you, the job seeker.
- *How many clients of the job bank who were referred to employers were actually interviewed by those employers?* If less than 50 percent, the quality of the match is suspect.
- *Are changes or updates of your résumé or profile permitted? Without a fee?* The answer should be yes to both questions.
- *What information about the job seeker is provided to employers?* A copy of your original résumé or profile should be forwarded to them.
- *What organizations endorse the Web site of the job bank?* If it can't provide testimonials, you are taking a risk.

Margaret Riley Dikel and Frances Roehm (2002) concur with many of the previous questions. They add some questions of their own and their reasons for asking them:

- *Is the information you are finding at the site advertising, or is it useful for your job search?* A Web page that is giving you advertising for its services isn't helping your job search now.

- *Is the information you find written by an expert in the job search field or the industry you are searching or is it written by other job seekers?* Although other job seekers may contribute tips that are useful from their individualized viewpoints, articles from authoritative experts who can see the "big picture" in job searching will contain more reliable information.
- *Do the lists of employers include schools, colleges, and nonprofit associations?* These organizations can be targeted or can connect you to places of which you were unaware.
- *Are the jobs listed actually real, or are they just "a sample list of jobs we are currently trying to fill"?* Samples are fine, but when you want the real thing, samples are frustrating.
- *If you don't see any dates of when the job was listed, can you obtain any relevant information about the employers who post jobs at the site? How much do employers pay to post their job opening, and how long will their jobs remain posted?* Most Web sites tell employers their job will be posted for a certain length of time for a specific fee. Can you send an e-mail message to the site's Webmaster and ask these two questions? You should get a specific answer. Without this information, the site goes to the bottom of your list. If there is no response at all, the site is removed from your list.
- *Do the owners of the Web site update and add new information on a regular basis?* Job leads and job search articles can become dated.
- *What are the backgrounds of the people running the Web site?* Hopefully, they are industry specialists, librarians, or recruiters. Many job search firms are operated by people with no background or training in what they are doing and who are in it for the fast buck.
- *Is there a name, a mailing (or e-mail) address, or telephone number for contacting the site when you have questions?* Legitimate Web sites will furnish this information.
- *Do you know anyone who has used the Web site? If so, how well did it work for them? If a fee was charged for the service, was it worth it?* These questions are used in networking. Gain from the experience of your friends and acquaintances.
- *What will your money get you?* If you are spending money to have your résumé forwarded to employers, find out how many employers will receive it (and their industry). You need to know that those employers are interested parties that have registered for the service and not people on a "spam" list assembled from other sources.
- *Does the job bank "guarantee results"?* If so, cross it off your list and have nothing to do with it. Nothing is guaranteed in the job search business.

WEB SITES OF JOB BANKS

Following is a small portion of the available job bank Web sites. With an estimated 40,000-plus sites (Weddle, 2002), we obviously cannot list all of them. Inevitably, some good sites will not be mentioned and more will be created after this printing. We used three basic sources for this list: (1) Dikel and Roehm's *Guide to Internet Job Searching* (2002–2003 edition), (2) *Weddle's Guide to Employment Web Sites* (2002), and (3) clearinghouses from the Career Resource Library of America's Career InfoNet (ACINET). All of the Web sites in this list were on at least two of the three sources' lists.

- *AllJobSearch.com (http://www.alljobsearch.com).* A "mega-site," AllJobSearch.com combines a number of (but not all) job search sites. You must supply a keyword for your search. You can specify the United States, Canada, and the United Kingdom, a state or province, city, job type, date of job posting (last one day, three days, seven days, and so on), and job category.
- *American Council of the Blind (ACB Job Bank) (http://www.acb.org).* ACB is an organization for blind and visually impaired people. Job listings are available

under the title of ACB Job Bank, which includes back issues of the Council's publication, *The Braille Forum*.

- *American Jobs (http://www.americanjobs.com)*. Users may search for job openings by keyword, state, and job categories. Résumés may be posted online and updated. Employer profiles are offered.

- *America's Job Bank (http://www.ajb.org)*. Click on Job Seekers when you reach this site. Operated by the U.S. Department of Labor, this site is a network that links the local offices of state employment services. AJB has a basic level of free service offering a database search by occupation, keyword, and military specialty code. You can match your skills to government jobs at this site. America's Job Bank also has a place to create cover letters and develop and submit a résumé. AJB allows you to search the databases of state, district, and territorial employment services, and also has links to employer and private agency sites. Toll-free help line: 1-877-US-2JOBS or TTY 1-877-899-5627.

- *Asia-Net (http://www.asia-net.com)*. Asia-related jobs requiring language proficiency in Japanese, Chinese, or Korean are posted.

- *Best Jobs USA (http://www.bestjobsusa.com)*. Offers job listings, articles from *Employment Review Online* published by the site's owner (Recourse Communications), company profiles, and information on career fairs.

- *The Black Collegian (http://www.black-collegian.com)*. Online site of a magazine that focuses on students of color seeking employment. Search by keyword or employer, post résumés, and look at resources about graduate schools.

- *Career Builder (http://www.careerbuilder.com)*. This Web site was started by six newspapers, and was originally called Career Path. You can begin with a "Quick Job Search" by entering a keyword(s) and a city (if desired) and select a state and a job category. A search can be made by a Web ID, which allows you to get more information. Look for a "FlexAd web code" (otherwise known as a Web ID) at the end of selected ads in the Sunday Career Builder section of your local newspaper. Enter the listed Web ID into the dedicated search box in CareerBuilder.com. You then have access to more information about the job and its company and you can apply online. You can search by company and by industry. For Spanish-speaking job hunters, you can search *en Español*. You can search for Canadian and international jobs, as well.

- *Career.com (http://www.career.com)*. After reaching the Career.com home page, click on "Job Seeker Home," register in "New Job Seeker Login," and begin searching for job leads by keywords, company, location, discipline, and "new grad-entry level."

- *Career Exchange (http://www.careerexchange.com)*. Search for jobs by location (United States, Canada, international) and by category (within the United States and Canada). You can post and edit your résumé. A "people match" feature can e-mail matching jobs to you.

- *CareerJournal.com (http://careerjournal.com)*. An excellent job bank, particularly for executive, managers, and professionals—plus articles and information from the *Wall Street Journal* and its online site. Click on "Salary and Hiring Info" for industry salary information and hiring trends.

- *Career Magazine (http://www.careermag.com)*. This site has a job openings database (search by location, title, and skills or by keyword), employer profiles, and articles about the job search.

- *Career Mart (http://www.careermart.com)*. Look at this site's list of employers and the positions it has posted by job category, state, region, keyword, and country. You can cut and paste your résumé onto a provided form even if you are not registered with Career Mart.

- *CareerSite (http://careersite.com)*. Start searching for job leads by selecting a region in the United States or Canada and an occupation; select a job title to view the entire job announcement and how to apply.

- *Career Web (http://www.careerweb.com)*. Search for job positions by location, employer, or health care jobs. Job listings are from regional *Employment Guide* magazines.
- *Chronicle of Higher Education (http://www.chronicle.com/jobs)*. The *Chronicle of Higher Education* bills itself as the No. 1 job marketplace for higher-education professionals. Career articles and job listings are culled from this weekly publication. Job lists are updated daily and are free to all users of this site.
- *College Grad Job Hunter (http://www.collegegrad.com)*. College Grad's home page gives you a selection from which to choose: preparation, career info, job search advice, résumés, cover letters, employer research, job postings, interview prep, salaries, job offers, new job, relocation center, startup center, and more.
- *FlipDog (http://www.flipdog.com)*. This site is an employment search engine for job seekers and employers. Job seekers registering with FlipDog.com can search and apply for job positions, post a résumé, and look at employment profile pages.
- *HotJobs (http://www.hotjobs.com)*. Job seekers can look for employment opportunities by keywords, job category, company, staffing firm, and locations in the United States and the world. Résumés can be posted online. Much competition here—8 million people visit this site each month.
- *IMDiversity (http://www.imdiversity.com)*. As the name implies, this site is intended for minority and diversity students and sponsored by *The Black Collegian* magazine. You can search for jobs with a diversity-sensitive employer, look up employer profiles, post résumés, and learn tips for your career development.
- *Internet Career Connection (http://www.iccweb.com)*. Lists of jobs, a résumé database, and career guidance services such as a free online occupational interest inventory are among the offerings of this site. Operated by Gonyea and Associates, it provides industry and occupational profiles, career advice, and information on state, government, and international jobs.
- *JobBank USA (http://www.jobbankusa.com)*. JobBank USA has its own directory of Internet employment services plus "Jobs MetaSearch" that accesses the Internet's largest employment resources; free résumé service available. Usually has a million job openings posted.
- *JobCenter (http://www.jobcenter.com)*. Maintains résumés from job seekers and matches them by a keyword search with its database of companies. Job seekers are informed about where their résumé was sent for review. As job ads come in to JobCenter, they are e-mailed to subscribers.
- *Job Find (http://www.jobfind.com)*. Focuses on New England job leads, but jobs are not confined to this region. Job openings may be searched by keyword and job category. Users can post a résumé and create a job search agent.
- *Job Hunter's Bible (http://www.jobhuntersbible.com)*. This site is an exception in this list (being an online guide to job searching rather than a job bank), but one that deserves to be mentioned. Job Hunter's Bible continues Richard Nelson Bolles's wisdom from his annually published book, *What Color Is Your Parachute?* Lots of good advice is given and many insightful comments are made about the job search and career decision-making process. One reason to tap into this site is that Bolles researches and directs you to the best job search sites.
- *JobWeb (http://www.jobweb.com)*. A service of the National Association of Colleges and Employers, this site is very helpful to college students and graduates who are entry-level job seekers. JobWeb features articles on career development, job listings, company information, salary information, and internships and also sponsors an online job fair.
- *Monster (http://www.monster.com)*. Probably the best known of all online job search companies, Monster.com has a vast array of services. You can hunt for a

"monster" number of jobs by category, keywords, company name, or location. Job descriptions, employer profiles, and international jobs are available. Build a résumé to gain access to many more job listings. Look into thousands of pages of career information and advice. You can compare salaries and cost of living estimates of different cities through this site's Salary and Cost of Living Wizard.

- *MonsterTRAK (http://www.monstertrak.com).* Originally JobTrak, this site caters to college students and graduates. Check to see if your school is registered and, if it is, contact the career services center to obtain the password.
- *NationJob Network (http://www.nationjob.com).* Job seekers tell "P.J. Scout" what they want and this free service automatically sends them any new jobs that match their choices via e-mail. Users can search job leads by specialty field, position, location, education, job type, and salary.
- *Net-Temps (http://www.net-temps.com).* This is an Internet recruiting center for the staffing industry, specializing in contract professionals. Users search for jobs by Career Channel. Net-Temps offers job lists, résumé posting, career development articles, and a weekly newsletter—and it does post full-time jobs despite its name.
- *Saludos Web (http://www.saludos.com).* Supported by *Saludos Hispanos* magazine, this site exclusively promotes Hispanic/Latino careers and education, job listings, internships, and scholarships.
- *TrueCareers (http://www.truecareers.com).* Designed to assist Sallie Mae's 7 million borrowers in locating job leads, this site is intended for job seekers who want college and entry-level professional job positions. TrueCareers includes articles on career advice and interview tips.
- *USAJOBS (http://www.usajobs.opm.gov).* This is a database of job listings for national, state, and local government jobs from the U.S. Office of Personnel Management.
- *Yahoo! Careers (http://careers.yahoo.com).* Perform nationwide searches for job leads by job family and keywords, city, and state. Yahoo! Careers tries to match you with jobs in your local area or the closest metropolitan area. If the local search doesn't come up with openings in your chosen field, it automatically reverts to a nationwide search. This is a heavily used site; 1.5 million people visit each month.
- *YouthPath (http://www.youth.gc.ca).* Established to help young Canadians in their job hunt, YouthPath is a cooperative venture among companies and various agencies of the Canadian government. This site is provided in both English and French. It promotes a job bank and gives help for starting your own business, along with offering career planning and self-assessment opportunities.

REFERENCES

Bolles, R. N. 2003. *What color is your parachute?* (annual editions). Berkeley, CA: Ten Speed Press.

Dikel, M. R., and Roehm, F. 2002. *Guide to Internet job searching.* Chicago: VGM Career Books.

Weddle, P. D. 1995. *Electronic resumes for the new job market.* Manassas Park, VA: Impact Publications.

Weddle, P. D. 2002. *Weddle's guide to employment web sites: The job seeker's edition.* Stamford, CT: Weddle's.

Word-Processed Résumés into Electronic Résumés: Converting, Pasting, Improving, and Formatting

CONVERTING YOUR WORD-PROCESSED RÉSUMÉ TO PASTE INTO AN ELECTRONIC RÉSUMÉ

1. In your word processor, with your résumé open, go to the "File" menu and then select the "Save As" option.
2. Scroll down and select "Text Only." (If you are using Word 2002 with Windows XP, choose Plain Text.)
3. Name the file something like "electronic resume." This will help you to recall where the electronic version of your résumé can be located.
4. Click "Save" on the dialog box that appears. You don't want to lose your file. A warning will immediately come on the screen telling you that features such as lines, boldface type, tabs, and other formatting will be stripped from your document (this is what you want). *Note:* The Office 97 and newer Microsoft Word programs automatically set your text at a 10-point font size. If you have converted your résumé to a 12-point font and Save As Text Only, the program will revert back to the 10-point font size.
5. Click "Yes" in response to the warning message.
6. Make a note of the folder or location in which you have saved your résumé so you can find it later.
7. Close the file (not the word processor program). Your original résumé is unchanged; it is still a .doc file. However, your new file will have a .txt extension. The résumé won't change in appearance until you close and reopen the file (Washington, 2003; Whitcomb and Kendall, 2002).

TO CONVERT YOUR RÉSUMÉ TO BE SENT AS AN E-MAIL MESSAGE

1. Reopen the Text Only version of your résumé. (In Microsoft Word, click on the File menu and scroll down to the document you want to open.)
2. To highlight all the text in your résumé, go to the Edit menu and click on "Select All."
3. Go to the File menu and click "Page Setup."
4. On Page Setup, enter 1.0 (for 1 inch) in the Top and Bottom boxes. For the left and right margins, set them so that you have 6.5 inches of text displayed. This makes your résumé easier to read and safe to print. An option is to set the left margin at 1.0 (1 inch) and the right margin at 2.0 (Whitcomb and Kendall, 2002). Then click OK.
5. Go to the Format menu. Click on "Font." Scroll through the font selection and set a "fixed-width" font (Courier is recommended). Fixed-width means each character will take the same amount of space; the letter "l" will be the same

width as "w". The 10-point size will position approximately 65 letters, punctuation marks, or spaces on each line; this fits the e-mail screen and won't have the "wraparound" effect you may have seen on some e-mail messages you have received.

6. Go to the File menu and click "Save As." Select Text Only With Line Breaks.
7. Click "Save." Make a note of where you have saved the file.
8. Click "Yes" to the warning message, which is simply telling you that formatting will be eliminated from your résumé (again, what you want).
9. Go to the File menu and click "Close" to remove the file from your screen. To review changes, open the new text document in a text editor. The most familiar text editor is Microsoft's Notepad.

IMPROVING THE READABILITY OF YOUR TEXT (WITHIN THE LIMITATIONS OF A PLAIN-TEXT RÉSUMÉ)

1. With all of the tabs gone, all of your text will probably be flush with the left margin. If you want to indent any part of the text, you can do so by putting the cursor in front of the first word you want moved and pressing the space bar.
2. Capitalize words you want emphasized (such as your name and section titles).
3. Use an asterisk (*), a hyphen (-), or a plus sign (+) in place of bullets. (Microsoft Word automatically converts bullets to asterisks. Other programs change bullets into question marks, which may be misleading to the reader.)
4. Scroll through your résumé to remove any glitches.
5. Double-space between sections to improve the readability of your résumé.
6. Tighten any spacing that needs it. Use only one space instead of two between sentences. Delete any unnecessary or repeated information (Whitcomb and Kendall, 2002).
7. Click "Save" to keep all format improvements you have made.
8. To view the results, close your document and your word processor and then reopen the résumé in a plain text editor such as Notepad. To do so, click on the "Start" button, then "Documents," and then your résumé. It should now appear in Notepad. (If not, click on "Programs," then "Accessories," and finally "Notepad" or another plain text editor. In Notepad, click on "File" and then "Open.") Text editors such as Notepad make sure your résumé is in Plain Text format, so when it is e-mailed to an employer or commercial databank, it will have the same appearance as you now see (Washington, 2003).

PASTING YOUR RÉSUMÉ INTO AN E-MAIL MESSAGE

1. Go to the File menu, click "Open," and scroll to the folder with your résumé.
2. Go to the Edit menu and click "Select All." You are highlighting the entire text of your résumé.
3. Stay with the Edit menu and click "Copy."
4. Open your e-mail software and start a new e-mail message. Place your cursor in the e-mail message area where your résumé text will be pasted.
5. In the Edit menu, click "Paste." Don't forget to paste your cover letter ahead of your résumé. Do not send the cover letter as an attachment.
6. Write a subject line for your e-mail message. If you are making a first-time contact, type in the word "Resume" and your name.
7. Complete the recipient's e-mail address and click "Send."

Use an attachment only when invited to do so; this request will come from employers who specify a formatted document. You can check your work by sending your résumé to yourself or a friend before e-mailing it to a recruiter (Smith, 2000).

FORMATTED RÉSUMÉS

What if ASCII plain text is too ordinary for you, and the company you are applying to will accept your formatted résumé because it has the software to handle it? You can:

1. Create your résumé using a word processing program such as Microsoft Word.
2. Decide how your résumé will look. Choose a font you like. Draw attention to items you want the employer to see by using boldface, italicized, and underlined words.
3. Use only the characters found on a standard keyboard. Use asterisks instead of bullets.
4. Save as "yourname.doc". You now have a formatted résumé for general use.
5. Print paper copies if you need them.
6. Send your formatted résumé directly into the applicant system from a Web portal or gateway. Web portals for submitting résumés include a company Web site's career portal, a job site such as Monster, or another Web site such as one run by a college career center or a professional society. Sending your résumé through a Web portal does away with the scanning procedure and gives the hiring manager a pleasing résumé to look at (Kennedy, 2003).

Using formats such as hypertext markup language (HTML), portable document format (PDF), and rich text format (RTF) and constructing Web-based résumés and portfolios are best left to books whose entire subject matter deals with résumés. Examples of these books are listed in the References section.

REFERENCES

Kennedy, J. L. 2003. *Résumés for dummies*, 4th ed. New York: Wiley.

Smith, R. 2000. *Electronic résumés and online networking: How to use the Internet to do a better job search, including a complete up-to-date resource guide.* Franklin Lakes, NJ: Career Press.

Washington, T. 2003. *Résumé power: Selling yourself on paper.* Bellevue, WA: Mount Vernon Press.

Whitcomb, S. B., and Kendall, P. 2002. *ERésumés: Everything you need to know about using electronic résumés to tap into today's job market.* New York: McGraw-Hill.

Web Sites for Company Information

- *Corporate Information (http://www.corporateinformation.com)*. Type in the name of a company or its stock ticker and receive a list of sites that cover the company. Over 350,000 profiles are indexed.
- *Dun and Bradstreet (http://www.zapdata.com)*. An Internet service of D&B's Sales & Marketing Solutions, this site gives information on more than 14 million U.S. businesses.
- *EDGAR (Electronic Data Gathering, Analysis, and Retrieval System) (http://www.sec.gov/edgar)*. EDGAR collects annual reports on Forms 10-K or 10-KSB, which are submitted to the U.S. Securities and Exchange Commission (SEC) by companies required to file with the SEC.
- *Fortune—Company Profiles (http://www.fortune.com/fortune/companies)*. Features information about the *Fortune* 500, Global 500, 100 best companies to work for, global most admired, 100 fastest growing companies, small business best 100, and 50 best for minorities.
- *Hoover's Online (http://www.hoovers.com)*. Search by company name, stock ticker or quote, industry keyword, and/or company keyword. Browse by companies *a–z*, geography, or industry.
- *Lexis/Nexis (http://www.lexis-nexis.com/businessresearchtask/)*. Company and individual profiles from news, business, financial, and legal sources along with annual reports, state corporation filings, and articles in newsletters, trade journals, and local business newspapers.
- *Monster Company Research (http://company.monster.com)*. Access company profiles listed alphabetically. You receive an overview of the company and can click on the company's Web site for job openings and other information.
- *Public Register's Annual Report Service (PRARS) (http://www.prars.com)*. This site provides free annual reports of public companies trading on the New York Stock Exchange (NYSE), NASDAQ, AMEX, and Over the Counter (OTC) exchanges.
- *Superpages (http://www.superpages.com)*. Business information for over 11 million businesses in virtually every city in the United States. Available in English or Español. Superpages.com has a simple search, detailed search, map-based search, and 11 other categories.
- *Thomas Register of American Manufacturers (http://www.thomasregister.com)*. Contact information on 173,000 U.S. and Canadian companies, with telephone, fax, and 800 numbers, plus addresses, subsidiaries, sales offices, and corporate affiliates.
- *WetFeet (http://www.wetfeet.com/research/companies.asp)*. Search by industry. This site offers snapshots of companies, their history and profitability data, and job opportunities.

- *Yahoo! Finance (http://biz.yahoo.com/i/).* Contains profiles of over 9,000 public companies, including contact information, business and earnings summaries, officer and employee information, and more.

Many companies have a home page or site on the Web. To locate these sources of information, start with a search engine such as Google (http://www.google.com), Yahoo! (http://www.yahoo.com), Infoseek (http://www.infoseek.com), AltaVista (http://www.altavista.com), Lycos (http://www.lycos.com), or Excite (http://www.excite.com), and perform a search for the company by name. Type "company profiles" or "research companies" in the dialog box. A tutorial for conducting online company research is offered by Debbie Flanagan (http://home.sprintmail.com/~debflanagan). The National Association of Colleges and Employers' JobTrak Web site has an "Index of Profiles" at http://static.jobtrak.com/profiles.

Reading Annual Reports

A publicly owned company sells shares of its stock and must publish an annual report of its financial condition for its stock holders. You can usually obtain a company's annual report by writing to the company and asking for one. The library often has on file the annual reports of local companies and some national or large companies. A career resource center may keep annual reports in its company file. Combining the data gained from an annual report with information written about a company in business magazines will give you valuable insights into the operation and financial condition of a company.

Try to obtain copies of a company's annual reports over the past four or five years. You can then make comparisons to learn about trends in growth and decline of sales, assets, liabilities, net worth, working capital, and numbers of employees and stockholders. Annual reports present financial highlights, the chief executive officer's letter to stockholders, an operations review, an income statement, the financial condition of the company, the balance sheet and cash flows, a financial summary, notes to the financial statements, and the auditor's report. Each of these sections will be considered in turn. Not all reports will be in this order, nor will they have the same kind of information.

FINANCIAL HIGHLIGHTS

The financial highlights section gives you a quick look at the financial health of the company. It usually appears a page or two ahead of the chief executive officer's letter and tells you at a glance how the company has performed financially over the past year. Listings can include the total amount of money received by the company or each division of the company, the total expenses of each division, and the net change in each compared to the preceding year. This section may have the number of stockholders, the number of shares held, the earnings per share of stock, the dividends per share, and the total number of employees working for the company.

LETTER TO THE STOCKHOLDERS FROM THE CHIEF EXECUTIVE OFFICER

In the letter to the stockholders, the chief executive officer gives information about the objectives of the company, developments during the past year, what went well and why, difficulties that were encountered, and how management is dealing with those problems. There is a natural tendency to describe operations in optimistic terms and gloss over setbacks. Sometimes, however, especially in economic downturns, you may read the flat statement, "The past year was not a good one for ABC Company," followed later by predictions or hopes of a better future. Financial goals, the condition of each division, and insights into the company's future are usually found in the letter. Watch for qualifying words such as "except" or "despite"; these are clues to problem areas. Qualifiers in annual reports often mention the rate of inflation or new government regulations.

OPERATIONS REVIEW (OR ANALYSIS OF OPERATIONS)

The operations review usually contains a review of the year, what the company sells, and an evaluation of the strengths and weaknesses of the organization, which may or may not be documented by statistics. Write-ups about products and/or services may resemble public relations articles that you could find in trade magazines or community business periodicals. The company could give its reasons for changes in sales, income, expenses, and taxes in this section. You may also find information on new product development, pricing actions, marketing strategies, relations with competitors, examples of corporate social responsibilities, and the handling of government policies.

CONSOLIDATED STATEMENT OF INCOME (OR STATEMENT OF CONSOLIDATED OPERATIONS)

Now you get into the world of numbers. The financial statement shows the amount of money the company made or lost over the past year compared with the previous two years, and other items such as the amount of tax paid. There may be reports of earnings and/or expenses, such as selling off a losing business or unexpected increases in expenditures. A crucial number in the income statement is net sales. Are sales increasing at a faster rate than before or going up faster than the rate of inflation? If sales are decreasing or the rate of sales increases is lower than before, the company may be headed for trouble. Growing sales increases are usually a sign of financial strength.

MANAGEMENT'S ANALYSIS OF THE FINANCIAL CONDITION

The management analysis of the financial condition explains how the company earned its money over the past year and how the money was spent. A new stock issue might be one way in which the company made its money. The company could also have borrowed money to stimulate growth. If sales grow and if the company has enough cash on hand to meet its payments, it can perform well on borrowed money. If sales fall, problems could lie ahead. If the company becomes liable for too much debt over several years, future profits could be affected, and it might be in trouble.

CONSOLIDATED BALANCE SHEET AND CASH FLOWS

Everything the company owns (assets) appears at the top or on the left side of the balance sheet. Anything that can be quickly converted into cash is a current asset. Liabilities are everything the company owes; these are shown following the total assets figure or on the right of the balance sheet. Current liabilities are debts that are due within one year. They are paid from current assets. Net working capital is the difference between current assets and current liabilities. This is a figure to watch from year to year, as well as in quarterly reports. The balance sheet lists cash on hand, value of inventories, where cash reserves are invested, long-term and short-term debts, and stockholders' equity, which is liabilities subtracted from assets.

SUMMARY OF FINANCIAL DATA

Income, expenses, profits, and dividends are compared over a span of 10 years. The financial summary gives you a long-term overview of the company's performance. It can provide information on whether sales have steadily increased, how well expenses have been controlled, changes in the number of shares of stock that have been held, and whether dividend payments have increased, remained the same, or decreased.

NOTES TO FINANCIAL STATEMENTS

The footnotes usually contain the most detailed information about a company's operations. Many people have problems with this section, because technical language is often used. The footnotes may deal with deferred costs, changes in accounting practices, retirement plans, lawsuits, lease obligations, and other technical matters.

AUDITOR'S REPORT

The auditor's report is a letter indicating whether the certified public accounting firm's examination of the company's accounts and financial statements found them to be satisfactory. Some accountants suggest counting the number of paragraphs in this section. Two paragraphs usually are a sign of a clean bill of health. More than three paragraphs indicates that a close reading of the footnotes is advisable. Professional investors start with the auditor's letter when they read an annual report. The auditor will immediately tell you if the company's annual report is in agreement with "auditing standards generally accepted in the United States." If problems are lurking in the figures, the auditor is expected to include them in the report.

The *Wall Street Journal Online* has a free Annual Reports Service. Companies can be accessed alphabetically or by industry. The Internet address is http://wsjie.ar.wilink.com/asp/WSJ3_search_eng.asp.

Index

TO THE OWNER OF THIS BOOK:

I hope that you have found *Job Search: Career Planning Guide, Book 2*, Fifth Edition, useful. So that this book can be improved in a future edition, would you take the time to complete this sheet and return it? Thank you.

School and address: _____

_____

Department: _____

Instructor's name: _____

1. What I like most about this book is:_____

_____

_____

2. What I like least about this book is: _____

_____

_____

3. My general reaction to this book is: _____

_____

_____

4. The name of the course in which I used this book is: _____

_____

5. Were all of the chapters of the book assigned for you to read? _____

   If not, which ones weren't? _____

6. In the space below, or on a separate sheet of paper, please write specific suggestions for improving this book and anything else you'd care to share about your experience in using this book.

_____

_____

_____

_____

_____

TAPE HERE. DO NOT STAPLE.   TAPE HERE. DO NOT STAPLE.

FOLD HERE

NO POSTAGE
NECESSARY
IF MAILED
IN THE
UNITED STATES

BUSINESS REPLY MAIL
FIRST-CLASS MAIL   PERMIT NO. 34   BELMONT CA

POSTAGE WILL BE PAID BY ADDRESSEE

Attn: Counseling Editor

Brooks/Cole Cengage Learning
10 Davis Dr
Belmont CA 94002-9801

FOLD HERE

OPTIONAL:

Your name: _____   Date: _____

May we quote you, either in promotion for *Job Search: Career Planning Guide, Book 2*,
Fifth Edition, or in future publishing ventures?

Yes: _____   No: _____

Sincerely yours,

Robert D. Lock